COCKTAIL CODEX

COCKTAIL CODEX

FUNDAMENTALS · FORMULAS · EVOLUTIONS

ALEX DAY · NICK FAUCHALD · DAVID KAPLAN

with Devon Tarby

Photographs by Dylan James Ho and Jeni Afuso

Illustrations by Tim Tomkinson

TEN SPEED PRESS
California | New York

CONTENTS

PREFACE

It was the winter of 2006 in New York City, and I was somewhere between a college student and an adult, finishing up my degree by day but mostly enjoying the city by night. One cold, snowy evening, almost certainly half in the bag already, I sought refuge in a bar on the corner of Seventh Avenue and Leroy Street. It was located inside a miniscule flatiron building with a door at its apex that opened to a stairway leading down, the *chunk-chunk-chunk* of cocktail shakers and the sound of a trumpet inviting me in. The details of the night are a bit fuzzy from there. I remember a tiny coupe being set down in front of me, a twist of lemon expressed across its top, and the bright aroma as my lips touched the edge of frozen glass and the velvety liquid of a Gin Martini came forth.

That sip changed everything.

My first trip to Little Branch planted a seed in my soul, one that sprouted from hobbyist-level interest in cocktails and spirits and quickly grew into my life's study. I soon found myself scouring the city for great drinks, eventually landing on a stool at Death & Co in early 2008. I immediately vowed to work there; not only did the bar serve impeccable cocktails, it did so while looking toward the future and making every guest feel welcome. Three years later, I became a partner at Death & Co, and the path toward putting these words on paper was well under way. Our first book, *Death & Co: Modern Classic Cocktails*, documented the first years of that special bar and all its creativity. This book reflects our evolution beyond those walls on East Sixth Street, extending to our work opening other bars and consulting on cocktail programs around the world.

For many people, the first strategy in studying cocktails is to memorize a bunch of recipes. However, it's a well-known (but rarely acknowledged) secret among bartenders that almost every cocktail in existence today can be traced back to a handful of seminal drinks. Many classic cocktails are organized into "families," or groups of drinks cut from the same cloth. This allows us to grasp a handful of recipes that connect to many more due to their similarities. While that helps in memorizing lots of "specs" (our lingo for shorthand recipes) and understanding their shared DNA, the approach has always felt a bit empty to me— it only scratches the surface of truly understanding cocktails. A bartender may know that a Martini and Manhattan are similar, but does that bartender understand why the recipes call for different vermouths, sometimes in different proportions? Memorizing families of drinks is helpful, but it does little to empower an understanding of why variations on a handful of formulas work (well or otherwise).

Over the past decade and a half, I've studied cocktails as a bartender working behind the stick, as an imbiber perched on any bar stool that would have me, and as a student with my nose stuck in a library of books on spirits, techniques, and the philosophies of great drinks. Those early visits to Little Branch and Death & Co (and so many other bars) were more than inspiring—they were also

perplexing. To a newcomer, cocktails are mysterious potions concocted from a seemingly endless collection of bottles and poured into tiny glasses with extravagant garnishes. Throw in the theatrics of a performative bartender, and the craft of making cocktails can be overwhelming. For those who are new to mixed drinks, the world of cocktails can intimidate as much as it can inspire. That you're reading this book means you're inspired. Stick with it; we've got your back.

As my colleagues and I have learned more about cocktails, we've begun to think of drinks less as families and more as intuitive progressions arising from a handful of well-known templates: the Old-Fashioned, Martini, Daiquiri, Sidecar, Highball, and Flip. This book seeks to teach the internal mechanics of *all* cocktails using these six templates to demystify recipes and inspire creativity. Through years of training bartenders and opening bars, we've come to the realization that cocktail makers can enjoy a more intuitive

relationship with the almost endless creative opportunities that a well-stocked back bar provides. Some bartenders have taken to studying the work of past masters to inform and drive their understanding of cocktails, while others have broken down the quantifiable data of various drinks' composition with scientific precision. While we find it important to study the classics and understand the scientific reasons for a great cocktail, our perspective involves both. After you have mastered the classics and have an understanding of the physical (cocktail) universe, you can apply that knowledge. With this book, we want to help you understand how cocktails truly, fundamentally work and help you use that knowledge to understand the ever-expanding universe of cocktails so that you can add your own new creations to it.

Cheers,
Alex Day

INTRODUCTION

This book aims to teach both novice and accomplished drink makers how to master a half dozen iconic cocktails—and invent new ones—using an approach that has become integral to our bar programs: root cocktails. The book is organized into six chapters, each using a classic, or root, cocktail to teach lessons you can apply to all cocktails.

This book isn't a study in cocktail history; that work is best left in far more capable hands (looking at you, David Wondrich, Gary Regan, and others). Nor is it a scientific study of cocktails (thanks, Dave Arnold!). Our six root cocktails are less a historical lineage than an approach to understanding the fundamentals. By studying each of these six drinks, you will learn the mechanics of a particular family of cocktails as well as important lessons in technique and ingredients that will elevate your overall cocktail game. We've spent much of the last fifteen years not only studying cocktails but also teaching them to countless other bartenders. In that time, we've found that this strategy—teaching these six drinks, studying their DNA, and explaining how they're connected with other drinks—is a proven method that demystifies the overwhelming diversity of cocktails.

This is where the written recipe enters the real world, where the abstract becomes real, and where the exactitude of technique can make the difference between a good cocktail and a great one. All great artists—from painters and poets to cellists and chefs—begin by studying the classics in their chosen field, and then they emulate and practice those classics until they've developed their own signature style and can create original works. We take a similar approach, examining each root cocktail, studying how others have made variations on each recipe—by substituting one ingredient for another or adding a touch of something new and flavorful—and considering what each new variation accomplishes.

Throughout the book we use a handful of terms that help explain the function of an ingredient (or collection of ingredients) in every cocktail. Together, three areas of focus—**core**, **balance**, and **seasoning**—help illuminate the inner workings of cocktails. We define the core as the primary flavor component of a drink. The core can be one ingredient or many. In the case of the Old-Fashioned, this is whiskey, while in the Martini, the core is comprised of both gin and vermouth. While the core is the heart of any cocktail, every cocktail is balanced by ingredients that enhance the drinkability of the core by adding sweetness, acidity, or both. Finally, we season our cocktails with ingredients that complement or contrast the core, adding intrigue and dimension. These three components (core, balance, and seasoning) are fundamental to understanding how cocktails work—and once you do, creating new cocktails is fantastically easy.

Be it your first foray into cocktails or your thousandth, this book is organized to incrementally build your knowledge as you progress through its pages. Each chapter begins with an examination of one of the six root cocktails, comparing its established **classic**

recipe to our (in our opinion) improved **root recipe**. We offer a simple **orthodoxy** that defines the key characteristics of that drink, then break apart the drink's **template**, or recipe, identifying its key components, which we then cover in depth. Next, we take a deep dive into the cocktail's core, balance, and seasoning, exploring the ingredients and techniques relevant to each component, including recommending bottles, most of which are widely available and reasonably priced for everyday use in cocktails.

When you're ready to stop reading and start drinking, we offer some hands-on experiments and recipes that illustrate these fundamentals to help you under-stand the connections between seemingly disparate cocktails, such as an Old-Fashioned and a Champagne Cocktail, a Martini and a Negroni, or a Flip and a Piña Colada. Then, after a quick love letter to the featured cocktail from one of the talented drink makers at our family of bars, we explore a specific **technique** that will help you further master the root

recipe (and its many brethren), and explain why a specific style of **glassware** is used to serve it.

Should you be here for recipes alone, flip toward the back half of each chapter, where we offer **variations** on each root recipe, as well as recipes for members of that cocktail's **extended family**. If fancy gear and advanced techniques are your game, each chapter concludes with a section on **next-level techniques** that can help you reimagine familiar ingredients and create new ones, delving into topics such as sous vide infusions and syrups, clarified juices, alternative acids, carbonated cocktails, and more.

You can read this book from cover to cover or just cherry-pick at your leisure. And while we'll be thrilled if you discover a handful of recipes that become new favorites, we hope you'll dig deeper than that. If you take the time to master these six classic cocktails—the Old-Fashioned, Martini, Daiquiri, Sidecar, Whisky Highball, and Flip—you can master them all.

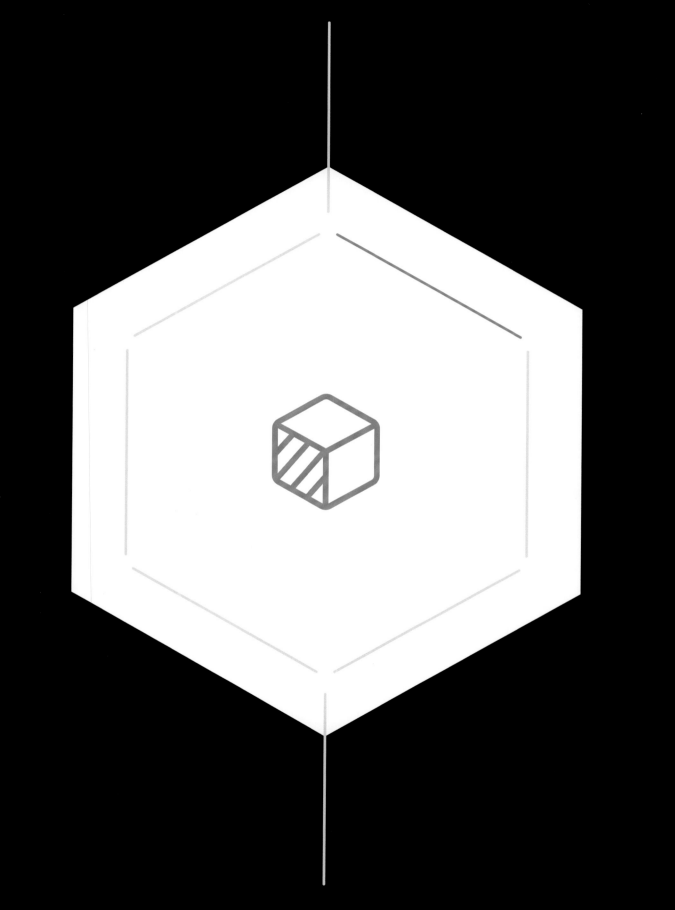

1

THE
OLD-FASHIONED

THE CLASSIC RECIPE

A version of the Old-Fashioned cocktail can be found in almost any respectable cocktail book. In its simplest form, it is just spirit, sugar, bitters, and water (in the form of ice) and frequently looks very similar to this recipe:

Old-Fashioned

1 sugar cube

2 dashes Angostura bitters

2 ounces bourbon

**Garnish: 1 lemon twist and
1 orange twist**

Muddle the sugar cube and bitters in an Old-Fashioned glass. Add the bourbon and 1 large ice cube and stir until chilled. Garnish with the lemon and orange twists.

OUR ROOT RECIPE

As you can see from the classic recipe, the Old-Fashioned is basically a glass of booze that's been sweetened with sugar and seasoned with bitters. That's the crux of what makes an Old-Fashioned an Old-Fashioned: a spirit makes up what we call the core—the defining flavor of the cocktail. Over years of making Old-Fashioneds, we've tweaked the classic "spec" (bartender slang for recipe) into our ideal Old-Fashioned in several ways.

First, we select a bourbon that's distinct without being too dominant. The world of bourbon has many options that can take the Old-Fashioned in different directions. Bourbons are bottled to various proofs and can be made from different mixes of sweet and spicy grains: more corn and the bourbon is sweeter; more rye and it will be dry and spicy. For the root recipe we'll present shortly, we chose a bourbon that sits in the middle of the spectrum, being both full-bodied and full of personality: Elijah Craig Small Batch. It also happens to be affordable.

Second, the classic Old-Fashioned starts with muddling a sugar cube. We find this technique outmoded because a sugar cube doesn't dissolve easily, so we use a sugar syrup to ensure that the sugar is distributed throughout the cocktail. But adding standard simple syrup in a proportion equivalent to the sugar cube—¼ ounce—would dilute the cocktail too much, given that simple syrup is comprised of equal portions of sugar and water. So we instead use our denser Demerara Gum Syrup (page 54), which adds a rich viscosity to the cocktail while also drawing out some of the whiskey's aged characteristics.

Third, to deepen the structure that Angostura bitters provides and create more intrigue, we include an additional dash of Bitter Truth aromatic bitters, which provides a barely perceptible layer of cinnamon and clove that further emphasizes the bourbon's flavor profile.

Fourth, and finally, we garnish the Old-Fashioned with both lemon and orange twists. We first squeeze, or express, the orange twist over the cocktail, and then rub it gently around the rim of the glass so the sweet orange oils not only perfume the cocktail but also become an element of the first sip. We then express the lemon twist over the cocktail, but because lemon oil is less sweet and more pungent than orange—and can ruin the drinker's palate for the entire cocktail—we don't rub it around the rim. Both twists are then inserted vertically into the cocktail so they continue to flavor the drink, or may be removed by the drinker if desired. (For an in-depth discussion of citrus twists, see "The Seasoning: Garnishes," on page 78.)

The result of all this tweaking is our ideal Old-Fashioned:

Our Ideal Old-Fashioned

2 ounces Elijah Craig Small Batch bourbon

1 teaspoon Demerara Gum Syrup (page 54)

2 dashes Angostura bitters

1 dash Bitter Truth aromatic bitters

Garnish: 1 orange twist and 1 lemon twist

Stir all the ingredients over ice, then strain into a double Old-Fashioned glass over 1 large ice cube. Express the orange twist over the drink, then gently rub it around the rim of the glass and place it into the drink. Express the lemon twist over the drink, then place it into the drink.

THE ORIGINAL COCKTAIL

What is an Old-Fashioned? Ask ten bartenders and you'll get ten different recipes, each deemed to be "the one true way" to make the drink. On paper they may look very similar, but take a sip and they may be wildly different. In musical terms, the Old-Fashioned is less like a five-piece band and more of a soloist with light accompaniment, the dominant core flavor, whiskey, being the star of the show.

The Old-Fashioned is an exercise in restraint, with a seemingly simple formula: booze, sugar, bitters. Its straightforward recipe seems to imply that mastering the drink would be a cinch, but its minimalism means the Old-Fashioned is an exercise in subtly. Use a touch too much sugar and the drink starts to get flabby—sweet, without sharply defined flavor. A heavy hand with the bitters bottle will make the drink taste disjointed and medicinal, yet too little bitters will yield a drink that may register as nothing more than iced whiskey. It's the perfect cocktail, then, to display how, with disciplined technique, a core flavor can be balanced and seasoned to create a harmonious result. Other root recipes, such as the Daiquiri (the topic of chapter 3), offer a bit more leeway in creating delicious results, but when it comes to the Old-Fashioned, the line is much finer. Precision is the name of the game.

In our view, the Old-Fashioned and its variations are best when the focus remains squarely on the spirit (or multiple spirits, though we generally stop at four) that makes up its core; any modifications should enhance the characteristics of that spirit. This cocktail is the most respectful way we can think to honor good booze. Other root recipes find their core flavor in multiple ingredients; for example, the Martini is defined by gin and aromatized wine. Because the Old-Fashioned keeps it simple, it's a great cocktail for zeroing in on core flavor.

UNDERSTANDING THE TEMPLATE

Those who gravitate to Old-Fashioneds tend to like boozy, or spirituous, cocktails. As a result, the Old-Fashioned can be a challenge for some people, as it may taste like firewater, especially if not made well. But if you like drinking spirits on their own, the Old-Fashioned and its many variations will probably appeal to you.

Drinking an Old-Fashioned activates all of your senses. The bottom-heavy glass with a large block of ice chills your hand, the bright aroma of citrus oil hits your nose as you lean in, and that first taste is sharp and boozy, yet smooth. And thanks to its high proof, an Old-Fashioned invites slow sipping and reflection.

Once you understand the Old-Fashioned's basic blueprint, it's easy to start manipulating it—which is exactly what we'll do in this chapter. You'll also start to notice how other iconic—and perhaps seemingly unrelated—cocktails, like the Mint Julep, Hot Toddy, and Champagne Cocktail—have surprisingly similar DNA. But first, let's dig into the core components.

THE CORE: AMERICAN WHISKEY

There are several things about American whiskey that make it a great base spirit for cocktails. First, it's one of the most tightly regulated spirits on the planet, so there's a high baseline standard—that is, the worst American whiskeys are still pretty decent, if simple—and there's also a high level of consistency within different styles: bourbon, rye, and so on. That said, due to increased global demand, there have been times when the whiskeys we love have been compromised in the interest of slaking a thirsty public. Producers that were once steadfast in only bottling whiskey above a certain age have started putting out younger whiskeys to meet market demand. So keep an eye on your favorite brands and taste them regularly.

All American whiskeys are made in a similar fashion. Cereal grains, predominantly corn, rye, wheat, and barley, are malted—a process wherein grains are germinated, converting their starch into sugars—and then fermented and distilled in either pot stills or continuous column stills. Most are aged in oak barrels.

Understanding the differences between various styles of whiskey and how they work in cocktails will help you choose the right bottles for your drinks. And although increased global popularity has pushed whiskey prices skyward, there are still plenty of affordable options for bartenders and home cocktail enthusiasts alike. Of course, there are lots of delicious high-priced whiskeys, but you don't need the most expensive whiskeys to make the best cocktails. In the section that follows, we'll outline the primary styles, then list our favorites for cocktails—Old-Fashioned and otherwise. While our suggestions don't represent every brand we use, all are perennial fixtures in our bars thanks to their flavor profiles, consistency, value, and availability.

THE *E* (OR LACK THEREOF) IN WHISKEY

You've probably noticed that whiskey is sometimes spelled without the e. The Scots spell it without the e, a naming convention that was adopted by Scottish settlers in Canada and distillers elsewhere whose spirits were inspired by Scottish styles. The Irish include the e, and thanks to the influence of Irish immigrants in American whiskey making, spelling has largely been standardized to include the e in American-made whiskeys. That said, there are plenty of exceptions, so we're reluctant to correct folks if they prefer one spelling over the other.

BOURBON

Bourbon is by far the broadest category of American whiskey, and because of that, it has the most stylistic variations. Our favorite mixing bourbons are those that spend enough time in oak barrels to develop rich flavor and texture, but not so much that the wood overtakes the spirit; we rarely mix with bourbons older than twelve or fifteen years. When choosing a specific bourbon for a cocktail, we also look at the makeup of the mashbill—that is, how much corn, rye, and/or wheat went into the product—and how each ingredient contributes to the flavor of the bourbon, and eventually the cocktail. Corn creates a perception of sweetness, rye a distinct spiciness, and wheat a delicate softness. While many of our preferred bourbons have a balance of these three ingredients, others showcase just one, so we reach for the latter when looking to amplify that flavor.

RECOMMENDED BOTTLES

Eagle Rare 10-Year: Made at the Buffalo Trace distillery—likely from the same mashbill as the eponymous (and also delicious) Buffalo Trace bourbon—Eagle Rare has a bit more age, along with a noticeable amount of rye, resulting in a whiskey with an extra hit of spice flavor. It's fantastic on its own in spirit-forward drinks, but we also love combining it with other base spirits, particularly Cognac.

Elijah Craig Small Batch: Our benchmark whiskey for Old-Fashioneds is this diplomat, which works equally well across the aisles of shaken and stirred cocktails. It balances the sweetness of corn with a healthy punch of rye and is aged long enough to stand up to a wide range of other ingredients. This is classic bourbon that tastes mature but is affordable enough for everyday cocktail making.

Old Grand-Dad 114: Typically, we steer clear of mixing with spirits over 100 proof. For one, they can cause our guests to get tipsy far too quickly. In addition, high-proof spirits tend to overshadow other ingredients. Given that this bourbon clocks in at 57% ABV and has a high amount of rye in the mashbill, it might seem too aggressive for cocktails, but nothing could be further from the truth. Thanks to some brilliant oak-aging alchemy, it's shockingly drinkable on its own, without ice or water. (For most other bourbons above 100 proof, we often add a bit of water to make them more palatable.) And while we often argue that a proper Manhattan should be made with rye whiskey, Old Grand-Dad has enough personality to make a damn fine one. Just one caveat: Sip slowly, please.

Old Weller Antique 107: Pappy Van Winkle gets all the attention these days, but we love its cousin Old Weller (both are made from the same mashbill at the Buffalo Trace Distillery). The Old Weller is a highly accessible, wheat-forward bourbon. Although wheat can sometimes make bourbon too soft for mixing in cocktails, allowing it to be overpowered by other ingredients, the high proof of this bottling means it will still shine through in boozy cocktails like an Old-Fashioned or a Manhattan. And if you use it in a sour-style cocktail, the wheat sings when balanced with citrus.

Wyoming Whiskey: The craft spirits market is more crowded now than ever before. While this means we have more products to choose from, it also means consumers have to do their homework. Not all of the new brands are transparent about where and by whom the booze was made, and many of the new products are just bulk commodity-grade whiskey packaged with marketing flair. Wyoming Whiskey is a producer that eschews shortcuts and makes their whiskeys, start to finish, in Kirby, Wyoming. Using local grain grown within one hundred miles of the distillery, Wyoming Whiskey's booze is stylistically bourbon but has a distinctive mineral note. It's a direct reflection of the unique characteristics of Wyoming.

RYE WHISKEY

Prior to Prohibition, rye was the most popular spirit in America. But then US drinking habits shifted in a sweeter direction, and the rye industry took decades to recover. Until its recent resurgence, there weren't many brands of rye that were widely available, and it still hasn't reclaimed its place as the American whiskey of choice. Unlike bourbon, which must include at least 51 percent corn in the mashbill, rye flips the equation, containing at least 51 percent rye.

Rye's spicy flavor blends well with other ingredients, acting a bit like bitters do in an Old-Fashioned. We conceptualize the flavor profile of rye much as we do the botanicals in gin: its distinct notes are like fingers that reach out and connect with other components of the drink.

RECOMMENDED BOTTLES

Rittenhouse Rye: Rittenhouse is a bonded whiskey, which means it must be aged at least four years and bottled at 100 proof. This high ABV makes it ideal for cocktails, giving it enough personality to come through in any style of drink. The downfall is that everyone knows it's awesome, so it tends to go out of stock quickly. If you find a bottle, buy it and immediately go home and make a Manhattan (page 84).

Russell's Reserve 6-Year Rye: The Russell family has been overseeing whiskey production at Wild Turkey for two generations, and over the years their craft has only gotten better. This whiskey has all the spicy rye character you would expect, but beautifully balanced by a floral aroma and fruity flavor. There's a subtle sweetness that makes Russell's rye fantastic in Old-Fashioned and Manhattan-style cocktails, and it's also soft enough to be mixed with citrus.

OTHER AMERICAN WHISKEYS

Bourbon and rye get all of the attention, but there are other styles of American whiskey worthy of use in cocktails, such as sour mash whiskey and wheat whisky. Though we don't mix with these styles of whiskey often, we want to address them because there's currently a boom in US production of whiskeys that don't necessarily fit into the mold of bourbon or rye.

Tennessee Sour Mash Whiskey: Based on the marketing, you might assume this whiskey is distinct because of the sour mash process (wherein a small amount of the previous grain mash is added in each new fermentation). However, this technique is also employed for all American bourbon. Whiskey from Tennessee is unique from other American whiskey because of the Lincoln County process, in which the spirit is filtered through sugar maple charcoal before being aged in oak barrels. This produces a lighter spirit that has a unique flavor profile: sweeter than bourbon, with an extra-long finish. Aside from that, Tennessee whiskey is much like bourbon and adheres to many of the same requirements. Of the two Tennessee whiskeys available (George Dickel and Jack Daniel's), we find the Dickel more complex. That said, we seldom use Tennessee whiskeys in cocktails because we consider bourbon and rye to be more versatile and think they contribute more meaningfully to drinks.

Wheat Whiskey: Though some bourbons have a high concentration of wheat, including Maker's Mark, Old Weller, Old Fitzgerald, and Pappy Van Winkle, true wheat whiskeys must contain 51 percent or more of the grain in the mashbill. There are only a couple of these on the market, one of which, Bernheim, we've used in drinks in the past. Its price point may be a bit prohibitive for cocktail use, but we've enjoyed some delicate Manhattan-style drinks made with it.

EXPERIMENTING WITH THE CORE

Riffs on the Old-Fashioned are almost as old as the cocktail itself. It didn't take long for other ingredients to find their way into the "original cocktail" to create now-classic variations. The easiest way to improvise on this, or any, cocktail is with what we often call the Mr. Potato Head approach, a term coined by former Death & Co head bartender Phil Ward. The process is simple: take out one thing and replace it with something similar. *Voilà!* Mixology.

The beauty of the Old-Fashioned is that nearly any spirit can be used as the core as long as the other ingredients support and accent that spirit. Want a spicier Old-Fashioned? Eagle Rare 10-year bourbon is a great choice. A bit more of a kick? Old Grand-Dad 114 will pack a boozy punch. Or if you're looking for a softer Old-Fashioned, try Old Weller Antique 107, with its wheat-heavy mashbill. We prefer an Old-Fashioned that balances these attributes, so in our root recipe (page 4) we use Elijah Craig Small Batch, which gives the drink a smooth core and a strong but not overwhelming personality.

Another way to alter the core is to modify it through infusions. Because the Old-Fashioned is composed mostly of a spirit, simply infusing that spirit with other flavors can create a strikingly different cocktail. In the appendix, we present a wide variety of infusions in depth, and as you'll see, we use a number of them in this chapter to explore the Old-Fashioned.

Finally, an Old-Fashioned need not use a strong spirit as its core; a fortified wine or amaro can also fulfill this role, though either substitution would require adjustments to the basic template. For example, using sweet vermouth in place of bourbon means you need to use less sweetener and more bitters to yield a balanced drink. Or if you use an amaro, you'll probably need to use smaller quantities of both bitters and sugar—or perhaps eliminate one entirely.

Golden Boy

ALEX DAY AND DEVON TARBY, 2013

Alex has long been captivated by the combination of scotch and raisins, an obsession born from late-night snacks accompanied by big glasses of whiskey. Indeed, the concentrated fruitiness of raisins pairs perfectly with the lusciousness of a blended scotch like Famous Grouse. In addition to flavor, the madeira and Bénédictine bring a balanced amount of sweetness to the cocktail, making any extra sweetener unnecessary.

1½ ounces Raisin-Infused Scotch (page 292)

½ ounce Barbeito 5-year rainwater madeira

¼ ounce Busnel Pays d'Auge VSOP Calvados

¼ ounce Bénédictine

2 dashes Peychaud's bitters

Garnish: 1 lemon twist

Stir all the ingredients over ice, then strain into an Old-Fashioned glass over 1 large ice cube. Express the lemon twist over the drink, then place it into the drink.

Vermouth Cocktail

CLASSIC

In the early days of cocktails, vermouth was becoming popular in America and found its way into the Old-Fashioned template, resulting in this nuanced, low-ABV sipper. This classic recipe also demonstrates that not all Old-Fashioned-style drinks are served over ice in rocks glasses.

2 ounces Carpano Antica Formula vermouth

½ teaspoon simple syrup (page 45)

2 dashes Angostura bitters

1 dash orange bitters

Garnish: 1 lemon twist

Stir all the ingredients over ice, then strain into a chilled coupe. Express the lemon twist over the drink, then set it on the edge of the glass.

Ti' Punch

Exit Strategy

NATASHA DAVID, 2014

Amaro shows off its versatility when used as the core of an Old-Fashioned; it also provides seasoning and sweetness, so neither bitters nor sugar syrup is needed. In this recipe, the brandy primarily provides a focused boozy flavor and dries the drink out, and a generous amount of salt solution rounds off the bitter edges.

1½ ounces Amaro Nonino

¾ ounce Germain-Robin Craft-Method brandy

¼ ounce Amaro Meletti

6 drops Salt Solution (page 298)

Garnish: 1 orange twist

Stir all the ingredients over ice, then strain into an Old-Fashioned glass over 1 large ice cube. Express the orange twist over the drink, then gently rub it around the rim of the glass and place it into the drink.

Ti' Punch

CLASSIC

It's said that in Martinique, where the drink originated, Ti' Punches are served up and consumed in one gulp. Our version is served over ice and meant to be sipped. If you were to change the proportions of the ingredients and shake the drink, you'd have yourself a Daiquiri, but the Ti' Punch is an Old-Fashioned, through and through, with the lime peel standing in for the bitters to season the drink. Make sure you include a bit of the lime flesh, as it will brighten the drink nicely.

1½-inch-thick disk of lime peel with some flesh attached

1 teaspoon Cane Sugar Syrup (page 47)

2 ounces La Favorite Couer de Canne rhum agricole blanc

In an Old-Fashioned glass, muddle the lime and syrup. Add the rum, fill the glass with cracked ice, and stir briefly. No garnish.

THE BALANCE: SUGAR

Balance in an Old-Fashioned is achieved by bridging the core flavor (whiskey) with the seasoning (bitters), which is exactly what the sugar is there for: it curbs the high-octane nature of the base spirit and brings out the spice of the bitters. Some folks like a sweeter Old-Fashioned, others drier. We're in the drier camp, preferring an Old-Fashioned with only just enough sugar to slightly round the rough edges of the booze.

You may think you don't like "sweet" cocktails, but just try to make a balanced drink without sugar. Providing sweetness is just one of several functions sugar serves in a cocktail; in the right amount, it amplifies other flavors and adds body and richness, much like fat does in cooking. Of course, too much sugar dumbs down other flavors to the point of making them unrecognizable, overshadowing the core spirit and making the cocktail taste boring.

Most of the time, the sweetener takes the form of a sugar-based syrup. Many cocktails call for simple syrup, a mixture of equal parts water and sugar. Before syrups came into wide use, sugar, by the cube or the spoonful, was used. But as alluded to earlier, this is an inconsistent and time-consuming process: sugar granules take time to dissolve, and anything that slows the drink-making process is devastating in a busy bar. Plus, a spoonful of sugar granules is harder to measure precisely than a syrup is. Suffice it to say that beyond nostalgia, we believe there's very little reason to make an Old-Fashioned with undissolved sugar.

EXPERIMENTING WITH THE BALANCE

In the Old-Fashioned, there are two main considerations in regard to sweeteners: the type of sweetener and how it's manipulated. While it makes sense that the neutral flavor of simple syrup can help keep the focus on the base spirit—especially in an Old-Fashioned—in practice, simple syrup thins out the cocktail too much, at least for our liking. To keep whiskey as the star of the Old-Fashioned, we use a syrup made from two parts demerara sugar to one part water, which deepens the richness already found in the spirit. Demerara sugar is an unrefined version of cane sugar that retains much of the molasses character that otherwise gets stripped away in the refining process. To add even more body to an Old-Fashioned without the cloying baggage that comes with added sugar, we use gum arabic to thicken our Demerara Gum Syrup (page 54). This powder, made from the hardened sap of the acacia tree, has been used in cocktails almost as long as they've existed. The result is a syrup that can bring a surprising amount of body to the drink, even when added in very small quantities. The difference in texture is difficult to describe, but it's clearly perceptible. The gum arabic amplifies the roundness of the cocktail in a way that comes across as an added layer of complexity; it's more of a sensory enhancement than noticeable change in flavor.

Sugar isn't the only way to balance an Old-Fashioned–style drink. Sometimes an implication of sweetness can be just as valuable as actual sweetness. Aged spirits (think añejo tequila, aged scotch, or older rums) often seem sweeter than young spirits because the aging process adds compounds—specifically, vanillin and spice from the oak barrels—that seem sweet. Using such spirits will definitely influence the balance of an Old-Fashioned. For example, a heavily aged whiskey will probably taste sweeter, and may also have lots of woody spices and therefore provide more seasoning. In that case, you may want to back off on the sweetener a bit, using perhaps ½ teaspoon of syrup as a starting point, and use a light hand with the bitters.

Fancy-Free

This vintage cocktail is an early example of bartenders swapping out sugar for a sweet, flavorful liqueur. Maraschino liqueur isn't as sweet as simple syrup (not to mention that it also has proof), so we up the quantity to ½ ounce.

2 ounces Rittenhouse rye
½ ounce Luxardo maraschino liqueur
1 dash Angostura bitters
1 dash House Orange Bitters (page 295)
Garnish: 1 orange twist

Stir all the ingredients over ice, then strain into an Old-Fashioned glass over 1 large ice cube. Express the orange twist over the drink, then gently rub it around the rim of the glass and place it into the drink.

Monte Carlo

In the classic Monte Carlo, Bénédictine, a sweet liqueur with herbal and honey flavors, stands in for the sugar.

2 ounces Rittenhouse rye
½ ounce Bénédictine
2 dashes Angostura bitters
Garnish: 1 lemon twist

Stir all the ingredients over ice, then strain into an Old-Fashioned glass over 1 large ice cube. Express the lemon twist over the glass and place it into the drink.

Chrysanthemum

A low-proof Old-Fashioned that doesn't contain a base spirit, sugar-based sweetener, or traditional bitters—and that gets served up in a coupe? Say it ain't so. Though the Chrysanthemum looks like it hails from the Manhattan or Martini family, the proportion of ingredients give away its lineage, with small amounts of Bénédictine and absinthe dutifully sweetening and seasoning the herbaceous vermouth core.

2½ ounces Dolin dry vermouth
½ ounce Bénédictine
1 teaspoon Pernod absinthe
Garnish: 1 orange twist

Stir all the ingredients over ice, then strain into a chilled coupe. Express the orange twist over the drink, then gently rub it around the rim of the glass and place it into the drink.

Stinger

Reimagining the core and balance of the Old-Fashioned can yield some interesting effects. The Stinger, a pre-Prohibition drink of untraceable origin, classically consisted of just brandy and crème de menthe, the latter providing both seasoning and sweetening. For our version of this classic, we include a bit of simple syrup to boost the flavor of the crème de menthe and curtail the brandy's strength. Though it's traditionally served up, we like to dress up our Stinger like a Julep and serve it with two straws for two-person consumption, à la *Lady and the Tramp*.

2 ounces Pierre Ferrand Ambre Cognac
½ ounce white crème de menthe
1 teaspoon simple syrup (page 45)
Garnish: 1 mint sprig

Shake all the ingredients with ice for about 5 seconds, then strain into an Old-Fashioned glass filled with crushed ice. Garnish with the mint sprig and serve with a straw.

Stinger

THE SEASONING: BITTERS

Before modern pharmaceuticals, there were bitters. Up through the Industrial Revolution, bitters were advertised as a cure-all: Can't sleep? Bitters. Want more pep in the bedroom? Bitters! Truth be told, this wasn't pure fiction, as many of the ingredients in bitters do have curative powers.

Bitters are highly concentrated macerations of barks, roots, herbs, and dried citrus—these days along with nearly anything you can think of—in high-proof alcohol. They're intentionally made to be unpalatable in higher doses, and they're used in tiny amounts in cocktails—just drops and dashes. Think of them as akin to cooking spices: a tiny amount can go a long way in adding flavor and complexity to drinks.

As recently as ten years ago, there weren't many options when it came to bitters. Typically, you could always find the iconic Angostura, Peychaud's when you were lucky, and perhaps a couple of brands of orange bitters (thank you, Gary Regan, for bringing a great orange bitters to market just when we needed it). The first wave of the bitters revival, in the early 2000s, was fostered by brands like Bitter Truth in Germany and Bittermens in New York. Their bitters were often homages to vintage recipes and, in some instances, wild new creations. But the real bitters explosion happened a few years later, and now there are hundreds of producers making bitters inspired by every imaginable flavor. Our friend Louis Anderman at Miracle Mile Bitters will, we swear, figure out a way to make bitters using this physical book.

Bitters are one of the most alluring cocktail ingredients. With a single dash from a mysterious bottle, they can change the flavor and entire experience of a cocktail, bind ingredients together, or introduce aroma on top of a drink. The amount of bitters added to an Old-Fashioned is a subtle balancing act, like seasoning soup with salt. The moment the bitters distract from the base spirit is when you've gone too far.

BITTERS TYPES: AROMATIC, CITRUS, AND SAVORY

Angostura is the world's most widely available brand and their traditional offering represents the most common bitters category: aromatic bitters. You might be thinking, *Aren't all bitters aromatic?* But in this context, bitters designated "aromatic" (as opposed to citrus or savory, for example) have a dense and sweet base, a bitter backbone, and a spice component. Gentian root (for bitterness) and warming spices like clove and cinnamon tend to dominate.

Produced in Trinidad using a highly guarded recipe, Angostura bitters is an indispensable tool in any cocktail kit—an ingredient that, on its own, tastes like a rum-fueled Christmas party. There are certainly other similar bitters, but Angostura is the king.

Citrus bitters have become almost as invaluable in our cocktails. Along with grapefruit, blood orange, Meyer lemon, and yuzu bitters, to name a few, orange bitters brighten a drink's overall flavor profile. While aromatic bitters are good friends with aged spirits, especially in Old-Fashioneds and Manhattan-style drinks, orange bitters are great with unaged spirits—gin and tequila in particular, especially when paired with a fortified wine. Orange bitters are also an easy companion for other bitters. Many people prefer an Old-Fashioned made with both Angostura and orange bitters.

Savory bitters, on the other hand, add a layer of complexity via pepper or vegetal flavors. Currently, one of the most popular savory bitters is Bittermens Xocolatl mole bitters, which has rich chocolate flavor and a hint of chile heat. Other favorites include celery bitters (surprisingly great with bourbon), cardamom bitters, and lavender bitters.

HOW BITTERS FUNCTION IN COCKTAILS

As the variety of bitters available increases, we've started to lump them into two categories based on how they function in cocktails. They can add a distinctive flavor, or they can amplify other flavors, drawing out and heightening the dominant flavors in the drink. To draw a culinary analogy, flavoring bitters are the pepper, while amplifying bitters are the salt. Sometimes bitters can do both.

For example, in our root Old-Fashioned recipe, we include a dash of Bitter Truth aromatic bitters in addition to the Angostura bitters. The Angostura acts as the flavoring bitters, binding the whiskey and sugar together, while the dash of Bitter Truth adds clove and cinnamon notes, which amplify the spice flavors within the Elijah Craig bourbon. If you were to use those same Bitter Truth aromatic bitters in a cocktail that includes a heavily spiced ingredient—cinnamon syrup, for example—it would amplify the spice even more.

Flavoring Bitters: Examples include Angostura aromatic bitters, Dr. Adam Elmegirab's Boker bitters, Fee Brothers whiskey barrel–aged bitters, Bitter Truth aromatic bitters, yuzu bitters, eucalyptus bitters, toasted pecan bitters, and celery bitters.

Amplifying Bitters: Examples include Fee Brothers West Indian orange bitters, Regan's orange bitters, and Bittermens Xocolatl mole bitters.

EVALUATING BITTERS

Here's a method you can use to taste unfamiliar styles of bitters: Fill two glasses with cold seltzer (not mineral water, which has more flavor). Use one to refresh your palate (continuing to do so while tasting), and add a few dashes of bitters to the other glass and stir briefly. The seltzer will stretch out the bitters' concentrated flavor profile, and its bubbles will lift its volatile aromas to your nose. If you can't smell or taste much in the glass, add more bitters until you can.

After taking a few sips of the bittered seltzer, place a drop of bitters on the back of your hand and lick it off. The flavors that were previously diluted will now be intense and pungent. This tasting of the bitters straight from the bottle is important for analyzing the sweetness of the bitters, which can vary widely from product to product, in part depending on whether caramelized sugar is used to add color. Many brands also contain some glycerin, which has a somewhat sweet flavor; with these, adding too much to a cocktail can make the drink taste oddly cloying without being noticeably sweet.

If you still feel unclear about the qualities of the bitters, put a drop of bitters on the palm of one hand, rub your hands together, and then cup your hands around your nose and mouth. This activates the intense aromas in the bitters.

EXPERIMENTING WITH THE SEASONING

The Old-Fashioned is an excellent template for exploring bitters, since they are such an integral part of the template. Swap in different styles of bitters and see what happens: Does a given bitters provide greater flavor dynamics (flavoring bitters), or does it allow you to taste other ingredients in the drink in a new light (amplifying bitters)? If neither of these things occurs, try another type—or rethink how you're using the bitters. It may be that the type of bitters you're using is too weak and another one would come through more assertively.

You don't need to add bitters to every cocktail, and more bitters won't necessarily make a better cocktail. Esoteric combinations of bitters won't be interesting if they lack context or if they don't provide thoughtful seasoning. Yuzu bitters might sound great on paper and be delicious in a different context, but add them to a bourbon-based Old-Fashioned and you're in questionable territory, as the astringency of yuzu may clash with the tangy bite of bourbon.

Normandie Club Old-Fashioned

ALEX DAY AND DEVON TARBY, 2015

In this Old-Fashioned, one of our most popular cocktails at the Normandie Club, we've manipulated both the core and the balance, using an infused bourbon and a spiced syrup. This cocktail showed us that coconut can shine in spirituous concoctions beyond the usual tiki drinks if it's incorporated into an infusion; just as with nuts, it adds rich body and toasty flavors.

2 ounces Coconut-Infused Bourbon (page 289)

1 teaspoon Clear Creek 8-year apple brandy

1 teaspoon Spiced Almond Demerara Gum Syrup (page 56)

1 dash Angostura bitters

Garnish: 1 dried apple slice on a skewer

Stir all the ingredients over ice, then strain into an Old-Fashioned glass over 1 large ice cube. Garnish with the dried apple slice.

Improved Whiskey Cocktail

CLASSIC

In the Fancy-Free (page 13), the addition of just one dash of orange bitters draws out flavors in the spirits, but the Angostura bitters still serve as the main seasoning agent. By contrast, the Improved Whiskey Cocktail, which was probably one of the first popular Old-Fashioned variations, turns to absinthe for seasoning, which adds a deep complexity to the cocktail. The sweet red-licorice and anise flavors from the Peychaud's bitters dial up the seasoning even more, while also increasing the impression of sweetness.

2 ounces Elijah Craig Small Batch bourbon

1 teaspoon Maraska maraschino liqueur

1 dash absinthe

1 dash Angostura bitters

1 dash Peychaud's bitters

Garnish: 1 lemon twist

Stir all the ingredients over ice, then strain into an Old-Fashioned glass over 1 large ice cube. Express the lemon twist over the drink, then place it into the drink.

Pop Quiz

DEVON TARBY, 2010

Substituting a sweet liqueur or amaro for the sugar in an Old-Fashioned–style cocktail is an amazing way to balance a drink while incorporating a unique seasoning. This approach led to the iconic Elder Fashion in our first book and has been a source of inspiration ever since. In the Pop Quiz, Devon includes an orange-flavored amaro, Ramazzotti, and swaps in spicy, chocolaty bitters.

2 ounces Elijah Craig Small Batch bourbon

½ ounce Ramazzotti

1 teaspoon simple syrup (page 45)

2 dashes Bittermens Xocolatl mole bitters

Garnish: 1 orange twist

Stir all the ingredients over ice, then strain into an Old-Fashioned glass over 1 large ice cube. Express the orange twist over the drink, then gently rub it around the rim of the glass and place it into the drink.

Night Owl

ALEX DAY, 2013

This riff on the Pop Quiz (see left) is an example of a Mr. Potato Head variation—making a new drink by swapping out one or more elements. Here, Alex wanted to make a drink that tasted like boozy chocolate without coming across as dessert in a glass. The seasoning comes from not only the bitters but also the amaro.

2 ounces Elijah Craig Small Batch bourbon

½ ounce Cacao Nib–Infused Ramazzotti (page 288)

½ teaspoon Demerara Gum Syrup (page 54)

3 dashes Miracle Mile toasted pecan bitters

Garnish: 1 lemon twist

Stir all the ingredients over ice, then strain into an Old-Fashioned glass over 1 large ice cube. Express the lemon twist over the drink, then place it into the drink.

DAVE FERNIE

Dave Fernie is a bartender and bar operator from Los Angeles who has worked at Honeycut, The Walker Inn, and The Normandie Club. Previously, Dave worked with Houston Hospitality and Sprout LA, both in Los Angeles, and at the River Café in New York City.

My first Old-Fashioned experience didn't sell me on the drink. I was at a holiday party at a sports bar, and some guy handed me a drink and said, "Try this Old-Fashioned. It's awesome!" It had a bright red cancer cherry and smashed-up orange in it. I took a sip and it was . . . so sweet . . . so gross. I wasn't sure what all the fuss was about and decided to stick to beer. It wasn't too long until I revisited the drink at the Campbell Apartment in New York City and had a much better experience. That Old-Fashioned set me on the path.

I eventually learned how to make one when I was bartending at the River Café in Brooklyn. I didn't know much about cocktails yet, and I had an epic fear of failure. (It wasn't unfounded. One time someone came in and ordered a Rob Roy. I made him a Roy Rogers, which is Coke and grenadine, a nonalcoholic drink.) So I spent my free time watching bartenders at the cool bars around town—Little Branch, Pegu Club, Milk & Honey—and reading old cocktail books. I think I made my first proper Old-Fashioned from a recipe in *The Savoy Cocktail Book*.

The thing I love most about the Old-Fashioned is how the drink can open your eyes to cool new cocktail ideas. I remember drinking a rum

Old-Fashioned at the Richardson in Brooklyn. I wasn't a big fan of rum at that point and had no idea what rhum agricole was, but this drink at the Richardson was made with Rhum JM VSOP and sweetened with honey. I remember thinking, *This simple thing is fucking ridiculous*. That started my obsession with rum and led me to trying and making other rum-based variations on the Old-Fashioned.

If you don't love an Old-Fashioned, it's pretty tough to be a bartender. You basically have to put some kind of Old-Fashioned-style drink on every cocktail menu. In many ways the drink is a great utility player at a bar: you can approach it from so many different directions, and its formula makes it easy to plug and play. For this reason it's often the last drink we add to a menu, because if we're missing a mezcal cocktail or one made with a peaty scotch, the Old-Fashioned template can easily showcase either of those spirits.

As for me, I don't like using top-shelf booze in my Old-Fashioneds. I understand the impetus for putting Pappy Van Winkle or Willett in an Old-Fashioned, but I think that misses the point of the drink. The original Old-Fashioned was a way to make

shitty booze taste better, and we should honor that. After all, you don't put Château Margaux in a Kalimotxo, you know? Beyond that, paying attention to the little nuances, like what sweetener you're using, and whether you express the orange twist and discard it or drop it into the drink, is what elevates the Old-Fashioned from a pedestrian cocktail to something elegant and memorable.

Dave Fernie's Old-Fashioned

2 ounces Evan Williams "Black Label" bourbon

1 teaspoon Demerara Gum Syrup (page 54)

2 dashes Angostura bitters

Garnish: 1 orange twist and 1 lemon twist

Stir all the ingredients over ice, then strain into an Old-Fashioned glass over 1 large ice cube. Express the orange twist over the drink, then gently rub it around the rim of the glass and place it into the drink. Express the lemon twist over the drink, then place it into the drink.

EXPLORING TECHNIQUE: UNDERDILUTED STIRRING

Many traditional recipes for Old-Fashioneds call for the drink to be built in the glass in which it will be served. The sugar goes in first (in granules or cube form) and is stirred or muddled with the bitters and a splash of water. Then the whiskey is added, followed by a large ice cube, and the drink is stirred until it's properly diluted.

Because the Old-Fashioned is served on ice, it continues to become more diluted while in the glass. The term *underdiluted* is relative to the full dilution we would seek in, say, a Martini (the topic of chapter 2), where the cocktail is served up after being stirred with ice until the ingredients have fully integrated, the cocktail is bracingly cold, and enough dilution has occurred to temper the intensity of the alcohol. For the Old-Fashioned, we have to pull our punch a bit, stopping short of full dilution and aiming for a point where the booze is still sharp and slightly abrasive.

With time and attention to detail, the traditional technique can yield a fantastic cocktail. But over years of training bartenders, we've found that in a bustling bar, there's never enough time or attention to ensure that the sugar is completely dissolved and the drink is adequately diluted. It takes about 3 minutes to properly make an Old-Fashioned using this method, which is about 2 minutes more than a busy bartender can spare. So sometimes the result is an underdiluted drink with a sludge of sugar at the bottom of the glass.

For these reasons, we usually build our Old-Fashioneds in a mixing glass, stirring the drink with 1-inch ice cubes until it's just shy of full dilution—that is, when the liquid is cold and the ingredients are well integrated, but the whiskey's alcoholic bite is still noticeable—then straining it into an Old-Fashioned glass over a single large cube of ice (though a few 1-inch cubes would also work). Stirring over the 1-inch ice cubes quickly cools and dilutes the drink, and then pouring it over a large cube of ice allows for slower dilution in the glass, extending the amount of time the drink will be in proper balance after it's been served.

The extra step of building the drink in a mixing glass not only saves time and makes it easier to mix consistent drinks, but also helps us adjust for different ingredients: higher-proof spirits (100% ABV and above) may need just a little more dilution than 80-proof liquors. Beyond Old-Fashioneds, we use this method for all stirred drinks that will be served on ice.

All of that said, building an Old-Fashioned in the glass is possible. You need an ice cube that's large enough to fill the glass and that won't shrink so much after stirring that it bobs in the liquid. This is a cardinal sin in Old-Fashioned making: if the ice floats, the drink will dilute rapidly. If building the drink in the glass is your preferred method, select a block of ice that seems slightly too large to fit in the glass. Add the ingredients to the glass and place the ice on top; it might not fully drop into the liquid right away, but while you carefully stir, it will begin to settle into the drink. Continue to stir, tasting the drink frequently until the abrasiveness of the core spirit tapers off, making sure to stop before the drink tastes watered down. It will take about 2 minutes, depending on the size of the ice and how fast you stir.

GLASSWARE: THE OLD-FASHIONED GLASS

Like the Martini and Highball, the Old-Fashioned is one of those cocktails lucky enough to have its own eponymous glassware. Also called a rocks glass, our ideal Old-Fashioned glass holds between 12 and 14 ounces of liquid, making it large enough to fit 2 to 3 ounces of cocktail and a large block of ice, with the ice resting below the rim of the glass without bobbing around in the drink. (A loose ice cube will melt and dilute the drink more quickly, and is also more likely to splash the drink in your face when you sip it.) This size of glass also accommodates drinks served over crushed ice, such as cobblers, and in a pinch can house a Julep.

The glass should have a thick, weighted base. We prefer the sides of the glass to be as thin as possible, though we usually have to compromise on thicker, sturdier glasses to withstand the rigors of bar service. The overall shape should ideally taper slightly toward the base, as this makes the drink easier to hold (and smell). There are some exceptions: for serving Sazeracs (page 33) and their variations, we usually use a smaller glass with straight sides, as this helps concentrate the aroma of absinthe (or other spirit) used to rinse the glass.

Old-Fashioned glasses don't come in as many styles as coupes or Martini glasses, but there are a few options that we love and buy repeatedly. As is typically the case with barware (or anything, really), the Japanese make some of the best glassware we can find; our favorite producer is Hard Strong, which makes beautiful glassware that's both delicate and sturdy. The Germans make some great glassware as well, especially Schott Zwiesel, particularly within the Charles Schumann line (see Resources, page 299). One can never be disappointed with Riedel, either, which has a slew of options. It all depends on your personal style.

OLD-FASHIONED VARIATIONS

Up to this point, we've outlined three different tactics for understanding and creating variations on the Old-Fashioned. But in actual practice, we often combine several of these tactics. The cocktails in this section were developed by playing with multiple elements of a cocktail—the core, the balance, and the seasoning.

Snowbird

DEVON TARBY, 2014

The split-base strategy that makes the Ned Ryerson (page 23) successful can be used to generate a wide variety of drinks. We particularly love pulling back on the base and adding another spirit, like apple brandy, to accent the primary spirit. Together, rye and apple brandy are a magical, crowd-pleasing combination, and St-Germain makes everything it touches taste better. A dash of celery bitters adds just enough savoriness to pull the drink back from excessive sweetness.

> 1½ ounces Rittenhouse rye
>
> ½ ounce Clear Creek 2-year apple brandy
>
> ½ ounce Cardamom-Infused St-Germain (page 288)
>
> ½ teaspoon Demerara Gum Syrup (page 54)
>
> 4 drops Miracle Mile celery bitters
>
> Garnish: 1 grapefruit twist

Stir all the ingredients over ice, then strain into an Old-Fashioned glass over 1 large ice cube. Express the grapefruit twist over the drink and place it into the glass.

Cold Girl Fever

DEVON TARBY, 2016

When coming up with new cocktail recipes, we often riff on an existing variation from our repertoire. This drink is based on the Golden Boy (page 10), and while it doesn't share any ingredients with that cocktail, it does take inspiration from its flavors: From the same starting point of raisins and whiskey, Devon took this cocktail to a smokier place by adding a touch of peaty Islay scotch to the core and balancing it out with raisin-infused honey syrup.

1¾ ounces Famous Grouse scotch

¼ ounce Laphroaig 10-year scotch

1 teaspoon Raisin Honey Syrup (page 286)

2 dashes Angostura bitters

Garnish: 1 orange twist and 1 lemon twist

Stir all the ingredients over ice, then strain into an Old-Fashioned glass over 1 large ice cube. Express the orange twist over the drink, then gently rub it around the rim of the glass and place it into the drink. Express the lemon twist over the drink, then place it into the drink.

Ned Ryerson

DEVON TARBY, 2012

In the Ned Ryerson, the core includes a small portion of young apple brandy, which adds a juicy flavor to the cocktail, and the Miracle Mile Castilian bitters in the seasoning are full of orange, licorice, and sarsaparilla notes. The result is an Old-Fashioned that's been reimagined with just modest changes.

1½ ounces Bulleit rye

½ ounce Clear Creek 2-year apple brandy

1 teaspoon Demerara Gum Syrup (page 54)

2 dashes Miracle Mile Castilian bitters

1 dash House Orange Bitters (page 295)

Garnish: 1 lemon twist

Stir all the ingredients over ice, then strain into an Old-Fashioned glass over 1 large ice cube. Express the lemon twist over the drink, then place it into the drink.

Deadpan

ALEX DAY AND DEVON TARBY, 2014

This is as rich and decadent as an Old-Fashioned gets, but there's not a drop of sugar syrup in it. Instead, the drink derives its sweetness from both a raisiny sherry and a vanilla liqueur, which provide a counterpunch to the nutty split base of Cognac and rum infused with sesame seeds. A dash of bitters is all that's required to zip these big flavors together.

1 ounce Pierre Ferrand 1840 Cognac

1 ounce Sesame-Infused Rum (page 292)

¼ ounce Lustau East India solera sherry

¼ ounce Giffard Vanille de Madagascar

1 dash Bitter Truth Jerry Thomas bitters

Garnish: 1 orange twist

Stir all the ingredients over ice, then strain into an Old-Fashioned glass over 1 large ice cube. Express the orange twist over the drink, then gently rub it around the rim of the glass and place it into the drink.

Autumn Old-Fashioned

DEVON TARBY, 2013

The Conference, a groundbreaking Old-Fashioned variation developed by former Death & Co head bartender Brian Miller, has a core that's divided between four different brown spirits. The Autumn Old-Fashioned is a richer, deeper expression of that drink. We usually like to use maple syrup as a sweetener when we combine this many big flavors; it has a brightness that keeps the spirits from becoming too heavy.

½ ounce George Dickel rye

½ ounce Laird's 100-proof straight apple brandy

½ ounce Tariquet VSOP Bas-Armagnac

½ ounce Bank Note scotch

1 teaspoon dark, robust maple syrup

2 dashes Bittermens Xocolatl mole bitters

1 dash Angostura bitters

Garnish: 1 orange twist and 1 lemon twist

Stir all the ingredients over ice, then strain into an Old-Fashioned glass over 1 large ice cube. Express the orange twist over the drink, then gently rub it around the rim of the glass and place it into the drink. Express the lemon twist over the drink, then place it into the drink.

Bad Santa

DEVON TARBY, 2015

This crystal clear drink tastes like minty dark chocolate, earning its place among what we like to call "mindfuck drinks." Vodka is a nontraditional base spirit for an Old-Fashioned-style drink for sure, but infusing it with cocoa butter and adding a splash of chocolate liqueur gives it the richness and complexity of an aged spirit. With a drink this rich and sweet, a bit of savory seasoning, in this case Salt Solution, is needed to brighten the flavors.

2 ounces Cocoa Butter–Infused Absolut Elyx Vodka (page 289)

¼ ounce Giffard white crème de cacao

¼ ounce Giffard Vanille de Madagascar

1 teaspoon Giffard Menthe-Pastille

1 drop Salt Solution (page 298)

Garnish: 1 small candy cane

Stir all the ingredients over ice, then strain into an Old-Fashioned glass over 1 large ice cube. Garnish with the candy cane.

Beach Bonfire

ALEX DAY, 2015

Developed for the inaugural Pacific Coast Highway–themed menu at the Walker Inn, the Beach Bonfire is designed to evoke the experience of sitting around a fire and taking alternating sips from a flask of whiskey and a cold beer. We start with our benchmark bourbon and add some cachaça for its chocolate and cinnamon notes, then sweeten the drink with pineapple syrup, which adds a nod to summer without making the drink taste tropical. At the bar, we'd hit the finished drink with a blast of hickory smoke before serving it next to a small glass of pilsner; at home you can skip the smoke and the beer if you like.

1½ ounces Elijah Craig Small Batch bourbon

½ ounce Avuá Amburana cachaça

1 teaspoon Pineapple Gum Syrup (page 56)

1 dash Angostura bitters

1 dash Bittermens Xocolatl mole bitters

Garnish: 1 dehydrated pineapple slice and a glass of pilsner

Stir all the ingredients over ice, then strain into an Old-Fashioned glass over 1 large ice cube. Using a PolyScience Smoking Gun or something similar, shoot some hickory smoke over the drink to create just a whisper of smoke aroma (see page 274 for instructions). Garnish with the dehydrated pineapple and serve with the glass of beer alongside.

Beach Bonfire

THE OLD-FASHIONED EXTENDED FAMILY

By manipulating the Old-Fashioned template, you can create whole new categories of drinks. What connects the root recipe and the recipes in the extended family is that they all focus on a core flavor and contain only small amounts of sweetener and seasoning. In the recipes that follow, we've highlighted our versions of some classic recipes, each followed by some of our own original cocktails inspired by these classics.

Champagne Cocktail

CLASSIC

A Champagne Cocktail is essentially an Old-Fashioned in which Champagne stands in for the whiskey. Because of the lower alcohol content of the Champagne, partially diluting the drink as you would an Old-Fashioned doesn't make sense, and, of course, the bubbles in the Champagne wouldn't be well served by stirring. Therefore, this drink is built in a flute. Given that it isn't stirred over ice, like an Old-Fashioned, be sure to start with cold Champagne.

1 sugar cube
Angostura bitters
Dry Champagne
Garnish: 1 lemon twist

Place the sugar cube on a paper towel. Dash the bitters over the sugar cube until it's completely saturated. Drop the sugar cube into a chilled flute and slowly top with Champagne; don't stir. Express the lemon twist over the drink, then place it into the drink.

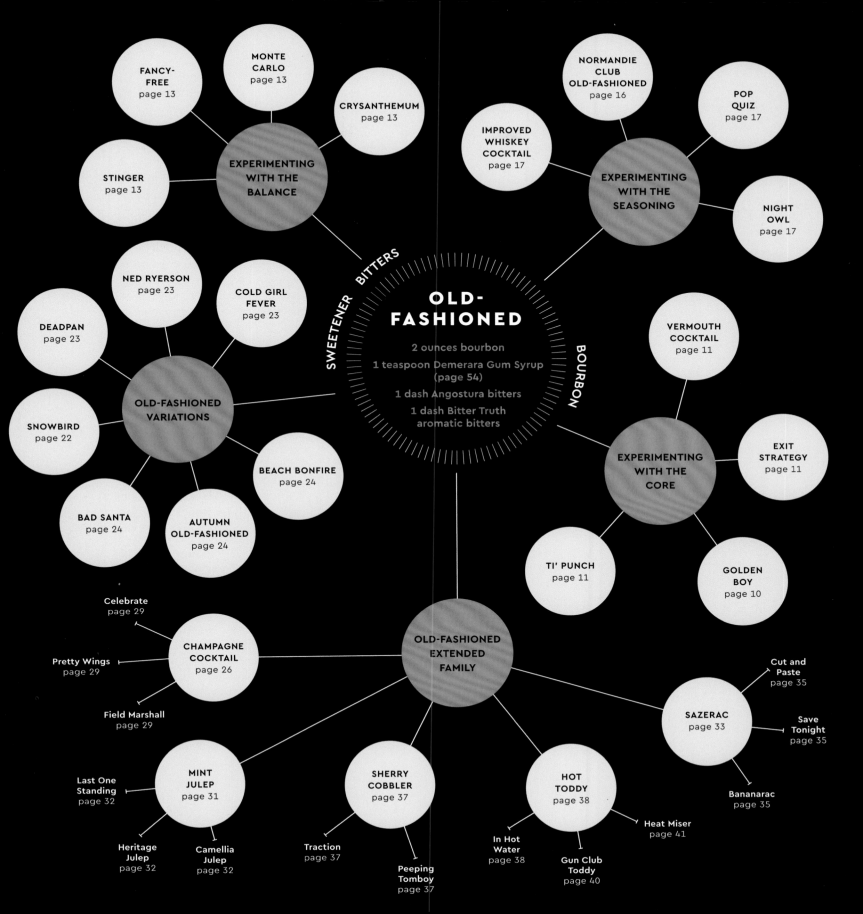

OLD-FASHIONED

2 ounces bourbon

1 teaspoon Demerara Gum Syrup (page 54)

1 dash Angostura bitters

1 dash Bitter Truth aromatic bitters

SWEETENER

BITTERS

BOURBON

EXPERIMENTING WITH THE BALANCE

FANCY-FREE
page 13

MONTE CARLO
page 13

CRYSANTHEMUM
page 13

STINGER
page 13

EXPERIMENTING WITH THE SEASONING

NORMANDIE CLUB OLD-FASHIONED
page 16

POP QUIZ
page 17

IMPROVED WHISKEY COCKTAIL
page 17

NIGHT OWL
page 17

OLD-FASHIONED VARIATIONS

NED RYERSON
page 23

COLD GIRL FEVER
page 23

DEADPAN
page 23

SNOWBIRD
page 22

BEACH BONFIRE
page 24

BAD SANTA
page 24

AUTUMN OLD-FASHIONED
page 24

EXPERIMENTING WITH THE CORE

VERMOUTH COCKTAIL
page 11

EXIT STRATEGY
page 11

TI' PUNCH
page 11

GOLDEN BOY
page 10

OLD-FASHIONED EXTENDED FAMILY

CHAMPAGNE COCKTAIL
page 26

Celebrate
page 29

Pretty Wings
page 29

Field Marshall
page 29

MINT JULEP
page 31

Last One Standing
page 32

Heritage Julep
page 32

Camellia Julep
page 32

SHERRY COBBLER
page 37

Traction
page 37

Peeping Tomboy
page 37

HOT TODDY
page 38

In Hot Water
page 38

Gun Club Toddy
page 40

Heat Miser
page 41

SAZERAC
page 33

Cut and Paste
page 35

Save Tonight
page 35

Bananarac
page 35

In cocktails, sparkling wine does multiple things: it adds effervescence, proof (alcoholic content), flavor, acidity, and sweetness. It's extremely helpful to become familiar with specific bottles and how each will impact recipes. But more fundamentally, it's useful to understand the most common styles, which we outline below. We haven't suggested specific bottles because the availability of certain brands is sporadic. Plus, any given wine changes from year to year.

Champagne is the king of sparkling wines. It's also expensive and probably best reserved for special occasions. If you do want to get fancy, we recommend using drier Champagnes (no sweeter than brut), which will have flavors of peach, cherries, citrus, almonds, and bread. Common styles are nonvintage (the house's consistent flagship bottle, aged for a minimum of fifteen months on the lees), blanc de blancs (made only from Chardonnay grapes), blanc de noirs (made only from Pinot Noir and Pinot Meunier), rosé (allowing contact with the grape skins for color), vintage (aged a minimum of three years on the lees), and special cuvée (aged for an average of six to seven years on the lees).

Crémant is our go-to sparkling wine for cocktails. Made in similar style to Champagne (though slightly lower age requirements), crémants are made in eight regions of France and can be phenomenally affordable. We prefer Crémant de Bourgogne and Crémant d'Alsace for their similarity to Champagne; using similar grapes grown in a nearby region, these are sparkling wines of incredible complexity. As with Champagne, we steer toward drier styles of crémant.

Cava is Spain's answer to Champagne, made in the same traditional method as Champagne. The grapes used for cava (Macabeo, Xarello, and Parellada) produce a sparkling wine that has whispers of its French counterpart but an entirely different flavor: fresh apple and pear, lime zest, quince, and just a bit of the almond found in Champagne. There are three quality levels to be aware of: cava is the standard marker, with at least nine months of aging on the lees; reserva spends a minimum of fifteen months aging on the lees; and gran reserva has a minimum of thirty months aging on the lees and vintage dating on the label.

Prosecco is made using the Charmant method, a process where the wine undergoes a secondary fermentation in a large container to create effervescence (as opposed to Champagne or Traditional method, which undergoes secondary fermentation within the bottle). Hailing from the Italian regions of Veneto and Friuli Venezia Giulia, prosecco has a fresh quality to it: green apple, melon, pear, and even a little dairy creaminess. It comes in three sweetness levels: (brut, extra dry, and dry). The flavor, body, and bubble size of prosecco are quite different from those of sparkling wines made using the traditional method, so we don't recommend stocking prosecco as your only mixing bubbly; however, it can be a great mixer in traditional Italian aperitif cocktails like the Aperol Spritz (page 223), where it acts as a soft supporting player to more powerful ingredients.

Lambrusco is Italy's other famous sparkling wine, but aside from using the same production method as prosecco, it could hardly be more different. Of the thirteen grape varieties named Lambrusco, the two most planted are Lambrusco Salamino and Lambrusco Grasparossa. The grapes are first made into a sweet, fresh red wine, which is then made into a sparkling wine. Expect strong flavors of strawberry, raspberry, and rhubarb. Lambrusco comes in three sweetness levels: secco (dry), semisecco (off-dry), and dolce or amabile (sweet). We don't use Lambrusco often in cocktails, but it can add a juicy complexity and slight fizziness to drinks.

The Field Marshall

ALEX DAY, 2013

Riffing on a Champagne Cocktail can be as easy as riffing on any other Old-Fashioned variation. In this case, the sugar is swapped out for a sweet liqueur. Combier is an orange curaçao, and the "royal" bottling has a base of Cognac, which provides a rich backbone. In a way, this variation lies somewhere between a classic Champagne Cocktail and an Old-Fashioned, being made with Armagnac and Champagne instead of whiskey.

1 ounce Tariquet Classique VS Bas-Armagnac

½ ounce Royal Combier

2 dashes Angostura bitters

2 dashes Peychaud's bitters

Dry Champagne

Garnish: 1 lemon twist

Stir all the ingredients (except the Champagne) over ice, then strain into a chilled flute. Pour in the Champagne, and quickly dip the barspoon into the glass to gently mix the Champagne with the cocktail. Express the lemon twist over the drink, then place it into the drink.

Pretty Wings

DEVON TARBY, 2016

Inspired by famed bartender Dave Kupchinsky's Lemonade cocktail at the Everleigh in West Hollywood, this drink also looks to the Champagne Cocktail for its simplicity and incorporates flavorful chamomile in an infusion of softly herbaceous and slightly bitter Cocchi Americano. It's exceedingly refreshing on a hot day.

½ ounce Chamomile-Infused Cocchi Americano (page 288)

1 teaspoon Suze

1 dash Bittermens hopped grapefruit bitters

5 ounces Champagne

Garnish: 1 lemon wheel

Stir all the ingredients (except the Champagne) over ice, then strain into a chilled flute. Pour in the Champagne, and quickly dip the barspoon into the glass to gently mix the Champagne with the cocktail. Garnish with the lemon wheel.

Celebrate

DEVON TARBY, 2016

While the components of this cocktail other than the Champagne—take up more volume than a sugar cube doused in bitters, they function in a similar way, enhancing the main spirit by amplifying flavors it already possesses: stone fruit, breadiness, nuttiness, and spice. Here we've added a new ingredient, Champagne acid, a combination of tartaric and lactic acid that enhances the tang of a dry Champagne.

½ ounce Clear Creek pear brandy

¼ ounce Lustau Jarana fino sherry

1 teaspoon Fortaleza reposado tequila

¼ ounce Cinnamon Syrup (page 52)

½ teaspoon Champagne Acid Solution (page 298)

4 ounces dry Champagne

Stir all the ingredients (except the Champagne) over ice, then strain into a chilled flute. Pour in the Champagne and quickly dip the barspoon into the glass to gently mix the Champagne with the cocktail. No garnish.

JULEP

In essence, a Julep is like an especially refreshing Old-Fashioned that substitutes mint for the bitters. Many Southerners will cry foul at this explanation, insisting that the ritual of making a Julep, a sacred heritage below the Mason-Dixon Line, is something Yankees are incapable of understanding.

Be that as it may, we'll stick our necks out and devote a few extra words to Julep-making technique. Begin by grabbing four or five healthy mint sprigs, enough to create a tight bouquet that spreads to about 4 inches in diameter, and trim the stems to 6 inches. Trim off the lower leaves (hopefully reserving them for another use). Holding an empty Julep tin by the edge (to avoid getting the oils from your hands on the tin, which will prevent frosting), insert the bouquet, upside down, into the Julep tin and lightly rub the leaves against the interior of the tin, using just enough force that you smell mint but not enough to bruise the leaves. Set the mint aside. Add the spirits and sweetener to the tin and stir briefly with a barspoon to combine. Add crushed ice until the tin is about four-fifths full and slowly stir until frost begins to form on the exterior of the tin. Once the tin is frosted, top with a cone of crushed ice and insert a straw along one side. Jiggle the straw in a small circle to create a small channel, then carefully slide the mint bouquet into this channel so that the leaves are tightly bunched together and the sprigs look like they're growing from the ice.

Mint Julep

CLASSIC

1 mint bouquet
2 ounces Buffalo Trace bourbon
¼ ounce simple syrup (page 45)

Rub the interior of a Julep tin with the mint bouquet, then set the mint aside. Add the bourbon and syrup and fill the tin halfway with crushed ice. Holding the tin by the rim, stir, churning the ice as you go, for about 10 seconds. Add more crushed ice to fill the tin about two-thirds full and stir until the tin is completely frosted. Add more ice to form a cone above the rim. Garnish with the mint bouquet and serve with a straw.

EXPERIMENTING WITH OTHER HERBS

Mint is a wonderfully versatile herb for cocktails. It can be incorporated via muddling or steeping, or it can aromatize the top of a drink when it's used as a garnish. That said, we highly recommend playing with the Julep template by substituting other herbs, whether other mint varieties (such as pineapple mint or chocolate mint) or basil in its many varieties, sage, and even thyme. Keep in mind that some herbs, like certain varieties of sage, can taste off-putting when muddled, and that muddling thyme creates a big mess and doesn't taste that great. When substituting such herbs, you may want to use them simply as an aromatic garnish, or you might try extracting their flavor through an infusion or syrup instead.

Last One Standing

NATASHA DAVID, 2014

The combination of Cognac and Jamaican rum appears frequently in older cocktail recipes. Here, the duo creates a big, funky core flavor that plays off the bright fruit of the peach liqueur. The amaro acts as a bridge between these two opposing camps, working in much the same way that bitters do, balancing other disparate flavors.

1 mint bouquet

1 ounce Pierre Ferrand 1840 Cognac

½ ounce Hamilton Jamaican pot still gold rum

¾ ounce Amaro CioCiaro

1 teaspoon Giffard Crème de Pêche

Garnish: 1 peach slice and confectioners' sugar

Rub the interior of a Julep tin with the mint bouquet, then set the mint aside. Add the remaining ingredients and fill the tin halfway with crushed ice. Holding the tin by the rim, stir, churning the ice as you go, for about 10 seconds. Add more crushed ice to fill the tin about two-thirds full and stir until the tin is completely frosted. Add more ice to form a cone above the rim. Garnish with the mint bouquet and peach slice, then lightly dust the top of the mint with confectioners' sugar. Serve with a straw.

Heritage Julep

ALEX DAY AND DEVON TARBY, 2015

The baked stone fruit and warm autumn flavors of this cocktail make it a great option for an Old-Fashioned lover who's looking for something on the more refreshing side. We double down on pear, bringing the spirituous heat and pear-like gritty texture thanks to pear brandy and the supple fruitiness of the pear liqueur. The addition of Amaro Montenegro brings this drink into the aperitif category.

1 mint bouquet

1¼ ounces Busnel Pays d'Auge VSOP Calvados

½ ounce Clear Creek pear liqueur

¼ ounce Clear Creek pear brandy

¼ ounce Amaro Montenegro

1 teaspoon Cinnamon Syrup (page 52)

2 dashes phosphoric acid solution (see page 194)

Garnish: 3 apple slices on a skewer and confectioners' sugar

Rub the interior of a Julep tin with the mint bouquet, then set the mint aside. Add the remaining ingredients and fill the tin halfway with crushed ice. Holding the tin by the rim, stir, churning the ice as you go, for about 10 seconds. Add more crushed ice to fill the tin about two-thirds full and stir until the tin is completely frosted. Add more ice to form a cone above the rim. Garnish with the mint bouquet and the apple slices, then lightly dust the top of the mint with the confectioners' sugar. Serve with a straw.

Camellia Julep

DEVON TARBY, 2013

When we use an unaged spirit as the core of a cocktail, we often add other ingredients to mimic the flavors typically contributed by oak and time. Here, we use a clean, straightforward pear distillate that's been infused with bitter cacao nibs, enhanced with the nut and spice flavors from the amontillado sherry.

1 mint bouquet

1½ ounces Cacao Nib–Infused Pear Brandy (page 287)

½ ounce Lustau Los Arcos amontillado sherry

1 teaspoon Demerara Gum Syrup (page 54)

Rub the interior of a Julep tin with the mint bouquet, then set the mint aside. Add the remaining ingredients and fill the tin halfway with crushed ice. Holding the tin by the rim, stir, churning the ice as you go, for about 10 seconds. Add more crushed ice to fill the tin about two-thirds full and stir until the tin is completely frosted. Add more ice to form a cone above the rim. Garnish with the mint bouquet and serve with a straw.

Sazerac

Truly great cocktails become iconic. A Sazerac is such a drink. When you look at the Sazerac's composition—spirit, sugar, bitters, citrus—it's so obviously linked to the Old-Fashioned, yet there are differences: While both are served in an Old-Fashioned glass, the Old-Fashioned is served on ice, whereas the Sazerac is served neat. The Old-Fashioned is garnished with twists of citrus in the glass, whereas the Sazerac has a lemon twist expressed over the glass, but the twist is then discarded. Most dramatically, the Sazerac plays a trick on the drinker's senses: Before the cocktail is poured, the glass is rinsed with absinthe, creating a pungent anise and citrus aroma that persists until the glass is empty—an aroma that contrasts with the cool, boozy liquid below. It's this technique—rinsing the glass with a highly aromatic spirit—that sets a Sazerac apart and defines it and the variations on it that follow.

The Sazerac also provides a good example of how classic cocktails evolved based on regionally available ingredients. In the mid-1800s, the spirit of choice in Francophilic New Orleans—the Sazerac's birthplace—was Cognac, but by the end of the century a shortage of French brandy due to a phylloxera outbreak that plagued France's vineyards shifted the Big Easy's focus to rye. New Orleans–made Peychaud's bitters, with its distinctive anise flavor, has remained a constant, but we've found that French absinthe and Angostura bitters are welcome additions to the benchmark recipe.

Vieux Pontarlier absinthe

1½ ounces Rittenhouse rye

½ ounce Pierre Ferrand 1840 Cognac

1 teaspoon Demerara Gum Syrup (page 54)

4 dashes Peychaud's bitters

1 dash Angostura bitters

Garnish: 1 lemon twist

Rinse an Old-Fashioned glass with absinthe and dump. Stir the remaining ingredients over ice, then strain into the glass. Express the lemon twist over the drink and discard.

ABSINTHE

In many ways, absinthe and bitters are cut from the same cloth. Just like bitters, absinthe is a highly concentrated flavoring that can be added to cocktails in small quantities as a seasoning, to contribute a bright herbal punch. We sometimes incorporate it by rinsing a glass with absinthe before pouring in the cocktail, a defining technique that sets a Sazerac (page 33) apart from an Old-Fashioned. Because of its proof, absinthe clings to the edge of the glass and perfumes the cocktail, creating a unique aroma that complements or contrasts with the cocktail. Absinthe can also be used in small volumes in a drink to create a bright herbal flavor that creates layers of complexity under a cocktail's core flavor. An example is the Chrysanthemum (page 13), where a teaspoon of absinthe enhances the herbaceousness of dry vermouth and the honeyed spices of Bénédictine. We rarely use more than ¼ ounce absinthe in a cocktail, as it can quickly overshadow the core flavor and bully the other ingredients.

There are several styles of absinthe. We prefer Swiss or French styles for their clean flavors. Some of our favorite bottlings are from Pernod, Emile Pernot, and St. George Spirits.

Cut and Paste

ALEX DAY, 2012

Although it's aged for eight years, the apple brandy in this drink doesn't taste much like an aged spirit, so we also include pot-distilled Irish whiskey, with its vanilla and spice flavors, in the core. And because Irish whiskey has a nice affinity for honey, we use a honey syrup for the sweetener, which keeps the drink light and crisp, whereas Demerara Gum Syrup would probably be too cloying.

Vieux Pontarlier absinthe

1½ ounces Clear Creek 8-year apple brandy

¾ ounce Redbreast 12-year Irish whiskey

¼ ounce Honey Syrup (page 45)

3 dashes Peychaud's bitters

1 dash Angostura bitters

Rinse a chilled Old-Fashioned glass with absinthe and dump. Stir the remaining ingredients over ice, then strain into the glass. No garnish.

Save Tonight

DEVON TARBY, 2017

In this cocktail, the tart bite of the cherry-infused rye whiskey is complemented by juiciness from the apple brandy, but alone those ingredients would come across as sweet and bland. However, just a couple of dashes of absinthe add an anise pop and complexity to the drink, accenting the tart and juicy flavors in an unexpected way—a great demonstration of the power of the seasoning.

Pernod absinthe

1½ ounces Sour Cherry–Infused Rittenhouse Rye (page 292)

½ ounce Clear Creek 2-year apple brandy

1 teaspoon Demerara Gum Syrup (page 54)

2 dashes Peychaud's bitters

2 dashes Pernod absinthe

Garnish: 1 brandied cherry on a skewer

Rinse a chilled Old-Fashioned glass with absinthe and dump. Stir the remaining ingredients over ice, then strain into the glass. Garnish with the cherry.

Bananarac

NATASHA DAVID, 2014

The idea of putting bananas in a boozy cocktail once seemed questionable at best. Then the liqueur company Giffard introduced Banane du Brésil to the US market, a banana liqueur that far exceeded our expectations. When our team first tasted it, we were excited to find it balanced and characterized by a true banana flavor—a rarity in liqueurs. It's also very versatile. Here, it plays a supporting role, seasoning a boozy drink.

Pernod absinthe

1 ounce Pierre Ferrand 1840 Cognac

1 ounce Old Overholt rye

½ ounce Giffard Banane du Brésil

½ teaspoon Demerara Gum Syrup (page 54)

1 dash Bitter Truth Aromatic Bitters

Garnish: 1 lemon twist

Rinse a chilled Old-Fashioned glass with absinthe and dump. Stir the remaining ingredients over ice, then strain into the glass. Express the lemon twist over the drink and discard.

Sherry Cobbler

Sherry Cobbler

CLASSIC

Replace the high-proof whiskey in an Old-Fashioned with a larger quantity of low-proof amontillado sherry, and swap muddled orange slices for the bitters, and you have a Cobbler. Amontillado sherry is a fortified wine that gives the cocktail both body and acidity, making it a strong backbone for the drink. When muddled, the orange wheels add not only a touch of sweetness from the flesh but also some seasoning from the bitter pith and the vibrant oils in the skin. This complexity is nicely counterbalanced by the levity and bright aroma of the fresh mint garnish.

When it comes to the garnish, don't limit yourself to the orange wedge and mint called for here; an array of seasonal fruits is traditional, so play around with whatever fruits or herbs you have on hand. It's become an inside joke among our bartender friends to make the most ludicrous, overgarnished cobbler any time one of us requests one.

3 orange slices

1 teaspoon Cane Sugar Syrup (page 47)

3½ ounces amontillado sherry

Garnish: 1 orange half wheel and 1 mint bouquet

In a Collins glass, muddle the orange slices and syrup. Add the sherry and stir briefly. Top with crushed ice and stir a few times to chill the cocktail. Top with more crushed ice, packing the glass fully. Garnish with the orange half wheel and mint bouquet and serve with a straw.

Traction

DEVON TARBY, 2014

Sherry cobblers were all the rage in nineteenth-century America and we, being obnoxious flag-waving fans of sherry and sherry-based drinks, are happy to keep them in modern rotation. Here, rum shines a light on the dried fruit flavors that are often somewhat hidden in amontillado sherry.

2 lemon wedges

2 strawberry halves

1½ ounces Lustau Los Arcos amontillado sherry

½ ounce Santa Teresa 1796 rum

¾ ounce Milk & Honey House Curaçao (page 295)

Garnish: ½ strawberry, 1 lemon wedge, and 1 mint sprig

In a shaker, muddle the lemon wedges and strawberry halves. Add the remaining ingredients and shake with ice. Double strain into an Old-Fashioned glass filled with crushed ice. Garnish with the strawberry half, lemon wedge, and mint sprig and serve with a straw.

Peeping Tomboy

DEVON TARBY, 2017

Almonds and stone fruits, such as apricots, peaches, and plums, are botanically related, and they tend to taste great together in cocktails. Amontillado sherry continues the nutty theme, while Cognac adds a bit of richness and proof. While fresh stone fruit can be a bit inconsistent in terms of sugar and acid, this template is nicely balanced to accommodate fruits of various ripeness.

1 lemon wedge

1 orange wheel

1 slice seasonal stone fruit

1½ ounces Los Arcos amontillado sherry

¼ ounce Pierre Ferrand Ambre Cognac

¼ ounce Toasted Almond–Infused Apricot Liqueur (page 293)

1 teaspoon Demerara Gum Syrup (page 54)

Garnish: 1 mint sprig, 1 lemon wheel, 1 orange wheel, and 1 slice seasonal stone fruit

In a shaker, muddle the lemon wedge and orange wheel with the syrup. Add the remaining ingredients and whip with a few pieces of crushed ice just until incorporated. Strain into a double Old-Fashioned glass and top with more crushed ice, cresting it over the top of the glass. Garnish with the mint sprig and fruit slices and serve with a straw.

Hot Toddy

CLASSIC

Water is an often overlooked element of cocktails. In our Old-Fashioned, the water comes from a bit of dilution, both while stirring the ingredients over ice and as the chunk of ice in the cocktail melts a bit. A toddy, then, is really just an Old-Fashioned that swaps in hot water for cold. This takes the cocktail in a different direction for two key reasons. First, heat increases the perception of alcohol. If you were to take the same amount of water present in a properly diluted Old-Fashioned—about 1 ounce—and warm it along with the spirit, sweetener, and bitters, you'd have a cocktail with an intensely alcoholic and unpleasant flavor. So for toddies the drink is lengthened. We've found that 4 ounces of water to 2 ounces of spirit is a good baseline.

Second, alcohol evaporates when heated, so when you drink a hot toddy, the volatile aromas will rise to your nose before you take your first sip. This can be off-putting if the drink is too high in proof, but it also allows the drink maker to play with aromas, whether infused into a spirit or inherent in it. Calvados, for example, is ethereal when heated, with a warming perfume that's almost reminiscent of putting on a thick sweater.

Because toddies are both heated and more diluted than other cocktails, they require a bit more sweetener and seasoning than Old-Fashioneds; otherwise, they feel thin. The small amount of lemon juice in the drink doesn't make it acidic; rather, it helps season the cocktail and bring the other components into harmony.

- **2 lemon wedges**
- **1½ ounces Elijah Craig Small Batch bourbon**
- **¾ ounce Honey Syrup (page 45)**
- **1 dash Angostura bitters**
- **4 ounces boiling water**
- **Garnish: 2 lemon wedges and nutmeg**

Squeeze the lemon wedges into a toddy mug, then add the remaining ingredients (except the water). Pour in the boiling water, then grate some nutmeg over the top of the drink and garnish with the lemon wedges.

In Hot Water

BRITTANY FELLS, 2014

If a traditional Hot Toddy isn't wintry enough for you, try this version, which was developed for the Rose, in chilly Jackson Hole, Wyoming. It evokes a boozy cup of coffee, with the Ristretto bringing dense espresso flavors to the mix, and cardamom-laced bitters offering savory flavors reminiscent of chicory.

- **1½ ounces Pierre Ferrand 1840 Cognac**
- **¼ ounce Galliano Ristretto**
- **½ ounce dark, robust maple syrup**
- **1 dash Fee Brothers Cardamom bitters**
- **4 ounces boiling water**
- **Garnish: 1 cinnamon stick**

Combine all the ingredients (except the water) in a mixing glass and stir. Pour into a toddy mug, then pour in the boiling water. Garnish with the cinnamon stick.

Hot Toddy

Gun Club Toddy

ALEX DAY, 2012

A toddy is supposed to be soothing, and in this variation we've tried to add as many comforting elements as possible. Built on a backbone of Calvados and Pineau des Charentes (an aperitif made from unfermented grape juice and young Cognac), and enhanced with the restorative combination of chamomile, lemon, and honey, this toddy is rich and nurturing.

1½ ounces Chamomile-Infused Calvados (page 288)

1 ounce Pineau des Charentes

½ ounce Honey Syrup (page 45)

¼ ounce fresh lemon juice

4 ounces boiling water

Garnish: 5 thin apple slices on a skewer

Combine all the ingredients (except the water) in a mixing glass and stir. Pour into a toddy mug, then pour in the boiling water. Garnish with the apple slices.

Gun Club Toddy

Heat Miser

DEVON TARBY,
KATIE EMMERSON,
AND ALEX DAY, 2015

There's a lot more at play here than in a traditional toddy. The chile-infused bourbon adds gentle heat without making the drink overtly spicy, and bright apple juice stands in for water, adding an extra layer of complexity.

1 ounce Thai Chile–Infused Bourbon (page 293)

½ ounce Luxardo Amaro Abano

½ ounce Alexander Jules amontillado sherry

3 ounces fresh Fuji apple juice

1 teaspoon Medlock Ames verjus

½ ounce dark, robust maple syrup

1 drop Salt Solution (page 298)

Garnish: 3 thin apple slices on a skewer

Combine all the ingredients in a small saucepan over medium-low heat and cook, stirring occasionally, until steaming hot but not simmering. Pour into a toddy mug and garnish with the apple slices.

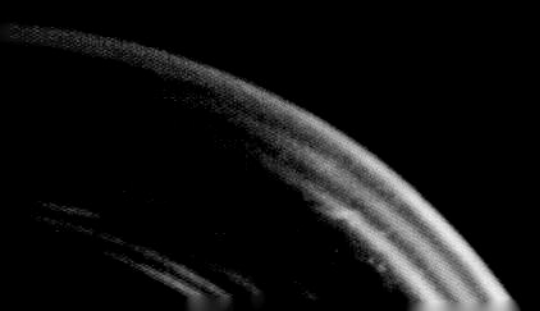

MAPLE SYRUP

Real maple syrup is expensive, and for good reason: it's a pain in the ass to produce. But there's no substitution for the real thing. We've tried a variety of maple syrups in cocktails and found our favorite to be those in the "Grade A Dark Color and Robust Flavor" category. Whereas with honey we seek more subtly, when we choose maple syrup it's because we want distinctive maple flavor. So while experimenting with lighter styles of maple syrup may yield great results, we've found that their subtlety tends to get washed out in cocktails.

Maple syrup's distinct flavor lends itself to some valuable flavor pairings. Maple loves whiskey, apple brandy, and rum, especially aged molasses rum. But it also has an affinity for herbs such as rosemary and sage, and spices like nutmeg. None of this should be surprising; anything that revolves around fall or winter or taps into a feeling of warmth is probably a good match for maple syrup.

We use maple syrup as is when mixing it into cocktails—no manipulation required.

NEXT-LEVEL TECHNIQUE: MAKING SYRUPS

Syrups are common enough in cocktail making, but they aren't always given the attention they deserve. A basic syrup (such as simple syrup, or equal parts water and sugar) is the best way to consistently and accurately add sweetness to a drink. The alternative, using sugar granules, introduces too many variables from sugar to sugar and bartender to bartender. To make the most accurate and consistent syrups, we have taken to making these ingredients with care, technique, and precision.

A basic sugar syrup is also a great platform to build upon, whether by adding another flavor or by using a thickener, such as the gum arabic in our Demerara Gum Syrup (page 54). You can also play with the proportion of sugar to water or substitute an alternative sweetener, such as honey, agave nectar, or maple syrup.

Water quality is an important consideration in making syrups. Some local water sources are perfect for making syrups, others less so. To ensure the best results no matter what the quality of your water, we recommend using filtered water. At some of our bars, we go so far as to soften the water or introduce particular minerals to ensure the quality is as good as possible for making syrups, but for most uses, a standard household water filter will suffice.

VOLUME VS. WEIGHT:
HOW WE MEASURE

As a general rule, we use a gram scale for measuring ingredients when making syrups, infusions, and other cocktail building blocks. Measuring volume by sight, even with measuring cups, tends to be less than accurate, whereas using a scale leads to consistent results. We use two different gram scales: one that can measure large quantities (up to 4 kilograms), and another that can accurately measure extremely small quantities (down to 0.01 gram).

HAND-MIXED SYRUPS

Hand-mixed syrups are simple enough: just mix the
sweetener and water by whisking or shaking. Most
hand-mixed syrups that use granulated sugar are made
with equal parts of sugar and water. Those that use a
liquid sweetener, such as honey, may need a much smaller
proportion of water. We mix syrups by hand when the
ingredients will integrate easily at room temperature,
but also when we want to maintain the ratio of water to
sweetener. For example, simple syrup is often made by
dissolving granulated sugar in boiling water; however,
we prefer to hand mix our simple syrup to ensure that
no water evaporates or boils off, which would alter
the 1-to-1 ratio of sugar to water. Heat also affects the
molecular structure of sugar. For example, if sucrose,
the disaccharide commonly known as white table sugar,
undergoes an extended period of boiling, it will eventually
convert to the monosaccharides glucose and fructose,
which taste sweeter (and cause nasty hangovers).

HOW TO MAKE HAND-MIXED SYRUPS

Gram scale
Bowl
Whisk
Storage container

1 Carefully measure the ingredients by weight.
2 Combine the ingredients in a bowl.
3 Whisk or shake until the sugar is completely dissolved.
4 Pour the syrup into a storage container, cover, and
   refrigerate until ready to use.

Simple Syrup

YIELD: 16 OUNCES

TECHNIQUE: HAND MIXED

Simple syrup is a mixture of equal parts white sugar and water. It has a very neutral flavor, which is one of its best attributes for drink making. We typically use very small amounts of simple syrup—between ½ teaspoon and ¼ ounce—to boost flat flavors or to curb bitterness without destroying it. We use it only in large quantities—¾ ounce to 1 ounce—to balance citrus.

250 grams white sugar
250 grams filtered water

Put the sugar and water in a bowl and whisk until the sugar has dissolved. Transfer to a storage container and refrigerate until ready to use, up to 2 weeks.

Honey Syrup

YIELD: ABOUT 16 OUNCES

TECHNIQUE: HAND MIXED

Most of the honey sold in grocery stores is clover honey. While you can make great drinks with high-quality clover honey, we find that most commercial clover honeys dominate other ingredients in drinks. We prefer lighter clover honeys for making drinks, or better yet, light floral varietals like acacia, which is our favorite for general cocktail use. Unfortunately, good-quality honey is becoming increasingly difficult to find and costly, making it harder for us to find consistent sources of our favorite honeys and even harder to continue justifying their extravagant expense. We've compromised by using a more generic wildflower honey, which has been successful thus far.

Because of honey's viscosity, we combine it with water (at roughly three parts by volume of honey to one part by volume of water) to make it more mixable in cocktails.

540 grams acacia or wildflower honey
100 grams warm filtered water

Combine the honey and water in a bowl and whisk until thoroughly blended. Transfer to a storage container and refrigerate until ready to use, up to 2 weeks.

BLENDER SYRUPS

Making syrups in a blender speeds the dissolution of sugar crystals and powdered ingredients, such as citric acid. We also use a blender for syrups that contain ingredients that would be negatively impacted by heat, such as strawberries.

HOW TO MAKE BLENDER SYRUPS

Gram scale
Blender
Fine-mesh sieve
Storage container

1   Carefully measure the ingredients by weight.

2   Combine the ingredients in a blender.

3   Blend at high speed until the sugar has dissolved and any solid ingredients are liquefied.

4   If solid ingredients are used, strain the syrup through a fine-mesh sieve.

5   Pour the syrup into a storage container, cover, and refrigerate until ready to use.

SYRUP SHELF LIFE

Because sugar is a preservative, many syrups will keep for a decent amount of time if stored properly. But when sugar is combined with fruit, it can become a breeding ground for bacteria. As a basic rule of thumb, we tend to avoid using syrups that are more than two weeks old. Those that are made with just a sweetener and water will probably keep longer, but others, such as strawberry syrup, are more prone to spoilage. Always taste homemade syrups before using them. If you detect any fizziness, don't use them—it means the syrup has begun to ferment.

Blended Strawberry Syrup

YIELD: ABOUT 16 OUNCES

TECHNIQUE: BLENDER

Anyone who's ever eaten a berry in peak season knows that most berry-flavored things offer only a pale imitation of the natural brilliance of the flavor of the actual fruit. This often has to do with how berries are processed into syrups and other flavorings. For example, as soon as heat is applied to strawberries, their flavor begins to develop an artificial taste. So to lock in the freshest strawberry flavor, we blend equal weights of strawberries and sugar, then pass the mixture through a fine-mesh sieve.

250 grams hulled strawberries
250 grams white sugar

Combine the strawberries and sugar in a blender and process until very smooth. Pass the mixture through a fine-mesh sieve, pressing the solids to extract as much liquid as possible. Transfer to a storage container and refrigerate until ready to use, up to 2 weeks.

Cane Sugar Syrup

YIELD: ABOUT 16 OUNCES

TECHNIQUE: BLENDER

Unbleached cane sugar isn't quite as refined as standard table sugar. It has a pale amber color and granules that are about twice the size of table sugar granules. It also has more flavor than white sugar but less than demerara, which makes it highly versatile. Adding just 1 teaspoon of this syrup to a spirituous drink can lift its flavors and add texture, and it can also play well with citrus, especially when the base spirit has plenty of personality, as in the case of tequila or rhum agricole. As with our Demerara Gum Syrup (page 54), we use it to make a rich syrup with two parts sugar to one part water to maximize its personality.

300 grams unbleached cane sugar
150 grams filtered water

Combine the cane sugar with water in a blender and process until the sugar has dissolved. Pour into a storage container and refrigerate until ready to use, up to 2 weeks.

House Grenadine

YIELD: 16 OUNCES

TECHNIQUE: BLENDER

Many bars make grenadine by reducing pomegranate juice and adding other flavorings. The result is a syrup that's murky and dense and, to us, tastes nothing like the grenadine we remember from childhood. Sure, that neon-red stuff in our Shirley Temples was made with high-fructose corn syrup, but it was pretty and we loved it. We wanted to develop a recipe for grenadine that uses high-quality ingredients while also honoring our memories of the stuff, and eventually came up with this simple, clean version that's incredibly simple to make.

250 grams POM Wonderful pomegranate juice
250 grams unbleached cane sugar
1.85 grams powdered malic acid
1.25 grams powdered citric acid
0.15 gram Terra Spice orange extract

Combine all the ingredients in a blender and process until the sugar has dissolved. Transfer to a storage container and refrigerate until ready to use, up to 3 weeks.

House Ginger Syrup

YIELD: ABOUT 16 OUNCES
TECHNIQUE: BLENDER

Ginger, typically in the form of ginger beer, is crucial in classic cocktails like the Moscow Mule (page 139) and the Dark and Stormy (page 140), as well as contemporary drinks like the Penicillin (page 282). Although there are many delicious ginger beers on the market, bartenders often prefer to use ginger syrup (often mixed with soda) to achieve a similar flavor profile. Our version of ginger syrup combines 1 part fresh ginger juice with 1½ parts unbleached cane sugar. The resulting syrup has a fiery pungency that almost burns—it's intense, for sure, but it can be balanced by other ingredients. If you don't have a juicer that can handle ginger, look for fresh ginger juice at specialty grocers or juice shops. Just be sure to start with plain ginger juice, free of added sweeteners or flavorings.

250 grams fresh ginger, washed and coarsely chopped

About 300 grams unbleached cane sugar

Juice the ginger (you don't need to peel it first) and pass the juice through a fine-mesh sieve. Weigh the ginger juice, then multiply the weight by 1.5 and weigh out that much sugar.

Combine the ginger juice and sugar in a blender and process until the sugar has dissolved. Pour into a storage container and refrigerate until ready to use, up to 2 weeks.

SPECIAL SYRUP INGREDIENTS

Gum arabic: Also known as gum acacia, this is hardened sap harvested from the acacia tree. It's mostly comprised of various sugars and a small amount of protein. Some of the proteins allow it to act as an emulsifier, thickening syrups and binding their ingredients together, as in our Demerara Gum Syrup (page 54) and Pineapple Gum Syrup (page 56).

Citric acid: This is the acid present in citrus fruits. We use citric acid powder as a flavoring agent for syrups, such as our Raspberry Syrup (page 51). We also use it to make a solution (5 parts water to 1 part citric acid) that we substitute for fresh citrus juice in certain cocktails when we want to add acidity without the particles in the juice. This is also important for carbonated cocktails, where pulpy juice can inhibit carbonation (see page 231).

Lactic acid: We sometimes use lactic acid, also known as milk acid, in very small quantities to add a round texture to certain syrups, such as our Vanilla Lactic Syrup (page 286).

Malic acid: First isolated from apple juice, malic acid has a flavor reminiscent of unripe green apples. We use it when we want to impart an impression of tartness, as in our House Grenadine (page 47).

Pectinex Ultra SP-L: This enzyme aids in clarification by breaking apart bonds in solids within a syrup. We only use Pectinex when we want to clarify ingredients that contain pectin, processing them either in a centrifuge, as with our Clarified Strawberry Syrup (page 57), or simply by mixing in Pectinex and allowing the liquid to sit.

IMMERSION CIRCULATOR SYRUPS

Cooking sous vide (French for "under vacuum") with an immersion circulator involves sealing ingredients in a plastic bag and cooking them in a temperature-controlled water bath. This helps maintain the fresh flavors of the ingredients. Our favorite example of this is raspberry syrup: raspberries are delicate, and when cooked at too high a temperature, their flavor changes, becoming more candy-like. But if you seal the raspberries, sugar, and water in a bag and cook the syrup in a temperature-controlled water bath (at a balmy 135°F in this case), the result is a syrup that beautifully captures the essence of fresh raspberries—and it's pretty to look at, too. We also use the immersion circulator method to help dissolve certain powders, such as gum arabic. This allows us to create our Demerara Gum Syrup (page 54) and Pineapple Gum Syrup (page 56) in a matter of hours, rather than days.

SUPERBAGS

A Superbag is a fine-mesh bag strainer that can be purchased online (we get ours from Modernist Pantry). Superbags are not only reusable, but also the material is so strong that you can squeeze the bag with force to speed up some filtrations. Superbags come in various sizes and micron perforations: 100, 250, 400, and 800 microns (800 is the coarsest size). For syrup preparation, we recommend a medium-size 250 micron bag.

HOW TO MAKE IMMERSION CIRCULATOR SYRUPS

Large water basin

Immersion circulator

Gram scale

Bowl

Resealable, heatproof plastic bag, such as a freezer bag

Ice bath

Fine-mesh sieve

Coffee filter or Superbag (see page 49)

Storage container

1 Fill the basin with water and place the immersion circulator inside.

2 Set the circulator to the desired temperature.

3 Carefully measure the ingredients by weight and combine them in a bowl.

4 Transfer the mixture to a sealable, heatproof plastic bag. Remove as much air as possible by sealing the bag almost completely, then dipping the bag (other than the unsealed portion) in the water. The counterpressure from the water will push the rest of the air out. Finish sealing the bag, then remove it from the water.

5 When the water has reached the desired temperature, place the sealed bag in the basin.

6 Carefully remove the bag when the specified time is up.

7 Transfer the bag to an ice bath and let cool to room temperature.

8 Strain the syrup through a fine-mesh sieve to remove any solids. If any particles remain in the syrup, strain it through a paper coffee filter or Superbag.

9 Transfer the syrup to a storage container and refrigerate until ready to use.

Raspberry Syrup

YIELD: ABOUT 16 OUNCES | TECHNIQUE: IMMERSION CIRCULATOR

Gently heating raspberries in a simple syrup allows the heat to extract the berries' flavor at a temperature below that at which they start to taste like jam. Unlike other raspberry syrups that either blend raspberries with sugar (which extracts bitter flavors from the fruit's seeds and makes a cloudy syrup) or that cook raspberries in simple syrup (creating a jam-like syrup with a deep purple hue), the immersion circulator extracts a vibrant, transparent pink syrup. This is pretty, sure, but it also means that there are no free-floating particles that would get in the way of carbonation, either in a fully carbonated cocktail or in a Collins.

500 grams simple syrup (page 45)
150 grams fresh raspberries
2.5 grams citric acid

Fill a large basin with water and place an immersion circulator inside. Set the circulator to 135°F.

Put all the ingredients in a bowl and stir to combine. Transfer to a sealable, heatproof plastic bag. Seal the bag almost completely, then remove as much air as possible by dipping the bag (other than the unsealed portion) in the water. Finish sealing the bag, then remove it from the water.

When the water has reached 135°F, place the bag in the basin and cook for 2 hours.

Place the bag in an ice bath and let cool to room temperature. Pass the syrup through a fine-mesh sieve. If any particles remain in the syrup, strain it through a paper coffee filter or Superbag. Transfer to a storage container and refrigerate until ready to use, up to 2 weeks.

Cinnamon Syrup

YIELD: ABOUT 16 OUNCES | TECHNIQUE: IMMERSION CIRCULATOR

Until recently, bartenders have made cinnamon syrup either by steeping cinnamon sticks in simple syrup overnight or by boiling the syrup and cinnamon sticks together. Neither is ideal. The first method produces a mild syrup that's somewhat bitter, and while the second one does produce a syrup with pungent flavor, the process skews the syrup to the sweeter side, as some of the water boils off. Using an immersion circulator allows a real breakthrough, producing a syrup with an incredible spectrum of cinnamon flavors, not just the typical Red Hots candy flavor. It has deep, woodsy undertones and a bright aroma similar to the smell of freshly grated cinnamon.

500 grams simple syrup (page 45)
10 grams crushed cinnamon sticks
0.1 gram kosher salt

Fill a large basin with water and place an immersion circulator inside. Set the circulator to 145°F.

Put all the ingredients in a bowl and stir to combine. Transfer to a sealable, heatproof plastic bag. Seal the bag almost completely, then remove as much air as possible by dipping the bag (other than the unsealed portion) in the water. Finish sealing the bag, then remove it from the water.

When the water has reached 145°F, place the bag in the basin and cook for 2 hours.

Place the bag in an ice bath and let cool to room temperature. Pass the syrup through a fine-mesh sieve. If any particles remain in the syrup, strain it through a paper coffee filter or Superbag. Transfer to a storage container and refrigerate until ready to use, up to 2 weeks.

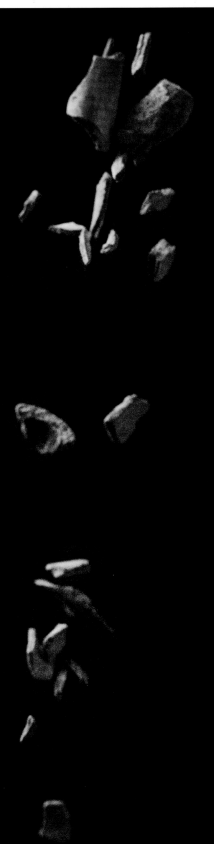

Grapefruit Cordial

YIELD: ABOUT 16 OUNCES | TECHNIQUE: IMMERSION CIRCULATOR

This method can be used to make a cordial from any citrus fruit. Consider trying it with Meyer lemons or any variety of tangerine or mandarin orange. Just be aware that you'll need to adjust the amount of citric acid depending on the type of citrus; since citric acid adds brightness, you'll want to use less with high-acid fruits. Note that we use a lower heat level in this recipe: just 135°F, as the cordial may lose its bright, fresh flavor if cooked at higher heat. As the cordial cooks, the zest and juice particles break down, creating a syrup that has multiple layers of grapefruit flavor.

250 grams strained fresh grapefruit juice

250 grams unbleached cane sugar

2.5 grams citric acid

10 grams grapefruit zest

Fill a large basin with water and place an immersion circulator inside. Set the circulator to 135°F.

Put all the ingredients in a bowl and whisk until blended. Transfer to a sealable, heatproof plastic bag. Seal the bag almost completely, then remove as much air as possible by dipping the bag (other than the unsealed portion) in the water. Finish sealing the bag, then remove it from the water.

When the water has reached 135°F, place the bag in the basin and cook for 2 hours.

Place the bag in an ice bath and let cool to room temperature. Pass the cordial through a fine-mesh sieve lined with several layers of cheesecloth. If any particles remain in the cordial, strain it again through a paper coffee filter or Superbag. Transfer to a storage container and refrigerate until ready to use, up to 2 weeks.

Demerara Gum Syrup

YIELD: ABOUT 16 OUNCES | TECHNIQUE: IMMERSION CIRCULATOR

Demerara sugar has large, dark granules. The dark color comes from the molasses naturally present within the sugar, which confers a rich toffee flavor. In cocktails, we often use Demerara Gum Syrup to round off the edges of intense spirits, as in Old-Fashioneds, or to add richness. However, because of demerara's molasses-y flavor, there are also limits to its use. If we're seeking a clean or sharp flavor in a cocktail, we typically don't use this syrup, as it could muddy the drink. In addition, the qualities that allow it to round the edges of fiery spirits can make it unsuitable for other applications; for example, we probably wouldn't use it in a Daiquiri, where it may dull the fresh, bright flavors we're looking for. In stirred cocktails like the Old-Fashioned, a gum syrup allows us to add more body to a cocktail without making it too sweet.

300 grams demerara sugar
18 grams gum arabic
150 grams filtered water

Fill a large basin with water and place an immersion circulator inside. Set the circulator to 145°F.

Combine the demerara sugar and gum arabic in a blender and process for 30 seconds. With the blender running, slowly add the water and continue to process until all the dry ingredients have dissolved, about 2 minutes.

Pour the mixture into a sealable, heatproof plastic bag. Seal the bag almost completely, then remove as much air as possible by dipping the bag (other than the unsealed portion) in the water. Finish sealing the bag, then remove it from the water.

When the water has reached 145°F, place the sealed bag in the basin and cook for 2 hours.

Place the bag in an ice bath and let cool to room temperature. Transfer to a storage container and refrigerate until ready to use, up to 2 weeks.

SCALING UP RECIPES

The syrup recipes in this book will generally produce about 16 ounces of syrup—enough to make a batch for a party, but not so much that it will linger in your fridge for a long time. If scaling up these recipes, be mindful of each ingredient's strength. When dealing with sugar or other sweeteners and water, scaling up is just a matter of simple math. However, ingredients like spices or extracts may be overly intense when scaled up. So if you're making a larger-than-double batch of a syrup that contains spices or extracts, start with two-thirds the amount, then taste and adjust from there.

Pineapple Gum Syrup

YIELD: ABOUT 16 OUNCES | TECHNIQUE: IMMERSION CIRCULATOR

Because of the high pectin levels in pineapple juice, shaken cocktails that contain it have a beautiful frothy head, much like that on a cocktail that contains egg white. But pineapple juice quickly separates out from the rest of a drink, and it can also spoil in fairly short order. To combat both of these issues, we often incorporate fresh pineapple juice in the form of this syrup, which includes a bit of citric acid, which gives the syrup more sharpness and clarity, cuts through the sweetness of the sugar, and brightens the natural pineapple flavor. As we were developing this syrup, we found that we wanted to use it not just in shaken cocktails, but also stirred. So, as in our Demerara Gum Syrup (page 54), we add a bit of gum arabic, which also has the benefit of keeping the sugar and pineapple juice in solution. As the ingredients are heated in the immersion circulator, the gum arabic dissolves and makes the liquid translucent, and the pineapple's pulp and juice break down into a homogenous liquid syrup without losing the fruit's bright, tropical flavor.

- **250 grams unbleached cane sugar**
- **15 grams gum arabic**
- **1.5 grams citric acid**
- **250 grams fresh pineapple juice**

Fill a large basin with water and place the immersion circulator inside. Set the circulator to 145°F.

Combine the sugar, gum arabic, and citric acid in a blender and process for 30 seconds. With the blender running, slowly add the pineapple juice and continue to process until all of the dry ingredients have dissolved, about 2 minutes.

Pour the mixture into a sealable, heatproof plastic bag. Seal the bag almost completely, then remove as much air as possible by dipping the bag (other than the unsealed portion) in the water. Finish sealing the bag, then remove it from the water.

When the water has reached 145°F, place the bag in the basin and cook for 2 hours.

Place the bag in an ice bath and let cool to room temperature. Strain through a Superbag, transfer to a storage container, and refrigerate until ready to use, up to 1 week.

DIRECT-HEAT SYRUPS

We rarely make syrups over direct heat, as gas, electric, and induction ranges all work differently, which makes it hard to present a recipe that will yield consistent results, especially when working with fragile ingredients. Also, water evaporates when heated, causing the syrup to become more concentrated. Nevertheless, there are times when direct heat can help extract flavor more quickly: heat causes the molecules to get moving, resulting in more surface contact, and therefore more flavor, faster. For example, in our Spiced Almond Demerara Gum Syrup (see right), we get the best results when we lightly simmer a base of Demerara Gum Syrup with the flavorings.

HOW TO MAKE DIRECT-HEAT SYRUPS

Gram scale
Saucepan
Stove
Fine-mesh sieve
Storage container

1   Carefully measure the ingredients by weight and combine in a saucepan.

2   Bring to a simmer, stirring frequently. Don't allow the ingredients to stick to the bottom of the pan. Simmer for the specified period—usually just a very short time.

3   Remove from the heat and cover the pan. This will ensure that any additional evaporation is contained; the water will condense, preventing the syrup from becoming more concentrated.

4   Let the syrup cool, then strain it through a fine-mesh sieve.

5   Transfer the syrup to a storage container and refrigerate until ready to use.

Spiced Almond Demerara Gum Syrup

YIELD: ABOUT 16 OUNCES

TECHNIQUE: DIRECT HEAT

This syrup was created to add both balance and seasoning to the Normandie Club Old-Fashioned (page 16). Cinnamon, clove, and cardamom add bright spice notes, while the almonds bring a fatty roundness that, in the Normandie Club Old-Fashioned, complements the coconut-infused bourbon. When we use spiced syrups in small quantities to season drinks, they perform in much the same way as bitters do. In other applications, such as when we want to incorporate a larger quantity in a citrus-based cocktail, we often find that the best strategy is to use a neutral syrup, such as simple syrup, in place of part of the spiced syrup so its flavor won't be overwhelming.

500 grams Demerara Gum Syrup (page 54)
30 grams sliced almonds
6 grams crushed cinnamon sticks
0.25 gram whole cloves, preferably Penang cloves
1 green cardamom pod

Put the gum syrup in a small saucepan over low heat. Add the remaining ingredients and stir to combine. Bring to a simmer, then cook, stirring constantly, for 10 minutes, maintaining a simmer throughout; don't let the mixture reach a rolling boil. Let cool to room temperature, then strain through a fine-mesh sieve. Transfer to a storage container and refrigerate until ready to use, up to 1 month.

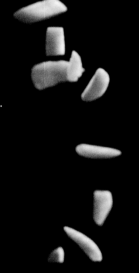

CENTRIFUGE SYRUPS

Centrifuge syrups can begin with any type of syrup, which is then spun at an incredibly high speed (up to 4,500 rpm) to separate out any solids. Although this requires advanced equipment, it can produce beautiful results. We use this technique when a translucent syrup will create a more visually appealing drink or when we plan to carbonate the cocktail (see page 228).

We use refurbished laboratory centrifuges from Ozark Biomedical. Our preferred unit—the Jouan CR422, which costs around $3,500 to $4,000—can spin 3 quarts of liquid at a time and clarify it in just 10 to 15 minutes. That said, there are now units available for culinary use that are far less expensive. One of the latest is Dave Arnold's Spinzall, which costs about $800.

Don't have a centrifuge? That's okay; you can follow much of the method below, then allow the syrup to sit overnight and strain the syrup through at least four layers of cheesecloth overnight in a refrigerator.

HOW TO MAKE CENTRIFUGE SYRUPS

Gram scale
Large gram scale
Bowl
Centrifuge containers with lids
Centrifuge
Superbag or paper coffee filter
Storage container

1 First prepare a base syrup using one of the previously described methods.

2 Measure the weight of a centrifuge container using a gram scale, then add the syrup and calculate the difference. (Or, if your scale has a tare function, place the container on it, zero the scale, then add the syrup and determine its weight.)

3 Calculate 0.2% of the weight of the syrup (multiply by 0.002) to get X grams.

4 Stir X grams of Pectinex Ultra SP-L into the syrup. Cover and let sit for 15 minutes.

5 Weigh the filled container and fill each of the other containers with an equal weight of water. Each container in a centrifuge must weigh exactly the same in order to keep the machine in balance. (Off-balance centrifuges are dangerous!)

6 Run the centrifuge at 4,500 rpm for 12 minutes.

7 Remove the containers and carefully strain the syrup through a paper coffee filter or Superbag, being careful not to disturb the solids that have collected on the bottom of the container.

8 If any particles remain in the syrup, strain it again.

9 Transfer to a storage container and refrigerate until ready to use.

Clarified Strawberry Syrup

YIELD: ABOUT 16 OUNCES

TECHNIQUE: CENTRIFUGE

Although blended strawberry syrup is delicious on its own, you can take it a step beyond by clarifying it—something that's especially important if you want to use it in stirred or carbonated cocktails.

250 grams hulled strawberries
250 grams unbleached cane sugar
0.5 gram Pectinex Ultra SP-L

Combine the strawberries and sugar in a blender and process until very smooth. Once the sugar has dissolved, add the Pectinex to the blender and process for 10 seconds. Transfer to a centrifuge container. Weigh the filled container and fill each of the other containers with an equal weight of water. Run the centrifuge at 4,500 rpm for 12 minutes. Remove the containers and carefully strain the syrup through a Superbag or a paper coffee filter, being careful not to disturb the solids that have collected on the bottom of the container. Transfer to a storage container and refrigerate until ready to use, up to 1 week.

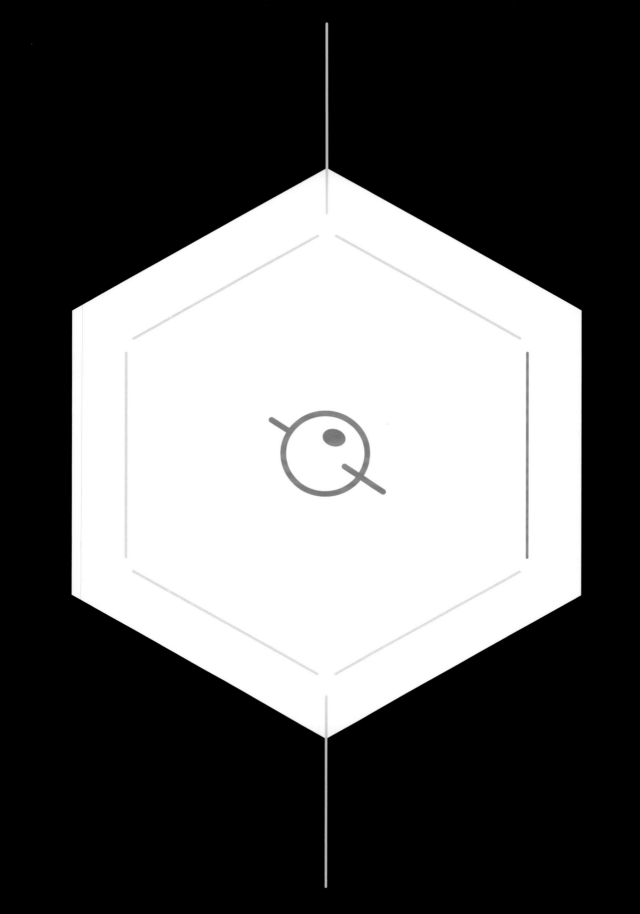

2

THE
MARTINI

THE CLASSIC RECIPES

There are Martinis made with gin or vodka and dry vermouth, and "Martinis" that call for apple schnapps, chocolate liqueur, purees of exotic fruit, and pretty much any other flavor you can imagine. For our purposes, we begin our exploration of the Martini with the standard recipe that can be found in most cocktail books, classic and modern alike: gin paired with dry vermouth, served up and garnished with either a lemon twist or an olive.

Gin Martini

2 ounces gin
¾ ounce dry vermouth
Garnish: 1 lemon twist or olive

Stir all the ingredients over ice, then strain into a Nick & Nora glass. Garnish with the lemon twist (expressed over the drink and set on the edge of the glass) or olive.

But when vodka is the core, the amount of vermouth is frequently decreased. Whereas gin has a strong botanical flavor (more on this later) that stands up to the vermouth, the flavor profile of vodka is highly streamlined and can easily be overshadowed by the vermouth. Some Vodka Martini recipes forgo vermouth altogether, but in our view, a bit of vermouth adds a touch of complexity, yielding a cocktail that's more than just chilled vodka.

Vodka Martini

2½ ounces vodka
½ ounce dry vermouth
Garnish: 1 lemon twist or olive

Stir all the ingredients over ice, then strain into a chilled Nick & Nora glass. Garnish with the lemon twist (expressed over the drink and set on the edge of the glass) or olive.

OUR ROOT RECIPES

As we'll explore in this chapter, gin comes in many different flavor profiles and varying proofs. Dry vermouths can also be dramatically different depending on the producer's recipe, and also how fresh the bottle is (an open bottle of vermouth deteriorates just like wine). The flavor of vodka can also vary depending on the source ingredient. All of these variables mean the Martini is highly customizable, with a key factor being the drinker's preference regarding intensity: high proof and less vermouth versus low proof and more vermouth.

For our Gin Martini root recipe, we take the classic version and push it in a vermouth-heavy direction. For the core, we use citrusy Plymouth gin, a crowd-pleasing choice. For the seasoning, our favorite bottle of dry vermouth, Dolin dry, with its flavors of alpine herbs, matches perfectly with the Plymouth gin. Because we're always using fresh vermouth in the context of our bars, we boost the amount to a full ounce. Consider this a baseline for further customization: you may want your Martini drier (with less vermouth) or more herbaceous (with more vermouth, a personal favorite of ours).

We like a Martini in which the gin serves as the core but vermouth is very present, collaborating equally with the gin, typically two parts gin to one part vermouth. As you'll see, we also include orange bitters. There are many historical references to such cocktails, though, depending on the source, it may be viewed as an entirely different cocktail. Be that as it may, we include orange bitters in our root recipe because it amplifies the flavors of both the gin and the vermouth and creates a harmonious cocktail without fundamentally changing the drink.

Finally, we express a twist of lemon over the top of the drink and then rest it delicately on the rim of the glass. As with the lemon twist in our Old-Fashioned recipe (page 4), we avoid rubbing it around the rim of the glass, as the powerful lemon oils will linger on the drinker's tongue and overwhelm the other flavors.

Our Ideal Gin Martini

2 ounces Plymouth gin
1 ounce Dolin dry vermouth
1 dash House Orange Bitters
(page 295)
Garnish: 1 lemon twist

Stir all the ingredients over ice, then strain into a chilled Nick & Nora glass. Express the lemon twist over the drink, then set it on the edge of the glass.

Personal taste plays an even greater role in the Vodka Martini than in one made with gin. We recognize that some people love nothing more than an ice-cold glass of vodka with little else getting in the way, but we prefer a cocktail with a bit more complexity. That said, with Vodka Martinis we prefer to err on the side of dry and clean by using less vermouth so that it exerts only a small, modifying influence on the cocktail, keeping the vodka front and center. Then, because vodka makes up such a large proportion of the drink, we use one that brings more than just proof to the party: Absolut Elyx, which makes a beautiful Martini, thanks to its smooth, slightly sweet flavor and softness. Finally, we garnish with an olive to add a hint of salt, which helps blend the flavors of the spirits.

Our Ideal Vodka Martini

2½ ounces Absolut Elyx vodka
½ ounce Dolin dry vermouth
Garnish: 1 olive

Stir all the ingredients over ice, then strain into a chilled coupe. Garnish with the olive.

HOW DO YOU LIKE IT?

A guy walks into a bar and orders a Martini . . .

No, no. That's not right.

A guy walks into a bar and orders a Gin Martini, straight up, stirred, with a twist.

That's more like it!

There's no cocktail that's ordered with more specific requests than the Martini: spirit type (gin or vodka), the quantity of vermouth (from dry to wet), technique (shaken or stirred), and a variety of garnish options ranging from olives and pickled onions to a citrus twist. How a person orders a Martini can communicate a lot: gin for traditionalists; vodka for rebels. A lemon twist and extra vermouth for poets; extra dry with a side of olives for bankers.

Furthermore, as cocktails have become a bigger part of American culture, our tastes have evolved. In the earliest days of the modern cocktail revival, back in the early 2000s, big, aggressive flavors were king: Jamaican rum, Italian bittersweet amari, and peaty scotch dominated cocktail menus at certain types of bars. But now the trend is toward finding beauty in the smallest and most delicate of details. The preference for one brand of gin over another, the influence of minerals in the ice used when stirring a cocktail, the perfume of a certain variety of lemon—these are differences that are revealed to those educated by experience, not by cocktail books, and that can elevate a cocktail into the realm of artistry.

We view understanding these kinds of fine details as the pinnacle of cocktail mastery, and perhaps no cocktail can exemplify this better than the Martini. Whereas many cocktails are defined by the strong personalities of their ingredients, the Martini is defined by minutiae—the small changes that can push the drink in many directions. By our definition, a Martini can be called a Martini if it's made with both booze and vermouth, without much else added. You can make a great Martini with either gin or vodka.

MARTINI ORTHODOXY

The defining traits of the Martini and its extended family of cocktails:

A Martini is composed of alcohol and aromatized wine, typically gin or vodka and dry vermouth.

A Martini is flexible in regard to the proportions of those ingredients, and its balance is dependent on the preference of the drinker.

A Martini's garnish has a big impact on the overall flavor and experience of the drink.

The choice of garnish can confer the brightness of lemon oil, the saltiness of an olive, the savory kick of a pickled onion, or nothing at all. And it's perfectly possible to shake a Martini, though we'll do our best to convince you otherwise.

The Martini is built on the collaboration between a base spirit and an aromatized wine, be it vermouth or another flavorful wine-based modifier. This marriage of two ingredients to make a greater whole will define the core flavor of all drinks in this chapter. The Martini also lacks the rigidity found in other root cocktails; it can be flexible to preferences of alcoholic strength and sweet or dryness.

Take, for example, the Old-Fashioned. Increasing the amount of sweetener quickly sends the drink into cloying territory. Adding too many dashes of bitters means they're all you'll taste. The flexibility within the standard Old-Fashioned (and other root cocktails) is narrow, but not so with the Martini and its brethren. Add more vermouth and the Martini is deliciously herbaceous; reduce the vermouth so that it's only a whisper and the Martini is dry and bracing, but still tasty. The Martini can be whatever you want it to be, and so this chapter is devoted to not only defining the skills and knowledge necessary to make a great Martini, but also guiding you to understanding how you take yours. Are you a poet or a banker?

UNDERSTANDING THE TEMPLATE

Understanding why the Martini template works requires understanding how balance can be found between a high-proof spirit and an aromatized wine. The spirit (gin or vodka) brings proof and flavor to the cocktail, while the aromatized wine (vermouth) adds flavor, acidity, and sweetness and also curbs the alcoholic intensity of the spirit. These qualities make the Martini (and its many variations) a highly spirituous cocktail that's texturally smooth and soothing.

We chose to focus this chapter on the Martini, not the Manhattan, its likely historical predecessor, because in a Martini there's less to hide behind: the ingredients are nuanced enough that slightly shifting the proportions will have more dramatic results than, say, building a Manhattan upon stronger or sweeter ingredients.

THE CORE: GIN AND VODKA

Unlike the Old-Fashioned, which is solely focused on one spirit, the Martini has a core that's a collaboration between gin or vodka and dry vermouth. And because there's no sweetener, the vermouth must also balance the intensity of the base spirit. This is a big part of what makes the Martini so interesting—the fact that the core extends beyond the base spirit and actually lies in the interaction of the base spirit with the vermouth.

How can something as delicate as dry vermouth mingle with the assertiveness of gin to create a new, utterly unique core flavor? Our general rule is that the stronger the base spirit, the more vermouth necessary to create a balanced core. Our root Gin Martini recipe is for what would traditionally be called a "wet" Martini, meaning it has a fair amount of vermouth, in this case 1 full ounce. Our root Vodka Martini, by contrast, calls for only ½ ounce of vermouth. Don't get us wrong; a Vodka Martini with 2 ounces of spirit and 1 ounce of vermouth is a beautiful thing. The vodka acts as a background against which the herbaceous and slightly bitter vermouth can shine. But because of vodka's more nuanced flavor, that much vermouth will overshadow any characteristics that make a particular vodka unique. Yes, some people think plain vodka has a neutral flavor, but this is far from the truth, and we believe that a Martini should highlight the personality of a given vodka. That's why we bump up the vodka and dial back the vermouth.

Once you understand how to create a balanced spirit-vermouth core, you can start playing around with base spirit; for example, the Manhattan (page 84) uses the same ingredient ratios but swaps in rye and sweet vermouth. Or you can tinker with the balance, exploring the wide world of aromatized wines beyond vermouth; for example, the Vesper (page 71) substitutes Lillet blanc for the vermouth. Finally, this chapter will explore Martini variations that bring in flavors that accent the core and balance, from amari (as in the Negroni, page 89) to small amounts of liqueurs (as in the Martinez, page 86). These riffs on the Martini may look and taste very different from our root recipe, but they maintain a balance between spirit and aromatized wine while amplifying the template's seasoning.

GIN

Gin is unique in the world of spirits because, at least in its modern form, it was developed specifically to be mixed with other ingredients in cocktails. Put simply, gin is flavored vodka. It starts with a neutral grain spirit, essentially high-proof vodka, which is then flavored with a variety of botanicals, most notably, juniper berries—indeed, in the United States and European Union, it can't be labeled "gin" if it doesn't include these fragrant berries. Other common botanicals in gin include coriander, orris root, angelica, citrus peel, star anise, and licorice. Some gins have only a few flavorings, whereas others are intricate tapestries of dozens of ingredients, and it is this composition that gives each gin its personality. And as is often the case, the whole is greater than the sum of its parts; beyond the aromas and flavors of the individual botanicals, a successful combination can create a unique and unexpected flavor profile.

On the nose, gins are bright, alcoholic, and noticeably forest-y thanks to the juniper. But because different brands have unique characteristics, each will steer cocktails in different directions. A juniper-heavy high-proof gin like Tanqueray will be more assertive than a citrusy standard-proof gin, such as Plymouth. So we don't consider one particular gin to be the best; we choose different gins for different reasons.

AQUAVIT

A native of Scandinavia, aquavit is a powerfully flavorful, clear (lightly aged) spirit that makes an extraordinary addition to cocktails. Where gin is predominantly flavored with juniper, aquavits are dominated by either caraway or anise, making for a spicy, savory flavor. In cocktails, the flavors can overwhelm, so we recommend using aquavit in collaboration with other spirits. Our favorite brands include Linie (Norway) and Krogstad (Oregon).

While no two gins are the same, we categorize most gins into one of two groups: London dry and contemporary. These aren't industry- or government-dictated terms; rather, they're our shorthand for thinking about them and deciding which gin might be best for a particular cocktail. For the recommended bottles that follow, we've suggested brands that are versatile and work well in a variety of applications, beyond just Martinis. Also, please note that in contrast to other categories of spirits, where substituting a similar brand is often totally acceptable, this doesn't work as well with gin because of how unique these spirits are. So in our recipes, we call for specific brands, with each being carefully chosen for its unique flavor profile. A cocktail recipe that simply calls for "gin" is leaving a great deal to interpretation, for better or (usually) for worse. If you do need to make a substitution, try to stick with a gin from the same category: London dry or contemporary.

LONDON DRY

London dry is the most pervasive style of gin, accounting for most of the widely available brands, including familiar names like Plymouth, Beefeater, Tanqueray, and Gordon's. These gins are characterized by a clean, nearly neutral foundation and sharp, spicy flavorings dominated by woodsy juniper berry. When most folks ask for gin, they usually mean London dry.

RECOMMENDED BOTTLES

Beefeater London Dry: In our view, there are few gins that are as versatile for cocktails as Beefeater—and specifically the bottling exported to the United States. Clocking in at 47% ABV, Beefeater has sufficient proof to cut through anything you throw at it (amari, citrus, fruit syrups . . .), but it's also delicate enough that it doesn't overpower the vermouth in a Martini. If you had to choose only one gin to stock in your bar, this would probably be it.

Fords Gin: Full disclosure: This gin is named after our dear friend Simon Ford, a spirits expert who worked for Plymouth and Beefeater before starting his own company. We aren't just name-dropping; the value of this information becomes clear when you taste Fords gin alongside Plymouth and Beefeater, as it falls somewhere between the two in terms of both flavor profile and proof. Simon created this gin for use in all styles of cocktails: citrusy, boozy, and bitter. So although you might find that another brand really shines in a particular cocktail, the balance between delicacy and assertiveness in Fords gin makes it an extremely versatile bottle to have on hand.

GIN AND PROOF

The proof of a specific brand of gin may vary depending on where you purchase it. This largely has to do with taxes: some gin makers are deterred from producing a higher-ABV gin or exporting it because the taxes would be prohibitively high—even if they believe a higher-proof version has a more desirable flavor. As an example, this is why you may find Beefeater available at 47% ABV in America, but only at 40% ABV in the United Kingdom and elsewhere. Peek at the label before mixing: a higher-proof gin will be more assertive than a lower-proof gin, so you may need to pull back on its measurement in a cocktail. While this can be true of other spirits, proof has a noticeable impact on how the botanicals in a certain gin are expressed. Higher-proof gins will be spicier, while lower-proof gins are often more citrusy.

Plymouth: Traditionally, we've tended to use Beefeater in our boozy drinks and Plymouth in our citrusy drinks. This rule of thumb reflects Plymouth's delicacy compared to higher-proof gins: at 41.2% ABV and with a botanical blend that's soft and citrusy with pronounced juniper undertones, Plymouth almost always works in citrus cocktails. We also use Plymouth (and similar gins) when we want the gin to serve as the foundation of a cocktail, with its flavors gently emerging in collaboration with the other ingredients. But Plymouth also works extremely well in stirred cocktails, where it can provide a softer foundation on which other delicate flavors are built.

Sipsmith: Born out of a collaboration between spirits industry experts, Sipsmith was developed to be the perfect Martini gin, and indeed, we do love using it in cocktails that, like the Martini, have gin at the core. While it can make a tasty gin and tonic and could certainly be mixed with citrus, Sipsmith is most successful when put center stage.

Tanqueray: Tanqueray is one of the most recognizable bottles on any bar, a squat green vessel that has held a distinguished place in the arsenal of gin fans for almost two hundred years, coming to market in the 1830s as the first spirit in the category now referred to as London dry gin. The US version of Tanqueray is sold at 47.3% ABV and, much like Beefeater, its high proof allows it to work well in many styles of cocktails. However, it also has a highly juniper-dominant flavor profile that makes it our greatest asset in spirituous and bitter cocktails, particularly the Negroni and its many variations, because it can cut through sweet and bitter flavors while asserting itself cleanly. For that very reason, it's often too assertive to use in refreshing, citrus-heavy drinks.

A once defunct style of gin that's slightly sweet, Old Tom is distinct from London dry gin and is thought to predate it. That said, it's similar enough that we tend to reach for it in some situations where we might otherwise go for a soft London dry, like Plymouth or Fords. Many gin cocktail recipes in nineteenth-century cocktail books specifically call for Old Tom gin, and it's believed that the Martinez (page 86) and Tom Collins (page 138) were both originally made with Old Tom. Now the style has been revived by both small and large producers, and as with gin more broadly, these offerings all have distinctive qualities. Some, like Hayman's Old Tom, are sweetened but heavy on the botanicals, while Ransom Old Tom is lightly aged. Hayman's was the first to reach the United States and is recognized as a standard of the style. Its slight sweetness allows the botanicals to blossom, and it has a fresh citrus quality (compared to the dried citrus qualities of London dry) and pronounced licorice flavor.

CONTEMPORARY GINS

Contemporary gins are the avant-garde artists of the spirits world. While they do satisfy the "must have juniper" requirement, they tend to eschew conventions. For this reason, it's generally best to devise cocktails using contemporary gin by working from the gin backward.

RECOMMENDED BOTTLES

Aviation Gin: Instead of using a neutral base alcohol, Aviation is made from a malty rye spirit, and although it pays homage to a classic London dry, it pulls back on the juniper and features sarsaparilla, which lends it a distinct root beer impression, with lavender adding an incredible sub-aroma. The result is a full-bodied and extremely flavorful gin that, at 42% ABV, has enough alcoholic strength to work well in various styles of cocktails. And because it's so distinctive, it also works well for seasoning cocktails, a role it plays in Beth's Going to Town (page 87).

St. George Botanivore, Terroir, and Dry Rye Gins: It's hard to pick one bottle of gin that best captures the essence of the contemporary style, so if you're game, we recommend exploring this trio of St. George gins to understand the unique and often dramatic variations in this style. It seems that many contemporary gins are driven by a narrative, telling a story or expressing a specific point of view. St. George Spirits has always been a producer that's unafraid to express a strong identity and worldview. It could be easy to dismiss those last two sentences with an eye roll (unless you live in San Francisco, in which case you probably nodded knowingly), but hear us out. The Botanivore, the most traditional of the trio, contains a variety of oddball botanicals, including dill, hops, and bergamot—nodding to gin's history, but also pushing the boundaries of what we'd expect from a London dry gin. The Terroir is a love letter to California, throwing everything from Douglas fir to sage in the mix, resulting in a woodsy little beast. Finally, the Dry Rye is made from a 100 percent rye base spirit and contains only six botanicals (compared to the Botanivore's nineteen and Terroir's twelve); the spicy base reinforces the peppery character of juniper to produce an extremely flavorful gin.

VODKA

Bartenders talk a lot of smack about vodka, and in the past, we've admittedly been some of the worst offenders. In the early 2000s, we were all doing our best to get the world to try new things, and we wanted to distance ourselves from the sort of drinks that people were accustomed to. The "-tinis" of the 1990s had severely sullied the reputation of the classic Martini, but to their credit, they also popularized cocktails. Though we may look back on that era as a time of blunt-force cocktails made from bad booze and industrial-grade ingredients, mixed drinks were suddenly fun again.

Vodka's relative neutrality with all the big mixers of the 1990s (sour apple liqueur, peach schnapps, highly processed juices, etc.) made it an easy target for many of us, who decried it as simply bringing booze to the party without making the party any more fun. Then, as the 2000s rolled around, enterprising bartenders were deep into pinching long-forgotten recipes from dusty pre-Prohibition bar manuals. They seldom found vodka in those pages, but they did find a lot of gin, whiskey, brandy, and rum, and those historic cocktails provided inspiration for bartenders who wanted to resurrect attention to ingredients, fresh products, and focused drink making. Along the way, we sewed a bunch of buttons onto our pants for attaching suspenders and spent hours yelling at YouTube while learning how to properly tie a bow tie, dappering up so people would take us more seriously.

But to deny the value of vodka is to sit on a pulpit of arrogance and, frankly, it's inhospitable. Lots of people love vodka, and it's probably not just because they saw a clever advertisement for it. They love it because of its honesty: you get what you see. When we choose to use it in cocktails, we do so because it works—because its character, clarity, and focus can be helpful for achieving very specific results.

Modern definitions of vodka talk about its "neutrality" and "flavorlessness," but this misses the point entirely. To the untrained palate, tasting undiluted vodka may be a lot like sipping rubbing alcohol. The reality is that to understand what characterizes a specific vodka, you must dig much deeper than with other spirits, which often offer a good understanding of their character through their aroma and a couple of sips. Vodka doesn't give its secrets away so easily.

A good starting point is to become familiar with the different styles of vodka and what each can bring to a cocktail. Vodka is defined by both what it's made from and how it's made. It can be distilled from any fermentable plant or fruit. Grain-based vodkas have predictable, if subtle, characteristics: wheat-based vodka is soft and sweet, rye is spicy, corn is rich, and so on. Regarding how it's made, vodka is almost always distilled to a very high proof—around 95% ABV (nearly pure alcohol). As a result, many of the potential flavors are stripped away, with only their essence left behind. That high-proof distillate is then diluted to 40% ABV (drinking proof), with water.

In most classic cocktail templates, vodka will be over-shadowed by other ingredients. That said, the subtle differences between vodkas can come into focus in nearly unnoticeable ways. You may not taste the qualities of wheat when using Absolut Elyx, a wheat-based vodka, but in a cocktail, it will provide softness and rich body—qualities that are less a flavor and more a sensation. The situation is similar with vodkas made from other bases: vodka made from rye has a whisper of peppery spice; one made from potatoes tastes earthy and almost beet-like; corn vodka may be slightly sweet; and grape vodka has a floral perfume. Although all are subtle, try tasting them side by side so you can pick out the differences.

The Martini is a great way to study the subtleties of vodka, far better than citrusy cocktails. This may sound unorthodox to cocktail nerds, who tend to favor gin. But as mentioned, a Martini gives you very little to hide behind, so the choice of vodka and the importance of technique are amplified.

Absolut: Though perhaps best known for its iconic marketing campaigns, Absolut is an exceptionally well-made product and a favorite among bartenders. A distillate made from winter wheat grown in southern Sweden, it has a softness that lends itself to many cocktail applications, particularly drinks made with citrus, though it also works well in savory cocktails like the Bloody Mary. We're particularly fond of a Martini made with equal parts Absolut and Dolin dry vermouth, with a dash of orange bitters and a lemon twist.

Absolut Elyx: Using wheat sourced from a single Swedish estate and a specific type of copper pot still, the folks at Absolut set out to explore the nature of terroir in a spirits category that lacks diversity, and they've succeeded. Though it can be rather expensive, Absolut Elyx has become one of the few vodkas in our arsenal that cannot be swapped out for another brand; its richness, creaminess, and depth of flavor combine to become a defining characteristic of any cocktail it touches.

Belvedere: Made from a base of rye, Belvedere is another big-name brand with plenty of marketing dollars behind it. It's a well-made product that excels in cocktails, bringing a subtle peppery spice note that's especially welcome in dry Martinis.

Hangar 1: Many of the small, craft brands of vodka popping up owe their success to the path forged by Hangar 1, a small(ish) distillery near San Francisco. Their Hangar 1 straight vodka is made from a distillate of grains and grapes. It therefore has some of the softness of wheat, along with the fruitiness and floral character of grapes. In addition, Hangar 1 produces three flavored vodkas that rise a cut above the competition: Buddha's Hand Citron, Mandarin Blossom, and Makrut Lime.

EXPERIMENTING WITH THE CORE

Swapping the base spirit (aka Mr. Potato Head) is the first strategy for building and understanding Martini variations. This is the logic on which countless cocktails have been created, and it's led to some of our favorite, and simplest, original cocktails. Just bear in mind that when you substitute a new base spirit, the integrity of the core—in this case, the relationship between the spirit and the aromatized wine—must be maintained if the cocktail is to be focused. In short, any change to the base spirit will probably demand a change to the vermouth to rebalance the cocktail, as you'll see in the variations that follow. A bit later in the chapter, in "Experimenting with the Balance" (see page 75), we'll explore how changes in the aromatized wine can profoundly affect the balance and have a major impact on the cocktail's flavor.

As you create your own cocktails, it may be tempting to use these strategies to push the Martini orthodoxy to its limits, veering toward sweet, bitter, or powerful in ways that fall beyond the parameters of balance. Sometimes this is successful and creates bold cocktails, but it often results in overindulgence, where the personality of the substitution distracts from the core flavor.

Vesper

CLASSIC

Though we called out gin and vodka as the core of Martinis in the preceding section, we've also emphasized that the true core of these cocktails is a combination of spirit and aromatized wine. In the Vesper, the two core spirits are combined—something that works in this classic cocktail because of a corresponding shift in the balance, wherein the vermouth has been replaced with Lillet blanc. The Lillet has a similar alcohol content, but it adds a fruitier quality, as opposed to vermouth's savoriness, and its flavors are delicate enough that using just gin as the base—even a softer gin, like Plymouth—would overpower the drink. Replacing some of the gin with vodka helps to stretch out the gin's botanicals and allows the Lillet to shine.

1½ ounces Plymouth gin
¾ ounce Aylesbury Duck vodka
½ ounce Lillet blanc
Garnish: 1 lemon twist

Stir all the ingredients over ice, then strain into a Nick & Nora glass. Express the lemon twist over the drink, then set it on the edge of the glass.

Dean Martin

DEVON TARBY AND ALEX DAY, 2015

Splitting the base with other spirits can be an easy way to keep the form of the Martini largely intact while creating an entirely new cocktail. The Dean Martin is a great example of this strategy, replacing some of the gin with a highly flavorful Douglas fir brandy. Because that changes the balance too, we added woodsy La Quintinye blanc vermouth to accent the Douglas fir eau-de-vie. The result is a cocktail that answers the question that inspired it: "What would a Martini consumed on a mountaintop in December taste like?"

1¾ ounces Tanqueray gin
¼ ounce Clear Creek Douglas fir brandy
½ ounce La Quintinye Vermouth Royal blanc
½ ounce Boissiere dry vermouth
1 drop Salt Solution (page 298)
Garnish: 4 sprays of Après-Ski Tincture (page 297)

Stir all the ingredients over ice, then strain into a Nick & Nora glass. Mist the top of the drink with the tincture.

THE BALANCE: VERMOUTH AND OTHER AROMATIZED WINES

Gin or vodka's collaborator in the Martini is an aromatized wine, most commonly vermouth. Aromatized wine is simply wine (usually a fairly neutral white wine) that has been flavored with herbs, barks, or citrus and fortified with additional alcohol. This increased proof preserves the life of the wine, but also means that it can stand up to other ingredients (like gin or vodka) without fading to the background. Vermouth can be thought of as a style of aromatized wine.

Most aromatized wines contain a residual sweetness (either naturally from the base wine or from added sugar), which is vital in balancing a Martini. Be it a dry French vermouth or a bitter and sweet Italian vermouth, this sweetness curbs the strength of a high-proof spirit like gin or vodka.

VERMOUTH

By its simplest definition, vermouth is a flavored, or aromatized, fortified wine—and just like wine, it has a shelf life. Therefore, we suggest purchasing the smallest bottle possible (usually 375 ml) so there's less to use once you've opened the bottle.

All aromatized wines, including vermouth, can also be called aperitif wines, which is shorthand for wines that have been flavored with slightly bitter ingredients, making them suitable for consumption before a meal to stimulate the appetite. Both sweet and dry vermouths are built on a base of wine, often white wine with a neutral flavor and aroma. Herbs and other botanicals are macerated in the wine for weeks, and although formulas vary from producer to producer, common ingredients include wormwood, chamomile, and gentian. (Interestingly, although vermouth gets its name from

wormwood, that ingredient is often omitted or included in only very small quantities due to various regulations outlawing it in the early twentieth century.) After the infusion process, sugar is added (a small amount for dry vermouth, more for blanc, and lots more for sweet) and the wine is fortified with alcohol so that most bottles end up with an ABV between 16% and 18%.

Though the history of vermouth is a bit murky, many credit the Italian distiller Antonio Benedetto Carpano for creating modern vermouth in 1786. Carpano's vermouth established the roots of the style now often referred to as Italian, sweet, or red vermouth: dark red and often bitter, with sweet cherry flavors and typically a lingering impression of vanilla. Despite being dark, it's usually made from white wine, with the flavorings and caramel coloring being responsible for its color.

The French soon adopted vermouth and made it their own, incorporating local alpine ingredients and stripping away some of the sweetness, leading to the style now known as French or dry vermouth, which is completely clear and colorless.

There are several other styles of vermouth, but the one most salient to cocktails is blanc (French) or bianco (Italian) vermouth, which is said to have been invented by the French and copied by the Italians. In terms of sweetness, it's similar to red vermouth, but it has fewer spicy flavors and more in the way of herbs (specifically thyme), and it's perfectly clear, like French dry vermouth. It's become a fixture in our cocktails, especially Martini variations. Blanc vermouths from French producers tend to be delicate, sweet, and herbal, whereas bianco vermouths from Italian producers have more amplified flavors, often adding a big vanilla note to any drinks they touch.

Many large vermouth producers make multiple styles, but we've found that our favorites in each style are from that style's country of origin; that is, we usually use an Italian brand for sweet vermouth and a French brand for dry. As for blanc or bianco, it depends on the application, but we more often use Dolin blanc, from France.

RECOMMENDED BOTTLES OF SWEET RED, OR ITALIAN, VERMOUTH

Carpano Antica Formula: Though this is said to be a reproduction of Antonio Benedetto Carpano's 1786 recipe, this particular brand didn't hit the market until the 1990s. But all marketing subterfuge aside, Antica Formula is one of our favorite vermouths, and it's considered a standard, stylistically, for vermouths from Torino, Italy. It's big and bitter and packs one hell of a vanilla kick. We love using it with aged spirits; few vermouths are as luscious a counterpoint to the peppery spice of rye in a classic Manhattan (page 84). However, all of that flavor does have a downside: when mixed with more delicate spirits—gin, vodka, and even tequila—Antica Formula can be a rambunctious guest who doesn't know when to shut up.

Cinzano Rosso: While it shares a common heritage with other sweet vermouths from Torino, Cinzano isn't as aggressive as Carpano Antica Formula, so it's a bit more versatile. While it doesn't make the best Manhattan, we'd never throw it out of bed. It's also a great companion to gin in a classic Martinez, or gin and Campari in a Negroni.

Dolin Rouge: A sweet French vermouth? Didn't we just tell you that we prefer Italian vermouths for this style? Yes, but Dolin rouge is a different type of sweet vermouth. Although it shares some of the characteristics of its Italian cousin, it's much lighter and softer, which can be very useful when creating a cocktail with a spirit that needs to be coddled a bit. For example, if you were to make a Manhattan with a wheated bourbon—such as Maker's Mark—a sturdy red vermouth, like Carpano Antica or even Cinzano, would overwhelm the bourbon. Dolin rouge won't. For the same reason, it also works well with other spirits that don't have the punchy spice of rye whiskey, including Cognac, Calvados, and some aged rums.

RECOMMENDED BOTTLES OF DRY, OR FRENCH, VERMOUTH

Dolin Dry: If we could only stock one bottle of dry vermouth, this would be it. It's extremely dry and clean—a benchmark for dry vermouth and the Martini's best buddy. With subtle flavors of alpine herbs and a slight bitterness, it's uniquely refreshing. In that way, Dolin dry is an excellent example of how terroir can define vermouth: it has deep roots in Chambéry, France, at the base of the Alps, where it's been made since 1821. If you want to see Dolin dry shine, make a fifty-fifty martini with equal parts Plymouth gin and vermouth, a dash of orange bitters, and a lemon twist.

Noilly Prat Extra Dry: Before the modern spirits revival, Noilly Prat, from Marseille, France, was one of the few bottles of dry vermouth available in the United States, and thanks to its lovely flavor and wide availability, it has remained as a staple bottle ever since.

RECOMMENDED BOTTLES OF BLANC, OR BIANCO, VERMOUTH

Dolin Blanc: Though we had used other blanc vermouths before Dolin's became available in the United States, it was Dolin's that made us fall in love with the style. A versatile player, Dolin blanc is useful in a wide range of cocktails: in Martini variations made with every imaginable base spirit (tequila, mezcal, gin, rum, whiskey, brandy . . .), as an herbaceous split base in sour-style cocktails, or as a base ingredient in spritzes and low-ABV drinks. We're particularly fond of pairing Dolin blanc with eaux-de-vie. If you visit one of our bars, you'll probably run into this combination somewhere on the menu.

La Quintinye Vermouth Royal Blanc: Whereas most blanc vermouths are based on a very neutral white wine, La Quintinye's blanc vermouth is built on Pineau des Charentes, an aperitif from France's Cognac region made from unfermented wine grape juice fortified with a young Cognac distillate, providing a broad and flavorful base for this extremely savory blanc vermouth.

Martini & Rossi Bianco: While the preceding two bottles are great, they aren't always easy to find. Among the blanc or bianco vermouths made by the big vermouth houses, our favorite is Martini & Rossi. Be warned that it exerts its personality a bit more than Dolin blanc, but that makes it an excellent companion to spirits like blanco tequila, mezcal, and gin.

OTHER AROMATIZED WINES

There are many other wine-based products that function similarly to vermouth in cocktails and are somewhat stylistically similar, and we often use them as creative substitutions for vermouth. Where they differ is in the flavorings that are added. Many focus on a single flavoring or small number of ingredients, as opposed to the wide range of flavorings used in vermouth. And while some are similar enough to vermouth that they can easily be substituted for it, others emphasize quite different flavors or have a higher alcohol content, requiring more adjustment to a cocktail's balance.

RECOMMENDED BOTTLES

Bonal Gentiane-Quina: Slightly bitter from a combination of cinchona bark (the source for quinine) and gentian root, Bonal tastes like a bitter amontillado sherry, with an impression of raisin on the nose, though it's dry on the palate. It pairs well with aged rum, either in a Manhattan-style drink or alongside citrus. Its astringency can be problematic in a sour-style cocktail, especially if made with lime juice.

We recommend a softer approach, pairing it with lemon or orange juice instead and keeping the amount of Bonal below 1 ounce.

Cocchi Americano Bianco: Cocchi Americano bianco and Lillet blanc (described below) share a similar slightly bitter, orangey flavor, leading many bartenders to think they're so similar that they can be used interchangeably. This can sometimes work, as in the classic Corpse Reviver #2 (page 188), but it isn't always successful. Cocchi packs a good deal more bitterness from cinchona, so we often use it when we need more structure to balance other big flavors. Our Little Victory (page 77) is a good example of this: as the base of a root beer infusion, Cocchi Americano's flavors are enhanced with a woodsy root beer extract, which balances the strength of both gin and vodka in the cocktail. We've tried the same infusion with Lillet and it falls flat; Cocchi's bitter backbone can be a great asset in building complex flavors.

Lillet Blanc: Though Lillet blanc doesn't have the bitter kick it used to (the original formula, called Kina Lillet, had a bit more cinchona than the current product), it's a wonderfully elegant aperitif wine. On its own, it's slightly bitter, with a modest honey-like sweetness, a floral aroma, and the brightness of orange zest. It can make cocktails "juicy," giving them the kind of balanced sweetness found in fresh apple juice and a rounded flavor. As a simple substitution for dry vermouth in cocktails, Lillet can yield excellent results, though it does express itself a bit more due to its flavorings. We often use it in small amounts to add body to a drink.

Lillet Rosé: In 2012, Lillet introduced this product—a mix of Lillet blanc, Lillet rouge (which we don't often use), and fruit liqueurs—to near-universal excitement. What's not to love about a fruity pink aperitif? It shares some of the characteristics of Lillet blanc but has a touch more sweet fruit flavor, particularly strawberry. It can work well in a variety of cocktails, from Martini variations to spritzes.

EXPERIMENTING WITH THE BALANCE

As mentioned, the reason the Martini recipe is so flexible is because it's not just about one spirit; the drink's core is a harmonious collaboration between a base spirit and . . . something else. As discussed, that "something else" is traditionally vermouth, but many other spirits can take its place: other types of aromatized wine (such as Lillet blanc in the Vesper, page 71), fortified wine (such as fino sherry in both Normandie Club Martinis, pages 77 and 282), or even a combination (for example, amontillado sherry, dry vermouth, and blanc vermouth in the low-ABV Bamboo, page 91). The point is, a Martini's core is not composed of just one ingredient, and this has a major bearing on its balance.

As for the balance, it's flexible and depends on personal preference. For those new to Martinis, and especially those who don't have an appreciation for dry vermouth, we love to offer three Martinis with different amounts of vermouth. If you choose to conduct this experiment at home, feel free to cut the recipe for each in half—though we highly recommend enjoying this line-up of Martinis with a friend or loved one. When gauging them, bear in mind that there's no "right" answer; one of these might be just right for you, while another might suit the preferences of your drinking pal. Especially for this experiment, be sure to use fresh vermouth—a bottle that's been open no longer than one week. Note that for the purposes of this experiment, we've removed the orange bitters and the garnish to keep the focus solely on the balance between the gin and the vermouth.

The first Martini, by far the driest, is mostly about the flavors of the gin, with the vermouth being a background player. This drink is potent and cooling and may take your breath away. The second, our root Martini recipe sans bitters and garnish, marries the gin and vermouth together nicely; both are discernable, but they've also melded to create a concise and harmonious flavor. The third, the Wet Martini is citrusy and light; it has a more herbal focus, with the gin bowing to the vermouth. Do you have a preference? The truth is, we like all three—it just depends what mood we're in.

As mentioned earlier in the chapter, changing the core or, in this case, the base spirit, generally necessitates changing the balance. But this works both ways: if we change the balance, substituting one vermouth for another, let alone swapping in a different aromatized wine, this is likely to change the proof, sweetness, and flavor of the drink, all of which need to be accommodated.

Little Victory

Martini (Very Dry)

2½ ounces Plymouth gin
¼ ounce Dolin dry vermouth

Stir all the ingredients over ice, then strain into a chilled Nick & Nora glass. No garnish.

Martini (Our Root Recipe)

2 ounces Plymouth gin
1 ounce Dolin dry vermouth

Stir all the ingredients over ice, then strain into a chilled Nick & Nora glass. No garnish.

Martini (Wet)

1½ ounces Plymouth gin
1½ ounces Dolin dry vermouth

Stir all the ingredients over ice, then strain into a chilled Nick & Nora glass. No garnish.

Normandie Club Martini #1

DEVON TARBY AND ALEX DAY, 2015

This cocktail, in which fino sherry replaces the vermouth, offers a great example of how a fairly simple change to the balance calls for further adjustments. Because fino sherry is so dry, we've used more than the amount of vermouth called for in our root Vodka Martini recipe (page 62) and have also added a bit of honey syrup to give the cocktail greater body. Then, because sherry is a more delicate modifier than vermouth, in this cocktail we showcase the subtle texture of a wheat-based vodka—a quality that vermouth would overshadow. The final touch is a spritz of a mineral-rich sea salt solution, which gives the drink an added layer of briny aroma.

2 ounces Aylesbury Duck vodka
1 ounce Alexander Jules fino sherry
1 teaspoon White Honey Syrup (page 286)
Garnish: 3 or 4 sprays of Sel Gris Solution (page 298)

Stir all the ingredients over ice, then strain into a chilled Nick & Nora glass. Mist the top of the drink with the Sel Gris Solution.

Little Victory

ALEX DAY, 2013

A more sensational way to change the balance is to infuse the aromatized wine with flavorings. This drink a riff on the Vesper (page 71), in which an aromatized wine (Cocchi Americano bianco) is flavored with a few drops of root beer extract. On its own, the infused Cocchi is tasty, but when mixed into the cocktail it gets a little lost, so we add a bit of orange marmalade, which introduces a touch of sweetness and a pleasant bitterness that bridges the flavors and helps highlight the infused Cocchi.

1½ ounces Beefeater gin
½ ounce Absolut Elyx vodka
1 ounce Root Beer–Infused Cocchi Americano (page 292)
1 teaspoon orange marmalade
Garnish: 1 orange wedge

Stir all the ingredients over ice, then double strain into a double Old-Fashioned glass over 1 large ice cube. Garnish with the orange wedge.

THE SEASONING: GARNISHES

A garnish can be a lavish, carefully composed artistic ensemble that sits atop the drink, or it can be a modest, simple adornment. If the garnish's functional contribution to the drink's flavor is essentially the same in either case, this provides an opportunity for the bartender to display some creativity. That said, while it is true that people experience a cocktail first with their eyes, we tend to take the Coco Chanel approach to garnishes: less is more. When we start to get outlandish with a garnish, we stop and ask ourselves, *Does this add anything?* If not, we simplify.

A garnish can also allow the drinker to personalize the drink; for example, the lime wedge on a Daiquiri allows drinkers to modify the drink along the sweet and sour spectrum. As for the topic of this chapter, the Martini, a garnish can be a powerful tool for seasoning the drink. That seasoning function is the focus of this section.

One advantage of using citrus twists as garnishes is the fragrant oils in their outer peel. Lemons and oranges are best for twists. Grapefruit can also work, but lime rarely does, as its pungent aroma can easily overwhelm other flavors. Though you've probably seen many bartenders rub the rim of a cocktail glass with a citrus twist, we rarely do it because we find the oils are too potent—the exception being the sweet, not-too-pungent oils of an orange twist. But expressing that oil over the top of the drink by squeezing or twisting the citrus peel over the cocktail disperses its flavors and aromas more evenly, enhancing the entire drinking experience. Finally, don't assume you need to drop a citrus twist into the drink; sometimes simply expressing it over the top is enough. Dropping it into the drink will further flavor the cocktail, which can be a good thing or a bad thing, depending on the drink.

For a Martini, we often express the twist over the top of the drink, then set it on the rim of the glass, where it will continue to offer its aroma without throwing off the balance of the drink.

EXPERIMENTING WITH THE SEASONING

A favorite experiment we use to illustrate this is to line up six Martinis, each made using the exact same recipe, but with different garnishes (see opposite page). Of course, we don't advise drinking six full-size Martinis, so we make three and portion them out into six glasses. For this experiment, we use Beefeater gin because we find it's a perfect middle-road gin: high enough in proof to be assertive but not overly flavorful to be off-putting to most people. Also, note that rather than following our usual practice of placing the expressed twist on the rim of the glass, for this experiment we drop it into the cocktail to explore how that affects the flavor of the drinks.

Taste each of the Martinis, one at a time. Notice anything different? The unadorned Martini doesn't have much aroma. In the second Martini, the olive adds just a hint of brininess, which gets more pronounced as the cocktail sits. The onion does much the same, though its flavor and aroma are more pronounced. The lemon twist is brightly perfumed. The Martini with the orange twist probably tastes sweeter than previous variations. And the Martini with the lime twist will probably have an off-putting taste, with the aroma and flavor of the lime clashing with the gin and vermouth.

After letting the Martinis sit for ten minutes, taste them again. The Martinis garnished with olive and onion will be even more savory, though similar to the first sips, while those with the citrus twists will probably have a bitter flavor, as more of the citrus oils have suffused the cocktail. If choosing to dip the lemon twist into the Martini, pull it out of the drink after a few minutes, giving it just enough time to add a hint of bitter complexity but long before it takes over the drink.

Six Ways to Season a Martini: A Garnish Experiment

6 ounces Beefeater gin

3 ounces Dolin dry vermouth

Garnish: 1 cocktail olive, 1 pickled onion, 1 lemon twist, 1 orange twist, and 1 lime twist

Stir all the ingredients over ice, then strain into six coupes. Leave the first glass without a garnish, add the olive to the second, add the onion to the third, and express the citrus twists over each of the remaining glasses, then place the peels into the drinks.

DAVID KAPLAN

David Kaplan is a cofounder of Proprietors LLC.

Martinis always remind me of my Aunt Anne, who's a fabulous Chicago designer and socialite. She threw the best parties and always had a giant, 10-ounce Martini in her hand as part of her ensemble. I was probably twelve or thirteen when I tried my first one. I definitely didn't understand the allure of the drink at the time, but I loved how elegant Anne looked with her Martini and loved the iconic glass, so I tried a couple of sips. I remember that, even at that tender age, I thought, *This is just a glass of rapidly warming vodka.*

I didn't really fall in love with the Martini until I was twenty-two or twenty-three, around the time I was set on opening a bar in New York. I was actively trying to learn as much about cocktails as possible. Somewhere along the way I tried a proper 5-to-1 Gin Martini at the Pegu Club. That was a revelation. And then I ordered one at Milk & Honey, and like every experience there, it was perfect. The glass and drink were impossibly cold and showed me what a Martini could be. It was transformative the way a great dish at a restaurant can be, and the Martini has been my drink of choice ever since.

Back in the day when I worked the floor at Death & Co, I'd order a fifty-fifty Martini over a big ice cube so I could slowly sip it during my shift as it diluted, much to the disdain of our bartenders, who didn't share my affection for a Martini on the rocks.

For me, the Martini is definitely an evening drink. The drink's proof alone kicks it out of the day-drinking category, for me at least. And there's this notion, steeped in history, that having a Martini signifies that it's time to unwind and relax—that you're done with work for the day. It's great before dinner, but you can also drink Martinis straight through the meal because you can tweak them to match whatever you're eating: you can bring the proof down by upping the percentage of vermouth, you can make it more savory or more citrusy, or whatever the meal calls for. In this way, it can take me from the first cocktail of the evening to the last drink of the night.

The Martini can also be a liquid resume. A Martini tells me a lot about the bartender who made it. Every bartender has a personal Martini spec, but the best results depend less on proportions of ingredients than on being a master of temperature and dilution and understanding all of the subtle variations that can influence a Martini. Making the drink correctly takes time, devotion, and a lot of practice, more so than any other cocktail.

For imbibers, it's also the most personal cocktail out there. Every bartender—whether in a dive bar or the fanciest cocktail den—expects guests to have some kind of preference: Shaken or stirred? Vodka or gin? Wet or dry? Olive or lemon twist? And just those few variables can produce such wildly different drinks. Every little decision becomes pronounced in the glass.

The Martini is enduring. It isn't a drink that comes in and out of fashion. The best one lives where the glass is cold as fucking hell, the cocktail itself is ice-cold, and that first sip transports you somewhere else. *Ahhhhh …*

David Kaplan's Favorite Martini

2½ ounces Tanqueray gin
¼ ounce Dolin dry vermouth
¼ ounce Dolin blanc vermouth
1 dash House Orange Bitters (page 295)
Garnish: 1 lemon twist

Stir all the ingredients over ice, then strain into a chilled Nick & Nora glass. Express the lemon twist over the drink, then set it on the edge of the glass.

EXPLORING TECHNIQUE: FULL-DILUTION STIRRING

Water is essential to life. Water is also essential to cocktails. (Does this make cocktails essential to life? Maybe.) Understanding how much water to add to a cocktail—that is, finding its dilution sweet spot—is one of the most important skills in making drinks.

We usually dilute drinks by shaking or stirring them with ice. In chapter 1, we covered why we deliberately underdilute certain stirred drinks (see page 19), such as the Old-Fashioned. In this chapter, we'll talk about the technique appropriate to Martinis: stirring to full dilution—a technique that's used for almost all stirred drinks served neat, without ice.

If you know exactly how much dilution is desired and at exactly what temperature you want to serve a cocktail, you could theoretically mix the drink at room temperature, add water, and place it in a freezer calibrated to the ideal serving temperature. And in fact, that's what our mad scientist friend Dave Arnold does. Of course, that takes time and special equipment—two resources often in short supply in busy bars, so here we'll stick with the more practical and common approach: stirring with ice.

Knowing when a drink is optimally chilled and diluted is a tactile thing that's easiest to demonstrate in practice. When we train our bartenders, we spend hours stirring and tasting drinks to help them recognize when they've hit the right levels of temperature and dilution. To help you gain similar experience, we recommend that you try the following experiment.

Start with the recipe for your favorite Martini or Martini variation; it's a good template to play with because its flavors change dramatically as it gets colder and more diluted. Use a chilled mixing glass fresh from the freezer and 1-inch ice cubes. Thanks to thermodynamics, using a chilled glass will actually slow the process of diluting the cocktail, which is especially useful for this experiment. Build the drink in the mixing glass without ice, then add ice cubes until the glass is nearly full. This might seem like a lot of ice, but the ice on top pushes down the rest of the ice so that as much ice as possible is in contact with the liquid, speeding the chilling process. To speed the process when you aren't experimenting, you can crack some of the ice cubes—we crack about one-third of them—to increase the surface contact between the ice and the cocktail.

As soon as you've added the ice, give the drink one stir, then taste it with a straw or spoon. This allows you to experience what the drink tastes like with very little dilution and at slightly below room temperature: disjointed, with each component distinguishable and not yet assembled into a seamless whole.

Next, stir the drink for 10 seconds, then taste it again. You'll notice that the flavors are more integrated but the flavors still haven't been stretched out enough—a quality we refer to as "tight." More dilution will give the flavors breathing room. At this point, the temperature of the cocktail should be around 40°F—chilled, but not *cold*. We want a very cold cocktail.

Now, stir for 10 seconds once again, then taste. Better, right? You should be noticing even more cohesion, like a chord of flavors instead of disparate notes. The temperature will also be bracingly cold, just below the freezing temperature of water. (The physics of this are complex, but in brief, the freezing point of alcohol is lower than that of water, and melting ice actually absorbs heat, so the net effect is to cool the cocktail below the freezing point of water.)

Finally, for the sake of education, continue to repeat the stirring and tasting process until the drink begins to taste weaker and less interesting. As soon as you can taste water getting in the way of the cocktail's flavors, you've exceeded the target dilution; the whole is no longer better than the sum of its parts. Yes, you're left with a less-than-ideal drink, but you've also discovered its sweet spot—the point at which the ingredients have reached harmony thanks to full-dilution stirring.

GLASSWARE: THE NICK & NORA GLASS

The Martini glass is the most iconic serving vessel for cocktails, but it's also the most flawed. Have you ever ordered a Martini and been served a swimming pool of booze that warmed to room temperature before you could drink even half of it? Blame the glassware—and the bartender who decided to use it.

So what's wrong with the traditional Martini glass? For starters, the deep, cone-shaped bowl encourages the cocktail to slosh around the glass—and out of it. It's also a clumsy glass to hold by the stem, so people are often inclined to pick it up by the bowl, in which case their hand will warm the drink. Then there's the fact that many Martini glasses are much too large for the drink they're designed to serve. A 10- or 12-ounce Martini glass begs to be filled with three or four drinks' worth of booze. Unless you're drinking for purposes other than to experience the refreshing harmony of a cold Martini, it's better to stick with the standard recipe's 3-ounce measure of booze and a serving vessel that will hold 4 to 6 ounces of liquid.

For Martinis, their variations, and many other stirred drinks that are served neat, we prefer a Nick & Nora glass. Named after the hard-drinking husband-and-wife sleuths featured in Dashiell Hammett's 1934 novel *The Thin Man*, this style of glassware has a deep, curved bowl, often tapering in slightly toward the top. They're less top-heavy than V-shaped Martini glasses and standard bar coupes and are therefore easier to hold by the stem. More importantly, Nick & Nora glasses have a thin, delicate lip that helps a velvety Martini slide onto your tongue. If this sounds like cocktail snobbery at its worst, try this little experiment: prepare two identical Martinis and serve one in a fine-edged Nick & Nora glass and the other in a coupe or Martini glass with a thicker edge. Now do you see what we mean?

No matter what type of glass you use for Martinis and their ilk, chilling it first will greatly enhance your drinking experience. If you don't have room in your freezer for glassware, fill the glass with ice water and let it sit for a few minutes while you assemble your cocktail, then dump it out just before straining and serving. A chilled glass will keep your drink colder while you sip it, something that's especially important with Martinis. And beyond that, visual appeal of a frosted glass and the tactile sensation of holding a chilled stem far exceed the experience with a room-temperature glass. One final note: Sometimes you may not have the luxury of chilling your glassware; that's totally fine, but please avoid using a warm glass.

Abbot Kinney,
page 90

THE MARTINI EXTENDED FAMILY

As we mentioned at the beginning of this chapter, everything we know about cocktail history suggests that the Manhattan was invented before the Martini. So why didn't we choose the Manhattan as the focus for this chapter? Because there's more leeway in executing a great Manhattan versus a Martini. The ingredients of a Manhattan are more boldly flavored, which means it's harder to perceive subtle differences when you change the ingredients or ingredient quantities.

Manhattan

CLASSIC

A Manhattan is basically a Martini that uses rye whiskey rather than gin, and sweet vermouth rather than dry. The yang to the Martini's yin, it nicely demonstrates how altering one element of a cocktail generally calls for other adjustments. Aged spirits, especially higher-proof ones, need to be paired with modifiers that can support their intensity without being smothered. If we were to simply substitute rye whiskey for gin in a Martini, the rye would overshadow the vermouth. Classic Angostura bitters connect the peppery rye and sweet vermouth, and offer yet another avenue for exploration, as you'll see in some of the variations that follow.

2 ounces Rittenhouse rye
1 ounce Cocchi Vermouth di Torino
2 dashes Angostura bitters
Garnish: 1 brandied cherry

Stir all the ingredients over ice, then strain into a chilled Nick & Nora glass. Garnish with the cherry.

From there we can begin exploring the larger Martini extended family, starting first with a cocktail from the earliest days of American cocktails, the Martinez, which introduces a small amount of highly flavorful liqueur to the Martini formula. As more flavors get introduced—for example, the slightly bitter seasoning of Bigallet China-China Amer in the Brooklyn—the Martini's extended family reaches a favorite among bartenders, the Negroni, a bitter-and-sweet cocktail that has inspired many of its own variations. Finally, we'll detour to a low-ABV Martini riff, the Bamboo, which swaps out high-proof spirit for sherry at its core.

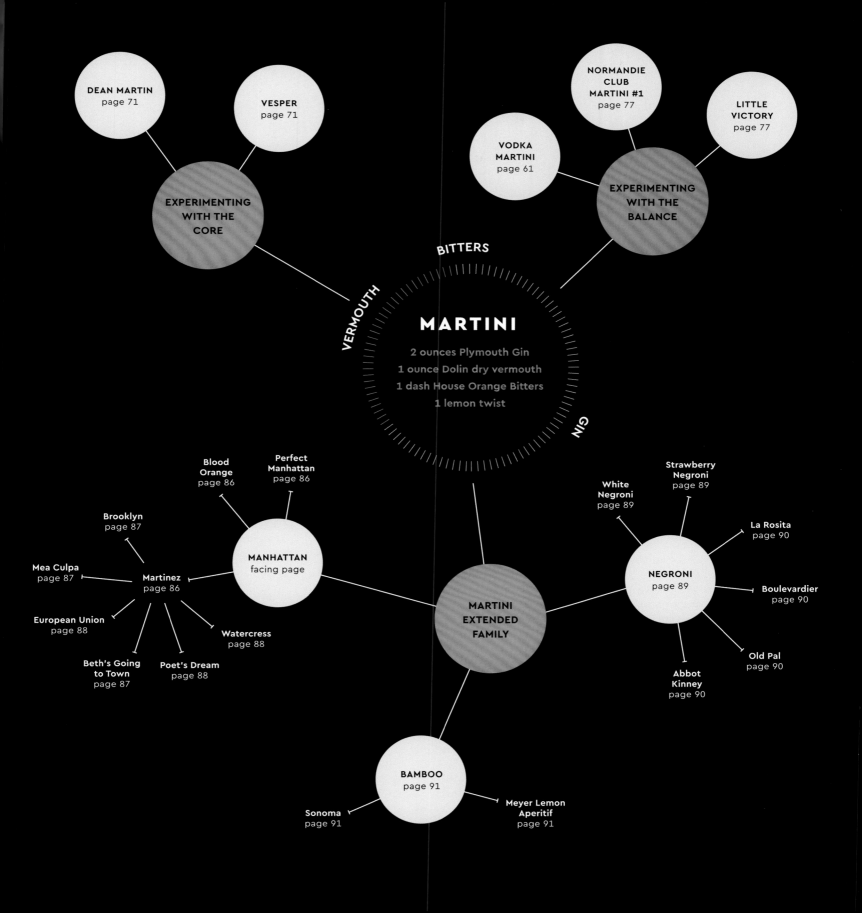

DEAN MARTIN
page 71

VESPER
page 71

EXPERIMENTING
WITH THE
CORE

VODKA
MARTINI
page 61

NORMANDIE
CLUB
MARTINI #1
page 77

LITTLE
VICTORY
page 77

EXPERIMENTING
WITH THE
BALANCE

BITTERS

VERMOUTH

GIN

MARTINI

2 ounces Plymouth Gin
1 ounce Dolin dry vermouth
1 dash House Orange Bitters
1 lemon twist

Blood
Orange
page 86

Perfect
Manhattan
page 86

Brooklyn
page 87

Mea Culpa
page 87

Martinez
page 86

MANHATTAN
facing page

European Union
page 88

Watercress
page 88

Beth's Going
to Town
page 87

Poet's Dream
page 88

MARTINI
EXTENDED
FAMILY

White
Negroni
page 89

Strawberry
Negroni
page 89

La Rosita
page 90

NEGRONI
page 89

Boulevardier
page 90

Old Pal
page 90

Abbot
Kinney
page 90

BAMBOO
page 91

Sonoma
page 91

Meyer Lemon
Aperitif
page 91

Blood Orange

Martinez

CLASSIC

True, the Martini and its variations typically involve a simple harmony of spirit and vermouth, but as just mentioned, a host of cocktails in its extended family also include a small amount of liqueur. In the Martinez, just 1 teaspoon of maraschino liqueur brings both fruitiness and astringency, qualities that pair beautifully with the vanilla flavors in aged spirits and sweet vermouth. When coming up with Martinez variations, the liqueur is a great place to start, given that there are so many interesting choices to explore, from Bénédictine, which introduces a honeyed sweetness and herbal undertones, to fruit liqueurs, such as peach, apricot, or raspberry.

1½ ounces Hayman's Old Tom gin

1½ ounces Carpano Antica Formula vermouth

1 teaspoon Luxardo maraschino liqueur

2 dashes House Orange Bitters (page 295)

Garnish: 1 lemon twist

Stir all the ingredients over ice, then strain into a chilled Nick & Nora glass. Express the lemon twist over the drink, then set it on the edge of the glass.

Perfect Manhattan

CLASSIC

In cocktail parlance, the term *perfect* refers to a drink that contains equal parts sweet and dry vermouth. Sounds easy enough, but splitting modifiers is tricky, especially in a Manhattan. If you use the wrong combination of vermouths, one (or both) will fight with the whiskey for attention. But in this recipe, the crispness of the dry vermouth, reinforced by the lemon twist garnish, results in a lighter, brighter Manhattan.

2 ounces Rittenhouse rye

½ ounce Cocchi Vermouth di Torino

½ ounce Dolin dry vermouth

2 dashes Angostura bitters

Garnish: 1 lemon twist

Stir all the ingredients over ice, then strain into a chilled Nick & Nora glass. Express the lemon twist over the drink, then set it on the edge of the glass.

Blood Orange

BRYAN BRUCE, 2016

While gorgeous blood oranges are tempting to use in cocktails, the flavor of their juice is flabby and leaves something to be desired. However, blood orange zest is fragrant, with a bright, almost savory orange flavor; here, it makes an appearance in an infused vermouth. The Cognac acts as a bridge in this Manhattan variation, linking the spiciness of the rye with the vermouth's bitter notes.

1 ounce Rittenhouse rye

½ ounce Pierre Ferrand 1840 Cognac

1½ ounces Blood Orange-Infused Carpano Antica Formula (page 287)

Garnish: 1 blood orange wheel

Stir all the ingredients over ice, then strain into a chilled coupe. Garnish with the blood orange wheel.

Mea Culpa

DEVON TARBY, 2015

We often say that bitter and sweet ingredients can act as glue, binding disparate components of a drink together, and this cocktail provides a great example. Small amounts of two liqueurs—bittersweet China-China Amer and rich apricot liqueur—marry the vodka with not one but two sherries, giving this drink a quiet backbone of dried fruit and nuts with a pleasant lingering bitterness.

2 ounces Grey Goose vodka

¾ ounce Alexander Jules fino sherry

¼ ounce Williams & Humbert Dry Sack sherry

1 teaspoon Giffard Abricot du Roussillon

1 teaspoon Bigallet China-China Amer

2 drops Salt Solution (page 298)

Garnish: 1 lemon twist

Stir all the ingredients over ice, then strain into a chilled Nick & Nora glass. Express the lemon twist over the drink, then set it on the edge of the glass.

Beth's Going to Town

DANIEL ZACHARCZUK, 2015

Here's a complex, Martinez-style drink that uses a soft scotch and a rich, spicy contemporary gin in place of the traditional Old Tom gin. This is a great example of the value of knowing your ingredients: The unique sarsaparilla flavors of the Aviation gin marry well with the cola notes found in both the sweet Spanish vermouth and the Ramazzotti amaro; substituting another brand of any of these ingredients will yield markedly different results.

1 ounce Highland Park 12-year scotch

1 ounce Aviation gin

½ ounce Carpano Antica sweet vermouth

¼ ounce Giffard Abricot du Roussillon

¼ ounce Ramazzotti

Garnish: 1 mint leaf

Stir all the ingredients over ice, then strain into a chilled Old-Fashioned glass. Garnish with the mint leaf.

Brooklyn

CLASSIC

Another strategy for experimenting with the balance is to substitute small amounts of amari or liqueurs for a portion of the vermouth or aromatized wine. The most classic example of this is the Brooklyn, a riff on the Manhattan that uses a bit of amaro and just a teaspoon of maraschino liqueur. Despite its Manhattan-adjacent name, you can quickly recognize this drink as a rye-based variation on the Martinez (page 86) because of the liqueur. Though the Brooklyn was historically made with Amer Picon, an orange-flavored French liqueur, modern bottlings of Amer Picon—if you can even find them—are less bitter and flavorful than older versions, so in its place we use China-China Amer, a bittersweet aperitif crafted with the classic Amer Picon recipe in mind.

2 ounces Rittenhouse rye

¾ ounce Dolin dry vermouth

¼ ounce Bigallet China-China Amer

1 teaspoon Maraska maraschino liqueur

Garnish: 1 brandied cherry

Stir all the ingredients over ice, then strain into a chilled Nick & Nora glass. Garnish with the cherry.

Watercress

DEVON TARBY, 2016

When you glance at this drink's ingredients, you might expect a savory cocktail to emerge, but using a centrifuge to make the Watercress-Infused Gin releases all of the plant's peppery flavors without making the gin taste like a liquid salad. Don't have a centrifuge? No sweat: just lightly muddle a few watercress leaves with the vermouths and peach liqueur, then remove them and build the cocktail. Just as you might add dried fruit to a salad of bitter greens, here we add a small measure of a peach liqueur to add a fruity complexity to the cocktail.

1½ ounces Watercress-Infused Gin (page 294)

½ ounce Absolut Elyx vodka

¾ ounce Dolin dry vermouth

¼ ounce Dolin blanc vermouth

½ teaspoon Giffard Crème de Pêche

1 drop Salt Solution (page 298)

Garnish: 1 Golden Delicious apple slice

Stir all the ingredients over ice, then strain into a chilled Nick & Nora glass. Garnish with the apple slice.

Poet's Dream

CLASSIC

As you may recall from the Improved Whiskey Cocktail (page 17) in chapter 1, the term *improved* refers to adding a bit of highly flavorful liqueur to a basic cocktail. This is a valuable way of thinking about how seemingly minor adjustments can create distinctive new variations. In the Poet's Dream, a basic Martini is "improved" by backing off on the vermouth a bit and including a bit of herbaceous Bénédictine.

2 ounces Beefeater gin

¾ ounce Dolin dry vermouth

¼ ounce Bénédictine

2 dashes House Orange Bitters (page 295)

Garnish: 1 lemon twist

Stir all the ingredients over ice, then strain into a chilled Nick & Nora glass. Express the lemon twist over the drink, then set it on the edge of the glass.

European Union

ALEX DAY, 2009

Before creating this drink, we'd only encountered Calvados in drinks as a base spirit. In this Martinez variation, a small amount of Calvados softens the Old Tom gin and adds a fruity depth to the drink, while a touch of Strega adds complexity, acting much like bitters. All the (pre-Brexit) European friends in one glass.

1½ ounces Hayman's Old Tom gin

½ ounce Busnel VSOP Calvados

¾ ounce Carpano Antica Formula vermouth

1 teaspoon Strega

1 dash Bitter Truth aromatic bitters

Garnish: 1 brandied cherry

Stir all the ingredients over ice, then strain into a chilled coupe. Garnish with the cherry.

Negroni

CLASSIC

By and large, the cocktails in this chapter are characterized by a core flavor of spirit and vermouth or another aromatized wine, and generally speaking, they fail when those components aren't in balance. However, there is an exception to this rule (as there always is): the Negroni, a deeply bitter cocktail made with a full ounce of Campari. Because Campari brings a lot of proof to the drink, the Negroni has less gin, and it finds its balance in the typical core of gin and vermouth, but in an equal-parts combination in which the amaro is a unified part of the core, with the gin providing a clean structure upon which the bitterness of Campari is balanced by the richness of the sweet vermouth. In the variations that follow, you'll find a few other cocktails that employ a similar tactic, substituting high-alcohol liqueurs or other amari for the Campari, and adjusting the balance of ingredients so they harmonize as a whole.

1 ounce Tanqueray gin

1 ounce Carpano Antica Formula sweet vermouth

1 ounce Campari

Garnish: 1 orange half wheel

Stir all the ingredients over ice, then strain into an Old-Fashioned glass over 1 large ice cube. Garnish with the orange half wheel.

Strawberry Negroni

Negroni

White Negroni

Strawberry Negroni

TREVOR EASTER AND DEVON TARBY, 2017

This Negroni riff doesn't veer too far from the original cocktail, but does so in ways that are profoundly delicious. A touch of Clarified Strawberry Syrup rounds off the bitter edges of the Campari, while drops of chocolatey (but dry) Cacao Nib Tincture deepens the bittersweet connection between Campari and sweet vermouth.

1 ounce Beefeater Gin

¾ ounce Campari

¾ ounce Dolin Sweet Vermouth

¼ ounce Clarified Strawberry Syrup (page 57)

5 drops Cacao Nib Tincture (page 97)

Garnish: 1 strawberry slice

Stir all the ingredients over ice, then strain into an Old-Fashioned glass over 1 large ice cube. Garnish with the strawberry slice.

White Negroni

WAYNE COLLINS, 2000

Replacing the Negroni's rich, red cloak of sweet vermouth and Campari with light, citrusy Suze (a French aperitif) and floral Dolin blanc, yields the White Negroni. We think of it as a seasonal wardrobe swap, and though we do drink classic Negronis year-round, in summer we like to go with the white.

1½ ounces Beefeater gin

1 ounce Dolin blanc vermouth

¾ ounce Suze

Garnish: 1 orange twist

Stir all the ingredients over ice, then strain into an Old-Fashioned glass over 1 large ice cube. Express the orange twist over the drink, then gently rub it around the rim of the glass and place it into the drink.

La Rosita

CLASSIC

Is this a tequila-laced Perfect Manhattan (page 86) with the addition of Campari, or a tequila Negroni that splits the vermouths? Either way, the addition of dry vermouth is key in our version of Gary Regan's adaptation of a recipe found in an old copy of *Mr. Boston: Official Bartender's Guide*, as the savory flavors of the Dolin blanc amplify the vegetal quality of the tequila.

1½ ounces Siembra Azul reposado tequila

½ ounce Carpano Antica Formula vermouth

½ ounce Dolin dry vermouth

½ ounce Campari

1 dash Angostura bitters

Garnish: 1 orange twist

Stir all the ingredients over ice, then strain into a chilled Nick & Nora glass. Express the orange twist over the drink, then gently rub it around the rim of the glass and place it into the drink.

Boulevardier

CLASSIC

The Boulevardier dates back to the 1920s, when it made an appearance in *Barflies and Cocktails*, a seminal cocktail book written by Harry MacElhone, the owner of Harry's New York Bar in Paris. The original recipe called for equal portions of each ingredient, a ratio that has shifted, over the years, in favor of whiskey. Now that you understand the basic orthodoxy of the Martini (and, likewise, the Negroni), this shouldn't come as a surprise: although a perfectly delicious Boulevardier can be made with equal measures, using more bourbon and less Campari and vermouth promotes the whiskey's flavor just enough that it asserts itself.

1½ ounces Elijah Craig Small Batch bourbon

¾ ounce Carpano Antica Formula vermouth

¾ ounce Campari

Garnish: 1 brandied cherry

Stir all the ingredients over ice, then strain into a chilled coupe. Garnish with the cherry.

Old Pal

CLASSIC

The Old Pal is almost identical to the Boulevardier, with dry vermouth being substituted for the sweet, and rye whiskey instead of bourbon. Though this Old Pal teeters toward sweet, it's also spicy thanks to the rye, with a bright backbone from the French vermouth, and a bitter finish via Campari.

1½ ounces Rittenhouse rye

¾ ounce Dolin dry vermouth

¾ ounce Campari

Garnish: 1 lemon twist

Stir all the ingredients over ice, then strain into a chilled Nick & Nora glass. Express the lemon twist over the drink, then place it into the drink.

Abbot Kinney

DEVON TARBY, 2015

Although this cocktail is still, it works like a spritz, having a low ABV and enough acidity to be a refreshing palate cleanser when consumed with a meal (pictured on page 83).

¾ ounce Fords gin

1½ ounces Dolin blanc vermouth

¼ ounce Suze

¼ ounce St-Germain

¼ ounce Fusion Napa Valley verjus blanc

2 dashes Miracle Mile celery bitters

Garnish: 1 celery ribbon

Stir all the ingredients over ice, then strain into a chilled Nick & Nora glass. Twist the celery ribbon into a spiral and balance it on the rim of the glass.

Meyer Lemon Aperitif

Meyer Lemon Aperitif

ALEX DAY, 2016

A lighter, brighter riff on the Bamboo, this is our take on a root-to-stem cocktail that uses the entire Meyer lemon. We combine the ingredients and infuse the cocktail with the fruit's fragrant zest, then we use the leftover juice to make a Meyer lemon cordial (page 285) that can be made into a carbonated soda and served alongside this cocktail. The recipe below makes about 1 liter—the perfect sophisticated and refreshing aperitif for a party.

12 ounces Lustau Puerto fino sherry

6 ounces Dolin blanc vermouth

6 ounces Dolin dry vermouth

4 ounces Campo de Encanto Moscatel pisco

Zest from 2 Meyer lemons

1¼ ounces Cane Sugar Syrup (page 47)

8 dashes House Orange Bitters (page 295)

8 ounces water

Garnish: 10 Meyer lemon wheels

Combine half of the sherry, vermouths, pisco, and zest in an iSi whipper (see page 97). Following the pressure infusion method explained on page 97, infuse the mixture. Strain through a fine-mesh sieve and transfer to a large bowl. Repeat with the remaining sherry, vermouths, pisco, and zest. Add the syrup, bitters, and water to the mixture and stir to combine, then transfer to a 1-liter bottle. Seal and refrigerate until cold. Serve in chilled coupes (this recipe makes ten drinks), garnished with the Meyer lemon wheels.

Bamboo

CLASSIC

If there's one unifying theme among all the Martini variations in this chapter thus far, it's that they're very boozy. But here's an iteration that's lower in ABV while still reflecting the spirit of the Martini: the classic Bamboo, which swaps out gin for amontillado sherry. Because the sherry is lower in alcohol and not as pungently flavored as gin, the proportion of vermouth is increased to balance the cocktail—the vermouths surround the sherry and add sweetness and depth of flavor. The Bamboo is a very old drink, having originated in Japan in the late nineteenth century, but it remains one of our favorite cocktails today—so much so that we often serve it on tap at our bars.

1½ ounces Lustau Los Arcos amontillado sherry

¾ ounce Dolin blanc vermouth

¾ ounce Dolin dry vermouth

2 dashes House Orange Bitters (page 295)

Garnish: 1 lemon twist

Stir all the ingredients over ice, then strain into a chilled Nick & Nora glass. Express the lemon twist over the drink, then place it into the drink.

Sonoma

DEVON TARBY, 2015

What would it taste like to drink wine while standing in a Sonoma farm? To answer the question that inspired this riff on the Bamboo, we start with a fruity Chardonnay and add a touch of sweet honey; the bright grapey acidity of verjus; and Calvados, an apple brandy native to Normandy, France, another bucolic agricultural region. Topping it off is a spray of a white pepper aroma, which has the distinct smell of a barn.

2½ ounces dry, unoaked Chardonnay

½ ounce Busnel VSOP Calvados

1 teaspoon Fusion Napa Valley verjus blanc

1 teaspoon Honey Syrup (page 45)

1 drop Salt Solution (page 298)

Garnish: 4 sprays of White Pepper–Infused Vodka (page 294)

Stir all the ingredients over ice, then strain into a chilled Nick & Nora glass. Mist the top of the drink with the infused vodka.

NEXT-LEVEL TECHNIQUE: MAKING INFUSIONS

In our early days of creating new cocktails, the wide variety of spirits and liqueurs on our back bar provided plenty of inspiration. But now that there are so many amazing bartenders creating delicious drinks every day, we've had to up the ante in our search for new and unique flavors to add to our repertoire. Infusions are one of the easiest ways to accomplish this; once flavors have been added to a base spirit or modifier, the infusion can be swapped into recipes, opening up a vast new realm of combinations. (By the way, an invaluable resource for developing new drinks is *The Flavor Bible*, by Karen Page and Andrew Dornenburg. Organized by ingredients, it's a compendium of what goes with what, from obvious to unexpected combinations.)

For us, coming up with new ideas for infusions is generally a matter of simple problem solving. When we work on a new drink, we often begin by zeroing in on a desired final flavor profile. Then we pick a base formula—inspired by one of the six foundational recipes featured in this book—and develop the drink from there. For example, let's say we want to use lemon as a key flavor. Lemon matches nicely with honey, no surprise there. We then look at honey and consider that it loves chamomile. Then we ask ourselves what base spirit might work best with this combination of flavors while also being unexpected. The combination of lemon, honey, and chamomile is warming and, for some people, tinged with nostalgia. What if we were to take advantage of that connection and choose a warming spirit, like calvados, that reinforces the comforting qualities of the other

ingredients? Once we've envisioned a Calvados-based cocktail with lemon, honey, and chamomile, we could express these flavors in a couple of different ways in a drink: as a sour made with lemon juice, perhaps (the La Valencia, page 188, which uses yellow Chartreuse's honeyed flavor matched with chamomile and rye whiskey); as a Collins (the Fuji Legend, page 280); or even a Hot Toddy (Gun Club Toddy, page 40).

Tea extraction in vodka after thirty seconds, one minute, and two minutes.

Making an infusion can be as simple as steeping an ingredient in a spirit, and that's pretty much the way people have done it for years. Alcohol is a great solvent because it excels at extracting flavor. In fact, sometimes it works too well and can pull out undesired flavors, along with the desirable ones. For example, when you eat a ripe raspberry, you'll mostly taste the fresh berry flavor. But if you soak raspberries in alcohol for an extended amount of time, the infusion will develop an unpleasant bitterness from compounds in the raspberry seeds.

For this reason, we use a number of different infusion techniques—cold infusion, room-temperature infusion, sous vide (or immersion circulator) infusion, pressurized infusion, and even a centrifuge method—choosing among them depending on the ingredients and flavors we're trying to extract. The first step in making that decision is to look at the ingredients and predict how their flavors will be expressed in the final infusion. Then we try one or more infusion methods to test our predictions. In the case of fresh fruits, macerating (soaking them in liquid) for a long time can draw out unwanted flavors, and cooking them at high temperatures can destroy their fresh flavor. The volatile aromatic compounds present in fresh fruits can be also be muted by an overly long infusion process. In this case, our solution would be to use an immersion circulator to heat the infusion at a very low temperature for a short amount of time (a process we'll describe in depth shortly). This allows us to extract only the flavors we desire and also has the benefit of speeding the process—most of our infusions are complete within a couple of hours.

We also give a lot of thought to our base liquid (spirit, liqueur, fortified wine, and so on). A key consideration is alcohol content. Common wisdom holds that spirits with a higher ABV yield better extractions, but that isn't universally true. A highly alcoholic spirit, such as Everclear, will extract flavors quickly and thoroughly, especially from dry ingredients, but the higher the proof, the more the ingredients' bitter flavors will be pulled out. That can be great for making homemade bitters, but not so hot for when using fresh ingredients. We've found that using spirits between 40% and 50% ABV generally produces great results no matter what infusion technique we use, and if we're using fresh fruits that have bitter elements, such as citrus peels, spirits at the low end of that spectrum extract the best flavors. It's also possible to use lower ABV spirits, such as liqueurs, fortified wines, and even still wines. But this requires taking care to prevent oxidization, which causes flavors to change quickly.

In the sections that follow, we'll provide detailed instructions on how to make infusions using five different techniques. Specific infusion recipes, including all of the infusions called for in the recipes in this book, are located in the appendix.

COLD INFUSIONS

When working with ingredients from which we want to extract as much fresh, vibrant flavor as possible (coffee beans, for example), cold maceration helps draw out the desired flavors. Chilling slows the process of flavor extraction, which means the flavoring ingredients can interact with the alcohol longer. A more mellow process, it yields infusions with deep, complex flavors that could be lost or changed for the worse in a room temperature or heated infusion. Importantly, we only use this method when an ingredient doesn't have unpleasant flavors that will be extracted over time—for example, berries with seeds that can impart an acrid flavor.

We also use lower temperatures in a process known as fat washing, which was pioneered by our friends Don Lee and Eben Freeman. When alcohol is combined with a fatty ingredient (such as butter, cream, oil, or animal fats) and then frozen, the fat will congeal into solids that can easily be strained out, leaving just the flavor of that fat in the alcohol. This is a great technique for introducing richness into cocktails that aren't rich, such as the Root Beer Float (page 283).

One word of caution on cold infusions: Ensure that there aren't any pungent ingredients in your freezer or refrigerator when making these infusions, as those aromas and flavors may find their way into the infusion.

COLD INFUSION METHODS

Fat washing: If using a solid fat, gently melt it in a saucepan or microwave. Combine the fat and spirit in a wide container, as this will maximize contact between the fat and spirit, producing better flavor, and stir or whisk to combine. Cover and freeze until the fat has solidified into a layer on top of the liquid, usually 12 hours or less. Carefully poke a hole in the fat layer and drain the liquid out; reserve the fat for another use (or discard). If any particles remain in the liquid, strain it through a fine-mesh sieve lined with several layers of cheesecloth or through a Superbag (a flexible, heat-resistant sieve). Though you can store fat-washed infusions at room temperature, we find they retain their flavor better when refrigerated. See Milk-Washed Rum (page 291) and Coconut-Infused Bourbon (page 289).

Eggs: Line a shallow, resealable container with paper towels. Arrange a layer of the flavoring ingredient (such as lavender) on top of the paper towels, then arrange whole, uncooked eggs, still in their shells, in a single layer on top. Seal the container and refrigerate overnight.

ROOM-TEMPERATURE INFUSIONS

With ingredients that infuse very quickly, generally an hour or less, we simply combine the ingredients and let the alcohol do its job at room temperature. These ingredients are often very flavorful and temperamental—such as jalapeños in tequila, which can overinfuse in a heartbeat; or black tea, which can become tannic if overextracted—so it's important to taste them every couple of minutes throughout the infusion process. This will help you develop a baseline standard for comparison and decide when to stop the infusion process. A case in point is our Thai Chile–Infused Bourbon (page 293), which we typically infuse for just 5 minutes—or less! Another example is the Oolong-Infused Vodka (page 291), which develops a distinctive color from the tea within about 20 minutes, providing a visual indicator that it's time to strain the infusion.

Also, keep in mind that some ingredients, like dried or fresh chiles, vary; thanks to nature, no two jalapeños are the same. So even if you've made a specific chile infusion before, taste often during the process every time you make it.

As discussed, the alcohol content of the spirit will play a large part in how quickly the infusion occurs. If you use a higher-proof spirit, the amount of time needed for optimum extraction will probably be short. If you use a lower-proof spirit, such as vermouth, it will take much longer. For example, we allow our Cardamom-Infused St-Germain (page 288) to infuse for about 12 hours because the St-Germain, at 20% ABV, is somewhat low in proof, and because the cardamom is more delicate. On the other hand, our Madras Curry–Infused Gin (page 291), made with fiery curry powder and equally fiery 44% ABV Dorothy Parker gin, is only infused for about 15 minutes.

HOW TO MAKE ROOM-TEMPERATURE INFUSIONS

Gram scale

2 large containers with lids

Fine-mesh sieve and cheesecloth, or a Superbag (see page 49)

1 Weigh the ingredients on a gram scale.

2 Combine the ingredients in a container. Whisk or stir to combine.

3 Taste the infusion often: every minute or so at first, then every 15 minutes, then every hour (depending on the ingredients used). For longer infusion times, keep the container covered except when tasting.

4 When the infusion is ready, strain it through a fine-mesh sieve lined with several layers of cheesecloth, or through a Superbag, into a clean container.

5 Transfer the infusion to a storage container and refrigerate until ready to use.

SOUS VIDE INFUSIONS

At our bars, we use the sous vide technique not only to extract flavor for syrups (see page 49), but also to flavor alcohol. We've adopted this method for two reasons. First, heat speeds the infusion process. Second, heating the mixture at a precise temperature without allowing any liquid to evaporate yields infusions that are more subtle and nuanced than those made using any other method. Importantly, the temperature remains consistent throughout the process, allowing us to select exactly the right temperature to preserve the flavors we want (typically the flavor of the raw ingredient) without extracting off-flavors. For example, in our Coconut-Infused Bourbon (page 289), the sous vide process results in a final product with fresh coconut flavor, whereas an infusion made by simply macerating coconut flakes in bourbon at room temperature for a few days will be far less vibrant, though still tasty.

Most of our sous vide infusions employ temperatures between 135°F and 145°F, with the lower end of that range being suitable for delicate ingredients such as fruits and the higher end being best for sturdier flavors, like coconut, nuts, or dried spices. As you'll see in the method that follows, at the end of the cooking time we submerge the infusion in an ice bath, which condenses any vapor present in the bag and preserves the alcohol content.

HOW TO MAKE SOUS VIDE INFUSIONS

Large water basin
Immersion circulator
Gram scale
Bowl
Resealable, heatproof plastic bag, such as a freezer bags
Ice bath
Fine-mesh sieve
Storage container

1 Fill the basin with water and place the immersion circulator inside.

2 Set the circulator to the desired temperature.

3 Carefully measure the ingredients by weight and combine them in a bowl.

4 Transfer the mixture to a sealable, heatproof plastic bag. Seal the bag almost completely, then remove as much air as possible by dipping the bag (other than the unsealed portion) in the water. The counterpressure from the water will push the rest of the air out. Finish sealing the bag, then remove it from the water.

5 When the circulator has reached the desired temperature, place the sealed bag in the basin.

6 Carefully remove the bag when the specified time is up.

7 Transfer the bag to an ice bath to cool.

8 Strain the infusion through a fine-mesh sieve to remove any solids.

9 Transfer the infusion to a storage container and refrigerate until ready to use.

PRESSURIZED INFUSIONS

Manipulating pressure is a valuable way to extract flavor from ingredients that are extremely fragile: those that perish too quickly to allow for extended maceration, or those that change dramatically with any amount of heat. We use two different techniques for pressurized infusions: rapid infusions using an iSi whipper (a gadget more typically used to make whipped cream) and nitrous oxide (N_2O), and vacuum infusions using a chamber vacuum machine.

In rapid pressurized infusion, flavors are extracted quickly by using compressed gas to force liquid into a solid ingredient. All of the ingredients are placed in the chamber of an iSi whipper and charged with N_2O, which forces the liquid into the cells of the solid ingredient, somewhat like a sponge sucking up water. When the pressure is released, the liquid is pulled back out of the solid ingredient, now carrying its flavor. Rapid infusions are particularly useful for extracting delicate flavors, such as those of fresh herbs, as well as with ingredients that have a wide range of flavors, such as cacao nibs. Because the infusion process is so quick—usually around 10 minutes—it doesn't run the risk of extracting any of the off-flavors that can come with long maceration times.

The vacuum infusion process is similar but requires a very expensive piece of equipment: a chamber vacuum machine. Instead of forcing liquid into solid ingredients using pressurized gas, it does so by removing all of the air inside the chamber. When a liquid and a solid are combined under vacuum, the pores of the solid open, letting the air within out and forcing the liquid into the vacated spaces. Then, when the chamber returns to the ambient atmospheric pressure, all of the liquid is sucked back out of the solid ingredient, now infused with flavor.

HOW TO MAKE VACUUM INFUSIONS

Gram scale
Wide plastic or metal container, such as a baking pan
Chamber vacuum machine
Plastic wrap
Fine-mesh sieve and cheesecloth, or a Superbag (see page 49)
Storage container

1   Carefully measure the ingredients by weight.

2   Put the ingredients into the widest high-walled container (at least 2 inches deep) that will fit into the chamber and put it into the vacuum machine. Cover with plastic wrap, poking about ten holes into the top (this will help hold back any splashing liquid when the vacuum is released—it can get messy).

3   Turn the machine on to full vacuum, keeping your finger on the stop switch. As the air is vacated, dramatic boiling will occur. Stop the machine if the infusion ever risks boiling over. Run the machine at full vacuum for 1 minute. Repeat the cycle at least two times for the best results—you'll notice that the boiling will subside.

4   Remove the container and use a straw to taste the infusion.

5   If your infusion is weak, there are two options for extracting more flavor: First, you can simply run the vacuum cycle multiple times until you achieve the desired flavor. Or, another great way to pull more flavor from the infusion is to turn the machine to full vacuum, then turn it off. The machine will hold at vacuum and the infusion will continue until you turn it back on. We recommend doing this for 10 minutes, then checking the infusion's flavor.

6   When you're satisfied with the flavor, strain the infusion through a fine-mesh sieve lined with several layers of cheesecloth or through a Superbag.

7   Transfer to a storage container and refrigerate until ready to use. Because these infusions extract delicate flavors, they are best used within 1 week (though they will remain usable for up to 4 weeks).

HOW TO MAKE RAPID PRESSURIZED INFUSIONS

Gram scale

iSi whipper, preferably 1 quart capacity

2 N$_2$O cartridges

Large, deep container

Fine-mesh sieve and cheesecloth, or a Superbag (see page 49)

Storage container

1   Carefully measure the ingredients by weight.

2   Put the ingredients in an iSi whipper, taking care not to fill it higher than the "Max" line. Seal tightly. Charge with one of the N$_2$O cartridges, then shake the canister about five times. Change the cartridge, then charge and shake again. We recommend allowing the mixture to sit under pressure for 10 minutes and shaking it every 30 seconds or so.

3   Point the canister's nozzle at a 45-degree angle into a container. Vent the gas as quickly as possible without spraying liquid everywhere; the quicker the venting, the better the infusion. When all of the gas is out, open the canister and take a listen. Once there is no longer audible bubbling, you can proceed. Strain the infusion through a fine-mesh sieve or Superbag.

4   Funnel the infusion back into the original liquor bottle and refrigerate until ready to use. Because these infusions extract delicate flavors, they are best used within a month—though some delicate flavors (such as herbs or citrus zest (see Meyer Lemon Aperitif, page 91) are most vibrant within 1 week.

ISI WHIPPERS

We highly recommend the whippers made by iSi. While other "culinary whippers" are available, we find that the longevity of an iSi stands up to their higher price point. Their whippers come in many sizes, and we recommend using the 1-liter Thermo Whip model for its high-quality components and insulated chamber. Aside from infusions, these whippers are perfect for making whipped cream (see White Russian, page 267), especially if you're making high volumes of cocktails.

CENTRIFUGE INFUSIONS

We learned this technique (among many others) from Dave Arnold, food scientist extraordinaire, and it has allowed us to create some of our most outlandish infusions, featuring flavors we'd never imagined we could use in cocktails, such as our Graham Cracker–Infused Bourbon (page 290) to make an Old-Fashioned variation (Campfire, page 279). Unfortunately, it does require a centrifuge, which is a very expensive piece of equipment.

Generally speaking, making a centrifuge infusion involves first blending solid ingredients with booze to maximize surface contact and speed the infusion process, then using a centrifuge to separate the solids and clarify the liquid. Note that with this process, some of the liquids from the solid ingredient end up in the infusion. For example, in our Strawberry-Infused Cognac and Mezcal (page 293, used in the Berry Picking, page 278), some strawberry juice ends up in the infusion. This can yield delicious results, but the infusion may be more prone to spoilage and therefore have a shorter life span. Also, be aware that if much liquid from the flavoring ingredients ends up in the infusion, this may decrease the proof of the final product.

It can take some trial and error to figure out the right proportion of booze to flavoring ingredient. With dry ingredients, such as dried fruits or graham crackers, start with a 1-to-4 ratio by weight of flavoring ingredients to booze. For ingredients that contain water, such as bananas or strawberries, start with a 1-to-2 ratio. With ingredients that have very subtle flavor, such as watermelon, you might use a 1-to-1 ratio.

HOW TO MAKE CENTRIFUGE INFUSIONS

Gram scale
Blender
Fine-mesh sieve
Bowl or other vessel
Centrifuge
Paper coffee filter or Superbag (see page 49)

1 Carefully measure the ingredients by weight.

2 Combine the ingredients in a blender and process until the solids are completely pureed.

3 Next, strain the mixture into a container. But first, weigh the container. (Or, if your scale has a tare function, place the container on it, zero the scale, then add the mixture and determine its weight.)

4 Strain the mixture through a fine-mesh sieve to remove any large particles.

5 Weigh the filled container, then subtract the weight of the container to determine the weight of the liquid to provide the baseline weight for the following calculation.

6 Calculate 0.2% of the weight of the liquid (multiply by 0.002) to get X grams.

7 Stir X grams of Pectinex Ultra SP-L (see page 48) into the liquid. Cover and let sit for 15 minutes.

8 Stir again to mix any separated liquid and divide the liquid evenly among the centrifuge containers. Weigh the filled containers and adjust the amount of liquid in each as needed to ensure their weights are exactly the same; this is important for keeping the centrifuge in balance. (Off-balance centrifuges are dangerous!)

9 Run the centrifuge at 4,500 rpm for 12 minutes.

10 Remove the containers and carefully strain the infusion through a paper coffee filter or Superbag, being careful not to disturb the solids that have collected on the bottom of the containers.

11 If any particles remain in the infusion, strain it again.

12 Transfer to a storage container and refrigerate until ready to use.

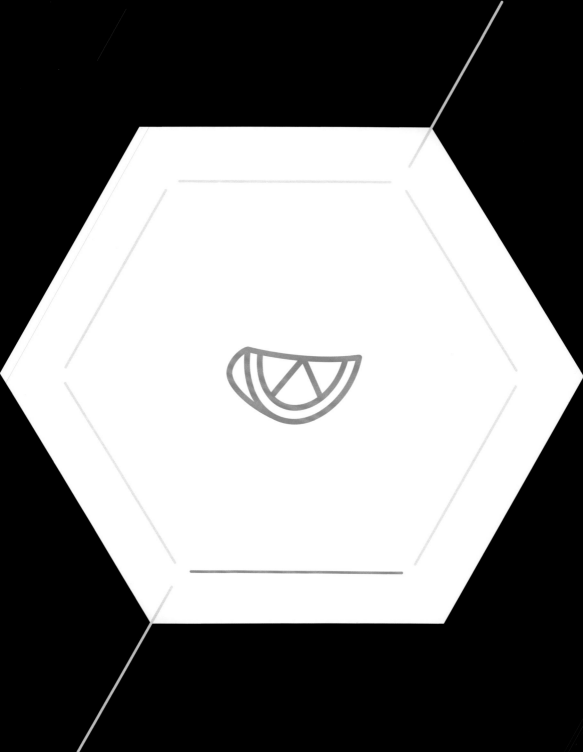

3

THE
DAIQUIRI

THE CLASSIC RECIPE

The Daiquiri is just one of many cocktails in the category referred to as sours—basically, a combination of spirit, citrus, and sweetener wherein the sweet and sour elements come together to temper the spirit's strength and flavor. These refreshing cocktails are great for people who steer clear of straight spirits or spirituous cocktails like Old-Fashioneds or Martinis. Though there are thousands of sours, we chose the Daiquiri as the focus for this chapter because of its universal appeal. If you think you don't like Daiquiris, that's just because you haven't tried a good one yet! We also chose the Daiquiri because of the wide variety of rums available, so choosing your favorite for making Daiquiris can entail an enjoyable voyage of discovery.

The Daiquiri has enjoyed sensational popularity—with the unfortunate side effect that this simple, sour-style cocktail often manifests as a blender catastrophe. Though a frozen Daiquiri blended with a produce stand of fresh fruits can be plenty tasty, the classic Daiquiri is a modest combination of rum, lime juice, and sugar, shaken and served up, and versions of the classic recipe can be found in countless vintage cocktail books.

Daiquiri

2 ounces rum
¾ ounce fresh lime juice
¾ ounce simple syrup (page 45)
Garnish: 1 lime wedge

Shake all the ingredients with ice, then strain into a chilled coupe. Garnish with the lime wedge.

OUR ROOT RECIPE

One thing we love about the Daiquiri is that it's a phenomenal way to explore the diverse world of rum. For our root recipe, we veer slightly from the classic by using a split base of light Spanish-style rum accented with a tiny amount of flavorful rhum agricole. We also bump up the lime juice a touch for a brighter hit of citrus. This recipe yields a drink that's simultaneously deeply refreshing and pleasantly complex.

Our Ideal Daiquiri

1¾ ounces Caña Brava white rum

¼ ounce La Favorite Rhum Agricole Blanc Coeur de Canne

1 ounce fresh lime juice

¾ ounce simple syrup (page 45)

Garnish: 1 lime wedge

Shake all the ingredients with ice, then strain into a chilled coupe. Garnish with the lime wedge.

THE DRINK OF A THOUSAND FACES

You can find something called a Daiquiri on Bourbon Street in New Orleans, dispensed from a large slushie machine and spiked with every imaginable flavoring—except, strangely, rum. You can also find Daiquiris at island resorts, blended or on the rocks, served in comically large glasses; if you're lucky these may be made with fresh fruit. This chapter is *not* about those kinds of Daiquiris.

Another type of Daiquiri can be found at the world's best cocktail bars: a foggy white, frothy tipple served in a dainty stemmed glass. At these establishments, industry folks know that the Daiquiri is the ultimate handshake, because making a great Daiquiri requires more attention to technique than most cocktails. While the proportions of the Daiquiri's three ingredients are important, how those ingredients are combined to create the finished cocktail is even more critical, from the freshness of the lime juice and the choice of rum to the shaking method and the temperature of the cocktail glass. In this way, the Daiquiri is an ideal cocktail to work with for mastering both technique and improvisation.

The Daiquiri may have a reputation as an easygoing cocktail, but its success hinges on your ability to understand how its components—strong, sweet, and sour—collaborate to make a unified whole. Beyond mastery of the formula and proper technique, the Daiquiri also requires thinking on your feet. While your choice of rum and shaking technique certainly have a role in making a successful Daiquiri, paying attention to the inconsistency of citrus (which can vary in acidity and sweetness from fruit to fruit) and adjusting accordingly can help you not only make a great Daiquiri but also inform your approach to all sour-style cocktails.

UNDERSTANDING THE TEMPLATE

Understanding the Daiquiri template really boils down to understanding sour-style cocktails in general, so that's where we'll start. Here's the basic sour formula:

Basic Sour

CLASSIC

2 ounces spirit
¾ ounce fresh lemon or lime juice
¾ ounce simple syrup (page 45)

Shake all the ingredients with ice, then strain into a chilled glass. No garnish.

This formula is a great starting place for any cocktail involving lemon or lime juice—and fundamental to understanding the Daiquiri and its many variations. (We'll address other citrus juices later in the chapter, including the adjustments that are necessary to accommodate their varying levels of sweetness and acidity.) In the basic sour template above, the components are in harmony: the strength of the alcohol is matched by a balance between sweet and sour. For most people, this combination—2 ounces spirit, ¾ ounce lemon or lime juice, and ¾ ounce simple syrup—strikes the right note. Then, this can be tweaked to suit individual preferences, with more lemon juice making for a tarter cocktail, and more sugar producing a sweeter one. What we don't recommend is increasing both, as that would overshadow the spirit's flavor. We love good-quality spirits and think cocktails are at their best when the characteristics of the spirits come through.

At this point, we want to briefly address the distinction between sours and daisies. We cover the latter in more detail in chapter 4, on Sidecars (see page 149); for now, we'll just say that whereas sours typically rely on a solitary base spirit, daisies include liqueur, which also contributes to the drink's sugar content. Two famous cocktails, the Margarita and the Cosmopolitan, both call for a fair amount of Cointreau—a high-proof orange liqueur—which places them firmly in the daisy category, even though they are both refreshing and somewhat sour. Also note that even though some of the recipes in this chapter contain small amounts of sweet liqueur, here it functions primarily as seasoning, rather than being part of the core, as in daisies.

COCKTAILS, HISTORY, AND A GRAIN OF SALT

According to legend, a white guy was the first person to have the bright idea to put together rum, lime juice, and sugar. That was Jennings Cox, an American mining engineer living in Cuba. As the story goes, at a rambunctious dinner party in 1898 he ran out of gin. Sobriety not being an option, he grabbed a bottle of local rum and whipped up a simple punch with citrus juice, sugar, and mineral water. His guests loved it, and he named it after a local beach, Daiquiri. It's a fishy narrative, and it also provides a good example of the problems that plague cocktail history: misinformation, revisionism, and the reality that documenting the history of cocktails is an activity often accompanied by drinking cocktails. We take stories like the tale of Jennings Cox with a grain of salt, and that's part of the reason why we haven't included much history in this book. If you're looking for a deeper dive into the past, we highly recommend anything written by David Wondrich, one of the foremost cocktail historians of our time.

THE CORE: RUM

If ever there was a pirate spirit, it's rum—not because rum is so closely tied to maritime history or because popular culture has aligned it with villainous pirate goons, but because rum, as a category of spirits, is downright resistant to rules. The styles of rum vary depending on where the rum comes from, if and how it's aged, and how it's distilled.

The single thread connecting all rums is the base material: sugarcane. Historically speaking, modern-day rum originated as a very unglamorous industrial by-product of sugarcane processing. During colonial times, the Caribbean's many islands were prized for their agricultural resources, chief among them was sugarcane. Once the sugar was refined and shipped off, an awful lot of molasses was left behind. And because molasses ferments easily, locals quickly seized the opportunity to distill that molasses into a fiery spirit. Though it lacked the refinement of contemporary rums, it was the precursor to what we now use in our Daiquiris.

The evolution of rum into the spirits we know today has a lot to do with the political history of colonization in the Caribbean region. Because different Caribbean islands and territories were controlled by different European nations, various distilling traditions were brought to bear on rum production. Rum is still unofficially classified in keeping with the old colonial borders: Spanish, English, and French, as well as Jamaican. The reality, though, is that modern rums has evolved dramatically and don't neatly fit into such categorization. Stylistic lines have blurred over the centuries. Plus, many producers now blend rums from different locales and of varying styles into their bottlings or otherwise buck convention, often in an effort to stand out in the market.

One upshot of these dynamics is that there's a great deal of variation from producer to producer—much more so than with most other strong spirits. Aside from a handful of former French colonies that adopted production standards similar to those for Cognac, rum production methods are beguilingly broad. That said, much of a rum's personality is determined by the type of still used to make it: a column still or a pot still (with some blends incorporating rums from both). Spirits distilled in column stills are bright and fresh, even after they've been aged in oak. Pot stills are less efficient, yielding a lower-proof spirit, but this can be a good thing, allowing the spirit to retain more flavor and have a richer texture. As you start to explore rums and choose your favorites, taste them blind to see whether you can pick out the qualities of one made in a column still versus one made in a pot still. If it's focused and light, it's probably the product of a column still. If it's big and funky, it was probably produced in a pot still.

As with all spirits covered in this book, for the recommended bottles that follow we've chosen rums that should be available in most major markets. Within each style, we've organized the recommended bottles from light to dark to aged so you can easily find recommendations suited to a given application. Be aware, though, that light rums are often aged; the "light" quality comes from being filtered heavily, which removes a good deal of color, along with some of the flavors associated with aging. We typically lump so-called gold rums into this category because they often have a similar personality, with just a bit more oak flavor, and tend to perform similarly in cocktails. Dark rums are usually aged but also contain added coloring to deepen their hue and, in some cases, to enhance certain flavor characteristics. Aged rums, by comparison, get their deep color primarily through contact with oak barrels.

RUM, RHUM, AND RON

The Spanish word for "rum" is *ron*, which is what it is called in Puerto Rico and other Spanish-speaking islands. In French, it is *rhum*, and this is the name for rums made from fresh sugarcane distillate in former French colonies in the Caribbean, as well as Guadeloupe and Martinique, which remain French overseas *départements*. On islands formerly under British rule, where rum is made from molasses, the English word *rum* is used.

Light rums are often found in citrusy cocktails like the Daiquiri, as a base or in collaboration with other light spirits. Dark rums are the stuff of Dark and Stormys and are often used in complex tiki-style drinks in which multiple rums are combined to create the core. Aged rums can certainly work in many styles of cocktails—a Daiquiri with aged rum is decadent and delicious! Give an aged Spanish-style rum enough years in oak, where it will develop deep, rich flavors of sweet vanilla and spice, and it will emerge as a beautiful sipping rum. Yet it will also shine in spirituous cocktails like Old-Fashioneds or Manhattans. We particularly like pairing aged Spanish-style rums with Cognac, as in Thick as Thieves (page 284)—though, to be fair, we like almost everything with Cognac.

SPANISH-STYLE RUM

The most popular category of rum, Spanish style, includes much of the rum produced in Puerto Rico, Cuba, the Dominican Republic, Venezuela, Guatemala, Nicaragua, Panama, Colombia, Costa Rica, and Ecuador. This style originated with some extremely savvy distillers who, in the nineteenth century, saw the invention of column distillation as an opportunity to create a new path for rum. Using this exceedingly efficient distilling method, they were able to produce rums that were high in proof and largely stripped of the aggressive flavors of pot still rum. Spanish-style rums range from unaged to aged for many years in oak barrels, but most are heavily filtered to remove the fiery personality of the molasses distillate. When aged and filtered, the result is a smooth, rounded rum with lots of vanilla undertones, a lovely companion for the brightness of lime juice in a Daiquiri.

RECOMMENDED BOTTLES

Caña Brava (Panama): Created specifically for cocktail use by our friends at the 86 Co., Caña Brava is an homage to old-style Cuban rums like Havana Club (which still isn't available in the United States, though there is a brand on the market called Havana Club, which isn't the same thing). Straw-yellow in color, with subtle flavors of coconut, banana, and a hint of vanilla, this rum is a must-have in our cocktail-making tool kit, specifically Daiquiris and their variations, most deliciously the Mojito.

Boukman Daiquiri,
page 129

Flor de Caña 4-Year White (Nicaragua): This has a bit more funk than other light rums (in a good way), and although that may be intimidating in the straight spirit, its personality comes through distinctively—and pleasingly—in cocktails. We love this rum paired with berries, such as strawberries and raspberries, as well as in uncommon combinations, such as with sarsaparilla and birch (see Root Beer Float, page 283).

Plantation 3 Stars White (Jamaica, Barbados, and Trinidad): Though the rums used in the blend are not all from islands following the Spanish tradition, the finished rum performs very much like one. This rum shines in a Daiquiri and other streamlined sours, but because it's somewhat mild, if you add too many ingredients with strong personalities, such as potent liqueurs or amari, it's character can get lost.

Gosling's Black Seal (Bermuda): A Dark and Stormy is not a Dark and Stormy without the dark, molasses flavor of Gosling's Black Seal rum at the core. Dense in color, it's surprisingly drinkable on its own. Though notes of rich molasses come through, we find there's an undeniable banana flavor, along with some spice, that works in a variety of cocktails, especially when matched with another spirit, as in the Ginger Rogers (page 280).

Ron del Barrilito Three Stars (Puerto Rico): Though its availability comes and goes due to inconsistent distribution in the United States, this rum is one of our favorites. Though it's aged between six and ten years, it has a freshness that reminds us of lighter rums. We love it as a base in cocktails and also use it to stretch out rums with a strong personality, such as Jamaican rums or rhum agricole.

Zacapa 23 (Guatemala): A blend of rums aged between six and twenty-five years, Zacapa XO delivers on the promise of older rums; years of aging in a solera system (see page 245) results in a deeply complex spirit that's perfect for sipping and also fantastic as a base for spirituous cocktails, such as riffs on the Old-Fashioned or Manhattan. And because it's aged in former whiskey barrels, there's also an affinity between Zacapa rum and American whiskey, in particular rye, which can add spice to Zacapa's richness to create a complex but balanced flavor.

ENGLISH-STYLE RUM

Many of the rums produced in the former Caribbean colonies of the United Kingdom and its current overseas territories are similar to Spanish-style rums; however, there are some distinguishing features that make them unique in cocktail applications. While they are primarily made from molasses, as are Spanish-style rums, they often have more richness and funkiness thanks to the blending of rums from different distillation processes that yield light-, medium-, and full-bodied rums.

RECOMMENDED BOTTLES

El Dorado White Rum (Guyana): This is a great and inexpensive rum for use in Daiquiri-style cocktails. Its modest personality can get overpowered in spirituous cocktails, though, so we suggest sticking to sour-style drinks with this one.

Cruzan Black Strap (US Virgin Islands): Dark as a moonless night and with distinct flavors of rich molasses and maple syrup, this rum is definitely not a utility player. We most often use it in small quantities to add depth to cocktails, as in the Piña Colada (page 269).

Plantation Old-Fashioned Traditional Dark Overproof (Trinidad and Tobago): Warning: High octane! The strength of this rum (69% ABV) is masked by a big punch of smoked fruit flavors, making it dangerously easy to sip straight. It's the perfect ingredient for deepening the complexity of tiki-style cocktails.

El Dorado 15-Year (Guyana): This rum, with its dark amber color and complex nose, is a great example of the type of rum that shares some of the qualities of a fine aged brandy. We'll gladly sip this lovely rum any day of the week, but it also works well in cocktails, either as the sole core spirit or as a companion to other aged spirits in Old-Fashioneds, Juleps, or Manhattan-style drinks.

JAMAICAN-STYLE RUMS

Whereas Spanish rums are clean and have a green-grass freshness and English rums have a bit more body and depth, Jamaican rums are an entirely different animal. Stylistically, Jamaican rum has a distinctive, profound funkiness. It's hard to describe the peculiarity of their flavor profile, but understanding how the spirit is made can provide some illumination. Jamaican rum is always made in pot stills, which gives it both richness and an intense, grassy aroma. Because of its strength and pungency, we rarely use Jamaican rums as the sole base of a cocktail and more often combine it with other spirits or fortified wine (Fair Game, page 280, or Last One Standing, page 32).

RECOMMENDED BOTTLES

Wray & Nephew White Overproof Rum (Jamaica): Clocking in at a highly potent 126 proof, this rum's alcoholic kick suppresses the funk of Jamaican rum—a strange neutralization that can be dangerous when it's mixed into a Daiquiri: delicious, but a little too drinkable. We most often use it when we like the flavors of a drink but find them a bit dense; a small dose of Wray & Nephew will spread them out.

Hamilton Jamaican Pot Still Gold (Jamaica): Ed Hamilton is a man who knows rum. The renowned drinks writer is now importing personally selected

rums of all varieties, including this bottling, which falls somewhere between the feistiness of Wray & Nephew and the density of the dark and aged Jamaican rums described below. We love using this, along with other rums, for the core of a Mai Tai.

Smith & Cross (Jamaica): This is, hands down, the least nuanced spirit we've ever experienced: funky, deeply sweet, high proof, and not too far from what we imagine a mixture of gasoline and molasses would smell like after years of aging in oak barrels. But strangely, that can be a good thing! Used in very small quantities, Smith & Cross will shine through, adding a tropical slant to a cocktail. Think of it almost like less-potent bitters, a highly flavorful ingredient that can coax tropical character out of other spirits.

Hamilton Jamaican Pot Still Dark (Jamaica): With just as much personality as Smith & Cross but less sweetness, this rum is refined enough to use in larger quantities but still packs a pungent aroma. A Daiquiri made with this rum will be simultaneously rich and refreshing, with a lingering banana flavor.

Appleton Estate Reserve Blend (Jamaica): Less pungent than other Jamaican rums, those produced by Appleton are almost elegant in comparison. While the Reserve Blend retains a noticeable Jamaican personality—rich molasses flavor with a grassy finish—this blend of twenty aged rums has a bit more nuance. Of all the Jamaican rums, this is the one we use most often in cocktails. It works beautifully as a base in both shaken and stirred drinks, as well as in collaboration with other rums, brandy, whiskey, or even blended scotch. It has a bright, fresh, citrusy character, and whereas other aged Jamaican rums tend to have a stewed banana flavor, this one tastes like fresh fruit.

FRENCH-STYLE RUMS

During the Napoleonic Wars of the early nineteenth century, a British blockade made it difficult for the French to import sugar from their colonies in the Caribbean, so the French set out to find a way to make sugar in France. Their scientists developed a way to process beets to yield something very similar to sugarcane crystals. At the same time, French colonial economies in the Caribbean built nearly entirely on sugar production were devastated. With decreased European demand for Caribbean-made sugar, excess sugarcane was juiced and used to make rum—a departure from using molasses, a by-product of sugar production, as the base. This produced a rum that was quite distinct from its molasses-based cousins, with an intense fruity aroma and vegetal flavor. Each sip offers the distinct impression of chewing on raw sugarcane.

Today, French-style rums are produced primarily on the islands of Martinique, Guadeloupe, Marie-Galante, and Haiti. Like other rums, French-style rums may be unaged or aged for many years. But whereas other rum styles don't have strictly standardized aging categorizations, French-style rums use many of the same age classifications borrowed from Cognac. In fact, many are also made using copper pot stills, just as Cognac is.

These distillates are called rhum agricole, and in cocktails, they behave differently than other rums. Whereas the softness and richness of molasses-based Spanish- and English-style rums provides a broad structure on which to build flavor, the grit and personality of rhum agricole has a sharpness that enhances citrus. Molasses-based rums do allow citrus to come through, and they keep it front and center; rhum agricole, on the other hand, makes its presence known with a bright tropical tang that's deeply refreshing.

In addition to using rhum agricole to enhance citrus, we also use it in ways similar to most unaged eaux-de-vie: as a modifier alongside another base ingredient. This can be another rum with a lighter flavor, to give it greater complexity (like our Root Daiquiri), or it can be a completely different type of spirit. Unaged rhum agricole mingles well with tequila or gin, and aged rhum agricole is particularly delicious with Cognac. In low-ABV cocktails based on sherry or fortified rum, small quantities of flavorful rhum agricole can boost the overall flavor of a cocktail, making a lower-octane cocktail drink like a full-strength one.

RECOMMENDED BOTTLES

Barbancourt White (Haiti): Veering in a different direction than the punchy rums from Martinique, Haitian rums from the Barbancourt distillery have enough personality to be distinctive, but not so much that they dominate cocktails like other French-style rums. Though we also love Barbancourt's aged bottlings, the white is a beautiful addition to any Daiquiri lover's bar.

La Favorite Coeur de Canne (Martinique): Rhum agricole can be a bit pricier than other rums, but this is a fantastically affordable option. A light rum, it's fruity with the aroma of fresh green grass. We love using it in tropical-style cocktails, where it works especially well with pineapple, in either juice or syrup form.

Rhum JM VSOP (Martinique): This rum has orange and chocolate flavors that are balanced by just enough time in oak. Its lingering, buttery finish makes it a fine sipping rum, and it's also useful in spirituous cocktails as a soloist or alongside bourbon or Calvados.

Neisson Réserve Spéciale (Martinique): For the opulent cocktail maker, this pricy bottle will not disappoint. Spirit snobs who believe that it should only be drunk neat may bemoan tossing this nutty and highly aged spirit into a Daiquiri, but try it . . . just once! Truth be told, we do generally suggest reserving it for sipping; however, it also makes for a truly unique Old-Fashioned.

CACHAÇA

It wasn't that long ago that quality cachaças were hard to find outside Brazil. In fact, back in those days, we often used rhum agricole when making cocktails that called for cachaça. But times have changed.

A native of South America, and particularly Brazil, cachaça can be a bit confusing for spirit novices: it's a distillate from sugarcane juice, so why don't we just call it rum—or, more appropriately, rhum agricole? The difference lies in two key factors: the process of distillation used to make cachaça, and the unique nature of its aged styles. Cachaça must be made from Brazilian sugarcane and must be distilled only once (whereas rhum agricole is generally distilled twice) and result in a spirit between 38% and 48% ABV. This single distillation to such a low proof produces a liquor that is rich in body and pungently flavorful. In comparison to rhum agricole, which is distilled to about 70% ABV, a quality cachaça is softer and easier to drink, with sweet flavors due to the restrained distillation.

Many cachaças are unaged, but some end up in wood for years. If unaged, cachaça is referred to as white (*branca, clássica, tradicional,* or *prata*—the latter meaning silver), indicating that the spirit has been stored in neutral stainless steel containers or woods that don't color the spirit. If aged (*envelhecida*), it could also be referred to as gold (*ouro*).

WHITE CACHAÇA

For cocktail use, it may be best to think of lighter cachaças as similar to a light rhum agricole: they're grassy and complex, with broad flavors of banana and dried stone fruit. Pairing them with citrus, especially lime, is a great start, though some of the more floral white cachaças can stand up to vermouth in a Martini-style cocktail. As with rhum agricole, add cachaça in smaller amounts to prevent it from dominating the party.

RECOMMENDED BOTTLES

Avuá Prata Cachaça: While this cachaça has the grassy aroma of rhum agricole, it also boasts uniquely pretty aromas of cinnamon and violets. A touch of vanilla rounds off the finish, which makes the spirit fantastically useful in cocktails. We use it as the base in many drinks, or let ½ ounce mingle with dry sherry or vermouth.

Novo Fogo Silver: In the United States, this could be considered a benchmark cachaça. Rich, bold, and vegetal, it's a workhorse that has tons of character but isn't overly aggressive, and it's an excellent cachaça for Caipirinhas.

AGED CACHAÇAS

Because cachaça can be aged with many varieties of wood, it offers a great opportunity to study the effects of different woods on spirits. Most spirits are aged in American and French oak, both of which impart flavors of clove, cinnamon, vanilla, and stewed fruits. But in Brazil, a wide variety of indigenous woods are used to age cachaça, resulting in a range of unique flavors in the final product.

RECOMMENDED BOTTLE

Avuá Amburana Cachaça: Aged for two years in Latin American amburana wood, this cachaça has become one of our secret weapons in variations on both the Old-Fashioned and the Manhattan. The aging process lends the spirit a pronounced cinnamon spiciness unique to the wood, while the vanilla-heavy base spirit gives it a broad and sweet substructure similar to that of spirits aged on oak. These elements combine to create an effect almost like liquid French toast. It blends beautifully with many aged spirits, especially when used in a small quantity, as a modifier. As the core of a cocktail it can be a little overwhelming, so we tend to use it in a split base with at least one other spirit.

EXPERIMENTING WITH THE CORE

Rum comes in many styles, and you can smell and taste the differences. But how do those different styles of rum interact with other ingredients in cocktails? The Daiquiri is the perfect starting point for exploring this. Here's an experiment that displays the unique nature of three different rums. Assemble the ingredients and equipment for three recipes below. Ideally, you would shake them at the same time; if that isn't possible, make them all in close succession so they'll have a similar temperature and frothy texture when you taste them side by side.

These three Daiquiris are made using exactly the same recipe, but isn't it amazing how different they are? Daiquiri (Light Rum) is most similar to our root recipe, and you will probably note that it's exactly the same as Daiquiri (More Lime Juice) in the experiment on page 118. It's undeniably refreshing, and the star of the show is the bright and unmistakable flavor of freshly pressed lime juice. In Daiquiri (Funky Rum), the focus shifts to the complex rhum agricole and its grassy flavor, which makes for a vegetal, almost savory iteration. In contrast to both, Daiquiri (Aged Rum), made with an aged Jamaican rum blend, displays rich, fruity peach and nectarine flavors. Clearly, playing with the core spirit can lead a cocktail in many different directions.

Daiquiri (Light Rum)

2 ounces Caña Brava white rum
1 ounce fresh lime juice
¾ ounce simple syrup (page 45)

Shake all the ingredients with ice, then strain into a chilled coupe.

Daiquiri (Funky Rum)

2 ounces La Favorite Coeur de Canne rhum agricole blanc
1 ounce fresh lime juice
¾ ounce simple syrup (page 45)

Shake all the ingredients with ice, then strain into a chilled coupe.

Daiquiri (Aged Rum)

2 ounces Appleton Estate Reserve Blend rum
1 ounce fresh lime juice
¾ ounce simple syrup (page 45)

Shake all the ingredients with ice, then strain into a chilled coupe.

Amaretto Sour

CLASSIC

To extend the experiment even further, you can use a liqueur or even a fortified wine as the core. And indeed, some classic sours are made in just this way. The Amaretto Sour is a great example. Because it calls for a full 2 ounces of nutty, sweet amaretto, some adjustments to the other ingredients are needed; to keep the cocktail from being way too sweet, we decrease the amount of simple syrup.

2 ounces Lazzaroni amaretto

1 ounce fresh lemon juice

¼ ounce simple syrup (page 45)

1 dash Angostura bitters

Garnish: 1 orange half wheel and 1 brandied cherry on a skewer

Shake all the ingredients with ice, then strain into a double Old-Fashioned glass over 1 large ice cube. Garnish with the orange half wheel and cherry.

Fresh Gimlet

CLASSIC

A more dramatic way to experiment with the core is to use a completely different spirit. A classic gimlet is made with lime cordial, a syrup originally devised to preserve lime juice for long sea voyages. Here, we make a version with fresh lime juice—essentially a Daiquiri made with gin. In keeping with our root Daiquiri recipe, we've included a full ounce of lime juice for a bright pop of citrus.

2 ounces Plymouth gin

1 ounce fresh lime juice

¾ ounce simple syrup (page 45)

Garnish: 1 lime wedge

Shake all the ingredients with ice, then strain into a chilled coupe. Garnish with the lime wedge.

Fresh Gimlet

THE BALANCE: CITRUS JUICE

When we travel abroad, we often wonder why familiar drinks taste different, and generally much better, in faraway places. Is it the romance of travel? The thrill of being far from home? The answer may come down to something much more practical: cocktails made with fresh ingredients grown nearby taste better. A lime in Chicago will not taste the same as a lime in Thailand.

This is just one of the many reasons it's hard to make blanket statements about using citrus juice for balance in cocktails. Beyond that, there are so many varieties of various types of citrus. Consider oranges. Within this broad classification there are both bitter oranges and sweet oranges. Of the latter, there are several key types (common oranges, navel oranges, and blood oranges). Then, among common oranges, there are dozens and dozens of unique cultivars.

Of course, the flavor of any given citrus fruit can also vary due to a host of environmental and growing conditions. Lemons and limes tend to be fairly consistent, but we still recommend tasting the juice to make sure it isn't a great deal sweeter or more acidic than usual. Grapefruits and oranges tend to be more variable, so it's even more important to taste their juice.

Generally speaking, most citrus fruit have a similar structure: a peel composed of a thick outer skin (the exocarp, or flavedo) and the bitter pith beneath it (the mesocarp, or albedo), and within the peel, segments that contain numerous small vesicles filled with juice. Some varieties contain seeds, and others are seedless.

If you slice off a thin swath of citrus skin and hold it up to a light, you'll see a bunch of tiny round circles. These are pockets that hold flavorful oils. If you then squeeze the peel, it will expel a mist of oil, and depending on the fruit, you'll probably smell a pungent aroma. This mist is what's expressed over cocktails, and because it's an oil, it will float on top of the drink, perfuming the cocktail as it's sipped.

When using the skin as a garnish or as an ingredient in infusions or syrups, a zester is generally the best tool for the job. Be careful not to go so deep that you get to the white pith, because it's usually unpleasantly bitter. However, some citrus fruits, such as kumquats, have so little pith that the fruit can be eaten whole, and some have little enough that the entire peel can be used, such as some varieties of mandarin oranges.

With other citrus fruits—lemons, limes, oranges, and especially grapefruits—including any amount of pith on a twist can adversely impact a drink's flavor. For example, consider the lemon and orange peels we drop into the glass to garnish an Old-Fashioned (page 3). In addition to providing a bright aroma, they flavor the cocktail because they're submerged in it. If either twist includes some of the pith, the cocktail will become increasingly bitter over time.

It's also important to be aware of the pith when using a conical juicer. With too much pressure, the juicer can penetrate into the pith and extract its bitterness.

Citrus segments can also be muddled to take advantage of all aspects of the fruit: juice, aromatic peel, and bitter pith. We generally muddle citrus that is flavorful, has highly acidic juice, and contains aromatic skin oils: oranges (and orange varieties such as mandarins), lemons, and limes all fit the bill. When muddled, this spectrum of flavors can be extracted, creating a highly dynamic citrus expression in a cocktail—best shown in the classic Caipirinha (page 137). We rarely muddle grapefruits, as their oils will dominate a drink's flavor and overwhelm your palate. Also, be mindful of seeds: if a seedy piece of citrus is muddled, the drink can become quite bitter. Do your best to remove seeds from a piece of citrus before muddling.

One last note on citrus: As a general rule of thumb, we tend to pair lime juice with unaged spirits (light rum, gin, blanco tequila, vodka) and lemon juice with aged spirits (bourbon, scotch, Cognac). There are, of course, many exceptions to this rule.

USING GRAPEFRUIT IN COCKTAILS

Citrus juice can hit all four categories of taste: sweet, tart, salty, and bitter. Grapefruit juice is usually fairly balanced in terms of tartness and sweetness, but it does tend to be noticeably bitter. Therefore, we typically combine grapefruit juice with lemon or lime juice plus a sweet syrup to ensure good balance in cocktails.

Another issue is that the flavor of grapefruits can vary widely. When making cocktails that have a large proportion of grapefruit juice, be sure to taste the juice before using it, and if it's particularly acidic, consider adding some simple syrup to compensate. If, on the other hand, it's particularly sweet, you get the best results by decreasing the amount of other sweet ingredients in the cocktail.

As for the skin, grapefruit twists can add an intense perfume to a cocktail, but its oils can be powerful and numb the taste buds if used too liberally. So we caution against rubbing an expressed grapefruit twist on the rim of a glass. It's better to express the grapefruit twist well above the drink, then drop it in. Even so, the bitter oils, and especially any bitter pith present on the twist, will flavor the cocktail quickly, so we often recommend that guests remove grapefruit twists after a few minutes.

COMMON CITRUS FRUITS AND THEIR COCKTAIL APPLICATIONS

LIMES

Persian, Tahitian, and Bearss
- Large fruits with relatively high levels of juice
- Used more for juice than for wheels, wedges, or twists
- Seedless, which makes them especially good for muddling

Mexican and Key Lime
- Smaller fruits with less juice than Persian limes
- Juice more acidic than that of Persian limes
- Uniquely aromatic peels that are good for flavoring syrups

Kaffir and Makrut
- Not great for juicing (juice is astringent and unpleasant)
- Fragrant leaves are great for muddling and infusions

LEMONS

Eureka
- Sweet and tart juice, typical "lemon" flavor
- Thick skin is good for twists

Lisbon
- Similar juice to Eureka, usually more juice per fruit
- Thinner skin that's less well suited to twists

Meyer
- Incredibly juicy
- Highly aromatic zest that's great in infusions and syrups
- Juice more acidic than Eureka or Lisbon, so a good adjunct to either to bolster the tartness of a cocktail

GRAPEFRUIT

Ruby Red
- Extremely juicy, bright acidity and high sweetness
- Dark, thick red skin, great for twists

Star Ruby
- Sweet, slightly tart juice that's darker in color than that of other varieties
- Thinner skin than Ruby Red, less useful for twists than Ruby Red but great for half-wheel garnish

Duncan
- Juice is similar in sweetness to Ruby Red and Star Ruby, but with a crisper clarity
- White-fleshed fruit

ORANGES

Valencia
- Packed with sweet juice that works well in cocktails
- Uniform skin that's quite thin; include some pith in twists to give them structure

Navel
- Juice less vibrant than that of Valencias, so it's less dynamic in cocktails
- Thick skin that's great for twists

Blood
- Juice is dark red, but generally lacks much acidity or noticeable flavor
- Skin is dark orange and aromatic

OTHER CITRUS

Tangerines
- Complex, flavorful juice that can be an interesting substitute for orange juice
- Thin skin is packed with sweet, aromatic oils

Clementines
- Supersweet juice that works best when combined with lemon juice or Citric Acid Solution (page 298)
- Thick skin that's good for infusions
- Usually seedless, making it good for muddling

Mandarin Oranges
- Larger than clementines but with supersweet juice that can be used in similar ways
- Peel flimsy, so unsuitable for twists, but sweet and aromatic, making it great for syrups and infusions
- May have seeds, so be mindful when muddling

Satsumas
- Similar in size, flavor, and application to clementines, with supersweet juice
- Seedless variety with loose skin, making satsumas difficult to use as garnish but great for muddling

Kumquats
- Tiny fruits with extremely tart juice
- Supersweet and edible skin, perfect for muddling segments, or use whole fruit to make syrups

Yuzu
- Sweet and tart juice, sort of like a mix between a lime and a mandarin orange
- Intensely aromatic skin, used to make into cordial for use in cocktails or sour-style drinks

Pomelo
- Similar to grapefruit, though larger fruits, with slightly sweeter juice—can be used in similar ways to grapefruit
- Potent skin makes dramatic and aromatic twists

EXPERIMENTING WITH THE BALANCE

As we saw at the beginning of this chapter, the daiquiri's balance is found through the collaboration between citrus and sugar and there is some flexibility in the amount of each depending on your preferences for tart or sweet. Here's a fun Goldilocks experiment to test where your preferences for sweet and sour fall. Gather a shaker, jigger, cocktail strainer, three chilled coupes, ice, 2½ ounces of fresh lime juice, 2 ounces of simple syrup, and, of course, a bottle of rum. For the purposes of this experiment, we forgo the garnish in order to keep the focus on the sweet-tart balance in the cocktail itself.

We find this side-by-side test to be invaluable for learning about how to balance spirits, citrus, and sweeteners and seeing how small tweaks to a recipe can transform a cocktail from tasty to delicious. Daiquiri (Classic) is a fine drink. Daiquiri (Less Sweetener) isn't very pleasant; even a small decrease in simple syrup makes the cocktail both too boozy and too tart. But Daiquiri (More Lime Juice), where the amount of lime juice is increased by ¼ ounce, is fresh, lively, and deeply satisfying. Because the Caña Brava is a fairly light rum, the flavor of the lime juice (not just its acidity) becomes a bigger contributor to the cocktail's overall flavor.

You may very well think that Daiquiri (More Lime Juice) is too tart—that's okay! Daiquiri (Classic) is probably more to your taste. That simple realization will be so helpful in choosing recipes, modifying them, and developing your own.

Once you understand the basic sour template, you can swap in any spirit for the rum; though we can't promise the result will be delicious, it will be balanced. Likewise, you can substitute lemon juice for the lime juice, or you can use a different sweetener. This very flexibility has allowed the sour to proliferate into a huge family of cocktails.

Now that we've highlighted some of the key qualities of various citrus fruits, let's take a look at how experimenting with them can push a cocktail in new directions. Sure, lemon and lime juices are most commonly used in cocktails. In fact, for that very reason substituting or incorporating other citrus juices is a great technique for developing new recipes. It's also a time-honored tradition, as displayed in a classic Daiquiri variation from the 1920s: the Hemingway Daiquiri.

Daiquiri (Classic)

2 ounces Caña Brava white rum

¾ ounce fresh lime juice

**¾ ounce simple syrup
(page 45)**

Shake all the ingredients with ice, then strain into a chilled coupe.

Daiquiri (Less Sweetener)

2 ounces Caña Brava white rum

¾ ounce fresh lime juice

**½ ounce simple syrup
(page 45)**

Shake all the ingredients with ice, then strain into a chilled coupe.

Daiquiri (More Lime Juice)

2 ounces Caña Brava white rum

1 ounce fresh lime juice

**¾ ounce simple syrup
(page 45)**

Shake all the ingredients with ice, then strain into a chilled coupe.

Pisco Sour

CLASSIC

Some drinks benefit from using a combination of lemon and lime juices: lemon for its mild flavor and lime for its brightness. For our take on the classic Pisco Sour, this is exactly what we do, as we've found that this cocktail isn't nearly as delicious when we use just one or the other. The pungency of the lime juice plays well with the gritty texture of the pisco, and the relative neutrality of lemon juice prevents the lime from taking over.

2 ounces Campo de Encanto Grand and Noble pisco

½ ounce fresh lemon juice

½ ounce fresh lime juice

¾ ounce simple syrup (page 45)

1 egg white

Garnish: 3 drops Angostura bitters

Dry shake all the ingredients, then shake again with ice. Double strain into a chilled coupe. Carefully garnish the top of the foam with the bitters.

Hemingway Daiquiri

CLASSIC

Grapefruit juice has a delicious bitter-tart flavor that makes it one of our favorite alternatives to lemon and lime juice in cocktails. To get an idea of how grapefruit juice affects the balance of a drink, we'll break down the classic Hemingway Daiquiri. Because grapefruit juice isn't as acidic as lime juice, simply substituting 1 ounce of it for the lime juice in our root Daiquiri recipe would yield a thin cocktail. And as you can see, the recipe for this classic variation also contains a somewhat generous amount of lime juice. Then, because both the grapefruit juice and the maraschino liqueur add sweetness, the amount of simple syrup is dialed way back. This drink is very much about the relationship between rum, grapefruit juice, and maraschino liqueur, but it gets its amazing vibrancy from the lime juice and simple syrup.

1½ ounces Flor de Caña 4-year white rum

½ ounce Luxardo maraschino liqueur

1 ounce fresh grapefruit juice

½ ounce fresh lime juice

1 teaspoon simple syrup (page 45)

Garnish: 1 lime wedge

Shake all the ingredients with ice, then strain into a chilled coupe. Garnish with the lime wedge.

Lemon and lime will have varying levels of acidity and sweetness (and you should taste to ensure they're near what you usually get), but most that we get are relatively consistent. Grapefruits and oranges, however, can have varying levels of sweetness and acidity. When making cocktails that have a large proportion of grapefruit juice, like the Hemingway Daiquiri, this variability can be more noticeable. Taste the juice before using it, and if it's particularly acidic, consider upping the simple syrup to ¼ ounce instead of 1 teaspoon. If, on the other hand, it's particularly sweet, you may find the best balance by leaving out the simple syrup altogether.

Pisco Sour

THE SEASONING: CITRUS GARNISHES

In chapter 2, we established that aroma can season a drink. In the case of a Martini, that aroma can be introduced in the form of a citrus twist, olive, or pickled onion garnish. With the Daiquiri, the lime wedge garnish serves a similar function, as do citrus wedges, wheels, and half wheels in other cocktails.

But a wedge of citrus can do more: It can be squeezed into the cocktail to add acidity, which allows people to customize their drinks. Squeezing the wedge also releases citrus oils into the drink, so it serves as an aromatic seasoning, too. And even if the wedge remains untouched on the rim of the glass, it still provides a noticeable hit of bright citrus aroma.

Another way citrus can add seasoning to a drink is if you drop a wheel or half wheel of citrus into a drink before serving, as we do in the Negroni (page 89). Some of the juice will infuse the drink, and alcohol will draw out some of the citrus oils, gently seasoning the drink as it's consumed. This will slowly flavor the cocktail as it's consumed. In the Martini, we addressed how a lemon twist left too long in a cocktail can add bitter flavors (see page 78), and the same is true of a half wheel of citrus—though there's greater leeway. When drinking a cocktail with a citrus wheel dropped in, we recommend removing it when you're finished with about half of the drink.

EXPERIMENTING WITH THE SEASONING

A wedge of citrus can have a profound impact on a cocktail. Try the following simple experiment to see not only how the juice from a lime wedge can shift the flavor of the cocktail, but also how throwing a spent wedge into a drink can slowly change its flavor.

First, prepare two Daiquiris using your favorite recipe in this chapter. For the first Daiquiri, leave the citrus wedge perched on the rim of the glass. For the second, squeeze the lime wedge into the drink and then drop the spent wedge into the cocktail.

Take a sip of each. The first thing you'll realize is that the second Daiquiri is noticeably tarter than the first—no surprise there. You may also notice a difference in aroma due to the pungent oils that were released when you squeezed the lime wedge. You may detect a similar aroma, though much fainter, in the first Daiquiri, simply from the lime wedge on the edge of the glass.

Next, let both cocktails sit for 2 minutes, then taste again. The second Daiquiri may now taste more bitter; that's because the alcohol in the cocktail has begun to draw out bitter flavor compounds from the pith. After 5 minutes, the difference between the two Daiquiris will be even more noticeable: the first will still taste balanced and refreshing, if a little warm, whereas the second will be distinctly bitter and tart, unpleasant qualities that are only emphasized as the cocktail warms.

What does this reveal about citrus wedges and their impact on seasoning? For one, it provides insight into how a seemingly innocuous garnish can push the flavor of a cocktail out of balance. For another, it can inform how you use citrus wedges. Personally, we love a tart drink, so we squeeze the wedge into the cocktail and then discard it.

DEVON TARBY

Devon Tarby is a partner in Proprietors LLC and has worked behind the company's bars, as well as at the Varnish in Los Angeles.

The Daiquiri is my favorite drink of all time. It's always the right drink for the moment; you don't even have to think about it. If I'm tired, it revs me up. If I'm stressed, it lifts my spirits. If you want to get me to stay out later than I should, give me a Daiquiri. It's my Gatorade.

Eric Alperin taught me how to make a proper Daiquiri. Before I worked at his bar, the Varnish, I'd never made a classic Daiquiri before. We paid excruciating attention to every detail there, and our Daiquiris embodied the principles that made the Varnish a special bar. We hand-squeezed our limes right before service. We used hand-carved block ice at the perfect temperature, which we swapped out every twenty minutes. We chilled our glassware in a deep freezer. Once in a while, though, we'd let loose late at night and practice our free pour skills by making Daiquiris. Of course, the guy who had worked at a Miami nightclub always made the best ones.

The Daiquiri is a merciless cocktail. It's a demonstration of all the tiny things a person needs to do behind the bar to make a great cocktail—a true test of the skills of a bartender. Some drinks are more forgiving if you overpour or underpour, or if you shake too much or too little, but the Daiquiri will reveal any flaws if you fuck up.

The hardest part about making Daiquiris is getting the shake just right. In fact, it's the drink we use to teach proper shaking technique, and a "Daiquiri shake" is our shorthand for the longest shake. You really have to give it your all to get the right texture; it probably requires more physical exertion than any other cocktail. I adjust my gym schedule to skip cardio days when I'm working behind the bar—it's that good of a workout.

I have a few personal rules for making Daiquiri variations. First, it still has to taste and feel like a Daiquiri: it needs to be brightly flavored, with just enough sugar to curb the citrus but more acidic than other sour-style drinks. Second, it needs to be served in a coupe; as soon as you pour it over ice, it ceases to be a Daiquiri. I also try to stay away from any variations that contain more than ½ ounce of aged spirits, and I avoid using overproof rum. Lastly, you have to be able to drink it in a few sips.

I spend a lot of time making complicated, layered cocktails. I taste a lot of complex flavors on a regular basis. For me, drinking a Daiquiri is like taking a break from it all, like sinking into the couch and watching cartoons.

Tarby Party

- **1¾ ounces Diplomático Blanco Reserve rum**
- **¼ ounce Neisson rhum agricole blanc**
- **1 ounce fresh lime juice**
- **¾ ounce simple syrup (page 45)**
- **Garnish: 1 lime wedge**

Shake all the ingredients with 1 large ice cube until very cold and frothy. Strain into a chilled coupe. Garnish with the lime wedge.

EXPLORING TECHNIQUE: SHAKING TO DILUTION

We've said this before and have yet to find a better analogy: shaking a cocktail is like sex. Everyone has a motion and rhythm that works best for them, and it takes a lot of practice to develop your personal style. But there the similarities end. With any cocktail that's shaken and served up, which we call shaking to dilution or full-dilution shaking, the goal is the same: to create a drink that's cold, properly diluted, and well aerated. In the case of the Daiquiri, the aim is to create a frothy drink with a noticeable layer of white foam resting on top of the cocktail.

Your shake can take many paths to get to this goal, depending on the style and size shaker you use, the type of ice you add to the shaker, and your own personal shaking motion. The last of these is personal to you, so we won't address it here. As for the shaker, at all of our bars—and at many others—the preferred shaker setup is a pair of weighted stainless steel shaking tins, one small (18 ounces), and one large (28 ounces). This "tin on tin" setup is ideal for many reasons—read our first book if you want to learn them all! However, other setups, such as a Boston shaker, cobbler shaker, or whatever gear you prefer to use, will also work. Therefore, our discussion of shaking to dilution will focus on the final variable: the type of ice. In the sections that follow, we'll walk you through how we train our staff to shake cocktails using three styles of ice: 1 big block, 1-inch cubes, and what we refer to as "shitty" ice.

HOW TO SHAKE WITH ONE LARGE ICE CUBE

After shaking tens of thousands of drinks, we've landed on what we think is the best ice to use for drinks that are shaken to dilution, such as the Daiquiri: a single large cube that's about 2½ inches across. The single-cube method has a couple of advantages: a large chunk of ice moving through liquid creates a lot of aeration, and also doesn't create many tiny ice chips, which we don't like in our Daiquiris, eliminating the need to double strain the drink (first through a strainer, then through a fine-mesh sieve). Using one block of ice also makes it easier to develop a consistent shaking style and duration, because the ice is no longer a variable you have to adjust for.

Begin by building the cocktail in the smaller shaking tin. We usually add the cheapest ingredients, such as syrups and fresh juice, first in case we screw up and have to start over. Building the drink before you add ice also lets you control when the dilution begins.

Next, gently slide the block of ice into the tin, using a barspoon to gently lower it if that's helpful for you. Then, coming in at an angle, place the large tin over the small tin so one side of the connected shakers forms a straight line.

Hit the top of the large tin with the palm of your hand to seal the shaker; you'll know it's sealed when you can grab the top tin and the bottom tin stays attached.

Pick the shaker up with the top of the small tin facing your body. This will put you, not others, in harm's way if the tins should happen to separate during shaking. Place each hand in a comfortable position on either end of the shakers, using a secure grip that requires as little contact as possible; if your palms are all over the shaker, they'll warm the shakers and result in a cocktail that's warmer than desired when it reaches the target dilution.

Give the shaker a few slow turns to temper the ice. This will keep it from shattering when you begin to shake.

Shaking is all about cadence—not because the rhythm has anything to do with the quality of the cocktail, but because it helps you create a consistent style and duration each time you make a drink. Feel free to develop your own motion, but we find that the most ergonomic technique is to shake it in front of your chest using a push-pull motion that follows a gentle arc. The goal is to make the ice move around the inside of the shaker in an elliptical motion (versus a straight, piston-like motion), as this rounds the edges of the ice rather than shattering it into pieces.

Start to shake slowly, then progressively speed up until you reach an intensity that you can comfortably maintain for about 10 seconds. After 10 seconds at top speed, start to slow down, taking about as long as you did to speed up.

Set the shaker down with the large tin on the bottom. Squeeze the sides of the large tin as you push the small tin away to unlock and separate the halves. Strain the drink through a Hawthorne strainer as soon as possible.

Once you've developed a shake with a consistent duration and slow-fast-slow rhythm, you can begin to pay more attention to what's going on inside the shaker. The *chunk-chunk* sound of the big ice block will become more muted as its edges are rounded off, and you'll hear and feel the volume of liquid increase as the ice melts and dilutes the drink. And, of course, you'll also feel the shaker getting progressively colder. You'll need to shake many, many cocktails to get an accurate feel for when this audible and tactile feedback indicates that a drink is ready to strain and serve, but that's not a bad thing. Practicing making drinks can be a lot of fun, and we're sure you can find people to help you enjoy the results along the way.

HOW TO SHAKE WITH 1-INCH ICE CUBES

Shaking with multiple 1-inch ice cubes is quite similar to the preceding method. Ideally, you'd use ice from a commercial machine, such as a Kold-Draft. Ice from an ice tray in your freezer will also work, but it will contain trapped gases and impurities that make it more prone to shattering and thus diluting the drink more quickly.

Start as in the preceding method, building the cocktail in the small shaking tin. Then add enough ice cubes to the small tin that the liquid nearly reaches the top. Seal the shaker as directed above, and roll it a few times to temper the ice.

Using the same motion and rhythm described in the previous method, shake the drink. Because you're using smaller ice cubes, you won't need to shake as long; there's

more surface area of ice in contact with the liquid, so it will dilute more quickly. With this method you'll also hear a difference in sound as the ice rounds off and melts, but it won't be as pronounced as when you shake with one big block of ice. The more noticeable sound will be the increasing amount of liquid sloshing around the shaker.

Double strain the drink, through both a Hawthorne strainer and a fine-mesh sieve to catch any small ice chips, which will ruin the texture of Daiquiris and similar drinks.

HOW TO SHAKE WITH SHITTY ICE

Whether is comes from a hotel hallway, your freezer's ice maker, or ice cubes smaller than 1 inch made in a tray in your freezer, everyday shitty ice is the most difficult form to work with because of its small size, and because it's usually wet and full of impurities—all factors that speed the rate of dilution. So, though it may sound counterintuitive, when we have to work with shitty ice, we actually use *more* ice.

As in the previous methods, begin by building the cocktail in the small shaking tin. Fill the tin with ice so that the liquid nearly reaches the top, then add ice to the large tin until it's about one-quarter full. (If you're using a cobbler shaker, you can go ahead and fill that baby up to the rim with ice.) Seal the shaker. Then, in this case there's no need to temper the ice by rolling the shaker; instead, you want to work quickly to avoid overdiluting the drink.

Using the same motion and rhythm as in the previous methods, shake the drink. The overall duration of your shake will be even shorter than with 1-inch cubes. And because you've packed the shaker with so much ice, you won't hear much movement other than the sloshing of liquid. In fact, shitty ice often fuses together into one big mass.

Be doubly sure to double strain the drink.

One large ice cube	One-inch ice cubes	Shitty Ice
15 seconds	10 seconds	5 seconds

GAUGING THE EFFECTIVENESS OF YOUR TECHNIQUE

You can assess the effectiveness of your shaking technique by looking at what's called the wash line of the cocktail—the level of the liquid below the rim of the glass—after you've strained it into a glass. This isn't just about the amount of liquid in the glass, but also about what the top of the drink looks like. For a Daiquiri, you want a layer of white foam resting atop the drink, and that foam should stick around for 30 seconds or longer. This indicates that you've introduced enough air while shaking. If you don't see this foamy cap, you might not be shaking hard enough or for long enough during the most intense stage of shaking. A long, slow shake will never yield this foamy layer. And while a short, vigorous shake might create a foamy layer, in all likelihood the wash line won't be as high, which means the drink didn't reach full dilution.

GLASSWARE: TIKI MUGS

While cocktails within this chapter come in every form of glass, we thought it'd be the perfect excuse to talk about a famous Daiquiri variation, the Zombie Punch (at right), and the wide world of tiki glassware, which comes in so many shapes, sizes, and often ridiculous forms.

There are a handful of tiki-style mugs to choose from. The Mai Tai–style glass is squat and round and holds around 16 ounces of liquid. These are good for any sour-size cocktail (4 ounces before dilution) that's served over crushed ice. Cooler-style tiki glasses also hold about 16 ounces of liquid, but they're taller, narrower, and intended for coolers and swizzle-style drinks. The biggest and most iconic of the tiki glasses we use—not counting scorpion bowls and other outlandish vessels meant for communal imbibing—is the zombie glass, named after the cocktail and accommodating up to 20 ounces of tropical terror.

A couple of years ago, we designed our own tiki mug with the goal of creating an all-purpose vessel that could be used for all styles of tiki drinks. Ours holds 14 ounces and is tall like a zombie glass, but we avoided any hint of the Polynesian in favor of a flintlock-toting pirate atop a pile of skulls. (If we've offended any pirates—or zombies!—among our guests, we're sorry.)

Zombie Punch

DON THE BEACHCOMBER, 1934

Former Death & Co head bartender Brian Miller's reworked recipe set the stage for this version of our own. A tiki-head of unquenchable enthusiasm, Brian meticulously studied the Zombie form and built a delicious (and highly potent) cocktail (see our first book, *Death & Co: Modern Classic Cocktails* for the recipe). Our homage backs off slightly on the booze (only a little!) and tweaks the rum mix a bit. Depending on the availability of rum in your area, the key is to ensure the mix of a Jamaican rum, an aged Spanish-style rum, and aged 151 rum—also known as firewater. Drink with caution.

> 1¼ ounces Appleton Signature Blend rum
>
> 1¼ ounces Ron del Barrilito 3-Star rum
>
> ¾ ounce Hamilton Demerara 151 Overproof rum
>
> ½ ounce Donn's Mix No. 1 (page 295)
>
> ¾ ounce fresh lime juice
>
> ½ ounce Tailor Velvet Falernum
>
> 1 teaspoon House Grenadine (page 47)
>
> 2 dashes Pernod Absinthe
>
> Garnish: Mint sprig, 1 cherry, 1 orange slice, 1 parasol, and 1 pineapple wedge

Shake all the ingredients with ice, then strain into a Zombie-size tiki mug filled with crushed ice. Garnish with the mint sprig, cherry, orange slice, parasol, and pineapple wedge.

DAIQUIRI VARIATIONS

Variations of the Daiquiri can come in many different forms, so long as there's a core assemblage of spirit, acidity, and sweetness. Here we explore some of our favorite classic variations and some of our original takes on the form, demonstrating how swapping in different base spirits (or more than one in a single cocktail), adding flavorful syrups, or seasoning with herbs and bitters can create vastly different cocktails.

Southside

CLASSIC

In bartending circles, there's an ongoing debate about whether this classic Daiquiri variation should be made with lemon juice or lime juice. Frankly, it's delicious either way, but we lean toward lime for its brightness when combined with mint. The Southside is similar to our Fresh Gimlet (page 114) but even more refreshing thanks to the muddled mint. It's also slightly more complex because it includes a dash of bitters.

5 mint leaves
2 ounces Plymouth gin
¾ ounce fresh lime juice
¾ ounce simple syrup (page 45)
1 dash Angostura bitters
Garnish: 1 mint leaf

In a shaker, gently muddle the mint. Add the remaining ingredients and shake with ice. Strain into a chilled coupe and garnish with the mint leaf.

Boukman Daiquiri

ALEX DAY, 2008

The Daiquiri template is so simple that riffing on it is easy. One of our favorite starting points is to introduce another rum or spirit as part of the core. Here, we replace a bit of the rum with rich, smooth Cognac, then bolster the aged character of the Cognac with a spiced syrup. When choosing the citrus for this drink, it could be tempting to use lemon juice because it would complement the Cognac and cinnamon so well. The result would be a decent drink, but lime juice cuts through the cinnamon and Cognac and imparts an unexpected astringency, keeping the drink bright and refreshing (pictured on page 109).

1½ ounces Flor de Cana 4-year white rum

½ ounce Pierre Ferrand 1840 Cognac

¾ ounce fresh lime juice

¾ ounce Cinnamon Syrup (page 52)

Shake all the ingredients with ice, then strain into a chilled coupe. No garnish.

Jack Rose

Jack Rose

CLASSIC

Grenadine, made from pomegranate juice and spiked with orange oil, has a flavor that's both juicy and tangy, a character that highlights the apple brandy in this classic cocktail. Lime juice provides a counterpoint to the grenadine's richness, cutting through the deep sweetness of the syrup.

1½ ounces Laird's 100-proof straight apple brandy

½ ounce Clear Creek 2-year apple brandy

¾ ounce fresh lime juice

¾ ounce House Grenadine (page 47)

Garnish: 1 apple slice

Shake all the ingredients with ice, then strain into a chilled coupe. Garnish with the apple slice.

Bee's Knees

The Boukman Daiquiri (page 129) highlights an interesting way to play with the sour template: by substituting a flavorful syrup for the simple syrup. A good rule of thumb for matching flavorful syrups with citrus is that lemon juice has a soft acidity that doesn't distract from honey, whereas lime juice brings an astringency that can cut through a dense syrup or heighten the flavors in a syrup. If honey were paired with lime juice in this classic cocktail, its flavor would disappear into the background.

2 ounces London dry gin

¾ ounce fresh lemon juice

¾ ounce Honey Syrup (page 45)

Shake all the ingredients with ice, then strain into a chilled coupe. No garnish.

Pink Lady

CLASSIC

You can think of this classic cocktail as a mash-up between the Bee's Knees (see left) and the Jack Rose (page 129). Gin and a bit of apple brandy make up the core and are enhanced by juicy-tart grenadine. Lime juice would overpower the gin, whereas lemon acts as a soft bridge between the gin, brandy, and grenadine. The Pink Lady is also a good lesson in restraint; if it simply used a full ¾ ounce of grenadine in place of the simple syrup in the basic sour template, the cocktail would be all about the grenadine; instead, it calls for just ½ ounce of grenadine and supplements it with simple syrup. Why only ½ ounce of lemon juice? Grenadine also has some acidity, and combined with the drying effect of egg white, a full ¾ ounce of lemon juice would create a tongue-strippingly dry cocktail.

1½ ounces Plymouth gin

½ ounce Laird's 100-proof straight apple brandy

½ ounce fresh lemon juice

½ ounce House Grenadine (page 47)

½ ounce simple syrup (page 45)

1 egg white

Garnish: 1 brandied cherry on a skewer

Dry shake all the ingredients, then shake again with ice. Double strain into a chilled coupe and garnish with the cherry.

Whiskey Sour

CLASSIC

In many cases, pairing an aged spirit like bourbon with lime juice yields results that are less than pleasant. Trying making a Basic Sour (page 106) with whiskey and lime juice, and you'll see what we mean: the same properties that make bourbon so tasty—vanilla, spice, tannins—don't play well with the high acidity, astringency, and flavor of lime juice. That's why recipes for cocktails like the classic Whiskey Sour generally call for lemon juice rather than lime.

2 ounces Elijah Craig Small Batch bourbon

¾ ounce fresh lemon juice

¾ ounce simple syrup (page 45)

Garnish: 1 lemon wedge

Shake all the ingredients with ice, then strain into a double Old-Fashioned glass over 1 large ice cube. Garnish with the lemon wedge.

Cat Video

NATASHA DAVID, 2015

In this riff on the Pisco Sour (page 120), singani and Crème Yvette sit on opposite ends of pisco's aromatic flavor profile, a dynamic tension that elevates the grape-based pisco. Singani, another grape-based spirit, pulls out pisco's deep earthy notes, while Crème Yvette plays off the floral qualities of Kappa pisco.

1½ ounces Kappa pisco
1 teaspoon Crème Yvette
½ ounce Singani 63
½ ounce fresh lemon juice
½ ounce fresh lime juice
¾ ounce simple syrup (page 45)
1 egg white
Garnish: 1 lemon twist and
1 edible flower

Dry shake all the ingredients without ice, then shake again with ice. Double strain into a chilled coupe. Express the lemon twist over the top of the drink and discard, then garnish with the edible flower.

Smoke and Mirrors

Smoke and Mirrors

ALEX DAY, 2010

In this cocktail, as in the Kentucky Maid (page 132), a bit of highly herbaceous mint helps bridge the gap between seemingly mismatched aged spirits and lime juice—a function also served by the absinthe in this recipe. Note that this cocktail and the Smokescreen (page 132) have exactly the same ingredients with the exception of the accent—absinthe in this case and Chartreuse in the Smokescreen. Even though only small amounts of these two accents are used, the end result is two very different flavor profiles, showing how something simple and seemingly minor can make a world of difference in a cocktail's flavor.

4 mint leaves
¾ ounce simple syrup (page 45)
1 ounce Famous Grouse scotch
½ ounce Laphroaig 10-year scotch
¾ ounce fresh lime juice
2 dashes Pernod absinthe
Garnish: 1 mint sprig

In a shaker, gently muddle the mint with the simple syrup. Add the remaining ingredients and shake with ice. Strain into a double Old-Fashioned glass over 1 large ice cube. Garnish with the mint sprig.

Kentucky Maid

SAMUEL ROSS, 2005

Despite the conventional wisdom that lemon juice is a better partner for aged spirits than lime juice, well-chosen ingredients can be used to bridge these kinds of conflicting elements, leading to delicious and surprising combinations. One of our favorite examples of this is the Kentucky Maid, concocted by the legendary barman Sam Ross. Here, bourbon and lime are bridged by muddled cucumber and mint, resulting in an unexpectedly refreshing cocktail. The cucumber adds juiciness similar to how lemon would, and the mint provides herbaceous seasoning. Without question, the Kentucky Maid is our go-to "welcome to bourbon" cocktail—we haven't met anyone who doesn't like it.

- **5 mint leaves**
- **3 slices cucumber**
- **¾ ounce simple syrup (page 45)**
- **2 ounces Elijah Craig Small Batch bourbon**
- **1 ounce fresh lime juice**
- **Garnish: 1 mint sprig skewered through 1 cucumber wheel**

Put the mint in a shaker and top with the cucumbers. Add the simple syrup and muddle, making sure to break up the cucumber skins. Add the bourbon and lime juice and shake with ice. Strain into a double Old-Fashioned glass over 1 large ice cube. Garnish with the mint sprig skewered through a cucumber wheel.

Pompadour

TYSON BUHLER, 2015

The Pompadour explores another way to riff on a Basic Sour: by incorporating a low-ABV ingredient as part of a split base, in this case, the French aperitif Pineau des Charentes. As you can see, the volume of the Pineau des Charentes is higher than if a boozy spirit were swapped into the split base. The Pompadour strikes a great balance between the power of rhum agricole, the juiciness of the Pineau des Charentes, and the sweet roundness of vanilla.

- **1½ ounces Rhum JM VSOP**
- **1½ ounces Pasquet Pineau des Charentes**
- **¾ ounce fresh lemon juice**
- **½ ounce Vanilla Lactic Syrup (page 286)**

Shake all the ingredients with ice, then strain into a chilled coupe. No garnish.

Smokescreen

ALEX DAY, 2010

The Smokescreen follows the same model as the Smoke and Mirrors (page 131), but gets its herbaceousness from green Chartreuse instead of absinthe. Whereas the absinthe gives the Smoke and Mirrors an anise undertone that contrasts with the smoky scotch, the Chartreuse gives the Smokescreen a savory quality thanks to its grassy, tarragon-like flavor, which draws out the Laphroaig scotch's vegetal side.

- **4 mint leaves**
- **¾ ounce simple syrup (page 45)**
- **1 ounce Famous Grouse scotch**
- **½ ounce Laphroaig 10-year scotch**
- **¼ ounce green Chartreuse**
- **¾ ounce fresh lime juice**
- **Garnish: 1 mint sprig**

In a shaker, gently muddle the mint with the simple syrup. Add the remaining ingredients and shake with ice. Strain into a double Old-Fashioned glass over 1 large ice cube. Garnish with the mint sprig.

High Five

ALEX DAY, 2010

Riffing on the Hemingway Daiquiri (page 120) is a great way to create new cocktails that are both exciting and refreshing. In the High Five, we use a very similar formula but substitute gin as the core. We also use Aperol to amplify the bitterness of the grapefruit, and because Aperol isn't as sweet as the maraschino liqueur in the Hemingway Daiquiri, we add a bit more simple syrup.

1½ ounces Beefeater gin

½ ounce Aperol

1 ounce fresh grapefruit juice

½ ounce fresh lime juice

½ ounce simple syrup (page 45)

Shake all the ingredients with ice, then strain into a chilled coupe. Garnish with a high five—seriously!

High Five

Brown Derby

CLASSIC

When paired with robust aged spirits, grapefruit juice acts differently than it does when combined with lighter liquors. Whereas spirits like rum and gin enhance the refreshing flavor of grapefruit, aged spirits tend to draw out some of the denser flavors and sweetness in the juice. Though the classic recipe for a Brown Derby doesn't call for any citrus beyond the grapefruit juice, we like to add just a bit of lemon juice to cut through some of the richness of the syrup, which might otherwise overshadow the brightness of the grapefruit juice.

2 ounces Elijah Craig Small Batch bourbon

1 ounce fresh grapefruit juice

1 teaspoon fresh lemon juice

½ ounce Honey Syrup (page 45)

Shake all the ingredients with ice, then strain into a chilled coupe. No garnish.

THE DAIQUIRI EXTENDED FAMILY

Mojito

CLASSIC

While the Mojito is certainly a member of the Daiquiri extended family, using similar proportions of the same ingredients—rum, lime juice, and sweetener—the fact that it's served over crushed ice makes it a distant cousin, at least in our eyes. Introducing crushed ice into the equation means it's necessary to think about how the cocktail will evolve after it's served. The key is to pack the ice into the glass, using a greater volume of ice than the volume of the cocktail. This will keep the cocktail cold and also keep the ice from moving around. Why should it matter if the ice moves around? If it does, dilution will occur more rapidly and the cocktail will quickly become a watery mess.

To avoid this, we take a few precautions when building Mojitos and their variations. First, we use a glass that can hold both a full cocktail and an appropriate amount of ice. Either a Collins glass or a double Old-Fashioned glass that can hold at least 16 ounces will fit the bill. Second, we freeze the glass so it's extremely cold when the cocktail is poured in. Third, instead of shaking the drink, we use a technique called whipping: shaking the drink with a few pieces of crushed ice—just enough to mix the ingredients without diluting them too much. After all, there's no need to chill the cocktail as much as one served neat, since it's served over so much crushed ice, which will also serve the

function of diluting the drink. Fourth and finally, after we pour the drink into the glass, we add crushed ice to fill the glass about four-fifths full, then stir or swizzle for a few seconds, and then pack the glass with ice, mounding the ice on top, like a snow cone. The end result should be a glass full of crushed ice, all the way to the bottom, with an even distribution of liquid, and a cone of crushed ice above the wash line.

10 mint leaves
¾ ounce simple syrup (page 45)
1 white sugar cube
2 ounces Caña Brava white rum
1 ounce fresh lime juice
Garnish: 1 mint bouquet

In a shaker, gently muddle the mint leaves, simple syrup, and sugar cube until the sugar cube breaks apart. Add the remaining ingredients and whip, shaking with a few pieces of crushed ice, just until incorporated. Dump into a Collins glass and add crushed ice until the glass is about four-fifths full. Swizzle for a few seconds, then pack the glass with ice, mounding it above the rim. Garnish with the mint bouquet, placing it in the center of the ice and serve with a straw.

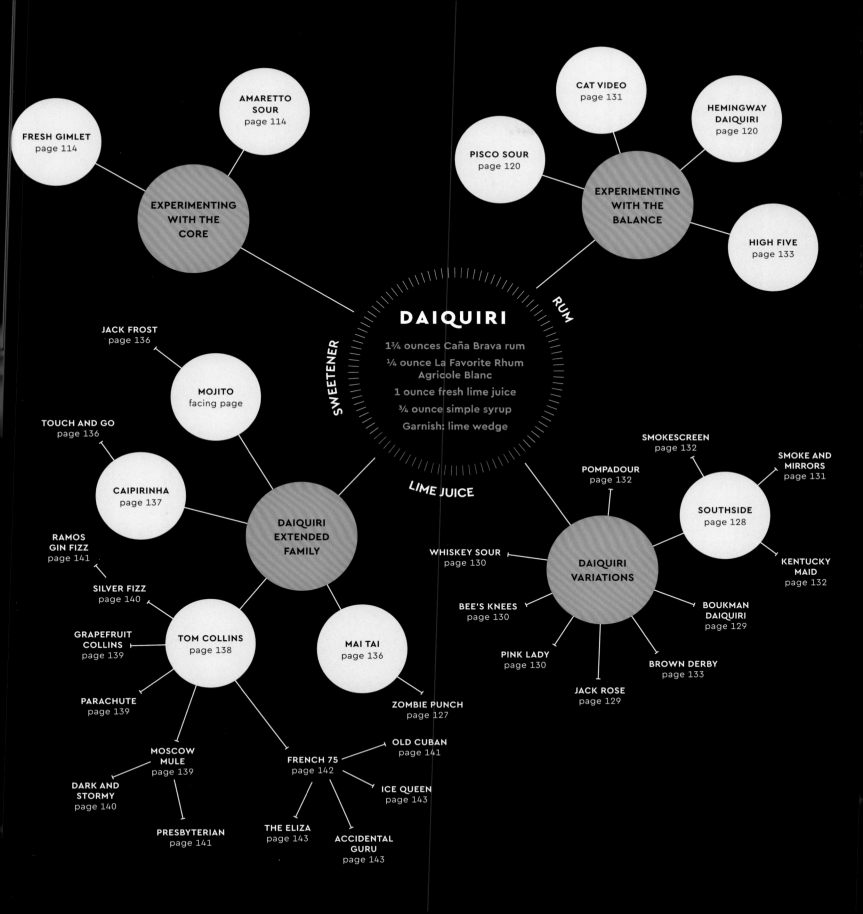

FRESH GIMLET
page 114

AMARETTO SOUR
page 114

EXPERIMENTING WITH THE CORE

CAT VIDEO
page 131

PISCO SOUR
page 120

HEMINGWAY DAIQUIRI
page 120

EXPERIMENTING WITH THE BALANCE

HIGH FIVE
page 133

RUM

SWEETENER

DAIQUIRI

1¾ ounces Caña Brava rum
¼ ounce La Favorite Rhum Agricole Blanc
1 ounce fresh lime juice
¾ ounce simple syrup
Garnish: lime wedge

JACK FROST
page 136

MOJITO
facing page

TOUCH AND GO
page 136

CAIPIRINHA
page 137

DAIQUIRI EXTENDED FAMILY

LIME JUICE

SMOKESCREEN
page 132

POMPADOUR
page 132

SMOKE AND MIRRORS
page 131

SOUTHSIDE
page 128

WHISKEY SOUR
page 130

DAIQUIRI VARIATIONS

KENTUCKY MAID
page 132

RAMOS GIN FIZZ
page 141

SILVER FIZZ
page 140

GRAPEFRUIT COLLINS
page 139

TOM COLLINS
page 138

MAI TAI
page 136

BEE'S KNEES
page 130

PINK LADY
page 130

JACK ROSE
page 129

BOUKMAN DAIQUIRI
page 129

BROWN DERBY
page 133

PARACHUTE
page 139

ZOMBIE PUNCH
page 127

MOSCOW MULE
page 139

OLD CUBAN
page 141

DARK AND STORMY
page 140

FRENCH 75
page 142

ICE QUEEN
page 143

PRESBYTERIAN
page 141

THE ELIZA
page 143

ACCIDENTAL GURU
page 143

Jack Frost

DEVON TARBY, 2015

The Jack Frost is a Mojito variation with a split base of tequila, pear brandy, and dry vermouth, accented with a bit of crème de menthe. Although the finished cocktail isn't overly minty, there is a cooling quality to the liqueur, like inhaling cold air on a snowy winter night—an effect that's enhanced by the crushed ice.

¾ ounce Cabeza blanco tequila

¾ ounce Clear Creek pear brandy

¾ ounce La Quintinye Vermouth Royal extra dry

1 teaspoon Giffard Menthe-Pastille

¾ ounce fresh lime juice

½ ounce simple syrup (page 45)

Garnish: 1 mint and sage bouquet and confectioners' sugar

Combine all the ingredients in a shaker and whip, shaking with a few pieces of crushed ice, just until incorporated. Dump into a Collins glass and add crushed ice until the glass is about four-fifths full. Swizzle for a few seconds, then pack the glass with ice, mounding it above the rim. Garnish with the mint and sage bouquet, and finish with a dusting of confectioners' sugar. Serve with a straw.

Mai Tai

CLASSIC

Crushed ice can help temper the sweetness of rich ingredients. A classic Mai Tai is a complex combination of funky rums, almond-laced orgeat, orange liqueur, and lime juice. The result is a complex cocktail that can easily teeter toward being too sweet. Serving it in a glass packed with crushed ice lightens the flavors just the right amount while still allowing their complexity to come through.

1 ounce Appleton Estate Reserve Blend rum

1 ounce La Favorite Coeur de Canne rhum agricole blanc

¼ ounce Grand Marnier

1 ounce fresh lime juice

½ ounce House Orgeat (page 285)

¼ ounce simple syrup (page 45)

1 dash Angostura bitters

Garnish: 1 mint bouquet

Combine all the ingredients in a shaker and whip, shaking with a few pieces of crushed ice, just until incorporated. Dump into a double Old-Fashioned glass, then pack the glass with crushed ice. Garnish with the mint bouquet.

Touch and Go

ALEX DAY, 2015

Muddling is a great technique for drawing out the flavors from less acidic citrus fruits, such as mandarin oranges, which have intensely aromatic peels and sweet juice. In the Touch and Go, a cross between a tequila-based sour and a Caipirinha that's balanced even without muddled citrus, we include the mandarin orange to add a layer of vibrant flavor.

½ mandarin orange, cut into 4 pieces

¾ ounce Basil Stem Syrup (page 285)

1½ ounces Espolòn blanco tequila

1 teaspoon Del Maguey Vida mezcal

¾ ounce fresh lemon juice

Garnish: 1 basil leaf

In a shaker, gently muddle the orange with the basil syrup. Add the remaining ingredients and shake with ice, then dump into a double Old-Fashioned glass. Garnish with the basil leaf.

Caipirinha

CLASSIC

As discussed earlier in this chapter, citrus skins are loaded with flavorful oils. These can be expressed from twists, but they can also be incorporated via muddling. The Brazilian Caipirinha, which includes almost an entire lime, provides a great opportunity to consider the finer details of muddling citrus. When we cut lime wedges to garnish a drink, we do so in such a way that they're easy to squeeze into a cocktail, cutting them into wedges from the top to the bottom of the lime. But for muddling, we prefer to cut them into pieces of a size and shape that make it easy to extract both the juice and the oils in the skin with one even pressing. So first we cut the lime in half across the middle, then we place the halves on a cutting board cut side down and slice them into quarters.

The lime is then muddled with sugar, which helps extract flavor from the lime skin. We prefer to use a sugar cube because it cuts into the lime skin to bring out more of its oils. We recommend putting the sugar cube in a small shaker tin, then adding the lime and simple syrup. Muddle each piece of lime by pressing down and twisting slightly to flatten the lime and break down the sugar. Stop muddling as soon as all of the pieces have been crushed.

Although we're typically militant about never pouring the ice we shake a cocktail with into the serving glass, we make an exception for the Caipirinha, which is traditionally served with not just the ice, but also the muddled lime. This allows the lime to continue to flavor the cocktail—though they can get bitter, we find that it's a pleasant limy flavor that builds toward the end of the cocktail. The brightly colored citrus also looks beautiful in a glass.

> 1 lime
> ¾ ounce simple syrup (page 45)
> 1 sugar cube
> 2 ounces cachaça

Cut the lime in half crosswise, then cut each half into quarters. Put 6 of the pieces in a shaker, reserving the other 2 for another use. Add the simple syrup and sugar cube and gently muddle the lime, carefully pressing each piece. Add the cachaça and shake with ice, then dump into a double Old-Fashioned glass. No garnish.

Tom Collins

CLASSIC

Another type of drink in the Daiquiri's extended family is sours that have bubbly ingredients added. This is such a broad category that it has several subfamilies: Collins-style drinks, fizzes, and numerous cocktails that include sparkling wine. We'll start with the Collins, which is basically a sour served in a tall glass with ice and seltzer.

The biggest challenge in preparing a Collins is avoiding overdilution. We like our Collinses as fizzy as possible, so rather than shaking them to full dilution, as for sours, we short shake them—just long enough to chill the ingredients without adding too much dilution, about five seconds. This leaves more room for the seltzer.

Traditionally, Collins-style drinks are topped with seltzer that isn't stirred into the drink. We view this as less than ideal. When the drink is sipped through a straw, the experience is often like drinking a sour that gradually dilutes and may not be bubbly at all. Our preferred method is to add a measured portion of seltzer to the empty serving glass, then pour in the contents of the shaker, an action that effectively mixes the cocktail, and then add ice at the very end—no stirring required.

To make the best Collins, use seltzer that's as cold as possible: keep it refrigerated and sealed before use or, better yet, build a carbonating rig and make your own very cold and highly sparkling seltzer (see page 232). Room-temperature seltzer is a waste of time; the bubbles will escape quickly and the seltzer will become flat. Add this to a drink and you're really just diluting it.

- **2 ounces cold seltzer**
- **2 ounces Beefeater gin**
- **1 ounce fresh lemon juice**
- **¾ ounce simple syrup (page 45)**
- **Garnish: 1 orange half wheel and 1 brandied cherry on a skewer**

Pour the seltzer into a Collins glass. Short shake the remaining ingredients with ice for about 5 seconds, then strain into the glass. Fill the glass with ice cubes and garnish with the orange half wheel and cherry.

Grapefruit Collins

SAM ROSS, 2005

When experimenting with the Collins template, keep in mind that seltzer contains a bit of carbonic acid, which increases the perception of acidity. For this reason, we often use a 1-to-1 ratio of citrus juice to sweetener in Collins-style cocktails unless we want an extra-tart drink (which we do for the basic Collins, but when adding other flavors we tend to back off on the acid). In the Grapefruit Collins, the grapefruit juice has a balanced sweet-tart flavor, so we remove it from the equation and then use equal amounts of lemon juice and simple syrup.

- **2 ounces cold seltzer**
- **2 ounces Beefeater gin**
- **1½ ounces fresh grapefruit juice**
- **½ ounce fresh lemon juice**
- **½ ounce simple syrup (page 45)**
- **4 dashes Peychaud's bitters**
- **Garnish: 1 grapefruit half wheel**

Pour the seltzer into a Collins glass. Short shake the remaining ingredients with ice for about 5 seconds, then strain into the glass. Fill the glass with ice cubes and garnish with the grapefruit half wheel.

Parachute

TYSON BUHLER, 2017

The Parachute is a great example of building a Collins-style cocktail on a low-proof base, here split between a juicy white port and the slightly bitter Salers aperitif. Because each of these ingredients has a powerful flavor, this cocktail drinks much like a full-proof sour but doesn't carry such a strong alcohol punch.

- **2 ounces cold tonic water**
- **1 ounce Quinta do Infantado white port**
- **1 ounce Salers Gentiane**
- **1 ounce fresh lemon juice**
- **¾ ounce simple syrup (page 45)**
- **2 dashes Peychaud's bitters**
- **Garnish: 1 grapefruit half wheel**

Pour the tonic water into a Collins glass. Short shake the remaining ingredients with ice for about 5 seconds, then strain into the glass. Fill the glass with ice cubes and garnish with the grapefruit half wheel.

Moscow Mule

CLASSIC

The Moscow Mule is famous for good reason: it has a strong ginger bite and is unquestionably refreshing. You may notice that this recipe uses slightly less lime juice than a typical sour-style cocktail. We do this to honor the original recipe, which was just a simple mixture of vodka and ginger beer topped with a squeeze of lime—more a Highball than a sour. In addition, ginger's powerful flavor has a zip somewhat like citrus, so when we use it, we often back down on any lemon or lime juice in the cocktail to let it shine.

- **2 ounces cold seltzer**
- **2 ounces vodka**
- **½ ounce fresh lime juice**
- **¾ ounce House Ginger Syrup (page 48)**
- **Garnish: 1 lime wheel and 1 piece of candied ginger on a skewer**

Pour the seltzer into a Collins glass. Short shake the remaining ingredients with ice for about 5 seconds, then strain into the glass. Fill the glass with ice cubes and garnish with the lime wheel and candied ginger.

Dark and Stormy

CLASSIC

In the Moscow Mule (page 139), the vodka core keeps the cocktail clearly focused on the interplay between ginger, lime juice, and the fizziness of seltzer. If a more flavorful spirit is used, the proportion of ingredients may need to be adjusted—a principle that's clearly illustrated in our version of the Dark and Stormy (which, like the Moscow Mule, was traditionally made with ginger beer). To balance the rich molasses flavor of Gosling's Black Seal rum, we up the amounts of both the ginger syrup and the lime juice.

2 ounces cold seltzer
2 ounces Gosling's Black Seal rum
¾ ounce fresh lime juice
1 ounce House Ginger Syrup (page 48)
Garnish: 1 lime wheel and 1 piece of candied ginger on a skewer

Pour the seltzer into a Collins glass. Short shake the remaining ingredients with ice for about 5 seconds, then strain into the glass. Fill the glass with ice cubes and garnish with the lime wheel and candied ginger.

Silver Fizz

CLASSIC

At their simplest, fizzes are basically Collins-style drinks served without ice. Although fizzes are most commonly associated with gin, they can be made with any spirit. This classic cocktail, the Silver Fizz, is a simple fizz to which an egg white has been added. When the cocktail is shaken, the egg white's tightly packed proteins unfold and trap air, forming bubbles. When the drink is then topped with seltzer even more frothiness ensues, as those proteins wrap around the carbon dioxide bubbles to create a light and fluffy foam.

2 ounces Beefeater gin
¾ ounce simple syrup (page 45)
¾ ounce fresh lemon juice
1 egg white
2 ounces cold seltzer

Dry shake all the ingredients (except the seltzer), then shake again with ice. Double strain into a fizz glass. Slowly add the seltzer, occasionally tapping the bottom of the glass on a table or flat surface to settle the foam. As you finish adding the seltzer, a white puck of foam should form on top of the drink. No garnish.

Silver Fizz

Ramos Gin Fizz

CLASSIC

Perhaps the most famous of the fizzes is the Ramos Gin Fizz, a New Orleans cocktail wherein the clean simplicity of a Silver Fizz is enriched with heavy cream. Traditionally, it's shaken for a full ten minutes to create a light, ethereal texture that's like a boozy liquid cloud. We've never found a full ten-minute shake to be necessary (it's more theater than necessary); five minutes is more than enough to create airy lightness needed for the Ramos. (See page 265 for the N₂O Ramos Gin Fizz, a version made in a whipper canister.)

2 ounces Fords gin
½ ounce fresh lime juice
½ ounce fresh lemon juice
1 ounce simple syrup (page 45)
1 ounce heavy cream
1 egg white
3 drops orange flower water
2 ounces cold seltzer

Dry shake all the ingredients (except the seltzer), then fill the shaker with ice cubes and shake for 5 minutes. Double strain into a pint glass. Slowly add the seltzer, occasionally tapping the bottom of the glass on a table or flat surface to settle the foam. As you finish adding the seltzer, a white puck of foam should form on top of the drink. No garnish.

Presbyterian

CLASSIC

As mentioned a few times earlier in this chapter, changing the core spirit in a cocktail may call for adjusting the type and amount of citrus in the cocktail. The classic Presbyterian is similar to the Moscow Mule (page 139) and the Dark and Stormy (page 140), being simply spirit combined with ginger ale. But in this case, the core spirit is rye whiskey, seasoned with lemon juice. For our version, we include both lemon juice, for its sweet and refreshing flavor, and lime juice, for its pleasant astringency.

2 ounces cold seltzer
2 ounces Old Overholt rye
½ ounce fresh lemon juice
½ ounce fresh lime juice
¾ ounce House Ginger Syrup (page 48)
Garnish: 1 lime wedge

Pour the seltzer into a Collins glass. Short shake the remaining ingredients with ice for about 5 seconds, then strain into the glass. Fill the glass with ice cubes and garnish with the lime wedge.

Old Cuban

AUDREY SAUNDERS, 2001

The legendary bartender Audrey Saunders created this deeply complex cocktail that livens up a Mojito with bubbles. To add greater complexity, Audrey relies on a lightly aged rum and seasons with Angostura bitters and mint, creating a drink that is both refreshing and sophisticated. We love the Old Cuban because it evolves as you drink it: with the first sips, you're met with tongue-tingling effervescence and fresh mint flavors. As the cocktail warms and the bubbles lose a bit of their intensity, the rum's richness comes to the front in a soothing way.

1½ ounces Bacardi 8-year aged rum
¾ ounce fresh lime juice
1 ounce simple syrup (page 45)
2 dashes Angostura bitters
6 mint leaves
2 ounces cold dry Champagne
Garnish: 1 mint leaf

Shake all the ingredients (except the sparkling wine) with ice, then double strain into a chilled coupe. Pour in the Champagne, and quickly dip the barspoon into the glass to gently mix the wine with the cocktail. Garnish with the mint leaf.

French 75

CLASSIC

Yes, Champagne *does* make everything better, including a Collins! Some
bartenders prepare a French 75 in a
tall glass with ice like a Collins, but we
opt for the swankier version in a flute.
Either way, introducing Champagne
(or a similar style of sparkling wine)
changes the cocktail's balance, adding
both proof and flavor. Therefore, the
formula for this classic cocktail calls
for decreased amounts of all three
elements of the sour base—in our
version, half the gin, and two-thirds of
the lemon juice and simple syrup.

1 ounce Plymouth gin
½ ounce fresh lemon juice
½ ounce simple syrup (page 45)
4 ounces cold dry sparkling wine
Garnish: 1 lemon twist

Shake all the ingredients (except
the sparkling wine) with ice, then
strain into a chilled flute. Pour in the
sparkling wine, and quickly dip the
barspoon into the glass to gently mix
the sparkling wine with the cocktail.
Express the lemon twist over the
drink, then place it into the drink.

The Eliza

DEVON TARBY, 2016

With careful adjustments, the subtle complexity of the French 75 (at left) can be modified to create exceptional variations. In this cocktail, we've replaced the citrusy Plymouth gin with sarsaparilla-forward Aviation gin in combination with Clear Creek pear brandy and savory French cassis, spiked with lavender bitters to provide a seductive floral hint.

- ½ ounce Aviation gin
- ¼ ounce Clear Creek pear brandy
- ¼ ounce Giffard Cassis Noir du Bourgogne
- ½ ounce fresh lemon juice
- ½ ounce simple syrup (page 45)
- 1 dash Scrappy's lavender bitters
- 4 ounces cold dry sparkling wine

Shake all the ingredients (except the sparkling wine) with ice, then strain into a flute. Pour in the sparkling wine, and quickly dip the barspoon into the glass to gently mix the wine with the cocktail.

Ice Queen

NATASHA DAVID, 2015

The Ice Queen expands on the French 75's flexibility by bringing in some elements from the Old Cuban (page 141)—rum, mint, and lime juice—and adding cucumber for a savory element.

- 1 cucumber slice
- ½ ounce simple syrup (page 45)
- 1½ ounces Plantation 3 Stars rum
- ½ teaspoon Giffard Menthe-Pastille
- ¾ ounce fresh lime juice
- 4 ounces cold dry sparkling wine
- Garnish: 1 lime twist

In a shaker, gently muddle the cucumber with the simple syrup. Add the remaining ingredients (except the sparkling wine) and shake with ice. Strain into a chilled coupe. Pour in the sparkling wine, and quickly dip the barspoon into the glass to gently mix the wine with the cocktail. Express the lime twist over the drink, then place it into the drink.

Accidental Guru

NATASHA DAVID, 2014

Beer and cider can also be used to add effervescence to Collins-style drinks. Because these ingredients can vary widely in alcohol content, flavor, sweetness, and acidity, using them requires careful attention to adjusting the amounts of the base spirit, citrus juice, and sweetener. In the Accidental Guru, just 1 ounce of strong spirit (whiskey) is used and the citrus juice is dialed back a bit. Less sweetener is also used, in this case because the drink is enhanced with peach liqueur.

- 1 ounce Bushmills Original Irish whiskey
- ½ ounce Giffard Crème de Pêche de Vigne
- ½ ounce fresh lime juice
- ½ ounce House Ginger Syrup (page 48)
- 3½ ounces cold Blanche de Bruxelles beer (or another wheat beer)
- Garnish: 1 lime wheel

Shake all the ingredients (except the beer) with ice, then strain into a large chilled fizz glass. Pour in the beer, then garnish with the lime wheel.

The Eliza

NEXT-LEVEL TECHNIQUE: CLARIFYING

Freshly pressed citrus juice is a key element of so many cocktails, and for good reason: it curbs the strength of alcohol and contributes flavor and texture. But it also adds color and opacity to cocktails. So, what if we want to add the flavor and balance without the color and density?

We've learned a lot about clarification from Dave Arnold in his excellent book *Liquid Intelligence* and his contributions to the blog *Cooking Issues*. Simply stated, clarification is the process of removing cloudy particles from a liquid, thereby making it transparent. This can be achieved easily with a filter. Consider the difference between filtered coffee and coffee prepared in a French press: The filtered coffee is lighter in color and more transparent, whereas coffee produced by a French press is cloudy. There's also a remarkable difference in flavor between the two, with the filtered coffee having a light, clear flavor and the French press coffee being dense and bold.

While we could clarify juices for our cocktails using a paper filter, we prefer to use either a mechanical centrifuge or agar. At our bars, we clarify a wide variety of juices: from citrus fruits (lemon, lime, grapefruit, orange, tangerine), fruit and vegetable juices (apple, pear, fennel root), and even purees (raspberry, strawberry).

Before we get into the nitty-gritty details, we want to answer the question that may be on your mind: Why bother with clarifying? Honestly, sometimes we just like to play with people's expectations: When they see a crystal clear drink that resembles a Martini, they assume it will be boozy and sharp. But if they take a sip and taste a shockingly bright and acidic Daiquiri, that's a fun surprise. Clarification also serves a practical purpose: when making fully carbonated cocktails (discussed at the end of chapter 5), removing any particulate matter allows the carbon dioxide to disseminate more uniformly throughout the drink.

One final note: Because clarified juices tend to be more fragile than fresh juices, we recommend using them within one day. The exception would be if they're mixed into batched or kegged cocktails (see page 236) with sweeteners and spirits that will help preserve their delicate flavor.

Clarified Lime Juice

Lime Juice

200 mL
PYREX

EXPERIMENTING WITH CLARIFIED JUICE

Our root Daiquiri recipe will help you understand how clarified juice can change a cocktail. Before you do the experiment, clarify some lime juice. Since you probably don't have a centrifuge (yet!), use the agar clarification method on page 146. Then make the two recipes below, noting that the second one calls for stirring, not shaking.

This experiment clearly reveals that clarified juice is a world apart from freshly pressed juice and has a completely different flavor that's lighter and less penetrating. As a result, the Clarified Daiquiri has a more pronounced rum flavor.

Clarification can also reset biases. For example, over the years we've mostly shied away from using orange juice in cocktails. A key reason is because the flavor of the juice can vary widely depending on the variety of orange, season, and where you live. (While this is true of all varieties of citrus, it seems more pronounced with oranges.) In addition, orange juice has a surprising homogenizing effect when mixed with other ingredients that tends to make drinks boring.

Take, for example, the Monkey Gland (page 146)—a cocktail we've always thought was a big glass of BS. Why? Because it lacks balance. The gin is nice and the grenadine can be vibrantly juicy and astringent, but the orange juice—high in sugar and low in acid—mutes the gin and dulls the grenadine. The ingredients aren't better for being put together; they're worse. With each sip, we're reminded of the bad old days, when the point of a cocktail was largely to mask the flavor of subpar booze. But in fact, the Monkey Gland is not irreparable. We can steer it toward a more pleasurable balance by swapping in clarified orange juice and stirring the drink rather than shaking it, resulting in a cocktail that has qualities somewhat akin to a Martini. (Another possible improvement would be to add a few drops of Citric Acid Solution, page 298.) We heartily encourage you to try this experiment, again using the agar method (see page 146) to clarify the orange juice.

Daiquiri

OUR ROOT RECIPE

1¾ ounces Caña Brava white rum

¼ ounce La Favorite Coeur de Canne rhum agricole blanc

1 ounce fresh lime juice

¾ ounce simple syrup (page 45)

Shake all the ingredients with ice, then strain into a chilled coupe. No garnish.

Clarified Daiquiri

1¾ ounces Caña Brava white rum

¼ ounce La Favorite Coeur de Canne rhum agricole blanc

1 ounce clarified lime juice (see page 146)

¾ ounce simple syrup (page 45)

Stir all the ingredients over ice, then strain into a chilled coupe. No garnish.

Monkey Gland (Classic)

2 ounces Plymouth gin

1 ounce fresh orange juice

1 teaspoon House Grenadine
(page 47)

2 dashes Pernod absinthe

Shake all the ingredients with ice,
then strain into a chilled coupe.
No garnish.

Monkey Gland (Made with Clarified Orange Juice)

2 ounces Plymouth gin

1 ounce clarified orange juice
(see right)

1 teaspoon House Grenadine
(page 47)

2 dashes Pernod absinthe

Stir all the ingredients over ice,
then strain into a chilled coupe.
No garnish.

HOW TO CLARIFY JUICE WITH AGAR

Juicer

Fine-mesh sieve lined with cheesecloth

Several bowls or other containers

Gram scale

Saucepan

Agar

Stove

Whisk

Superbag or paper coffee filter

1   Juice the fruit or other fresh produce, then strain the juice through a fine-mesh sieve into a bowl. Prepare an ice bath.

2   Measure the weight of a container using a gram scale, then add the juice and calculate the difference. (Or, if your scale has a tare function, place the container on it, zero the scale, then add the juice and determine its weight.) Record the weight of the juice.

3   Calculate 25% of the weight of the juice (multiply by 0.25). Measure out that amount of water and put it in a separate container.

4   Add the weights of the juice and water, then calculate 0.2% of the combined weight (multiply by 0.002) to get X grams; this is the amount of agar you'll use.

5   In a saucepan, combine the water and agar. Cook over medium heat, whisking constantly, until the agar is dissolved.

6   Remove from the heat, add the juice, and whisk until combined.

7   Pour the mixture into one of the containers, then put the container in the ice bath.

8   After about 10 minutes, the mixture will set up. Once it does, use a whisk to break it into curd-like chunks.

9   Transfer to a fine-mesh sieve lined with several layers of cheesecloth placed over a bowl.

10 Gently gather the edges of the cheesecloth and form the mass into a ball. Squeeze out the liquid; don't squeeze too hard, or some of the agar may come through.

11 If any particles are still present in the clarified juice, pass the liquid through a Superbag or paper coffee filter.

12 Transfer to a storage container and refrigerate until ready to use.

HOW TO CLARIFY JUICE WITH A CENTRIFUGE

Juicer

Fine-mesh sieve lined with cheesecloth

Gram scale

Centrifuge containers with lids

Pectinex Ultra SP-L

Kieselsol

Chitosan

Centrifuge

Superbag

1 Juice the fruit or other fresh produce, then strain the juice through a fine-mesh sieve.

2 Measure the weight of a centrifuge container using a gram scale, then add the juice and calculate the difference. (Or, if your scale has a tare function, place the centrifuge container on it, zero the scale, then add the juice and determine its weight.) Record the weight of the juice.

3 Calculate 0.2% of the weight of the juice (multiply by 0.002) to get X grams.

4 Stir X grams of Pectinex Ultra SP-L and kieselsol into the juice. Cover and let sit for 15 minutes.

5 Stir X grams of chitosan into the juice. Cover and let sit for 15 minutes.

6 Stir in X grams of kieselsol right before putting the container in the centrifuge.

7 Weigh the filled container and fill each of the other containers with an equal weight of water. Each container in a centrifuge must weigh exactly the same in order to keep the machine in balance.

8 Run the centrifuge at 4,500 rpm for 12 minutes.

9 Remove the containers and carefully strain the juice through a fine-mesh sieve lined with several layers of cheesecloth or through a Superbag, being careful not to disturb the solids that have collected on the bottom of the container.

10 Transfer to a storage container and refrigerate until ready to use.

SPECIAL CLARIFICATION INGREDIENTS

Kieselsol and Chitosan: Frequently used in the wine industry, where they are known as fining agents, kieselsol and chitosan are often sold as a set for clarifying suspended particles in wine, but they're also useful for clarifying ingredients for cocktails. Most of the suspended solids in a liquid have an electrical charge, either positive or negative. Fining agents also have a charge: kieselsol, which is added first, has a negative charge, and chitosan, added second, has a positive charge. Each will attract and bind particles with the opposite charge, forming clumps that are heavier than the surrounding liquid. With wine, the clumped sediments are allowed to settle for days before being separated, but when working with cocktail ingredients, we're often playing a game against time. Their freshness will rapidly deteriorate, so we can't let them sit around for a couple of days. Therefore, we typically start by using fining agents to clump the particles together, then run the liquid through a centrifuge to separate out the solids.

Agar: An alternative clarification method uses a gel approach wherein liquid is combined with an agent that turns the mix into a gel; the clarified liquid can then be expelled from the gel, leaving the particulate matter behind. A variety of agents can used, from egg whites to gelatin, but we prefer agar because it's derived from algae and is vegan-friendly, whereas many other gelling agents are animal products. Although kieselsol and chitosan are great for clarifying cocktail ingredients when used in tandem with a centrifuge, they don't produce the same results without one, so we use agar when we don't have a centrifuge or don't want to use one.

Pectinex Ultra SP-L: See page 48.

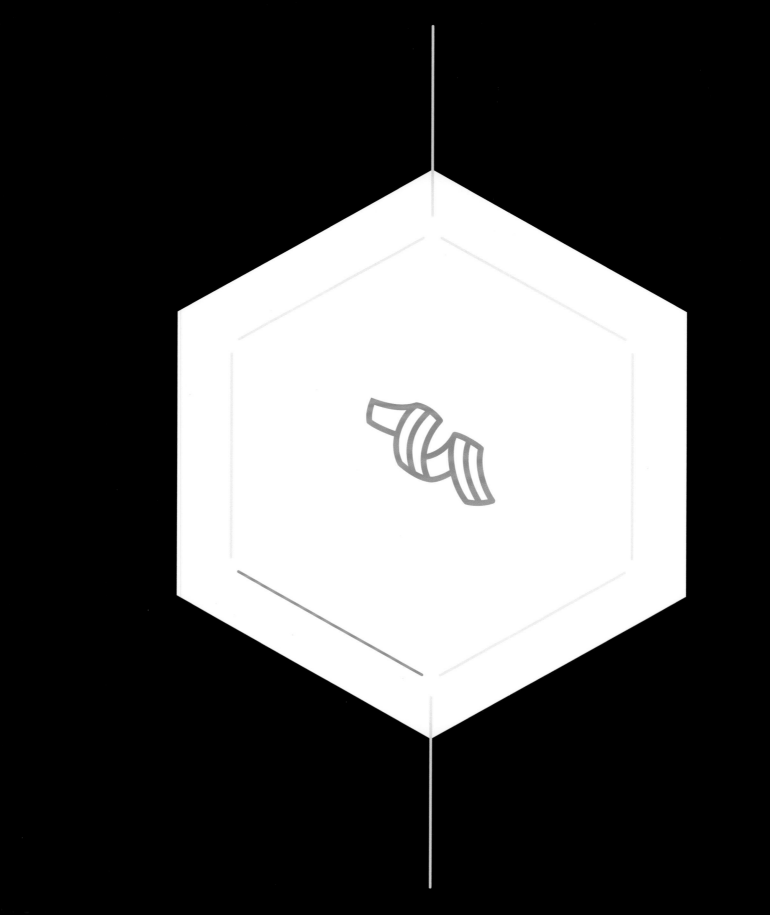

4

THE
SIDECAR

THE CLASSIC RECIPE

The Sidecar is rumored to have been created by an American army captain stationed in Paris during World War I (though, as usual, there are plenty of other origin stories). The captain rode around the city in a motorcycle sidecar, hence the name of the drink. The likely predecessor of the Sidecar was a drink known as the Brandy Crusta, which first showed up in Jerry Thomas's 1862 book *The Bar-Tender's Guide* and contained a large proportion of brandy and miniscule amounts of lemon juice and curaçao (along with a couple of dashes of bitters). As the Sidecar evolved, these proportions shifted. While some older French recipes call for equal parts of Cognac and Cointreau, we don't know many modern bartenders who make a Sidecar this way, as the Cointreau would overshadow the fruity qualities of the Cognac.

Sidecar

1½ ounces Cognac
1 ounce Cointreau
¾ ounce fresh lemon juice
Garnish: 1 orange twist

Shake all the ingredients with ice, then strain into a chilled coupe. Express the orange twist over the drink, then gently rub it around the rim of the glass and place it into the drink.

a specific Cognac and matching it with an orange liqueur. Pierre Ferrand's Ambre Cognac spends enough time in oak to provide a rich, flavorful foundation that's beautifully complemented by that producer's extremely dry curaçao. Then, because the dryness of the curaçao is so bracing, we add a bit of simple syrup to boost the flavors and bring the cocktail into harmony.

Ambre Cognac

1 ounce Pierre Ferrand dry curaçao
¾ ounce fresh lemon juice
1 teaspoon simple syrup (page 45)
Garnish: 1 orange twist

Shake all the ingredients with ice, then strain into a chilled coupe. Express the orange twist over the drink, then gently rub it around the rim of the glass and place it into the drink.

LIQUEURS COME TO THE PARTY

Whereas the Daiquiri is like a boisterous guest at a party—the guy who knows everyone—the Sidecar is an exotic, quiet foreigner brought by a friend who reads big, hardcover books and likes to talk about them. Though it contains only three ingredients, it's mysterious. When you first taste one, it may be hard to identify what's in the glass. That first sip delivers a punch of bright citrus, followed by an almost bracing dryness and then a finish that hangs around for a while. It's a complex, layered drink, and it evolves in delicious ways as it warms (unlike the aforementioned Daiquiri), from crisp and dry to rich and full.

Sidecars are related to Daiquiris, both having evolved from the sour template, but Sidecars are distinguished by the fact that they contain a significant amount of flavorful liqueur—generally between ½ ounce and 1 ounce. So whereas Daiquiris—and many sours—are defined by a rich texture and bright acidity, the Sidecar and members of its extended family are often drier and gain their complexity through the combination of liqueur and citrus. Therefore, when we teach our bartenders about cocktails, we separate Daiquiris from Sidecars. And because Sidecars contain a relatively large amount of liqueur and liqueurs vary in sweetness, proof, and tannins, they're trickier to master.

The same balance that is sought in a Daiquiri—the careful equilibrium between strong, sweet, and sour—is achieved in a Sidecar and its variations, but because the Sidecar is made with a liqueur (which brings proof, sweetness, and seasoning to the drink), the proportions of ingredients are different. To complicate matters, each liqueur has a different proof and sweetness, so there isn't one standard template: you must study the liqueur and tweak the proportions accordingly.

UNDERSTANDING THE TEMPLATE

You might have noticed that the Sidecar's template is similar to that of a couple of far more popular cocktails: the Margarita, made with tequila, curaçao, and lime juice, and the Cosmopolitan, made with vodka, curaçao, lime juice, and cranberry juice. We chose the Sidecar to represent this style of cocktail because its balance is difficult to achieve with three ingredients that can be so different from producer to producer—Cognac, curaçao, and lemon juice. This makes it a great example of the importance of properly balancing the inherent qualities of ingredients. Depending on its age, Cognac can be light and tannic or rich and luscious. Orange curaçaos can be bone-dry (like the Pierre Ferrand), sweet (Grand Marnier), or somewhere in between (Cointreau). Knowing the characteristics of each ingredient informs how you might put them together.

Here's an experiment to help you begin to explore this template. Juice some lemons, grab your shaker, and crack a bottle of Cognac. (As with most of these experiments, we'll forgo the garnish to keep the focus on the cocktail itself.) Let's start by returning to the Basic Sour template (page 106), with the generally agreed-upon formula of two parts spirit to one part lemon or lime juice and one part sweetener, which is broadly accepted as a tasty, balanced cocktail. So, in your shaker, build a simple Cognac Sour, followed by Sidecar (Boozy) and Sidecar (Balanced).

Cognac Sour

CLASSIC

**2 ounces Cognac
(preferably VSOP)**

¾ ounce fresh lemon juice

¾ ounce simple syrup (page 45)

Shake all the ingredients with ice, then double strain into a chilled coupe. No garnish.

What do you think? Sure, it may be tasty, but to us, it doesn't seem to be anything special. The Cognac is clearly the star of the show, but its woodsier notes are muted by the refreshing combination of lemon and sugar. Set that glass aside to reference in a few minutes and rinse your shaking tin. Then put together the following variation, which substitutes Cointreau for the simple syrup, yielding a basic Sidecar.

Sidecar (Boozy)

**2 ounces Cognac
(preferably VSOP)**

¾ ounce Cointreau

¾ ounce fresh lemon juice

Shake all the ingredients with ice, then double strain into a chilled coupe. No garnish.

What's the first thing you taste? We're guessing it's booze. This spec packs a hell of a punch, and though that's not necessarily a bad thing, alcohol dominates the flavor profile, creating a harsh, bitter drink. This is a widespread problem in cocktail making: ignoring the proof of higher-ABV modifying ingredients, like Cointreau, and simply substituting them for a sweetener without adjusting the ratios. At 80 proof, Cointreau is just as boozy as most base spirits, and while its sweetness will curb some of the effects of the lemon juice, the resulting cocktail is far too dry. That's why the classic Sidecar recipe calls for less Cognac, along with slightly more Cointreau, to provide a bit more sweetness. So, even if you've already made the classic recipe at the beginning of the chapter, make it again so you can do a side-by-side comparison.

Sidecar (Balanced)

**1½ ounces Cognac
(preferably VSOP)**

1 ounce Cointreau

¾ ounce fresh lemon juice

Shake all the ingredients with ice, then double strain into a chilled coupe. No garnish.

We find that this classic recipe achieves an almost perfect balance, with the full-bodied character of the Cognac being complemented by the bright sweetness of Cointreau and the refreshing quality of lemon juice. However, because this spec tends to be a bit dry for most people, our root recipe (page 152) also includes a tiny amount of simple syrup to achieve an ideal balance and boost the flavors of the cocktail.

THE CORE: BRANDY

Cognac provides a broad foundation for the Sidecar. It's rich enough to wrangle the acidity of lemon and structured enough to mingle deliciously with the Cointreau's bright citrus, spiciness, and mild sweetness. Cognac is one of the most famous brandies in the world, *brandy* being a catchall term for spirits distilled from fruits, including grape-based brandies, apple brandies, and eaux-de-vie.

Worldwide, brandies made from grapes are by far the most common, and among them Cognac, native to France, is the most popular. But Cognac is just one style of grape brandy: France also produces Armagnac, Peru and Chile produce the grape brandy known as pisco, and excellent brandies are also produced in the United States. Grape brandies can be made from grapes that are bright and acidic, or from grapes that are sweet and aromatic, and they can be either aged or unaged. As with other spirits, barrel aging produces brandies that tend to be rich and juicy, with deep, nuanced vanilla and spice flavors from the oak. By contrast, unaged brandies are fiery and sharp, offering the unadulterated essence of the grapes from which they're made. The latter can provide a real sense of both the character of the fruit and the distiller's skill in capturing it.

Different styles of brandy are rarely interchangeable. So while two Cognacs of a similar age could be substituted for each other in a cocktail, aged and unaged brandies have entirely different flavor profiles that will affect the balance of a drink. In the case of the Sidecar, a moderately aged Cognac provides the necessary richness to bring equilibrium to the cocktail, whereas a younger Cognac would fall flat.

In this chapter we'll explore a wide variety of cocktails based on the Sidecar template, and in the process we'll be experimenting with the core. So in this section we'll survey the various types of brandy: Cognac, Armagnac, Spanish brandy, pisco, apple brandy, eau-de-vie, and because the Sidecar's most famous variation is the Margarita, we also take a brief detour into the world of agave-based spirits.

COGNAC

Produced in southwestern France, Cognac has been made in much the same way for hundreds of years: a grape-based wine is distilled in specialized alembic stills and then aged in oak barrels. While all of those steps (making the wine, distilling it, and aging it) are important, even more vital to Cognac's personality is blending, with each house producing a final product that expresses its house style. This provides an assurance that Cognac from any given producer will have a fairly consistent flavor profile from year to year. There are three official grades of Cognac based on age—from youngest to oldest, VS, VSOP, and XO. The term *hors d'âge* is defined as being equivalent to XO, but producers primarily use it to indicate high-quality bottles that exceed XO in age. Since Cognac is pricy, we tend to use VS and VSOP bottlings in cocktails. VSOPs are usually our choice because they are full in flavor and body and versatile enough for all cocktail applications, often having a cooked banana–like flavor. VS Cognacs, on the other hand, have a woodsy flavor and tend to be too young for spirituous cocktails, though they are perfectly acceptable for citrusy cocktails, including the Sidecar.

RECOMMENDED BOTTLES

Hennessy VS: Hennessy is a juggernaut producer that makes as much as 40 percent of the world's Cognac supply. While this may diminish Hennessy's standing among those who gravitate toward small, craft producers, we're impressed by Hennessy's consistency and find it to be quite characteristic of Cognac: woody and sweet, with a mild clove flavor. As a bonus, Hennessy is almost always available.

Paul Beau VS: In contrast to most VS Cognacs, which are fine to sip but not complex enough to be versatile in cocktails, Paul Beau offers a fantastic balance between the alcoholic strength of a young spirit and the vanilla and toasty wood character of oak. It also has an attractive price point—typically between $30 and $40.

H by Hine VSOP: In response to increasing demand for cocktail-friendly Cognacs—affordable enough to mix and with a strong personality—Hine created the "H" bottling, a delicious Cognac that has a strong floral aroma, fresh stone fruit flavors, and just a little spice. Its elegance can get lost when it's mixed with assertive spirits, but it's a delicious solo base, as well as a great complement to light fortified wines, such as fino and amontillado sherries, as well as aromatized wines like Lillet blanc.

Park VSOP: Whereas many Cognacs in this age group are characterized by deep, juicy flavors, Park VSOP has a noticeably bright aroma and flavor. The telltale personality of cooked bananas is present, but a citrus and fresh peach brightness are layered on top, making this bottle a great choice for refreshing citrus-based cocktails.

Pierre Ferrand 1840: This is a relatively new product created specifically for mixing into cocktails. While Pierre Ferrand doesn't affix typical age statements to its Cognac, the 1840 and the Ambre (below) all mix like a VSOP. It has a powerful aroma of baking spices that extends into the flavor, and whereas most Cognacs are bottled at 40% ABV, it clocks in at 45% ABV. Together, these qualities allow the 1840 to take center stage in a cocktail and also allow it to collaborate with aggressive spirits like American rye whiskey without getting bullied.

Pierre Ferrand Ambre: This is our go-to Cognac for cocktail use. It has a sweet vanilla and apricot nose, and its flavor is deep and complex. The oak's influence is clear, but it also has a fresh-fruit quality—like biting into a sweet apple—that makes it a wonderful platform on which to build cocktails. We love it equally in shaken and stirred cocktails, on its own or in collaboration with other spirits, particularly aged rum, apple brandy, and bourbon.

A RIDICULOUSLY GOOD AND UNNECESSARY SIDECAR

In the interest of experiencing the finer things in life at least once, we recommend buying an expensive but perfect bottle of Cognac, Paul Beau Hors d'Âge, and making yourself a Sidecar using the following recipe. The difference between this recipe and our root recipe (page 152) reflects the qualities that this much older and denser Cognac brings to the cocktail.

> 1½ ounces Paul Beau Hors d'Âge Cognac
> 1 ounce Pierre Ferrand dry curaçao
> ¾ ounce fresh lemon juice
> Garnish: 1 orange twist

Shake all the ingredients with ice, then strain into a chilled coupe. Express the orange twist over the drink, then gently rub it around the rim of the glass and place it into the drink.

ARMAGNAC

Armagnac is a close cousin to Cognac, as both are produced in southwest France using similar ingredients. A key area in which they differ is in their flavor: Cognac is rich and fruity, and though Armagnac has some of the same flavors, it often has a much spicier character. We often think of it like this: bourbon is to rye whiskey as Cognac is Armagnac.

Another distinction is that Armagnac is frequently bottled in dated vintages, and because vintages can vary so much, it's nearly impossible for us to offer advice on which bottles to use in cocktails. However, there are some blended Armagnacs that make their way out of France, and these tend to be more affordable, making them a good choice for mixing into cocktails. These blends employ a similar age grading: VS, VSOP, XO, and hors d'âge, and we use them just as we do the different ages of Cognacs.

Tariquet Classique VS Bas-Armagnac: This bottle offers a great introduction to Armagnac at a fantastic price. Though it's young, it's surprisingly full-bodied, with flavors of dried apricots and toasted spices, primarily clove and a touch of cinnamon.

Tariquet VSOP Bas-Armagnac: Tariquet's Armagnac develops greater structure and complexity with more time in oak. In comparison to the younger bottle described above, which comes across as slightly wild, the VSOP has a more rounded quality, with sweet flavors of vanilla and cooked stone fruits. Its fuller body greatly complements the underlying flavors of toasted spices, making this Armagnac a tasty addition to stirred cocktails.

Domaine d'Espérance Blanche Armagnac: Blanche Armagnac is a highly flavorful spirit that can be a great substitution for other unaged grape brandies. Whereas piscos, the unaged brandies of South America, are intensely floral, the high acidity of the base wine for Armagnac lends this spirit a more savory aroma and flavor characterized by almonds and white pepper, but the spirit still has a lively freshness.

SPANISH BRANDY

Richer, darker, and often a bit sweeter than their French cousins, Spanish brandies are produced in different styles. Today, we have access to a handful of producers that are mostly bottling what's known as Brandy de Jerez, a rich and sweet brandy from the southern tip of Spain. There are other styles of Spanish brandy beyond the Jerez region, but they don't often find their way into our cocktails.

In cocktails, Spanish brandy works similarly to Cognac and Armagnac, but because of its aging process, it usually has a pronounced richness that comes through in the glass. When working with heavily aged Spanish brandies, we often add just a small amount to dose the cocktail

with a spiced fruitcake kick; in larger quantities, they can overwhelm the other flavors. The exception is an Old-Fashioned, which is a great template for allowing a very old Spanish brandy to shine through.

RECOMMENDED BOTTLES

Cardenal Mendoza Solera Gran Reserva: Aged between fifteen and seventeen years in both former oloroso and Pedro Ximénez sherry casks, Cardenal Mendoza's gran reserva is characterized by an onslaught of prunes and raisins, with a sweet nutty and chocolate flavor that lasts and lasts. Because it's so dense, we typically use it in a split base in a spirituous cocktail, such as alongside American whiskey in an Old-Fashioned.

Gran Duque de Alba Solera Gran Reserva: For many years, William & Humbert's Gran Duque de Alba was the only widely available Spanish brandy in the United States, so it largely set the tone for our expectations of the category. Rich and sweet on the nose, it's semidry but retains the iconic raisiny flavor of brandy aged in sherry casks (in this case, oloroso). It's a delicious sipping brandy that can also be used in a split base for a stirred cocktail.

Lustau Brandy de Jerez Solera: The bodega responsible for some of our favorite sherries also produces some of the best-priced Brandy de Jerez. The reserva is aged around three years in former amontillado sherry casks. It has dense aromatics but is dry, with notes of vanilla, toasted nuts, and fresh nutmeg. Although youthful, it's still full-bodied enough for both shaken and stirred cocktails. Lustau's gran reserva steps up the game. It's aged for more than ten years and spends a portion of that time in richer oloroso casks. The result is a mature brandy that's suffused with walnut and toffee flavors and has a lingering raisin finish. We love Manhattan variations made with the gran reserva.

PISCO

Pisco and its cousin singani are South American brandies made from intensely floral varieties of grapes, and both are often bottled unaged. This gives them qualities a world apart from the aged brandies of Europe and dictates using them differently in cocktails.

In popular culture, pisco is almost inseparable from the most iconic pisco cocktail on the planet: the Pisco Sour (page 120). In this cocktail, the sharp, floral spirit mingles with citrus for a pleasing flavor—an indicator that pisco can work beautifully as a flavorful and aromatic base for shaken citrusy cocktails. We particularly like it in collaboration with an amontillado-style sherry, as in the Daisy Gun (page 279), where it adds a layer of wine and grape-brandy flavors. And as more high-quality brands of pisco have made it to the United States, the spirit has proven to be quite versatile, also working well in stirred cocktails. In many drinks we use pisco much as we'd use blanco tequila, but whereas tequila confers a noticeable vegetal character, pisco adds a floral aroma coupled with an intense bite, which can be curbed by including blanc vermouth or another semisweet fortified wine.

RECOMMENDED BOTTLES

Campo de Encanto Grand and Noble Pisco: This pisco was born for cocktails. Made from a blend of Quebranta, Torentel, Moscatel, and Italia grapes, it's clean, brightly aromatic, smooth on the palate, and distilled to proof, without a drop of anything added. If you can only mix with one bottle of pisco, this should be it. That said, we do recommend keeping an eye out for Campo de Encanto's single-variety bottles, which offer a unique way to explore how specific grape varieties express themselves as spirits.

Capurro Pisco Acholado: While it has all of the iconic aromas and flavors of pisco—bright stone fruits and flowers—there's something uniquely earthy in this bottling that allows it to shine in stirred cocktails, especially Martini riffs with blanc vermouth. This pisco is made from a blend of grapes, but Capurro also offers single-grape varieties that are stunning—grab them if you find them!

Macchu Pisco: Produced in the same area as Campo de Encanto, Macchu pisco is made from only Quebranta grapes, a nonaromatic variety. The result is a spirit that's less floral than many other piscos but still full-bodied and flavorful. It's a great base for sour-style cocktails.

SINGANI

Although pisco gets most of the attention, Bolivia's native singani, which is also an unaged grape brandy, has a unique personality, with a depth of flavor that works well in both citrusy and spirituous cocktails. The difference between pisco and singani has a lot to do with where the grapes for singani are grown: a tiny, arid region in southern Bolivia, 5,200 feet above sea level, that produces highly aromatic Muscat de Alexandria grapes from which the spirit is produced. When developing cocktails with singani, the process can be inspired by how pisco is used, though the character of singani is often more floral. As with pisco, one of our favorite ways of using singani is to bolster a fortified wine, as in the Class Act (page 279), or in collaboration with another base spirit, as in the Cat Video (page 131). In Bolivia, the preferred method of consumption is in a traditional *chuflay*—singani and ginger ale with a slice of lime.

Singani 63: Currently, this is the only singani that's widely available in the United States. It strikes a great balance, featuring both the full-bodied flavor of the base wine and the qualities of a youthful distillate: floral and fruity, with a sharp texture on the palate.

APPLE BRANDY

Depending on how it's distilled and aged, an apple brandy can be either smooth and rich or spicy and pungent. While the types of apples and many production methods used for apple brandies combine to produce a huge spectrum of styles, one characteristic is always present: the inherent impression of apples. In this section, we'll discuss the two most common types: French Calvados and American apple brandy.

CALVADOS

Regal, beautiful, perfect—there is probably no spirit we adore more than Calvados. It's made from one or many of the two hundred varieties of apples and pears allowed by French law, which are pressed into juice and fermented into cider, which is then distilled and aged in oak barrels for at least two years.

Calvados is classified by both region, with Pays d'Auge being the most restricted region, and age statements. Though the age groupings are similar to those for Cognac and Armagnac, producers can use many different terms to cover each age. For use in cocktails, we generally favor Calvados aged for at least three years, though any older than that and it gets too pricy for mixing into drinks. Younger Calvados generally doesn't have a deep enough flavor to shine through in cocktails, and can get lost in the mix.

Busnel Pays d'Auge VSOP: For us, the aroma and flavor of Busnel's VSOP have become inseparable from Calvados in general—that's how much we use it. The aroma is sweet and spiced, characterized by baked apples with cinnamon, clove, and vanilla, and it has an off-dry flavor of butter, toffee, and just a bit of caramel. All of this comes together in a broad flavor that works well in many ways in cocktails, particularly as the core in both stirred and shaken drinks, or in small quantities for seasoning.

Dupont Pays d'Auge Réserve: This exceptionally elegant brandy is blended from spirits aged in oak casks, of which 25 percent are new. This produces a toastier flavor subtly seasoned with spice and just a hint of vanilla. This is a highly nuanced spirit that typically finds its way into our cocktails as the star of the show.

AMERICAN APPLE BRANDY

American apple brandy is as old as America itself. Apple trees flourished in the colonies, where hard cider, and later brandy, became the drink of choice for colonists. The first commercial distillery in the United States (established in 1780) made apple brandy. It a was popular spirit for much of our country's history, but over time, American apple brandy fell by the wayside—until the last couple of decades. During the intervening years, there was only one significant producer: Laird's. Laird's is important because it sheds light on American apple brandy in general. Their products have significant stylistic differences from French apple brandies: while Calvados is a close cousin to Cognac, the apple brandy made by Laird & Company is more akin to American whiskey. The company also makes applejack, which by law is a blend of apple brandy and neutral grain spirits, aged for at least four years in used bourbon barrels. Though applejack has its uses, we much prefer the 100-proof Laird's straight apple brandy, made only with apples.

As interest in American apple brandy has grown, the domestic industry has blossomed, with some producers following Laird's lead and making apple brandies with the soul of whiskey (aged in charred oak barrels), and others taking inspiration from French Calvados. In cocktails, the Laird's-inspired brandies work much like American whiskey, particularly bourbon. And, not surprisingly, those that follow the French lead can work much like Calvados in a cocktail. While there are several classic cocktails that call for applejack, that term is now associated with the legal designation described above. Given that *applejack* used to be the term for pure apple brandy, to reproduce those old-school drinks accurately, we suggest going with one of the following bottles.

RECOMMENDED BOTTLES

Black Dirt Apple Jack: Made in New York State in limited quantities, Black Dirt is a delicious spirit that takes inspiration from Laird's but forges its own path. Made entirely from apples and aged in newly charred oak barrels for at least four years (though many batches are aged between five and six years), Black Dirt has many of the spicy aged characteristics of Laird's but a more appley presence and a soft, not overly aggressive flavor.

Clear Creek 2-Year Apple Brandy: This brandy is a bit of an outlier, as it's aged differently from Laird's and Black Dirt Apple Jack. It's akin to a very young French-style apple brandy, and because of its youth, it has a lot of fire and personality. We tend to use it as we would either Laird's or Black Dirt—generally where we might otherwise go with an American whiskey.

Clear Creek 8-Year Apple Brandy: Made from Golden Delicious apples, distilled in a copper pot still, and aged for at least eight years in used and new French oak barrels, this brandy has the old soul of a French Calvados, infused with the distinctive personality of the Pacific Northwest. The sweetness of the apples creates a bright and full-bodied aroma that screams, *"I'm made from apples!,"* followed by flavors concentrated by oak, with vanilla, a slight woodsy flavor, and a semisweet and smooth finish. We absolutely adore this brandy for all types of cocktails, but particularly as an accent to other aged spirits, such as pure pot still Irish whiskey, as in the Cut and Paste (page 35).

Copper & Kings Floodwall Apple Brandy: Distilled in copper pot stills and aged for a minimum of four years in used bourbon and oloroso sherry casks, the apple brandy produced by Kentucky's Copper & Kings is a unique blend of European and American aging styles. With its spicy aroma and flavor reminiscent of apple skins, it's a spirit that has some of the qualities of scotch.

Laird's 100-proof Straight Apple Brandy: Produced from West Virginia apples and distilled in Virginia, this is the benchmark American apple brandy. It's highly potent and spicy and will dominate a cocktail if not kept in check. In sour-style drinks, pair it with flavors strong enough to stand up to it, as in the Jack Rose (page 129); or, in other styles of drinks, use it as a modifier to add an unexpected dimension, as in the Pink Lady (page 130).

Laird's 88-proof 12-Year Apple Brandy: While Laird's may be best known for its high-proof straight apple brandy, the company also produces a refined and elegant pot still apple brandy. The color is a deep amber, and it has a sweet chocolaty aroma and buttery flavor with the vanilla and nutmeg notes that often result from such long aging. Though it takes inspiration from European traditions, it still has a gritty and acidic quality that makes it perfect for Old-Fashioned-style cocktails.

EAU-DE-VIE, OR FRUIT BRANDY

Literally translated as "water of life," the French term *eau-de-vie* refers to clear, colorless brandies made with fruits other than grapes. Though eaux-de-vie are occasionally aged, most are not. For the latter, because additional flavors aren't developed after distillation, the concentration of flavor and aroma is guided by a highly refined distilling process. Eaux-de-vie are successful when they capture the flavor of the fruit, which makes exploring the world's different eaux-de-vie exciting: while it's impossible to simultaneously sample slices of pear from Alsace, Oregon, and California at the same time, you can sip distillates of all three side by side. Instant flavor travel . . . it's magical.

While there isn't a universal approach to using fruit brandies in cocktails, we often have success when we employ one of these two strategies: using ½ to ¾ ounce as part of a split base, or using a smaller amount, usually 1 teaspoon to ¼ ounce, in a low-ABV cocktail that lacks body to add a highly flavorful punch. Although there are many styles of fruit brandy, in this section we'll stick with the ones we use most frequently: pear, cherry, and apricot.

PEAR BRANDY, OR POIRE WILLIAMS

In cocktails, pear brandy can act almost like a concentrated flavor extract, and as such, it can reinforce another flavor or combine with other ingredients to create an entirely new flavor—or sometimes both. For example, if pear brandy is used in a tiny proportion in a drink with a base that includes apple brandy, it will lift and amplify the apple presence. The resulting flavor is not necessarily pear plus apple, but more like Technicolor apple. Thanks to pear brandy's versatility, it's also a good match with herbal flavors, as in our Jet Set cocktail (page 281), where the freshness of pear brandy is given greater dimension

by the cocktail's accents of mint liqueur and absinthe, with its herbaceous punch. The result is a refreshing cocktail with deep layers of complexity.

RECOMMENDED BOTTLES

Clear Creek Pear Brandy: Clear Creek's pear brandy is both a nod to traditional European eaux-de-vie and a celebration of Oregon's agricultural bounty. Made with pears grown on the slopes of Mt. Hood, not far from the Portland distillery, it's bright and slightly buttery but ultimately sharply focused. We cannot recommend it more enthusiastically, for both its quality and its affordability.

Massenez Poire Williams: Much like wines from Alsace (think bone-dry Rieslings full of minerality), the brandies from that region have a clarity and sharpness that's unmistakable. Indeed, many connoisseurs of eaux-de-vie regard those made in Alsace to be the finest in the world. Massenez makes a wide variety of great eaux-de-vie and liqueurs, and their Poire Williams is one of our favorites. The Williams pear is known Stateside as the Bartlett, a juicy variety with a flavor that comes through beautifully in the spirit.

CHERRY BRANDY

Often labeled as "kirschwasser" or "kirsch," cherry brandy can be intimidating. On the nose it's all alcoholic fire and grit, and whereas other brandies tend to mirror their base ingredient's flavor, kirsch can be beguiling. After a few sips, your brain will reset, and then you'll be able to smell and taste cherry beyond the immediate onslaught of alcohol. We highly recommend using cherry brandy in small quantities—generally 1 teaspoon to ¼ ounce. One of our favorite cocktails that utilize cherry brandy is the Rye Pie (page 283).

RECOMMENDED BOTTLES

Clear Creek Cherry Brandy: In this excellent eau-de-vie, made in Oregon from fresh Oregon and Washington cherries, the sweetness of the cherries comes through on the nose and the flavor is fruity and strong.

Massenez Kirsch Vieux: Not surprisingly, one of our favorite cherry brandies hails from Alsace. Compared to Clear Creek's cherry brandy, Massenez's has a nutty, almond-like quality.

APRICOT BRANDY

We've just started experimenting with apricot brandy—a rarity among eaux-de-vie—and we're excited about the prospects. The Unidentified Floral Objects (page 284) uses apricot brandy to add a juicy impression without sweetness, a difficult task when introducing fruitiness into a cocktail—and ultimately eau-de-vie's greatest contribution to cocktaildom.

RECOMMENDED BOTTLE

Blume Marillen Apricot Eau-de-Vie: With fruit sourced from the Danube Valley in Germany, this brandy is floral, with a highly concentrated aroma of the Klosterneuburger apricots from which it's made. This can trick the brain into expecting a sweet flavor, but like other eaux-de-vie, it's dry and focused on the palate. A little goes a long way, as our Rendezvous in Chennai (page 283) demonstrates.

THE CORE: AGAVE-BASED SPIRITS

Though it may seem like a bit of a detour to head to Mexico in a chapter dedicated to the Sidecar, there's good reason to do so. After all, as mentioned at the beginning of this chapter, we could easily have based it on the Margarita, rather than the Sidecar, because the formulas for the two cocktails are so similar. Bartenders tend to obsess about and even idolize agave-based spirits—tequila, mezcal, and their cousins *bacanora* and *raicilla*—because there's a level of honesty to them: the plant from which they are made is reflected in the flavor of the liquid. There's also a lot of romance involved in spirits that remained untouched by the modern world until very recently, giving them a rustic, genuine aura. As an interesting side note, *mezcal* refers to any spirit distilled from agave (just as *brandy* refers to any spirit distilled from fruit); therefore, tequila is actually a type of mezcal.

TEQUILA

The cultivation of agave is laborious and time-consuming, and the agricultural practices used seem, from the outside, decidedly old-world—quaint, even. So too is the distillation process that's touted on bottles and in marketing literature, where masters toil over ancient pot stills, producing the spirit largely through intuition. These are great stories, but beneath them is an even more exciting tale—that of a spirit that's shed the stigma of being cheap firewater to become highly respected alongside the world's most revered liquors.

There's a simple distinction between good and bad tequila: Those that are made with 100 percent agave and those that are *mixto*, meaning they're produced from a mixture of agave and other sugars. While mixto tequilas are more affordable than 100 percent agave tequilas, they are also hugely inferior. We only use 100 percent agave tequila. When made well, it's a refined and elegant spirit that highlights the vegetal personality of the agave plant.

Like many spirits, tequila is produced in a range of ages, and almost all have a role to play in cocktails. Blanco tequila, the lightest style, sees no time in oak, and at its best is a bright and vegetal spirit that's wonderful in citrusy cocktails like the Margarita. Reposado tequilas spend between two months and one year aging in barrels, which gives them some of the characteristics of other aged spirits: clove and cinnamon spice, vanilla, and a slight sweetness. Reposado tequilas are versatile, working well in citrusy and boozy cocktails alike. Añejos spend even more time in barrels—one to three years—and therefore have the deeper and spicier flavors of oak. Añejo tequila can be quite expensive, so we reserve it for the occasional Manhattan variation. The final age statement is extra añejo, for tequilas that are aged for three years or longer, but these are almost always far too expensive for mixing. The following recommended bottles are arranged by age.

RECOMMENDED BOTTLES

Cimarrón Blanco: An affordable high-quality blanco, Cimarrón has a broad vegetal flavor with notes of funky white pepper. The overall personality of this tequila tilts a little toward the savory, but it's just as versatile as the Pueblo Viejo described below. We use it as a go-to for shaken cocktails like the Margarita.

Pueblo Viejo Blanco: Pueblo Viejo's blanco is bright, peppery, strong in personality, wonderfully mixable—and surprisingly affordable. It's one of our favorites in Margaritas and other shaken cocktails that include citrus.

Siembra Azul Blanco: Produced by David Suro, a champion of ethical and quality tequila production, Siembra Azul is clean and floral in aroma and fruity on the palate. The quality of this tequila shines through in all cocktails, from citrusy drinks to stirred cocktails. As a bonus, it's also reasonably priced.

Siete Leguas Blanco: Blanco tequila isn't just for shaken cocktails; we love its vegetal character in stirred cocktails, too. Though the Cimarrón and Pueblo Viejo blanco tequilas can make good stirred cocktails, we tend to use bottles with a bit more sophistication when matching tequila with fortified wine. Siete Leguas is a beautifully produced blanco tequila: bright, earthy, and velvety smooth. The hint of vanilla in its flavor profile makes it a good match for blanc vermouth and liqueurs, especially peach liqueur.

Cimarrón Resposado: Cimarrón's reposado is a rare exception among aged tequilas, being only a bit more expensive than the company's blanco. While it isn't as refined as some reposados, it will add aged complexity to a cocktail without breaking the bank.

Don Julio Reposado: In tequila, we find ourselves steering our attention to smaller producers because they often offer spirits with more personality, using traditional methods to produce tequilas that are intensely flavorful and unique. Unfortunately, their tequilas aren't always widely available. Don Julio is a major producer of tequilas that are both widely available and of consistently high quality. The reposado strikes a good balance between rich, vegetal agave and the cinnamon and toasty oak spice of aging. It's a great addition to stirred cocktails, and can also be used in small amounts to season cocktails with its spice notes.

El Tesoro Reposado: We love everything made by El Tesoro, but the reposado is where their tequila shines. Here, the influence of oak aging has clearly been applied with grace, with used bourbon barrels creating a subtle oak sweetness that doesn't overpower the clarity present in unaged tequilas—a balance we prefer in aged tequilas. We love using this tequila for Old-Fashioned-style drinks, though it's equally at home next to sweet vermouth in Manhattan riffs.

Pueblo Viejo Añejo: Shockingly affordable for an añejo, this tequila is laced with sweet vanilla and orange notes that linger over the agave's vegetal personality. This makes it a great stand-in for bourbon, especially in citrusy cocktails. And if paired with bourbon, it can also work well in Manhattan-style cocktails. However, despite its age, it lacks the structure to be the star of the show in an Old-Fashioned.

MEZCAL

In recent years, mezcal has transfixed spirit and cocktail lovers because of its extremely distinctive flavor and the romance of its heritage as a peasant spirit created by artisan producers following many generations of traditions. Indeed, many spirit enthusiasts have all but abandoned tequila for mezcal because, unlike tequila, it is still a small-scale artisanal product. Mezcals are most frequently bottled unaged (blanco or *joven*—a term meaning "young"), though there are a handful of producers who age mezcal in oak barrels. In our opinion, the unique flavors of mezcal aren't universally benefited by oak, but there is one producer of a reposado that we love to sip neat: Los Amantes. (Their joven is exceptional, too.)

RECOMMENDED BOTTLES

Del Maguey Vida: The entry-level bottle in Del Maguey's growing collection of truly spectacular mezcals, Vida is meant for cocktails. With the smoky characteristics typical of mezcal and smooth vegetal undertones, Vida is versatile enough to be the primary spirit in a cocktail or to play a supporting role to another spirit, like a blanco or reposado tequila.

Nuestra Soledad La Compañia Ejutla: Another affordable option, this mezcal is a bit less smoky than others but is packed with bright herbal aromas and flavors (mint and cilantro) and fresh tropical fruits, including mango, and has a green bell pepper finish.

While other mezcals are often noticeably assertive and overpower other spirits, this bottle plays well with blanco tequila and even gin.

Los Amantes Reposado: Though they aren't as commonly available as other mezcals, time and again we find ourselves obsessed with the offerings from Los Amantes, particularly their reposado. We almost always prefer unaged mezcal, which celebrates the inherent qualities of agave and traditional production methods. However, this spirit, which is aged for up to eight months in French oak barrels, is beautifully balanced, with a very modest influence from the oak—more rounding off the edges of the mezcal than intensely flavoring it.

BACANORA AND RAICILLA

From the Mexican state of Sonora, made from the agave plant, Bacanora will often follow a similar production method and style to mezcal: the piña is cooked in earthen pits lined with volcanic rock and heated with mesquite charcoal. After fermentation and two distillation runs, Bacanora is cut with water to the desired proof, usually 40% to 50% ABV, depending on the producer. Bacanora has an intensely earthy and savory flavor, almost like barbecued meat.

Though it has a reputation as a Mexican form of moonshine, Raicilla is gaining traction with quality producers. Produced in the Mexican state of Jalisco, Raicilla is made from various types of agave that are cooked in above-ground ovens, though there's often a hint of the smokiness of mezcal. Raicillas often come in two types: de la coasta (of the coast) and de la sierra (of the mountains). Each have characteristics similar to the elevation differences in tequila: low, earthier flavors from the coast and sharper flavors from the mountains.

EXPERIMENTING WITH THE CORE

As we've demonstrated in previous chapters, one of the easiest ways to create new cocktails is to simply swap out the base spirit for a different one. Sometimes this works, but often it's necessary to adjust the amounts of other ingredients in the cocktails. Let's take a look at how that works by considering the Sidecar and its close relative, the Margarita. If you were to start with our Sidecar root recipe (page 152) and simply substitute blanco tequila for the Cognac and lime juice for lemon, the resulting drink would be dry, vegetal, and overwhelmingly orangey. Why is that? The answer lies in the base spirit. Cognac is softened by years in oak barrels and has a greater perceived richness than blanco tequila. In addition, the Cognac melds with the sweetness of the Cointreau to create a harmonious core flavor. Simply substituting tequila for the Cognac yields a drink that's disjointed and noticeably boozy, with the intense flavor of the liqueur overpowering the tequila. To correct this and allow the tequila to shine through, we back off on the Cointreau a bit, increase the amount of tequila, and add a bit more simple syrup to compensate for the sweetness lost due to decreasing the amount of liqueur, even though our personal preferences almost always skew toward the dry side.

That said, we know that people differ in their preferences for sweet and sour, so we recommend that you try the following Goldilocks experiment to determine where your own preferences lie. As usual, for the purposes of this experiment, we forgo the garnish.

Margarita

CLASSIC

Lime wedge

Kosher salt, for rimming

2 ounces Siembra Azul blanco tequila

¾ ounce Cointreau

¾ ounce fresh lime juice

¼ ounce simple syrup (page 45)

Rub the lime wedge along the upper ½ inch of a double Old-Fashioned glass, halfway around the circumference, then roll the wet portion in the salt. Put 1 large ice cube in the glass. Shake the remaining ingredients with ice, then strain into the prepared glass. No garnish.

¾ ounce Cointreau
¾ ounce fresh lime juice

Use the lime wedge and salt to rim a double Old-Fashioned glass as in the preceding recipe, then put 1 large ice cube in the glass. Shake the remaining ingredients with ice, then strain into the prepared glass. No garnish.

¾ ounce Cointreau
¾ ounce fresh lime juice
½ ounce simple syrup (page 45)

Use the lime wedge and salt to rim a double Old-Fashioned glass as in the preceding recipe, then put 1 large ice cube in the glass. Shake the remaining ingredients with ice, then strain into the prepared glass. No garnish.

Margarita (Sweet)

FURTHER EXPERIMENTING WITH THE CORE

Let's get even more specific with how individual spirit choices can impact balance. The classic Between the Sheets is a simple Sidecar variation that splits Cognac with rum—a recipe much like the one below can be found in countless books. Knowing what we do about Cognac (see page 156) and rum (see page 107), we know that there is huge difference in flavor and perceived sweetness between brands.

Between the Sheets

CLASSIC

The spec for the classic Between the Sheets cocktail has a split base of Cognac and rum.

- **¾ ounce Cognac**
- **¾ ounce rum**
- **¾ ounce Cointreau**
- **¾ ounce fresh lemon juice**

Shake all the ingredients with ice, then strain into a chilled coupe. No garnish.

Without guidance, you may choose a VS Cognac and an unaged Spanish-style rum, resulting in a boozy and thin-flavored cocktail. But what if you went to the other end of the spectrum and use a funky Jamaican-style rum mixed with a big XO Cognac? The drink would be rich, decadent, pungent—and totally out of balance. With an understanding of our spirits and how they interact, we're able to make choices that work in harmony together.

Between the Sheets

OUR IDEAL RECIPE

Between the Sheets is a good cocktail for exploring what specific bottles bring to a cocktail. Our house spec for this classic has a split base of youthful VS Cognac paired with the large personality of Jamaican rum, balanced by Pierre Ferrand's dry curaçao. If we had stuck with Cointreau, as in the classic Sidecar (page 151), we might not need any additional sweetener, but because the Pierre Ferrand is so dry, we include a bit of Demerara Gum Syrup to give the cocktail more body.

- **1 ounce Paul Beau VS Cognac**
- **1 ounce Appleton Estate Reserve Blend rum**
- **¾ ounce Pierre Ferrand dry curaçao**
- **¾ ounce fresh lemon juice**
- **1 teaspoon Demerara Gum Syrup (page 54)**

Shake all the ingredients with ice, then strain into a chilled coupe. No garnish.

White Lady

CLASSIC

Another instructive example of simple core substitution is the White Lady, an established riff on the Sidecar that plugs in gin for the Cognac. As with the Margarita, if the amounts of ingredients remain true to the Sidecar template, the gin would be overshadowed by the orange liqueur and have a punishing astringency. So to rebalance this classic cocktail, we increase the amount of gin to boost its personality, back off on the Cointreau, and add a bit of simple syrup.

The White Lady also illustrates how egg white affects a cocktail and impacts the drinker's perception of balance. Though we cover the use of egg whites elsewhere (see pages 253 and 264), within the Sidecar family they can take on another dimension. Because the egg white's frothiness expands the drink's overall volume, it spreads the cocktail's flavor throughout that volume.

2 ounces Plymouth gin
½ ounce Cointreau
¾ ounce fresh lemon juice
¼ ounce simple syrup (page 45)
1 egg white
Garnish: 1 lemon twist

Dry shake all the ingredients, then shake again with ice. Double strain into a chilled coupe.

Express the lemon twist over the drink, then set it on the edge of the glass.

Peaches
and Smoke

Rational Thought

DEVON TARBY, 2017

One of our favorite ways to show
novice bartenders how to use pear
brandy in a cocktail is by using it in a
split base in a classic Sidecar. In this
cocktail, it's paired with Paul Beau
Cognac, chosen specifically for its
textural earthiness, reminiscent of
pear skin. A hint of cinnamon spice in
the form of a syrup brings warmth that
rounds off the sharp boozy edges.

1 ounce Paul Beau VSOP Cognac
½ ounce Clear Creek pear brandy
1 ounce Pierre Ferrand dry curaçao
¾ ounce fresh lemon juice
**1 teaspoon Cinnamon Syrup
(page 52)**

Shake all the ingredients with ice, then
strain into a chilled coupe. No garnish.

Peaches and Smoke

ALEX DAY, 2014

Low-ABV cocktails are becoming
more popular, for a variety of good
reasons. For our part, we admit that
we love being able to enjoy multiple
drinks in a session without getting
too tipsy, and the same is true for
many of our guests. One approach
to creating them is to split the core
between a larger portion of fortified
wine and a small measure of strong
spirits. In a Sidecar, the strong spirit
can then work with a flavorful liqueur
to balance and season the drink. Note
that because fortified wine often has
some sweetness, it may be necessary
to use a bit less liqueur.

1 peach wedge
1½ ounces Lillet rosé
**½ ounce Pierre Ferrand Ambre
Cognac**
**1 teaspoon Laphroaig 10-year
scotch**
¾ ounce Giffard Crème de Pêche
¾ ounce fresh lemon juice
¼ ounce simple syrup (page 45)
Garnish: 1 peach wedge

In a shaker, muddle the peach. Add the
remaining ingredients and shake with
ice, then double strain into a chilled
coupe. Garnish with the peach wedge.

Beausoleil

DEVON TARBY, 2016

The Beausoleil's main flavor components (dry vermouth, limoncello,
and lemon juice) closely mirror those
in a classic Sidecar. But because the
vermouth is fairly low in proof, we
bolster it with a bit of grappa and also
increase the amount of simple syrup—
two adjustments that prevent the
cocktail from tasting watery.

1½ ounces Dolin dry vermouth
**½ ounce Clear Creek Pinot Noir
grappa**
1 ounce Meletti limoncello
¾ ounce fresh lemon juice
¼ ounce simple syrup (page 45)
Garnish: 1 thyme sprig

Shake all the ingredients with ice, then
strain into a Collins glass filled with
ice. Garnish with the thyme sprig.

THE BALANCE AND SEASONING: LIQUEUR

We would love to write a book about various liqueurs and their potential cocktail applications, as there are hundreds of different bottles, each with its own unique properties. But for the purposes of this book, we'll offer a broad outline of what liqueurs are and how their qualities, such as sweetness and alcohol content, interact in a cocktail.

Liqueurs are a combination of alcohol, flavoring, and sweetener. Though they may seem to be all about the flavor, when using them in cocktails, it's important to consider their sweetness and proof, as both can have a profound effect on a cocktail's balance. While their sweetness is sometimes derived from natural fruit sugars, it's much more common to add sugar. But the bigger issue is that bottles seldom give any indication of how much sugar is present. There are some broad categories of liqueur that can provide a rough indication of sweetness. Fruit-focused liqueurs such as cassis or framboise are often quite sweet, whereas citrus liqueurs like orange curaçao can be shockingly dry.

Regarding proof, this must, by law, appear on the label. Generally speaking, liqueurs must typically be at least 20% ABV in order to be shelf stable, though many are much higher proof, with green Chartreuse clocking in at a massive 55% ABV. Those with a low ABV will taste sweeter, whereas higher-proof liqueurs will be perceived as more dry.

FRUIT LIQUEURS

Almost any type of fruit you can think of has been used to flavor liqueur. One thing to watch out for with all fruit liqueurs: There's a huge difference between quality liqueurs and bargain brands. There's nothing delicious about an artificial flavor, so seek out the good stuff.

ORANGE LIQUEUR

A number of proprietary brands have become synonymous with orange liqueur (aka triple sec or curaçao), with Cointreau and Grand Marnier being the most famous. Importantly, curaçao isn't flavored solely with orange peels; it also includes spices that support the orange flavor. They can be made using a neutral spirit, as Cointreau is, or using a richer brandy base, as Grand Marnier is, with each bringing something different to drinks.

Because curaçaos are generally dry (at least by liqueur standards), they are exceptionally versatile. In the Sidecar, orange curaçao is a significant component in the drink—generally a full ounce—making it a key flavor in the cocktail. When used in lesser quantities, it can support the flavors of a fortified wine, as in the Troubled Leisure (page 284). It can also be used in tiny measures to add an orange-laced pop of flavor to a drink, as in Jump in the Line (page 262).

RECOMMENDED BOTTLES

Cointreau: The most iconic of the orange curaçaos, Cointreau is clean and versatile and a favorite in shaken drinks like Sidecars and Margaritas. Thanks to its relative dryness, it also works well in stirred cocktails, like the Nurse Hazel (page 282).

Grand Marnier: A foundation of aged Cognac gives this orange liqueur greater depth that's delicious, though it can limit Grand Marnier's usefulness in cocktails. We're particularly fond of mixing it with rum in classics like the Mai Tai (page 136) and the Dark Horse (page 280).

GRAPEFRUIT LIQUEUR

Often referred to as *pamplemousse* (French for "grapefruit"), grapefruit liqueur is a newcomer that's taken the sour cocktail category by storm. With a balanced sweet and tart flavor profile, grapefruit liqueur can be added to citrusy cocktails to deepen the impression of fruitiness. We rarely use more than ½ ounce, and we get some of our best results by adding ½ ounce of the liqueur and ½ ounce of simple syrup to sour-style cocktails.

RECOMMENDED BOTTLE

Giffard Crème de Pamplemousse: This liqueur is intensely aromatic and has a great balance between sweetness and bright acidity. It's become the new St-Germain—a liqueur that makes every drink it touches better.

BERRY LIQUEUR

Deeply sweet and juicy, berry liqueurs are pure decadence, mimicking the flavor of luscious ripe fruit, though some, such as cassis (black currant), have a tart astringency that can quickly overpower cocktails. In drinks, we use them in small quantities—generally ¼ to ½ ounce.

RECOMMENDED BOTTLES

Clear Creak Raspberry Liqueur: This bottle has a good balance of sweet and tart without being too jammy, but a little goes a long way. In citrus cocktails, we'll often combine this liqueur with an equal amount of simple syrup to balance fresh lemon juice. It's a particularly good companion for bitter aperitifs like Aperol and Campari.

Corpse Reviver #2,
page 188

Gabriel Boudier Crème de Cassis de Dijon: A classic addition to the Kir Royale (page 223), this fruity, tannic cassis is surprisingly dry, allowing as much as ¼ ounce to be added without making a cocktail cloying.

Giffard Crème de Fraise des Bois: Made from wild strawberries, this liqueur has a lot of depth and personality, with a subtle underlying herbal quality like fresh grass.

STONE FRUIT LIQUEUR

Of all the fruit liqueurs, apricot and peach are our favorites in cocktails; we use the former in our Normandie Club Martini #2 (page 282) to provide a whisper of tart fruit.

RECOMMENDED BOTTLES

Giffard Abricot du Roussillon: Made by macerating Roussillon apricots in alcohol, this liqueur has a Technicolor apricot color, and an aroma of dried apricot.

Massenez Crème de Pêche: Massenez's is by far our favorite peach liqueur: with little cooked flavor, it's useful in citrusy and stirred cocktails, where it keeps the overall flavor profile light and refreshing.

PEAR LIQUEUR

We like to use pear-flavored liqueurs to add a bit of sweetness and texture to cocktails.

RECOMMENDED BOTTLES

Clear Creek Pear Liqueur: The Clear Creek pear brandy on page 162 is the base for this liqueur, which makes for a deeply structured and complex spirit. While the flavor of the Mathilde pear liqueur described below is dominated by fresh pear, Clear Creek's offering has more roasted flavors, making it a brilliant match for

aged spirits and oxidized wines, such as amontillado and oloroso sherries.

Mathilde Pear Liqueur: With its focused aroma and flavor of fresh pears, Mathilde pear liqueur is versatile in many types of cocktails. Like Clear Creek's pear liqueur, it utilizes a pear brandy base, giving it a flavor profile that's all fresh pear, all the time. We opt for this liqueur when we want to add a sharp pear texture to citrusy cocktails.

MARASCHINO LIQUEUR

A beguiling liqueur that captures the attention of most cocktail enthusiasts at some point, maraschino liqueur is the secret weapon in many of the world's cult cocktails, vintage and contemporary alike. The Aviation (page 278) and the Martinez (page 86) wouldn't be possible without the funky punch of maraschino, a liqueur made from sour marasca cherries from the coastal region of Croatia. Because the liqueur is made from both the fruit and the crushed pits, it has an almond-like flavor. It's a powerful distilled spirit similar to a sweetened pomace brandy. The end result is a liqueur that has a funky and exceedingly complex flavor.

RECOMMENDED BOTTLES

Luxardo Maraschino: The most widely available maraschino liqueur, Luxardo is true to form: funky, complex, and sweet. The flavor of cherries is nuanced and like nothing you've experienced before. On its own, it can be a lot to handle, but when added to drinks in moderation, it enhances other flavors in incredible ways. We tend to use Luxardo maraschino liqueur in cocktails that contain citrus.

Maraska Maraschino: Though made from the same base material and using the same process as Luxardo's maraschino liqueur, the Maraska is sweeter and has a more pronounced cherry flavor. We tend to use it in tiny amounts (1 teaspoon to ¼ ounce) as a seasoning in stirred cocktails like the Brooklyn (page 87).

FLORAL AND HERBAL LIQUEURS

While fruit liqueurs get a lot of attention, several liqueurs showcase the aromas and flavors of flowers, with elderflower and violet liqueurs being the most widely used.

ELDERFLOWER LIQUEUR

Also known as "bartender's ketchup" because everything tastes better with it, St-Germain elderflower liqueur appeared on the market in 2007 and set the stage for elderflower liqueur to be tossed into damn near every type of drink. St-Germain started the trend, with several other producers rapidly following suit.

RECOMMENDED BOTTLE

St-Germain: You've probably been living under a rock if you haven't heard (or experienced) St-Germain. With its sweet, floral aroma and full-bodied flavor reminiscent of dessert wine, St-Germain is extremely versatile. We honestly can't think of a spirit it couldn't mix well with. In tiny amounts, St-Germain can add juiciness to a cocktail without making it noticeably sweet, as in the Night Light (page 282). In larger amounts, it can serve as one of the base spirits if balanced with a bit of acid, as in the Normandie Club Spritz #3 (page 225).

VIOLET LIQUEUR

Fundamental in several classic cocktails, the Aviation being the most famous, violet liqueurs can add a mysterious flavor to cocktails when used in moderation, but when used in larger amounts, they overpower drinks and make them taste like liquid soap or perfume. There are a couple of styles available: one is crème de violette, which is sweet and low proof; in the United States, the other style is represented by a single bottle, Crème Yvette, which is higher in proof and dosed with other flavors. These two styles aren't interchangeable unless you adjust the sweetness or base spirit of the cocktail.

RECOMMENDED BOTTLE

Giffard Crème de Violette: Deeply purple in color and with a vibrant violet aroma, this bottle has just the right level of sweetness to work well in cocktails. It is sweet, but the sugar doesn't dumb down the floral violets.

CRÈME DE MENTHE AND MENTHE DE PASTILLE

Mint liqueurs are a great way of adding a cooling and refreshing quality to drinks. A vital component of the Stinger (page 13) and the Grasshopper (page 268), crème de menthe is traditionally made by steeping dried mint in alcohol for several weeks and then straining out the leaves and adding sugar. There are versions that are colored green, either naturally or with food coloring; these are generally identical in flavor to the clear versions.

RECOMMENDED BOTTLES

Giffard Menthe-Pastille: Try it as the French do, over crushed ice, or in classic crème de menthe cocktails. Alternatively, add just a bit to a cocktail that features fresh mint to accentuate its minty quality, as in the Salvation Julep (page 283), or use a tiny bit in cocktails that include herbal liqueurs to amplify their flavors, as in the Greatest Dancer (page 281).

Tempus Fugit Crème de Menthe: Made with both peppermint and spearmint, plus secret botanical ingredients, this liqueur has a deeply complex spectrum of minty flavors. As always, complexity offers a great opportunity for flavors to match with the spirits or other ingredients in a cocktail.

HERBAL LIQUEURS

Up to this point, all of the liqueurs we've discussed draw their inspiration from a single flavor; even when other ingredients are added, such as spice, this is done to emphasize the key flavor. But liqueurs can also feature a combination of many powerful flavors that synergistically create a new flavor—Bénédictine, Galliano, and Chartreuse to name a few. Most of these liqueurs were originally created for medicinal purposes, the thinking being that a few sips of a highly flavorful elixir could ensure health and long life. Because so much flavor is crammed into then, they often aren't terribly pleasant to drink on their own; the experience can be a crushing onslaught of liquor-soaked herbs, barks, roots, flowers, and citrus. Indeed, they tend to be quite high in proof, so use them in small quantities and consider adding more sweetener to tame their flavors.

RECOMMENDED BOTTLES

Bénédictine: One of the more approachable liqueurs in this category, Bénédictine has broad flavor, with honey-like sweetness laced through earthy spices. It pairs well with aged brown spirits and apple brandies.

Chareau California Aloe Liqueur: There's more to this new aloe-based liqueur, introduced in 2014, than meets the eye. Built on a backbone of unaged brandy, it features layers of aloe, cucumber, lemon peel, muskmelon, and spearmint flavors that make for an incredibly complex liqueur. Although aloe dominates the first impression, let it linger and you'll find a refreshing and complex herbal quality that can contribute greatly to a drink. While it is a liqueur and therefore has added sugar, it's surprisingly dry. In cocktails, we tend to use it more like a spirit than a liqueur and often add a bit more sugar if substituting it for another liqueur, as in the Lily Pad (page 184).

Chartreuse: Produced by Carthusian monks at the base of the French Alps for several centuries, Chartreuse

has a long and storied history. There are two widely available types of Chartreuse: yellow (80 proof) and green (110 proof). Both have an unmistakable woodsy aroma and sweet, tingly herbal flavor that adds incredible dimension and complexity to cocktails. Thanks to its (relatively) lower proof, yellow Chartreuse can be used in larger quantities—typically up to ½ ounce. Green Chartreuse, on the other hand, can quickly dominate a cocktail, so it's best used in measured doses to add a distinct herbal complexity. Some exceptions, such as the Bijou (page 89), rely on a large dose of green Chartreuse to create a highly complex cocktail that's balanced by the bitterness of Campari.

Galliano l'Autentico: Galliano has strong flavors of anise, juniper berry, cinnamon, and especially vanilla. This dominance of vanilla sweetness sets Galliano apart from other herbal liqueurs and makes it a clever way of adding a subtle vanilla character to a cocktail, though we tend to use it in small quantities—typically less than ½ ounce (see Aces and Eights, page 278)—as it can quickly overshadow other flavors.

Strega: This liqueur has a distinctive yellow color courtesy of saffron, but that's just one of over seventy flavorings it incorporates. The result is a unique flavor that's savory with light anise notes. Strega can be used in much the same way as yellow Chartreuse, though its flavor is more challenging in cocktails. We typically use it in modest quantities: just 1 teaspoon will add dimension to a stirred cocktail, or it can be used alongside simple syrup in a sour.

RICH LIQUEURS

Chapter 6 explores the Flip and other rich cocktails, and that's where we'll focus on the use of rich, sweet liqueurs, such as crème de cacao, vanilla liqueur, coffee liqueur, and cream liqueurs. However, we'll go ahead and discuss them here, while we're on the topic of liqueurs. These liqueurs are often maligned for their sweetness, but many are highly versatile ingredients that can do more than just flavor a cocktail. Used in moderation, they can season cocktails without overpowering them.

CRÈME DE CACAO

Thanks to the former popularity of the Brandy Alexander (page 257), crème de cacao has been a bar staple for a century. The decadence of that cocktail typecast crème de cacao as a specialist in drinks at the rich end of the spectrum. However, other classic cocktails do use it in a more nuanced way, an example being the 20th Century (page 179), where it's combined with gin, Lillet blanc, and lemon juice. Crème de cacao is available in two versions: light and dark. The dark is often colored with caramel coloring, which deepens the flavor in a direction we usually avoid. The lighter variety, white crème de cacao, is our preferred choice for cocktail use.

RECOMMENDED BOTTLE

Giffard White Crème de Cacao: Made from cacao beans and a small amount of vanilla, Giffard's crème de cacao is a high-quality, reliable option. We tend to be very careful in how much is added to a cocktail: any more than ¾ ounce and this liqueur tends to make a cocktail taste like powdered chocolate milk.

VANILLA LIQUEUR

Though there are many liqueurs that contain vanilla, a handful focus on its flavor. Because vanilla can dumb down other flavors, we tend to use vanilla liqueurs in moderation, especially in cocktails featuring aged spirits that already have vanilla qualities thanks to the influence of oak. Vanilla liqueurs also tend to be quite sweet—another good reason to use them with restraint.

RECOMMENDED BOTTLE

Giffard Vanille de Madagascar: Flavored with extracts of Madagascar vanilla, this is a straightforward, single-flavor liqueur on its own. In cocktails, we find it most useful when we want to draw out sweet flavors already present in a drink without making it overtly sweet, as in see the Deadpan (page 23).

COFFEE LIQUEUR

If you've taken the plunge into artisanal coffee, you're probably all too aware of coffee's instability. The sweet and focused flavors of a freshly brewed cup of coffee from freshly ground beans can rapidly deteriorate. That illuminates the problem with some coffee liqueurs: while they do have coffee flavor, they don't have any of the complexity of extremely fresh, high-quality coffee. Luckily, a side effect of the explosion of quality coffee roasters is that there are now many artisanal coffee liqueurs in local markets. We highly recommend exploring any that are available to you. For our recommended bottles, we've chosen two that are widely available.

RECOMMENDED BOTTLES

Caffé Lolita Licor de Café: Produced in Mexico, this liqueur has a strong coffee flavor without being cloyingly sweet, making it more versatile in cocktails. While it can be used in larger quantities in classic recipes like the White Russian (page 267), it can also be added in small quantities to impart a subtle coffee accent, as in the Coco and Ice (page 279).

Galliano Ristretto: Taking inspiration from strong espresso, Galliano's coffee liqueur is intensely complex, with cinnamon and chocolate in addition to coffee. It's best used in tiny amounts to give the slight impression of coffee without overshadowing a cocktail's core flavor, as in the Aces and Eights (page 278).

EXPERIMENTING WITH THE BALANCE AND SEASONING

Given everything you've just learned about the wide world of liqueurs, you're probably eager to try some Sidecar variations that feature liqueurs other than curaçao. This can be a much more daunting proposition than experimenting with a Daiquiri, where citrus provides both the balance and the seasoning, precisely because liqueurs vary so widely in proof and sugar content, not to mention flavor.

There is a whole world of liqueurs that can, in theory, be inserted into the Sidecar template to create new drinks. Before doing so, we need to learn how a given liqueur stacks up next to orange curaçao in terms of proof, sweetness, and flavor. While an orange curaçao like Cointreau is relatively dry and mild in flavor, it nonetheless contains sugar and a low proof. What if we swapped in another liqueur with even more proof *and* sweetness, like green Chartreuse in the Last Word (page 179)? Or, in the other direction, what if you were to use a liqueur lower in proof and higher in sweetness (say, white crème de cacao in the 20th Century, page 179). You would need to accommodate by upping the core and lowering the liqueur to find balance. The following cocktails demonstrate how the characteristics of each substitution will dictate the ingredient amounts in the final cocktail.

Crop Top

20th Century

CLASSIC

Swap rich crème de cacao for the Cointreau—and a little Lillet blanc to stretch out the sweetness of the cacao—and you've got yourself the 20th Century, a chocolaty cocktail that doesn't taste like liquid dessert. (You'll notice that this cocktail calls for a full 1½ ounces of gin—an adjustment that's necessary because crème de cacao is sweeter and lower in proof than Cointreau.) Thanks to the bright botanicals from the gin and the acidity from both the lemon juice and the Lillet blanc, the drink gives the impression of fruity cacao nibs, rather than a decadent chocolate bar.

- **1½ ounces London dry gin**
- **¾ ounce Lillet blanc**
- **¾ ounce white crème de cacao**
- **¾ ounce fresh lemon juice**

Shake all the ingredients with ice, then double strain into a chilled coupe. No garnish.

Last Word

CLASSIC

The classic Last Word uses intensely herbaceous green Chartreuse and funky maraschino liqueur in place of the Cointreau. The two liqueurs are front and center and bring a lot of proof to the cocktail, thereby requiring the gin be reduced in proportion. In this case, the green Chartreuse and maraschino are both the dominant flavor, bringing sweetness to the cocktail and balancing the acidity of the lime juice, while the gin helps dry the cocktail out.

- **¾ ounce London dry gin**
- **¾ ounce green Chartreuse**
- **¾ ounce Luxardo maraschino liqueur**
- **¾ ounce fresh lime juice**

Shake all the ingredients with ice, then strain into a chilled coupe. No garnish.

Crop Top

DEVON TARBY, 2013

In this cocktail, we've modified the Last Word (see left), which packs a serious punch, to create a subtler, lighter cocktail. We use an amaro as part of the base, resulting in a drink that's significantly more refreshing than the dense Last Word. Its flavor combination, grapefruit-laden pamplemousse combined with the cinnamon spice notes of Amaro Montenegro, was directly inspired by Donn's Mix No. 1, a classic tiki syrup made with grapefruit juice and cinnamon syrup.

- **¾ ounce Beefeater 24 gin**
- **¾ ounce Amaro Montenegro**
- **¾ ounce Giffard Crème de Pamplemousse**
- **¾ ounce fresh lemon juice**

Shake all the ingredients with ice, then strain into a chilled Nick & Nora glass. No garnish.

EXPLORING TECHNIQUE: RIMMING

Because we feel that a properly balanced drink doesn't need an extra dose of sugar or salt, we rarely rim cocktails. But some classic cocktails, such as the Paloma, Margarita, Bloody Mary—and the Sidecar—are traditionally served in a rimmed glass, and we do honor that heritage when making those drinks—and sometimes when making variations on those drinks, as a way of connecting them with their history.

We divide rims into two sizes: skinny and fat. For salt, sugar, and other standard rims, we cover about half of the rim with a ½-inch swath of the rimming ingredients. When using more pungent ingredients, such as chile powder and other spices, we use a narrower rim. The reason we rim only half the glass is so the guest can customize each sip or avoid the rim altogether.

HOW TO RIM A GLASS

In most cases, we use a citrus wedge to wet the rim of the glass, preferably the same citrus used in the drink. (If there's no citrus juice in the drink, we use lemon juice, which has a more neutral flavor.) We also like how the flavors of citrus and salt and/or sugar balance each other out to create an unobtrusive rim, but in some cases we use alternate liquids, such as coconut oil or a sugar syrup, depending on the flavor profile of the drink. Importantly, we only wet the outside of the glass; any rimming ingredients on the inside of the glass will probably fall into the drink and affect its flavor.

After wetting the outside of the glass, we roll it in the rimming ingredient. We spread rimming ingredients in an even layer on a flat plate to make it easier to apply an even amount to the rim. Then, after rimming the glass, we hold it upside down and tap it lightly to shake off any excess granules.

RIMMING INGREDIENTS

The classic Sidecar is usually served in a glass with a sugared rim. This probably arose because of the inherent dryness of the cocktail, but it may also have been a case of gilding the lily, since sugar was still a luxurious commodity when the Sidecar was created. That said, we feel that our Sidecar recipe is balanced enough that it doesn't need any extra sugar, so we usually omit the rim when following our own spec. When we do add a sugar rim, we like to use fine-grain cane sugar. Denser sugars like demerara and muscovado are too chunky and also too flavorful, which can dumb down the flavor of the drink. Ultimately, it' a personal choice: Consider how a sugar rim will impact the balance of the cocktail. If you feel a drink will benefit from being tilted in a sweeter direction, go for it!

As for salt rims, though we do use them more often than sugar rims, we often accomplish the same things by adding a few drops of Salt Solution (page 298). Either way, a bit of salinity can help lift the flavors of bright fruit liqueurs or help tame bitter ingredients. Salt also enhances the savory or mineral flavors in sherry, gin, and other spirits with savory flavors. Lastly, salt can help meld the flavors of dense amari and other ingredients that have chocolate or caramel notes. When we opt for a salt rim, the type of salt depends on how much texture we want to add to the experience. While we typically use kosher salt, we sometimes choose a flaky sea salt to add some crunch.

These days, we often combine multiple ingredients in our rims. This allows us to add aromatic ingredients, such as black pepper and other pungent spices, or dehydrated citrus powder, which we make by drying citrus slices in a dehydrator, then pulverizing them into powder. Experimenting with more complex rim recipes is a lot of fun and can add another layer of creativity to cocktails. Just keep in mind that they should always enhance what's in the glass, not distract from it or overpower it.

OUR FAVORITE COCKTAIL RIMS

Specific salts: pink Himalayan, kosher, sea salt, sel gris

Smoked salt

Salt + pepper

Salt + fennel pollen

Salt + ground celery seed

Cayenne pepper or other ground chiles

Cayenne pepper + salt

Sugar + ground cinnamon

Dehydrated and pulverized fruit: strawberry, raspberry, and so on

Dehydrated and pulverized citrus: lemon, lime, or grapefruit

Pink Himalayan salt + pulverized dehydrated pink grapefruit + citric acid + coconut oil

GLASSWARE: THE COUPE

Our favorite glass for the Sidecar and other shaken drinks served up, as well as many stirred cocktails and the occasional Champagne Cocktail, is the coupe. It has a wide, shallow bowl, with sides that taper toward the top. For years we used standard, all-purpose coupes at our bars because they were the only affordable, widely available option. These hold only 5½ ounces of liquid, which means a standard cocktail fills the glass completely—until some of it inevitably sloshes out during transport. And unless you've perfectly dialed in the amount of dilution with your shake, it's likely that a bit of the cocktail will be left in the shaker after you've filled the glass. With a Sidecar (or Daiquiri, for that matter), that's especially problematic because the leftover bit in the shaker is often that fantastic white froth. A Sidecar without its desired foamy head is a bummer.

Now we use coupes that hold about 7 ounces of liquid. This extra capacity leaves room in the glass to play around with, allowing us to add bubbly ingredients and other flourishes to the top of the drink. Our current favorite model is the Retro Coupe Glass made by Urban Bar, which holds 7 ounces of liquid and is durable enough to withstand the wear and tear at a busy bar.

Whenever possible, we pre-chill our cocktail coupes. While one of the reasons for this is to keep the cocktail colder longer (the glass will hold onto cold temperature and let it seep into the liquid while you drink), another important reason is the sensory experience of sipping a freshly shaken cocktail from an ice-cold rim. It's one of those extra experiences that doesn't make the liquid taste better, but improves the drinking experience remarkably.

If you don't have coupes, you can always use Old-Fashioned glasses or small wineglasses to serve Sidecars and other similar cocktails. Heck, we'd rather drink a Sidecar in any vessel than not drink one.

SIDECAR VARIATIONS

The Sidecar is a great starting place for generating variations that become progressively more complex the more you play with the template. It's a cocktail that underscores the importance of balance: use too much liqueur and it will overpower the drink; use too much citrus and it will hit your tongue like sandpaper. Here, we'll show you how manipulating any one of the drink's three elements can have an impact on its balance, and ultimately its success. Then we'll extend this line of thought as we explore the Sidecar's extended family.

Why Not

DEVON TARBY 2017

A Whiskey Sour (page 130) meets a Sidecar (page 151) in the Why Not. Though a simple Sidecar made with whiskey would be a balanced and tasty drink, we substitute maple syrup for half of the Cointreau to add not only sweetness but also rich flavor, and opt for the herbal aroma of a sage leaf garnish. The result is a refreshing cocktail that's perfect for fall and winter.

> 1¾ ounces Evan Williams
> "Black Label" bourbon
> ½ ounce Cointreau
> ¾ ounce fresh lemon juice
> ½ ounce dark, robust maple syrup
> Garnish: 1 sage leaf and
> 1 lemon wheel

Shake all the ingredients with ice, then strain into a double Old-Fashioned glass filled with ice. Garnish with the sage leaf and lemon wheel.

Cosmopolitan

OUR VERSION FROM TOBY CECCHINI'S ORIGINAL, 1988

All Carrie Bradshaw jokes aside, it's hard to hate the Cosmopolitan. A Cosmo is beautifully refreshing, and if ever there was a gateway drink that led people to explore other cocktails, this would be the one. It also provides a great demonstration of how an established template can quickly be transformed into an entirely new cocktail. The Cosmo is a Sidecar that swaps citrus vodka for the Cognac and lime juice for the lemon, with a small amount of cranberry juice added. Where this drink can and often does go wrong is in using cranberry cocktail and adding too much of it. This makes the whole thing a sweet mess, which may be tasty for people unaccustomed to strong spirits, but it robs the cocktail of complexity, sophistication, and balance. Though cranberry cocktail is the ingredient originally called for in Cosmopolitans, we encourage you to try a version made with pure, unsweetened cranberry juice. Admittedly, it is very tannic and behaves quite differently in cocktails, so for our version, we balance the cranberry juice with an equal amount of simple syrup, and then increase the amount of vodka slightly to help it punch through the tart sweetness.

2 ounces citrus vodka

¾ ounce Cointreau

½ ounce fresh lime juice

½ ounce pure, unsweetened cranberry juice

½ ounce simple syrup (page 45)

Garnish: lime wheel

Shake all the ingredients with ice, then double strain into a chilled coupe. Garnish with the lime wheel.

Clarified Cosmopolitan

DEVON TARBY AND ALEX DAY, 2015

To make our ideal Cosmopolitan, we stick with high-quality ingredients and use clarified lime juice to mimic the clarity of what most folks know as a "Cosmo," minus the Rose's Lime Juice and crappy cranberry cocktail. In addition to using pure cranberry juice, we forgo flavored vodka and impart citrus flavor by shaking the drink with lemon and lime twists. This is a more flexible approach that allows us to accommodate guests who request a preferred brand of vodka.

1¼ ounces vodka

¾ ounce Cointreau

½ ounce clarified lime juice (see page 146)

½ ounce unsweetened pure cranberry juice

½ ounce simple syrup (page 45)

Lemon twist

Lime twist

Garnish: 1 orange twist

Shake all the ingredients with ice, then strain into a chilled coupe. Express the orange twist over the drink, then gently rub it around the rim of the glass and place it into the drink.

Cosmopolitan

Lily Pad

DEVON TARBY, 2015

Blanc vermouth can act like a liqueur in shaken cocktails due to its sugar content. Here, it partners with Chareau—an aloe-based liqueur—to serve as the liqueur element in this Sidecar variation. Because Chareau is so dry, we increase the amount of sweetener to add body to the cocktail.

   5 basil leaves, preferably Thai basil
   ½ ounce simple syrup (page 45)
   1½ ounces Bombay gin
   ½ ounce blanc vermouth
   ½ ounce Chareau aloe liqueur
   ¾ ounce fresh lemon juice
   1 dash St. George absinthe
   1 drop Salt Solution (page 298)
   Garnish: 1 basil leaf, preferably Thai basil

In a cocktail shaker, gently muddle the basil leaves and simple syrup. Shake all the ingredients with ice, then double strain into a chilled coupe. Garnish with the basil leaf.

Pegu Cub Cocktail

CLASSIC

Highly potent bitters can also be added to a cocktail to help adjust the balance. As you can see, this recipe follows the same basic template as our version of Between the Sheets (page 168). Gin acts in a supporting role to Cointreau's juicy flavor and sweetness, and so by adding a dash each of both Angostura and House Orange bitters, we are able to introduce seasoning that dries out the cocktail a bit while curbing the sharpness of the lime.

   2 ounces London dry gin
   ¾ ounce Cointreau
   ¾ ounce fresh lime juice
   1 dash Angostura bitters
   1 dash House Orange Bitters (page 295)
   Garnish: 1 lime wedge

Shake all the ingredients with ice, then double strain into a chilled coupe. Garnish with the lime wedge.

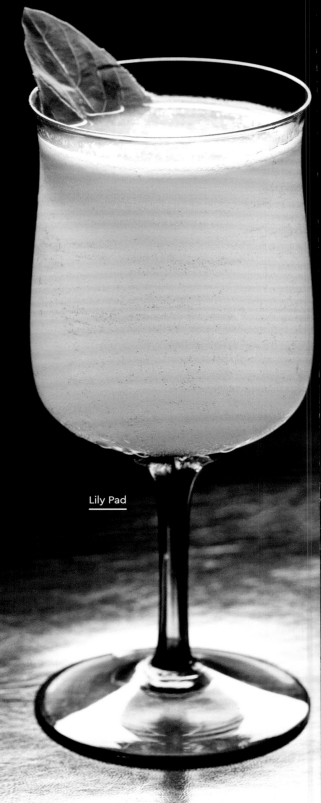

Lily Pad

NATASHA DAVID

Natasha David is a co-owner in the Manhattan bar Nitecap and runs the bar-consulting company You and Me Cocktails with her partner Jeremy Oertel.

When I first moved to New York for college, my sister hooked me up with a bartending job at an Irish pub in the East Village. I literally knew nothing about drinks and could barely pour a beer. When people ordered actual cocktails, I either made them up based on what I thought they should contain or consulted a little recipe book behind the bar. I had no concept of balance and had never heard of a jigger, so I eyeballed everything. I had a regular there who always ordered Sidecars, and I'd just dump some brandy, triple sec, and sour mix into a sugar-rimmed glass and serve it to him. I tried one of those Sidecars once, and it was revolting. But this guy, bless his soul, drank every single one I made for him.

Later I landed a job at a speakeasy—an actual speakeasy—called Woodson and Ford. My bosses there, Jim Kearns and Lynette Marrero, showed me how to make a real Sidecar: good brandy, Cointreau, fresh lemon juice. It was a perfectly balanced drink and a real *Aha!* moment. Not long afterward, I decided to quit my acting career and work in bars full time.

Expanding out from the Sidecar, I learned how to make a proper Margarita, my favorite cocktail, and other drinks in this family of sours. These drinks demonstrate how three ingredients can work in harmony and bring the best out in each other.

The Sidecar template is incredibly versatile, so I use it a lot when creating new cocktails. When I create Sidecar variations, it's all about splitting up the modifiers. Cointreau is interesting because it's both sweet and dry, so when I replace it, I like to use a combination of something sweet, perhaps a flavored syrup, and something dry, like sherry. And unless a guest specifically requests one, I don't put sugar rims on my drinks. I like making a balanced cocktail that doesn't need any extra sugar.

Most of all, I love the Sidecar for how it lets ingredients shine. The drink seems so simple, but when you take a sip you taste layer after layer of flavor. And because you can taste each of the drink's components, the quality of every ingredient is important; you can't hide any swill in there.

Modern Display

- 1½ ounces Pierre Ferrand 1840 Cognac
- ½ ounce Lustau Los Arcos amontillado sherry
- ½ ounce Giffard Crème de Pamplemousse
- ¾ ounce fresh lemon juice
- ½ ounce Vanilla Lactic Syrup (page 286)
- Garnish: 1 lemon twist

Shake all the ingredients with ice, then strain into a chilled coupe. Express the lemon twist over the drink, then set it on the edge of the glass.

Champs-Élysées

CLASSIC

In the classic Champs-Élysées, green Chartreuse replaces the Cointreau in a Sidecar. Because Chartreuse is high proof (110% ABV) and intensely herbaceous, the formula must be adjusted accordingly. As you can see, the amount of liqueur is dialed back. In addition, the amount of Cognac is increased slightly, and simple syrup is added to help push the cocktail back into balance.

2 ounces Cognac
½ ounce green Chartreuse
¾ ounce fresh lemon juice
½ ounce simple syrup (page 45)
1 dash Angostura bitters
Garnish: 1 lemon twist

Shake all the ingredients with ice, then strain into a chilled coupe. Express the lemon twist over the drink, then set it on the edge of the glass.

Four to the Floor

DEVON TARBY, 2014

When a liqueur drives the flavor of the cocktail, this usually requires some changes to the citrus. In the Four to the Floor, a variation on the Corpse Reviver #2 (page 188), the base is a beautiful marriage of pisco and grapefruit liqueur, so we opt to replace the more acidic citrus juice, which would over-shadow those flavors, with verjus. Technique comes into play here, with the finished cocktail having a smooth, silky texture because it's stirred, whereas shaking would introduce air bubbles.

1½ ounces Campo de Encanto Grand and Noble pisco
¾ ounce Giffard Crème de Pamplemousse
½ ounce Dolin blanc vermouth
¾ ounce Fusion Napa Valley verjus blanc
Garnish: 1 green grape on a skewer

Stir all the ingredients over ice, then strain into a chilled coupe. Garnish with the grape.

Four to the Floor

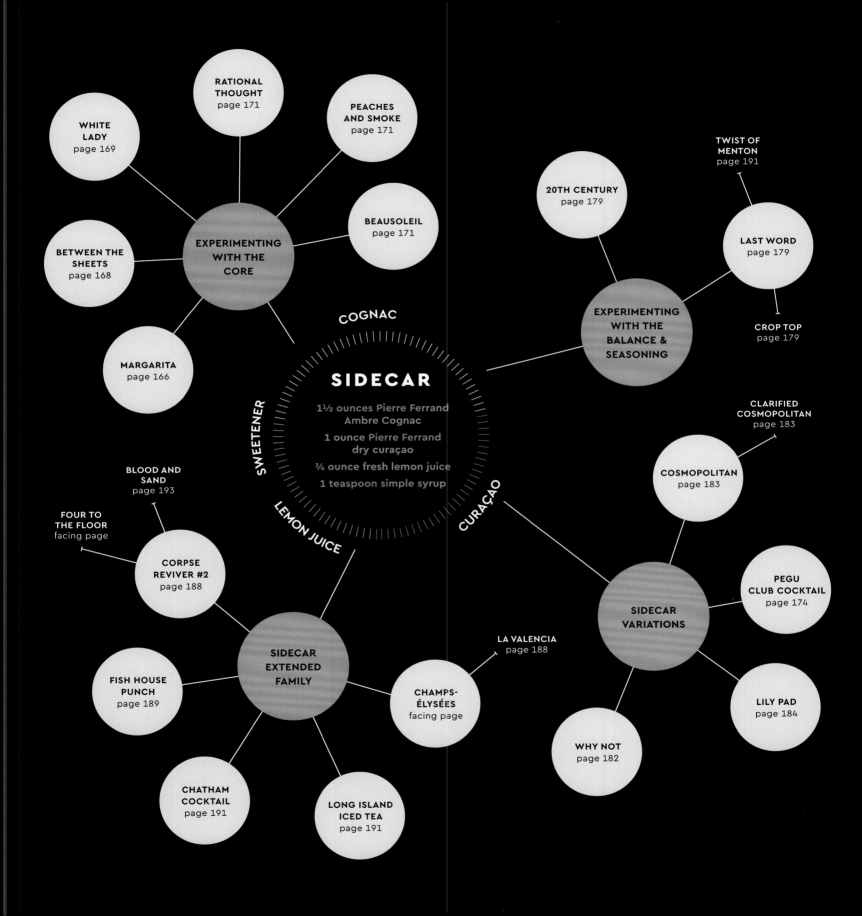

EXPERIMENTING WITH THE CORE

WHITE LADY
page 169

RATIONAL THOUGHT
page 171

PEACHES AND SMOKE
page 171

BEAUSOLEIL
page 171

BETWEEN THE SHEETS
page 168

MARGARITA
page 166

SIDECAR

1½ ounces Pierre Ferrand Ambre Cognac

1 ounce Pierre Ferrand dry curaçao

¾ ounce fresh lemon juice

1 teaspoon simple syrup

COGNAC

SWEETENER

LEMON JUICE

CURAÇAO

EXPERIMENTING WITH THE BALANCE & SEASONING

20TH CENTURY
page 179

TWIST OF MENTON
page 191

LAST WORD
page 179

CROP TOP
page 179

SIDECAR EXTENDED FAMILY

BLOOD AND SAND
page 193

FOUR TO THE FLOOR
facing page

CORPSE REVIVER #2
page 188

FISH HOUSE PUNCH
page 189

CHATHAM COCKTAIL
page 191

LONG ISLAND ICED TEA
page 191

CHAMPS-ÉLYSÉES
facing page

LA VALENCIA
page 188

SIDECAR VARIATIONS

CLARIFIED COSMOPOLITAN
page 183

COSMOPOLITAN
page 183

PEGU CLUB COCKTAIL
page 174

LILY PAD
page 184

WHY NOT
page 182

Verjus is French for "green juice." It's made by pressing wine grapes before they've ripened, then bottling the unfermented liquid. This vibrant nonalcoholic juice is fragile, and once a bottle is opened, it must be used within a few days, even if sealed and refrigerated. Producers bottle both white and red versions. We favor the more versatile white verjus for cocktails.

Verjus can be purchased bottled. Note the date of production: if it's more than two years old, it will lack vibrancy. Originally used in cooking, verjus adds both acidity and flavor to cocktails. On occasion, we use a fairly large proportion of verjus to create a bright acidic backbone, especially in stirred sour drinks. This results in a clear cocktail, like a Martini, with an unexpected flavor profile that's exceptionally refreshing.

La Valencia

ALEX DAY, 2008

This riff on the Champs-Élysées (see page 186) has a split base of dry and salty manzanilla sherry and a chamomile-infused rye. The honeyed and herbal flavor of yellow Chartreuse is perfect for drawing out the chamomile in the infused rye.

> **1 ounce Chamomile-Infused Rye Whiskey (page 288)**
> **1½ ounces La Gitana manzanilla sherry**
> **½ ounce yellow Chartreuse**
> **¾ ounce fresh lemon juice**
> **½ ounce simple syrup (page 45)**
> **1 dash Angostura bitters**

Shake all the ingredients with ice, then strain into a chilled coupe. No garnish.

Corpse Reviver #2

CLASSIC

The Sidecar's extended family includes many cocktails that contain a lot of booze, but there is precedent for heading in the other direction. In the Corpse Reviver, a split base of gin and Lillet blanc replaces the cognac. We view it as a highly democratic recipe: there's a harmonious balance among its ingredients, yet each pulls its own weight. Lillet blanc contributes qualities that mirror those of the other ingredients in the cocktail: proof, sweetness, and acidity. However, because the overall profile of Lillet is much softer and more subtle than the gin, Cointreau, and lemon juice, it effectively turns down the volume of the louder ingredients and allows them to happily coexist (pictured on page 173).

> **¾ ounce London dry gin**
> **¾ ounce Lillet blanc**
> **¾ ounce Cointreau**
> **¾ ounce fresh lemon juice**
> **2 dashes absinthe**

Shake all the ingredients with ice, then double strain into a chilled coupe. No garnish.

Fish House Punch

The classic Fish House Punch is clearly related to the Sidecar, containing Cognac, liqueur, and lemon juice in proportions quite similar to those in the Sidecar. The key difference is that it also includes seltzer, which increases the perception of acidity—much like our discussion of the Collins in the Daiquiri chapter (page 138). In this case, the classic recipe already includes ample richness in the core spirits and sweet peach liqueur, and the syrup bolsters those ingredients to increase the drink's body.

2 ounces cold seltzer

¾ ounce Pierre Ferrand Ambre Cognac

¾ ounce Appleton Estate Reserve Blend rum

¾ ounce Giffard Crème de Pêche de Vigne

¾ ounce fresh lemon juice

¼ ounce Cane Sugar Syrup (page 47)

1 strip lemon peel

Garnish: 1 lemon wheel and nutmeg

Pour the seltzer into a Collins glass or goblet. Short shake the remaining ingredients with ice for about 5 seconds, then strain into the glass. Fill the glass with ice cubes, then garnish with the lemon wheel and grate some nutmeg over the top of the drink.

Chatham Cocktail

Chatham Cocktail

DEVON TARBY, 2015

In the Chatham Cocktail, the core is a blend of fortified wines, which bring more sugar and acidity to the drink, and the drink is topped with Champagne, which brings even more acidity. Therefore, we use a smaller amount of both Grand Marnier and lemon juice and boost the amount of simple syrup.

¾ ounce Cocchi Americano bianco
¾ ounce Lustau Puerto fino sherry
¼ ounce Grand Marnier
½ ounce fresh lemon juice
¼ ounce simple syrup (page 45)
Pinch of salt
1½ ounces Champagne
Garnish: 1 grapefruit twist

Short shake all the ingredients (except the Champagne) with ice for about 5 seconds, then strain into a chilled flute. Pour in the Champagne, and quickly dip the barspoon into the glass to gently mix the Champagne with the cocktail. Express the grapefruit twist over the drink and then place it into the drink.

Twist of Menton

DEVON TARBY, 2015

In another riff on the Last Word (page 179), this recipe uses two types of bitter liqueur in place of the Chartreuse and maraschino liqueur. To add a necessary sweet counterpoint and boost the body of this cocktail, we add a luscious strawberry syrup.

¾ ounce Grey Goose vodka
¾ ounce Aperol
½ ounce Amaro Nonino
¾ ounce fresh lemon juice
½ ounce Strawberry Cream Syrup (page 286)
Garnish: 1 strawberry slice

Shake all the ingredients with ice, then double strain into a chilled coupe. Garnish with the strawberry slice.

Long Island Iced Tea

CLASSIC

No exploration of the Sidecar's extended family would be complete without the infamous Long Island Iced Tea. Of course, a key way in which this cocktail diverges from the standard Sidecar recipe is in the amount of spirits, with the core containing a whopping 3 ounces of strong spirits, split between vodka, gin, tequila, and rum. The amounts of Cointreau and lemon juice, however, aren't increased, so the added cola contributes a burst of sugar and acidity to bring the whole thing into balance.

2 ounces cold Coca-Cola
¾ ounce Aylesbury Duck vodka
¾ ounce Plymouth gin
¾ ounce Cimarrón blanco tequila
¾ ounce Plantation 3 Stars rum
¾ ounce Cointreau
¾ ounce fresh lemon juice
Garnish: 1 lemon wedge

Pour the cola into a pint glass. Short shake the remaining ingredients with ice for about 5 seconds, then strain into the glass. Fill the glass with ice cubes and garnish with the lemon wedge.

NEXT-LEVEL TECHNIQUE: USING ALTERNATIVE ACIDS

Lemon juice and lime juice are the backbone upon which so many cocktails are built, but the acidity they offer can also be found in other sources. Here we'll dive into the world of what we call alternative acids. We'll provide details on these acids shortly, but first we'll discuss how to use them three different ways: replacement, seasoning, and manipulation.

REPLACEMENT

One way to use alternative acids is to simply omit the lemon or lime juice in a cocktail and replace it with however much acid is required to add an equivalent amount of acidity. Just as we view clarified citrus juice as inherently different from unclarified juice (see page 144), we see these acids not as replacements for the flavor of lemon and lime juice, but as opportunities to express cocktails in a different way, similar to how the Clarified Daiquiri (page 145) in chapter 3 offers a surprising expression of a familiar form. One thing we like about the alternative acids in this section is how they can be used to create stirred versions of acidic drinks; in other words, cocktails that are typically associated with a shaken and frothy form can instead be expressed as smooth, stirred drinks. Here's a simple Sidecar experiment you can do to experience the effect yourself: Make the two Sidecar recipes below, then taste them side by side.

Sidecar (Classic)

1½ ounces Pierre Ferrand Ambre Cognac

1 ounce Cointreau

¾ ounce fresh lemon juice

Shake all the ingredients with ice, then double strain into a chilled coupe. No garnish.

Sidecar (with Citric Acid)

1½ ounces Pierre Ferrand Ambre Cognac

1 ounce Cointreau

1 teaspoon Citric Acid Solution (page 298)

Stir all the ingredients over ice, then strain into a chilled coupe. No garnish.

What do you think? The fact that there's perceptible acidity but no juicy pulp definitely confounds expectations of a Sidecar, but does replacing the lemon juice with citric acid make a tastier drink? (For the record, we don't think this stirred version of the Sidecar is a better cocktail.)

SEASONING

Alternative acids can also be used to season cocktails by amplifying the flavors in particular ingredients or the entire cocktail in subtle ways. Just as bartenders make sugar into a syrup for ease of use and consistency in cocktails, we often mix powdered acids into solutions and add them to cocktails by the drop. For example, sparing use of phosphoric acid (most commonly found in soft drinks) adds acidity yet no perceptible flavor, making it a favorite trick for exploring Highball variations. Likewise, just a couple of drops of Citric Acid Solution in a cocktail that contains orange juice can add a tart brightness that lifts the flavor of the juice, as the following experiment demonstrates.

The Blood and Sand is a Sidecar variation that uses ingredients more commonly found in stirred cocktails. Orange juice contributes moderate acidity to complement the sweet vermouth and Cherry Heering. Some versions of this recipe call for equal parts of scotch, vermouth, cherry brandy, and orange juice, but we find that bumping the scotch up a hair and adding a bit of lemon juice yields a cocktail that's more balanced and less cloying.

Blood and Sand

CLASSIC

1 ounce Famous Grouse scotch

¾ ounce Carpano Antica Formula vermouth

¾ ounce Cherry Heering

1 ounce fresh orange juice

Garnish: 1 brandied cherry

Shake all the ingredients with ice, then double strain into a chilled coupe. Garnish with the cherry.

Blood and Sand (Ours)

1 ounce Famous Grouse scotch

¾ ounce Carpano Antica Formula vermouth

¾ ounce Cherry Heering

1 ounce fresh orange juice

2 drops citric Acid Solution (page 298)

Garnish: 1 brandied cherry

Shake all the ingredients with ice, then double strain into a chilled coupe. Garnish with the cherry.

What do you think? Though the second cocktail may not taste more acidic, the brightness of the orange juice is clearer. Overall, we find the second cocktail more harmonious.

MANIPULATION

Finally, acids can be used to manipulate ingredients. As noted in the syrups section in chapter 1 (see page 42), we often include a small amount of powdered acid in our syrups to draw out desired flavors, as with the citric acid in our Raspberry Syrup (page 51). Acids can also be used to compensate for inconsistent flavor in citrus juices. As discussed in chapter 3, the flavors in citrus juices can vary from season to season, and even from fruit to fruit. Because lemons and limes tend to be fairly consistent, we seldom use alternative acids to adjust their flavor. But when working with fruits that tend to be more variable in acidity, such as oranges, we use citric acid when necessary to brighten the flavor of their juice.

ALTERNATIVE ACIDS AND HOW TO USE THEM

Alternative acids are not only an opportunity to make cocktails without lemon and lime, but also a method for reducing waste. It's shocking how much waste is produced by juicing citrus, so alternative acids can help us find balance in a refreshing cocktail with a fraction of the ecological impact. Is the flavor different? Absolutely. But progress should taste different, right? One important note: If you choose to work with powdered acids, it's essential that you have a high-precision gram scale that can accurately measure down to 0.01 gram.

PHOSPHORIC ACID

What it is: Coca-Cola as we know it wouldn't be possible without phosphoric acid. It's responsible for most of the acidity in commercial sodas—that refreshing quality that makes us come back for more. It's an odorless and flavorless liquid on its own, so it doesn't contribute flavor, as many other acids do; instead, it adds a tongue-tingly tartness.

How to prepare it: While it's possible to track down bulk phosphoric acid, it's no easy task. Plus, it's usually very concentrated and must be diluted. If you choose to go that route, please research safe methods for doing so. Don't want the headache? A ready-to-use product by the name of Extinct Acid Phosphate, produced by Darcy O'Neil, can be purchased online at Art of Drink (see Resources, page 299).

How to use it: Even diluted, phosphoric acid must be used in small quantities. You can add it to cocktails in two ways: using a couple of drops to enhance the acidity of other ingredients or as the solo acidic backbone. For the latter, we suggest experimenting with amounts between ½ teaspoon and 1 teaspoon. We advise against using more than 1 teaspoon; otherwise, it will add a metallic flavor.

CITRIC ACID

What it is: The primary acid in lemons and limes is citric acid, making this one of the most familiar of the acid alternatives. It's tart and lemony and unmistakable when tasted on its own.

How to prepare it: Citric acid powder can be used as is when preparing syrups, but for cocktails it's best to dissolve it in water. We make it into a solution for adding directly to cocktails. Using a gram scale to measure the ingredients, combine 100 grams filtered water with 25 grams citric acid powder and stir until dissolved. Store in a glass dropper bottle or other glass container at room temperature—no need to refrigerate.

How to use it: Though citric acid doesn't precisely emulate the flavor of lemon and lime juice, a few drops of citric acid solution can act as a close equivalent to lemon or lime juice in cocktails. A teaspoon of citric acid solution has roughly the same amount of acidity as the amount of lemon or lime juice (approximately ¾ ounce) used in a Sidecar or Daiquiri-style cocktail; simply swapping it in for fresh juice is an instructive experiment, but not terribly interesting. Instead of relying on citric acid to replace lemon or lime juice, we generally add a few drops of it to cocktails that are a little flabby and in need of more oomph, as in the Blood and Sand (page 193). We also use it to boost the acidity of syrups to be incorporated into carbonated cocktails.

LACTIC ACID

What it is: This is a versatile ingredient that can be used to impart a creamy texture to cocktails without adding the density of dairy or nut milks.

How to prepare it: Like citric acid and malic acid (below), lactic acid powder can be used as is when preparing syrups. It's about as strong as malic acid, so we use a 9-to-1 ratio of water to acid. Using a gram scale to measure the ingredients, combine 90 grams filtered water with 10 grams lactic acid powder and stir until dissolved. Store in a glass container at room temperature—no need to refrigerate.

How to use it: We love using lactic acid to give syrups a rounder texture, as in our Vanilla Lactic Syrup (page 286) and Strawberry Cream Syrup (page 286).

MALIC ACID

What it is: If you've ever bitten into a green apple, you've tasted malic acid—it's bright and exceptionally tart.

How to prepare it: In powdered form, malic acid can add a bright flavor to syrups. For cocktails, we use it as we do citric acid: in a solution. However, because it's more potent than citric acid, we make a weaker solution. Using a gram scale to measure the ingredients, combine 100 grams filtered water with 10 grams malic acid powder, and stir until dissolved. Store in a glass container at room temperature—no need to refrigerate.

How to use it: Our House Grenadine recipe (page 47) calls for a fair amount of malic acid in combination with citric acid to bolster the astringency of the pomegranate juice. In cocktails, malic acid solution adds a tart bite that can accent flavors already present in the cocktail. For the Apple Pop (page 222), we make a nonalcoholic carbonated soda from clarified apple and celery juices, to which we add malic acid to restore the fresh apple flavor lost when the apple juice is clarified.

TARTARIC ACID

What it is: Tartaric acid is a naturally occurring acid that's found in apricots, bananas, apples, and, perhaps most noticeably, grapes, where it largely determines the acidity of the wine made from that fruit. We use it in cocktails for the drying effect it has on drinks.

How to prepare it: We rarely use tartaric acid on its own. Should you want to try it in cocktails, make a 10-to-1 solution as above for malic acid.

How to use it: Our preferred method of using tartaric acid is to mix it with lactic acid to create what we call "Champagne acid," which mimics the yeasty richness of Champagne and has a tannic bite. To make Champagne Acid Solution, mix 3 grams each of tartaric acid and lactic acid with 94 grams of filtered water and stir until dissolved. It's an important ingredient in the cocktail Celebrate (page 29), where it enhances the tang of a dry Champagne.

ASCORBIC ACID

What it is: Also known as vitamin C, ascorbic acid has few flavor-amplifying applications. However, because it's an antioxidant, it's perfect for preserving fragile ingredients that are damaged by contact with oxygen.

How to prepare it: We only use ascorbic acid as is, in a powder form, to stave off oxidation in juices, syrups, and even infusions.

How to use it: Ingredients like fresh apple juice can oxidize and turn brown very quickly—a process that can be slowed or prevented by adding a bit of ascorbic acid. Likewise, rinsing fragile garnishes, such as apple or pear slices, in a solution of water and ascorbic acid can prevent them from browning. A general rule of thumb is that for every quart of liquid (be it a juice or water for preserving garnishes), add 1 teaspoon of ascorbic acid, stirring or whisking until it's completely dissolved.

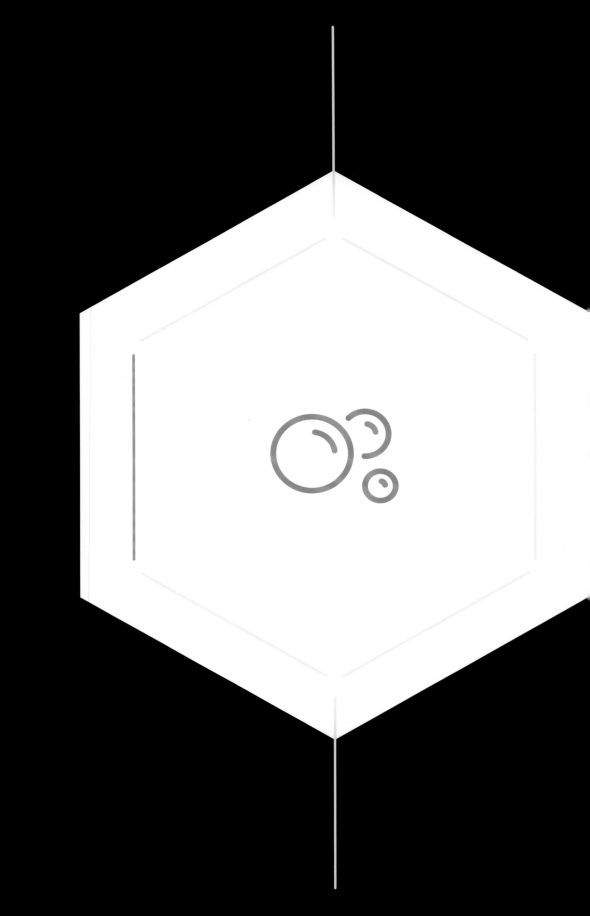

5

THE
WHISKY HIGHBALL

THE CLASSIC RECIPE

We'll never know who was first to mix scotch with sparkling water, but it seems fairly clear that this cocktail originated around the turn of the twentieth century, as did its name. The name may be a reference to the bygone days of steam-powered trains: When a steam locomotive gets up to speed, the full pressure pushes a ball to the top of a gauge—thus the train is "highballing." Or perhaps it's a reference to the train signals of the day, wherein a raised globe meant the track ahead was clear and a train could speed through quickly, which could be a metaphor for slugging down a scotch and soda. Less colorfully, the name may, in fact, just be derived from a common nineteenth-century term for a glass (a *ball*), indicating that this drink was a tall, or high, glass of scotch. Whatever the case may be, the tall glass that this drink is served in has become inseparable from the drink itself.

Whisky Highball

2 ounces scotch

6 ounces cold seltzer

Garnish: 1 lemon wedge

Pour the scotch into a Highball glass, then add 3 ice cubes. Stir for 3 seconds. Add the seltzer and stir once. Garnish with the lemon wedge.

OUR ROOT RECIPE

To construct our ideal Highball, we start by choosing the base spirit—a selection that's highly personal. Some people prefer a high-powered smoky Islay scotch, while others favor the fruity cereal grain flavor of a blended Irish whiskey. Because a classic Highball has no ingredients beyond whiskey and sparkling water, we lean toward a spirit that doesn't overpower the light tingle of sparkling water: Hakushu, a 12-year Japanese whisky that's soft and elegant and has only a whisper of smokiness. Then, although most bars garnish Whisky Highballs with a lemon wedge, we think that's unnecessary at best, so we deliberately omit it, allowing our root Highball recipe to stand as a testament to the drink's nuance, keeping the harmony of great whisky and tingly bubbly water intact.

Of course, the harmony of this ideal Highball largely stems from the delicacy of the Japanese whisky it calls for. If you lean toward stronger-flavored whiskies, such as Islay single-malt or American rye or bourbon, you may want to adjust the proportion of whiskey to sparkling water. Personally, we prefer 5 ounces of chilled seltzer to 2 ounces of whisky in Highballs with more assertive whiskies. Another solution is to keep a glass of chilled seltzer at hand to top off the drink as needed.

Our Ideal Whisky Highball

2 ounces Hakushu 12-year Japanese whisky
4 ounces cold seltzer

Pour the whisky into a Highball glass and add 1 ice cube. Let sit for 3 seconds. Add the seltzer and stir once. No garnish.

DEVIL IN THE DETAILS

On paper, the Whisky Highball is just whisky and carbonated water, similar to other familiar two-ingredient rail drinks—vodka and soda, gin and tonic, rum and Coke . . . These are the simplest drinks served at many bars, and while that may lead you to dismiss them as being less sophisticated than an ice-cold Martini or an expertly shaken Sidecar, we see mastering the Whisky Highball as a key accomplishment for any bartender. Executing a great one speaks volumes about the knowledge, preparation, and technique of its maker. If that seems far-fetched, bear with us. We'll discuss this in depth later in the chapter (see "Exploring Technique: Building Whisky Highballs," on page 214).

Cocktail nerds love to whisper tales of tiny bars in Tokyo's Ginza district where the modest Highball reaches its apotheosis. There, the few spare elements of the cocktail are carefully considered, both in isolation and in how they will collaborate with each other. These elements include the character of the whisky; the size, shape, and clarity of the ice; the temperature, effervescence, and mineral content of the water; the heft of the glass and the thickness of its rim; and the meticulous method by which the drink is assembled and placed in front of the guest. In short, the ritual of Japanese Highball service is pure craftsmanship with a dash of theatrical affectation wherein the process of making the drink is seemingly just as important as the guest's enjoyment of that drink. We heartily endorse this approach and believe that making a great Highball requires mastering both ingredients and tools—and elevating and refining both wherever possible.

UNDERSTANDING THE TEMPLATE

The success of any Highball depends on several factors. First, you must start with ingredients that work well together. On a basic level, this involves understanding fundamental flavor affinities, such as the magic that happens when gin and tonic meet in a glass. At a deeper, more nuanced level, it requires understanding the intrinsic qualities of the spirit and mixer, such as how the mineral content of a certain sparkling water will interact with the brininess of a particular scotch.

It also involves understanding that the Highball is a template that's both very simple and extremely flexible. Broadly speaking, a Highball is simply the combination of a spirit and some sort of mixer. Its flexibility stems from the fact that any spirit can compose the core, and the possibilities for mixers are equally wide: seltzer or tonic water, ginger ale or ginger beer, various colas and other sodas are typical, and even juices. A Mimosa, for example, is a Highball made with Champagne and orange juice, and a Greyhound is a refreshing mixture of gin and grapefruit juice. One of our favorite hangover cures is a savory Highball: the Bloody Mary.

Then, the possibilities can be expanded exponentially by splitting the core spirit, the mixer, or both. For example, the Americano (page 208) has a split core of Campari and sweet vermouth, topped with seltzer, and the Aperol Spritz (page 223) is a Highball that uses Aperol as the core spirit and splits the mixer between seltzer and prosecco. To create more complex cocktails, the template can be expanded to include small amounts of other flavorings, as in the Harvey Wallbanger (vodka, orange juice, and a float of Galliano) or a Tequila Sunrise (tequila, orange juice, and grenadine).

Finally, making a great Highball is a learned craft that can only be mastered through repetition. We view the craft of bartending as the careful study of ingredients and a refinement of technique built upon experience. Craft also involves knowledge: learning more about spirits, ingredients, tools, and techniques in order to be better at making drinks.

Art is something different, although it's built upon the shoulders of craft. Art is applying creativity to those studied skills. A musician must learn scales before writing a masterpiece; a sculptor must grasp form; a painter must know how to combine primary colors. And here, deep in chapter 5, is our true motivation for writing this book: by studying classic cocktails and explaining how we and others have interpreted those forms, we're providing the foundational knowledge necessary for developing your own artful creations based upon studied skills and knowledge. With that in mind, we see the Highball as the opportunity for all the skills and knowledge previously accumulated in this book to be fully articulated.

As this chapter progresses, we'll progress through those levels of variation, working toward cocktails that eventually start to stray quite a distance from the basic Highball template. This blurs the lines between what makes a Highball a Highball, and when it becomes another type of cocktail. And in fact, we don't have to go that far before the clear lines between a Highball and a Collins become diffuse, especially considering that the

mixer used in a Highball may have attributes reminiscent of elements of a traditional sour. We draw the line based on how much citrus juice is used: more than ¾ ounce and the drink is probably more closely affiliated with sours, such as the Daiquiri. In a Highball, citrus and other acidic components are used to accent the other flavors in the drink, not as a central component.

THE CORE AND SEASONING: WHISKY

The basis of a proper Highball is a high-quality spirit, since the cocktail doesn't contain much else to hide behind, especially in the Highball's simplest format: whisky and seltzer. Furthermore, because the seltzer has a fairly neutral flavor, the whisky also serves as the main seasoning.

At our bars, we make most of our whiskey-based cocktails with American whiskey. This isn't because of we view American whiskey as superior, but because of the sheer number of classic cocktails based on bourbon or rye, along with the important fact that domestic whiskeys are usually more affordable than those from other countries (shipping booze around the world is expensive). But as we've learned more about international whiskies and discovered more bottles that are affordable to mix with, we've started incorporating more of them across our cocktail repertoire.

In this section, we'll provide an overview of whiskies from Scotland, Ireland, Japan, and a few other countries and then recommend specific bottles. But first, here's a brief overview of the category in general. Just as with American whiskey, these whiskies are all made from grains that are first cooked into a mash, then distilled and aged in oak barrels. The differences between them lie in which grains are used, how those grains are processed before and during fermentation, the distillation process, the types of barrels used for aging, the duration of aging, and whether the aged whisky is bottled direct from the cask or blended with other whiskies.

SCOTCH WHISKY

Of all the world's spirits, none brings out the nerds like scotch does, and for good reason: the best bottles are treasures of human achievement, patiently aged for generations, and sometimes the product of distilleries that no longer exist. In a sense, the appeal of old scotch whisky lies in its ability to transport us to a bygone era. While this may sound overly nostalgic, the qualities that make scotch so unique truly are steeped in tradition, craftsmanship, and artistry—along with a good dose of clever marketing.

There are truly beautiful scotch whiskies that cost a small fortune, and those bottles deserve our adoration. But unless money is no object, you'll want to use something a bit more affordable—both for sipping and for mixing in cocktails—which can make finding the right bottles challenging as there is a wide gap between good quality, affordable, and mixable scotches. Our suggested bottles below represent our favorite go-to brands for versatility and affordability.

Scotch whisky can be divided into two broad categories: single-malt and blended. The notion that a single-malt scotch is inherently better than a blend is inaccurate; they are simply different.

SINGLE-MALT SCOTCH

The only ingredients allowed in single-malt scotch are barley and water. Single-malts must be distilled twice in copper pot stills, after which the distillate is aged in oak casks for a minimum of three years. The spirit must be produced by only one distillery, though it can be a blend of distillates aged for different numbers of years. If the label

has an age statement, such as 12-year, that represents the youngest whisky in the blend.

Scotch production is separated into several regions, with the Highlands, Lowlands, and Islands being the easiest way to group styles. The heart of scotch whisky making is the Highlands, and specifically the Speyside region. The vast majority of Scotland's whisky is made in this region, with an impressive collection of famous distilleries lying in close proximity to one another: Balvenie, the Glenlivet, Glenfiddich, the Macallan, and many more. Speyside scotch is either light and floral (Glenlivet) or rich and fruity (Balvenie), the latter resulting from the use of sherry casks for aging.

Scotland's Lowlands yield far less whisky than the Highlands, but there are some brands we use from time to time. They are often light-bodied and a bit sweeter, with very little peaty smoke. In cocktails, Lowland single-malts can act as a broad substrate on which to build flavor, but due to limited availability of our favorite bottling (Auchentoshan Three Wood), we rarely mix with them.

The most distinctive of all single-malts are the often-aggressive whiskies from Islay, an island off Scotland's southwestern coast. Islay whiskies are intensely smoky, but also rich and full-boded. In cocktails, the smokiness of Islay single-malts can quickly overpower other flavors, so we often split it with a blended scotch, as in Smoke and Mirrors (page 131). We sometimes keep Islay scotch in a dasher bottle for adding small pops of flavor to cocktails or in an atomizer to spray it atop a cocktail for a savory aroma, a trick we picked up from Sam Ross's neoclassic cocktail the Penicillin (page 282).

RECOMMENDED BOTTLES

Auchentoshan Three Wood (Lowlands): The result of three distillations (rather than the two typical of single-malt scotch), Auchentoshan is aged in three different types of oak: first in former bourbon barrels for up to twelve years, then in oloroso sherry barrels for one year, and finally in Pedro Ximénez sherry barrels for one year. The result is a dynamic, multilayered scotch with flavors from each of the different barrels in an impressive balance.

Bowmore 12-Year (Islay): Of all the Islay single-malts, Bowmore has the most restrained presence of smoky peat. It doesn't lack smoky flavors—far from it—but while other iconic Islays (Lagavulin, Ardbeg, and Laphroaig) have dense smoke aromas and flavors, this one is more nuanced, with an orangey citrus and vanilla flavor beneath the smoke.

The Glenlivet 12-Year (Highlands): Elegant and floral, with a touch of honey, the Glenlivet is one of those massively produced single-malt scotches that can be found around the world and is consistently delicious, if not terribly complex. However, that very lack of complexity makes Glenlivet a useful single-malt for mixing, since it won't aggressively overpower other flavors.

Highland Park 12-Year (Orkney Islands): This may be our favorite go-to sipping single-malt, thanks to its elegance and affordable price. It hails from the Orkney Islands, and the sea's influence lingers in the background, beneath its mildly smoky and slightly sweet flavor. Highland Park ages their whiskies primarily in former sherry barrels, which lends a soft apricot flavor to the whisky.

USING SINGLE-MALT SCOTCH WHISKY (AND OTHER EXPENSIVE BOOZE) IN COCKTAILS

For many whisky enthusiasts, a fine single-malt scotch should not be mixed with more than a few drops of water—even an ice cube is considered sacrilegious. Why? It's thought that the whisky should not be adulterated too far beyond its finished state in the bottle. Obviously we don't agree. When done right, cocktails show the ultimate respect for great spirits, emphasizing their qualities alongside other flavors in a composition that enhances the spirit—and this is how we approach mixing with fine spirits.

It's true that most single-malt scotches are far too pricy for most bars to mix with (unless you're willing to pay $50 per cocktail, in which case we have a great time-share opportunity to discuss). But at home we find that our favorite single-malts for sipping, especially those from Speyside and Orkney Island, make delicious cocktails. If you're making cocktails at home and cost is a concern, here's an approach that's worked well for us:

instead of using only a single-malt scotch in a cocktail, use it to accent another whisky. For the base, use a more affordable blended scotch, such as the Famous Grouse, then add a small amount of a single-malt for more depth of flavor. This strategy is particularly effective when working with intensely smoky Islay single-malts, which will quickly dominate a drink if used in larger amounts, all cost considerations aside.

Another strategy for mixing with single-malts is more romantic. Many of them are lovingly described in terms of the geography and climate of the location where they're aged—the smell of the sea, the softness of the heather growing nearby, and so on. These lyrical descriptions can provide wonderful inspiration for cocktails. For example, to accent the smell of the sea, we might base the cocktail on salty manzanilla sherry, or to amplify the heather, we might include floral St-Germain elderflower liqueur.

Laphroaig 10-Year (Islay): We love this Islay scotch not just because it's intensely smoky and briny and because just a few drops of it can flavor a cocktail, but also because it has complex spice flavors of black pepper, cardamom, and vanilla. It also has a lingering herbal note that makes it a great companion for mint, as in the Smoke and Mirrors (page 131) and Smokescreen (page 132).

BLENDED SCOTCH

Although single-malt scotch gets much of the attention these days, it wasn't long ago that blends dominated the Scottish whisky category. But as single-malt scotches have become increasingly more expensive, the tide is turning once again, and innovators like John Glaser, of Compass Box, are restoring honor to high-quality blends.

For cocktail purposes, blended scotch is both affordable enough for mixing and versatile, so we use it frequently in our drinks. We gravitate toward blends that are distinctive but not overpowering and look for an even balance between richness and the spice flavors conferred by aging. Most of our favorite blended scotches have an appley fruitiness and a smoked tobacco flavor that works especially well in citrusy drinks. They also work well in stirred cocktails, where the tobacco and smoky characteristics can shine through.

RECOMMENDED BOTTLES

Compass Box Asyla: Whereas most of the bottles described here are defined by richness, Asyla is all elegance. It has some of the characteristics that make blended scotch so useful in cocktails—a fruity core flavor topped with spice notes—but the flavors are gentler and more reminiscent of fresh apple than cooked. On its own, Asyla is light-bodied, but in cocktails it can shine through in sophisticated ways, especially in riffs on the Manhattan, such as the Bobby Burns (page 279).

The Famous Grouse: This is our favorite blended scotch for cocktails. The blend's single-malts are sourced from the Highland Park and Macallan distilleries, and after they're combined, the blend is aged for six months in oak. It has a creamy richness that melds into the flavor of cooked apples and a touch of spice gives it personality, but not so much that it overpowers. It's a truly versatile whisky for many cocktail applications and priced right for mixing.

Compass Box Oak Cross: This unique blend is comprised of three single-malts that are combined and aged for six months in both American and French casks. Its flavor is dense, with the sweetness of malty vanilla and baking spices. It's strong enough to make itself known even in cocktails that also include the bold flavors of vermouth—notably bitter Manhattan-style drinks, such as the Affinity (page 278).

IRISH WHISKEY

Thought to have been one of the first whiskeys, Irish whiskey has oscillated between prominence and near extinction for two centuries but is now experiencing a renaissance. Many heritage brands are finding their way into the export market, and this has expanded our concept of Irish whiskey beyond the handful of bottles we've known for years.

There are a few things that differentiate Irish whiskey from its Scottish cousin. The devil is in the details: Most Irish whiskey is distilled three times, not two, and when pot stills are utilized, they are typically much larger than those used in Scotland. And though there are Irish whiskeys that are the equivalent of a scotch single-malt—produced by a single distillery and made only from barley—Irish whiskey by far favors the art of blending many whiskeys with different grain compositions, barrel types and sizes, and distilling methods.

When using Irish whiskey in cocktails, we don't focus on style or region, as we do for scotch. This is largely because region has less influence than larger, countrywide styles of whiskey. Though these may have once been emblematic of certain places in Ireland, today the Irish whiskey industry has largely been consolidated into a few distilleries, though more are opening every year as Irish whiskey regains popularity. Lighter blends, such as Paddy, Jameson, and Tullamore Dew, have a soft and sweet personality much like a young bourbon. These blends are tasty in citrusy cocktails, too, but they tend to fall a little flat when tasked with playing the starring role, as in Manhattans or Old-Fashioned-style cocktails.

Pure pot still Irish whiskey is something entirely different. It has enough depth and body to be versatile in many cocktail applications. We love combining them with other ingredients that pull out their qualities and emphasize them.

RECOMMENDED BOTTLES

Bushmills Original: This whiskey, aged for five years in used American oak, leans toward a lighter style than others made by Bushmills. Its clarity makes it great for mixing in citrusy cocktails. For use in Manhattans and Old-Fashioned-style cocktails, we recommend Bushmills' other bottlings, such as Black Bush, which incorporates a high proportion of whiskey aged in oloroso sherry casks, or the various Bushmills single-malts, which develop progressively complex flavors depending on aging time.

Redbreast 12-Year: This whiskey epitomizes traditional pot still Irish whiskey. It's rich and almost oily, a result of unmalted and malted barley mash being distilled in a copper pot still. It has an almost coconut-like quality and a slight anise flavor. Blended from distillates aged in both American oak and sherry casks, it has a beautiful balance between spice and the rich, raisin-like

finish of sherry. That nuance may get lost in a sour-style drink (though won't try to talk you out of it), but Redbreast shines when used as the base in spirituous cocktails, such as the Cut and Paste (page 35), where it mingles with an aged apple brandy for a juicy riff on a Sazerac.

JAPANESE WHISKY

Gone are the days when Japanese whisky was an obscure player. Since it landed on US shores a couple of decades ago, skepticism about whisky from Japan has evolved into full-on fanaticism, and it now has the reputation of being some of the finest whisky in the world, thanks to a long string of awards and accolades. The relentless Japanese quest for perfection is represented in every drop of Japanese whisky that we've tasted, and we're endlessly frustrated by its scarcity in the United States.

There are surprisingly few regulations governing the production of Japanese whisky; its industry is shaped much more by tradition. One example of this is the barrels used for aging. While many Japanese producers rely on the same barrels used elsewhere, such as former bourbon, sherry, and port barrels, they also make heavy use of Japanese mizunara oak barrels, as well as plum wine casks. This has resulted in a wide spectrum of whiskies, from those that bear a striking resemblance to single-malt scotch to those that are quite like the blends produced in both Scotland and Ireland to distinctive types that are unique to Japan. This diversity is exciting to explore but makes it challenging to offer general guidelines about how to use Japanese whisky in cocktails, so we won't go there. Instead, in the descriptions of the recommended bottles below, we'll indicate what type of whisky a particular bottle most resembles—single-malt or blended scotch; Irish blend or pot still; or American—and address mixing from that perspective.

All of that said, you may be stymied by a far more practical consideration: most Japanese whiskies are available to the export market in only limited quantities, and the bottles we're able to obtain are often quite expensive. Fortunately, there are a few bottles that usually won't break the bank—if you can find them, that is. In our opinion, it's worth your while to try.

RECOMMENDED BOTTLES

Hakushu 12-Year: Among our recommended bottles of Japanese whisky, Hakushu 12-year is the most similar to single-malt scotch, yet it's far more than a Japanese rendition of Scotland's whisky in Japan; it's a beautiful example of how Japanese whisky making expresses a unique voice and distinctive style. The distillery is located 2,600 feet above sea level in a remote, forested location. The local water here is thought to have a great deal to do with Hakushu's soft flavor, and this, coupled with a mild peatiness from the pot distillation and aging in both bourbon barrels and sherry barrels, results in a mildly fruity and floral whisky. We're more than happy to mix finer, more expensive Japanese whiskies into our Highballs, but Hakushu's elegance produces an ideal benchmark Highball by which we judge all others.

Nikka Coffey Grain Whisky: While many Japanese whiskies take direct inspiration from single-malt scotches, Nikka Coffey Grain whisky lies somewhere between Irish whiskey and bourbon. It's made mostly from corn, producing the vanilla and spice flavors reminiscent of bourbon, then aged in various types of barrels, the products of which are then blended together to create a unique final flavor profile. In case you're wondering, the word *Coffey* in the name doesn't have anything to do with coffee; rather, it refers to the equipment used for distillation: a continuous still, also known as the Coffey still after its inventor, Aeneas Coffey.

Suntory Toki: A blend of whiskies from Suntory's three distilleries (Yamazaki, Hakushu, and Chita), this is a smooth and light whisky that's usually priced around $45, making it both affordable (for Japanese whisky) and a gentle introduction to whiskies from Japan. This bottle balances the refinement of a scotch-style single-malt with some of the grit and spice of grain whisky.

OTHER WORLD WHISKEYS

The global industry has been dominated by whiskeys from only a handful of countries (America, Scotland, Ireland, Canada, and Japan), but there are great whiskeys made in many other countries. To date, aged quality whiskey is being produced in India, Switzerland, Sweden, Denmark, Germany, Austria, France, South Africa, Australia, Thailand, and New Zealand—and that's just the countries we know of. More will undoubtedly emerge in the coming years.

If you choose to navigate these whiskeys, reflect back on everything we've outlined about whiskey above and in chapter 1. If the production method for a given whiskey is similar to that of a familiar style, this can provide an indication of what the whiskey might taste like, which will help you predict both its quality and its usability in cocktails. That said, studying a new offering also involves learning about where it comes from and what the climate is like there.

EXPERIMENTING WITH THE CORE AND SEASONING

When mixing with blended scotch alone, we often use a split core to bring in flavors that have an affinity for the whisky. One strategy is to use fortified wines, since many of the barrels used for aging scotch were previously filled with sherry, madeira, and port. American whiskey, especially bourbon, is a possible cohort for the same reason, though the aggressiveness of American oak may overpower a blended scotch. There are two primary ways to work with this. One is to use a split core consisting mostly of scotch (1½ ounces) with a small amount of bourbon (½ ounce) to give a drink a scotch-focused flavor with a bit of added spice. The other is to use inverse proportions—a bourbon-heavy core with a small portion of scotch—to create a cocktail with all the spice and personality of American whiskey but with a soft, earthy, apple-like undertone.

Of course, spirits other than whisky also work well in Highballs, in part because seltzer goes well with any spirit. Indeed, it's fun to see how seltzer can change the flavor of the core as its bubbles enhance the aroma and provide an acidic note. For example, blanco tequila is earthy and vegetal on its own, but when it's mixed into a Highball in place of whisky, it suddenly becomes citrusy. And although gin is famously paired with tonic water, substituting seltzer for the tonic makes for a delicious and sophisticated Highball, with seltzer allowing the botanical flavors to blossom. Because this too is a very simple way to experiment with the core, we'll just leave it at that and encourage you to experiment on your own.

The natural next step in experimenting with the core is to substitute other types of booze for the strong spirits. The sky's the limit here and we encourage you to follow your inclinations, but consider playing with ingredients that have distinctive flavors, such as fortified wines and bitter aperitifs. This is a traditional approach, as demonstrated by the classic Americano cocktail.

Americano

CLASSIC

A staple aperitif cocktail, the Americano is like a Negroni (a member of the Martini family, page 89) in which the gin has been replaced with seltzer, transforming it into a Highball with a split base of Campari and sweet vermouth. Both ingredients are rich and bitter, even though they're lower in alcohol, which allows this basic Highball format to work without any modifications. That said, the orange garnish is important for this cocktail: it perfumes the nose, and its flavors slowly seep into the drink as it's consumed. We highly recommend having extra cold seltzer on hand to frequently top off an Americano, ideally in the late afternoon with a good book.

1 ounce Campari

1 ounce Carpano Antica Formula vermouth

4 ounces cold seltzer

Garnish: 1 orange half wheel and a small bottle of cold seltzer

Pour the Campari and vermouth into a Highball glass, then add 3 ice cubes. Stir for 3 seconds. Add the seltzer and stir once. Garnish with the orange half wheel and serve with a bottle of seltzer.

THE BALANCE: SPARKLING WATER

Whereas most cocktails are balanced via ingredients that provide sweetness, acidity, or both, the classic Whisky Highball is balanced solely by sparkling water. This requires greater attention to the qualities of the sparkling water and a judicious hand in pouring it. So let's start by taking a closer look at this seemingly simple ingredient.

One role of sparkling water in a Highball is easy to grasp: it dilutes the spirit, stretching its powerful flavors and making it easier to drink. Yet this also transforms the flavor of the spirit. Flavors that had been tight and complex let their hair down and become easier to identify. A second role of the water is to add an impression of acidity. This doesn't come across as acidic in the same way as lemon or lime juice; rather, it creates a pleasant sharp tingle on the tongue. Finally, sparkling water also enhances the spirit's aroma, perfuming the space above the cocktail and lifting volatile fragrances to the drinker's nose.

For these reasons, we pay particular attention to how carbonated our sparkling water is, since more bubbles will have a greater effect on the cocktail. We also ensure that our sparkling water is well chilled in order to preserve the bubbles (carbon dioxide comes out of solution more quickly in warm liquid). The many ways in which bubbly water is labeled and sold can be confusing, so we want to be clear about the differences between sparkling mineral water, soda water or club soda, and seltzer.

Sparkling mineral water: Some natural springs produce water with relatively high concentrations of minerals, which are dissolved into the water from rocks underground. Though some sparkling mineral waters are naturally effervescent, others are mineral water that's been carbonated, so they can vary widely in terms of how bubbly they are. The types of minerals and their abundance, as well as the acidity, or pH, can also vary widely from source to source. Because of these natural variations, the category as a whole isn't consistent enough for different products to be used interchangeably. However, the flavor of certain mineral waters—as subtle as they may be—can be a delicious match with whisky in a Highball.

Soda water: Also known as club soda, soda water is a product that mimics the flavors that occur naturally in mineral water by adding small quantities of various minerals to still water (typically sodium bicarbonate, sodium citrate, and potassium sulfate) and then carbonating the water, resulting in a subtle salty flavor. The flavor of these minerals is nearly imperceptible in straight soda water; try tasting soda water side by side with seltzer to see whether you can detect a difference. However, in a cocktail those minerals can act to brighten the flavor of citrus and curb bitterness, just as adding a bit of Salt Solution (page 298) will. Because we want the most control in our cocktails, we don't often use soda water and instead use seltzer water, adding salinity if needed.

Seltzer: This is simply filtered water that's been carbonated. It has no additives, so it's a very neutral and consistent product. For this reason, we generally prefer it in cocktails and highly recommend it for Highballs, since its clean flavor won't appreciably alter the core spirit.

Finally, Highballs need not be bubbly; they can also be built with noncarbonated mixers, primarily juice. Old-style versions of such cocktails made with citrus juice, such as Screwdrivers and Salty Dogs, tend to have a bad reputation, and for good reason: the pasteurized and processed juices so often used to make them result in sad cocktails with a flat flavor. But when built with fresh ingredients, they can be delicious, if simple. At the extreme end of this spectrum lies one of the most unexpected Highballs of all: the Bloody Mary.

EXPERIMENTING WITH THE BALANCE

Because the mixer comprises such a large portion of the overall volume of a Highball and the choice of mixers is almost unlimited, changing out the mixer creates a vast canvas for exploration. This can be as straightforward as replacing seltzer with a different commercial mixer, such as tonic or cola, or as radical as using beer, sparkling wine, or even juice as the mixer, including vegetable juices to take the template in a savory direction, as in the Bloody Mary and its many variations.

Paloma

CLASSIC

Though the Margarita may get the world's attention, Mexicans are far more likely to mix up a Paloma, which is simply grapefruit soda and tequila with a squeeze of lime. This cocktail can also be made with mezcal, and we highly recommend trying that variation. Our Paloma takes the traditional version and amplifies its flavors, first by making our own grapefruit soda from fresh grapefruit, and then adding a touch of grapefruit liqueur for even greater complexity.

Lime wedge
Kosher salt, for rimming
1¾ ounces blanco tequila
¼ ounce Giffard Crème de Pamplemousse
¼ ounce fresh lime juice
4 ounces cold Homemade Grapefruit Soda (page 295)
Garnish: 1 grapefruit wedge

Rub the lime wedge along the upper ½ inch of a Highball glass, halfway around the circumference, then roll the wet portion in the salt. Pour in the tequila, Pamplemousse, and lime juices, then add 3 ice cubes. Stir for 3 seconds. Add the soda and stir once. Garnish with the grapefruit wedge.

Cuba Libre

CLASSIC

In the classic Cuba Libre, a humble Highball—rum and Coke—is elevated by adding a touch of lime juice. It's an inspired choice, because lime peel is a key ingredient in most colas, so the juice draws that flavor out of the cola while also cutting through its sweetness. The core spirit is also crucial to making this cocktail work: rum's sugarcane backbone complements the cola's round spice flavors, and whisky's spice can work wonderfully with cola's bitter and citrus flavors, but the subtlety of vodka would fall flat, and gin's botanicals would clash with the mixer.

2 ounces white rum
¼ ounce fresh lime juice
4 ounces cold Coca-Cola
Garnish: 1 lime wedge

Pour the rum into a Highball glass, then add 3 ice cubes. Stir for 3 seconds. Add the lime juice and cola and stir once. Garnish with the lime wedge.

Negroni Sbagliato

CLASSIC

Remember the Americano (page 208) from the section "Experimenting with the Core and Seasoning"? What if we were to replace the seltzer with sparkling wine? The delicious result is a classic Negroni Sbagliato. Because the sparkling wine has more flavor than seltzer, less is used, resulting in a cocktail that dances between bitter, sweet, and refreshing.

1 ounce Carpano Antica Formula vermouth
1 ounce Campari
1 ounce cold prosecco
Garnish: 1 orange wedge

Pour the vermouth and Campari into a Highball glass and stir to combine. Fill the glass with ice cubes, then pour in the prosecco and quickly dip the barspoon into the glass to gently mix the wine with the cocktail. Garnish with the orange wedge.

Screwdriver

CLASSIC

As mentioned earlier, Screwdrivers (and similar Highballs that use citrus juice as the mixer) can be quite disappointing when made with processed commercial juices. However, these simple drinks can be redeemed by using freshly pressed juice from oranges that are in season. The juice itself is balanced, thanks to its bright acidity and sweetness, which makes for a refreshing cocktail. Even so, sometimes even fresh juice can fall a little flat. No problem! Just add a bit of Citric Acid Solution.

4 ounces fresh orange juice
Citric Acid Solution (page 298), if needed
2 ounces vodka

Taste the juice before mixing. If the flavor seems a little flat, add a bit of Citric Acid Solution, a drop at a time, until the flavor is sweet with a tangy bite. Combine the orange juice and vodka in a Highball glass, then add 3 ice cubes. Stir for 3 seconds. No garnish.

EXPLORING TECHNIQUE: BUILDING WHISKY HIGHBALLS

Technique is important to all Highballs, but it's crucial to Whisky Highballs, so in this section we'll elaborate on our recommended technique for this simple but sophisticated drink. We build our Whisky Highballs with three things in mind: the proportion of whisky to seltzer; the temperature of the ingredients and glassware, and the style of ice. We also use a very specific mixing technique.

If we use too little seltzer, the whisky will taste diluted, and its bubbles will feel weak. If we use too much seltzer, the whisky's flavor will be dumbed down. The proportion of two parts seltzer to one part whisky allows the ingredients to work together well, positioning the whisky as the star of the show, lifted up on the sharply effervescent backbone of the seltzer. It's refreshing but also flavorful.

Our second key consideration is the temperature of the glassware and ingredients. We start by using glasses that have a smooth interior, as any etching provides a greater surface area for gases in the seltzer to attach to and come out of solution. In addition, we prefer to serve Whisky Highballs in chilled glasses and only use extremely cold seltzer for our Highballs. This isn't just about serving a bracingly cold drink; it also helps maintain the seltzer's bubbles throughout the life of the drink.

Our third and final consideration is the type of ice we use—a factor that also has a bearing on effervescence. This also has to do with surface area: many small pieces of ice have a much greater surface area than a few larger pieces; again, this allows more gases to come out of solution more quickly, resulting in a drink that rapidly becomes flat. While a single large chunk of ice with less surface area—say, a long spear of ice—would help keep the drink bubbly, it may not keep it very cold. We opt for the middle ground, choosing 1-inch ice cubes.

To build the drink, pull a chilled Highball glass out of the freezer and pour in the whisky. Carefully add 1 ice cube (preferably 1 inch or larger), taken directly from the freezer, slowly lowering it into the whisky with a barspoon so it doesn't crack. Let the ice sit for about 10 seconds; if you stir immediately, the huge temperature difference between the whisky and the ice will probably make the ice cube crack. After the ice has tempered, slowly stir until condensation forms on the outside of the glass, typically about 10 seconds. Add another ice cube or two, so that the ice comes two-thirds of the way up the glass, then stir briefly. Pour in some of the chilled seltzer— just enough that the ice doesn't float. Insert a barspoon into the glass, all the way to the bottom, and carefully lift the lowest piece of ice up about an inch, then lower it back to the bottom of the glass. This will gently mix the whisky and seltzer. Add a final piece of ice, then the remaining seltzer. Give it a final stir—one revolution only so as not to decrease the effervescence! Serve immediately.

GLASSWARE: THE HIGHBALL GLASS

The Whisky Highball and most of the cocktails in its extended family are all about the bubbles, so it's especially important to use a glass that will help keep that effervescence alive as long as possible. In a short, wide glass, such as an Old-Fashioned glass or a coupe, a cocktail will have a larger surface area exposed to the open air, so the gases in the mixer will come out of solution more quickly than in a tall, narrow glass.

Our ideal Highball glass holds 12 ounces of liquid. We prefer those with a thick, weighted base and sides that become quite thin at the rim. The heavy base gives the cocktail solid footing on the table, and the delicacy of the rim is as much sensorial as it is practical (those thin rims can chip easily, but boy are they sexy). Some Highball glasses have etching on the outside, which is mostly ornamental but also gives the drinker a little extra grip. You probably won't find it surprising that many of our favorite models hail from the Highball's promised land, Japan. Our favorite Japanese brand available Stateside is Hard Strong, which makes a couple of styles of very durable Highball glasses with that combination of heft and delicacy that we love.

We should point out that Highball glasses and Collins glasses aren't necessarily interchangeable, despite their similar shape. A proper Collins glass is larger, holding around 14 ounces of liquid. That difference in volume makes sense when you consider that a Highball is 2 ounces of booze plus a mixer, while a Collins is a full cocktail, shaken to dilution, then poured over ice and topped with bubbles. The larger Collins glass would be fine for serving Highballs, but if you try to fit a Collins-style drink in a Highball glass, you'll have to either use less mixer or sacrifice some ice cubes in order to save space for the cocktail. The same goes for swizzles and coolers, which also benefit from a larger glass that can hold the requisite amount of ice.

WASTE NOT

In most bars, Highball-style drinks are served with a plastic straw, and until recently, we did this at our bars. We've been phasing them out because of their environmental impacts: plastic straws eventually end up in a landfill, and, of course, manufacturing them also has an environmental impact. In all honesty, most cocktails don't really need straws. These days we do provide them if requested, but otherwise we only use them for drinks that genuinely, require straws—such as Juleps, swizzles, and other cocktails served over crushed ice, and we use metal straws, which can be washed and reused indefinitely.

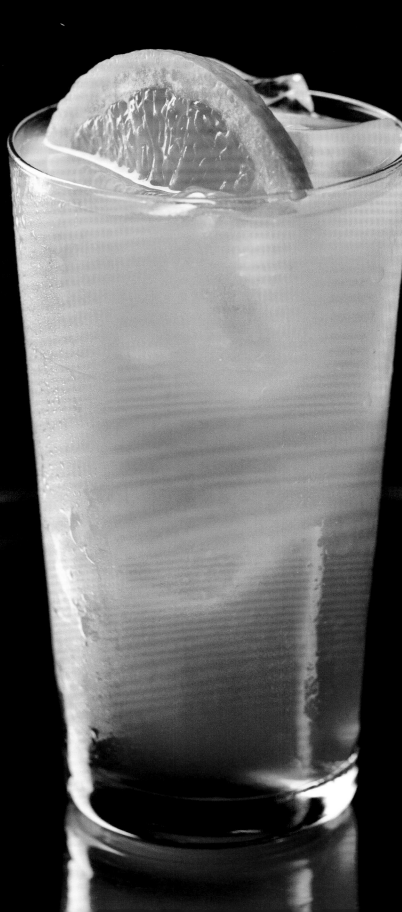

HIGHBALL VARIATIONS

Because of the Highball's simplicity, elements from the cocktails at the heart of each of the previous chapters can be used to generate balanced and tasty Highball variations. For example, the interplay between acidic lemon or lime juice balanced by sugar (the dynamic fundamental to Daiquiris) can be worked into a Highball in small quantities to boost flavor—but not so much that it becomes a sour! Similarly, the principles embodied by the Old-Fashioned and the Martini—using bitters to accent a spirit, or achieving harmony by marrying a spirit with fortified wine—can also be used in Highballs. Indeed, as you'll see, some of the drinks in the remainder of this chapter look a lot like riffs on sours, Old-Fashioneds, or Martinis stretched out with a mixer.

Tequila Sunrise

Tequila Sunrise

CLASSIC

Like the Screwdriver (page 213), the Tequila Sunrise is an oft-maligned classic cocktail that's greatly improved by using fresh, rather than commercial, juice. We also find the classic version a bit cloying because of the sweetness of the grenadine, so we compensate by adding just a bit of lime juice, which pairs well with the tequila. The result is a refreshing, juicy cocktail, perfect for daytime drinking.

2 ounces blanco tequila

4 ounces fresh orange juice

¼ ounce fresh lime juice

¼ ounce House Grenadine (page 47)

Garnish: 1 orange half wheel and 1 lime wedge

Combine the tequila, orange juice, and lime juice in a Highball glass, then add 3 ice cubes. Stir for 3 seconds. Add the grenadine and don't stir so it will settle to the bottom of the glass. Garnish with the orange half wheel and lime wedge.

Gin and Tonic

CLASSIC

The gin and tonic is perhaps even more popular than the Whisky Highball, perhaps because of how its two simple ingredients interact with each other. Tonic water isn't just a bitter seltzer; it also has a fair amount of sugar, giving it a sweetness that helps highlight the botanical flavors of high-proof English gin while curbing its alcohol heat.

2 ounces London dry gin

4 ounces cold tonic water

Garnish: 1 lime wedge

Pour the gin into a Highball glass, then add 3 ice cubes. Stir for 3 seconds. Add the tonic water and stir once. Garnish with the lime wedge.

Harvey Wallbanger

CLASSIC

Continuing our exploration of Highballs that have a bad reputation, consider the Harvey Wallbanger—basically a Screwdriver (page 213) with a float of Galliano on top—where just a small amount of liqueur adds flavor and complexity to a simple Highball. For our version of this classic, we pull back on the vodka a bit to compensate for the alcohol in the Galliano and, as with our take on the Tequila Sunrise (see left), we add a bit of citrus juice (in this case lemon) to compensate for the added sweetness. We also forgo floating the Galliano on top because we find that this creates an unbalanced cocktail, and the liqueur drops to the bottom anyhow.

1½ ounces Aylesbury Duck vodka

½ ounce Galliano l'Autentico

3 ounces fresh orange juice

½ ounce fresh lemon juice

Garnish: 1 orange half wheel

Short shake all the ingredients with 3 ice cubes for about 5 seconds, then strain into a Highball glass filled with ice. Garnish with the orange half wheel.

THE HIGHBALL EXTENDED FAMILY

The Highball extended family begins to play with the template—one part base to two parts mixer—in different ways. For savory Highballs like the Bloody Mary that are all about the mixer, we increase the amount of mixer used in each cocktail; in cocktails made with Champagne (like the Mimosa), we flip the equation and use a small amount of orange juice (mixer) as flavoring. Though these cocktails begin playing with the Highball formula, at heart they are all just a combination of alcohol and mixer.

Normandie Club Bloody Mary

DEVON TARBY, 2015

By now you know that we're big proponents of using fresh juices. But for years, we were confounded by tomato juice, since fresh versions have a thin flavor and tend to separate when mixed with booze. The answer, as it turns out, is to mix fresh tomato juice with a bit of bottled juice to stabilize the texture while still delivering fresh tomato flavor, so that's the approach we take in the Bloody Mary mix for this cocktail. Another pet peeve of ours is Bloody Marys with a grainy texture or particulates, such as spices or horseradish. So for this Bloody Mary mix, we forgo spices or horseradish and instead use a bit of fresh celery juice and bell pepper juice. With so much work dedicated to perfecting the mix, we chose savory aquavit to deepen the flavor even more. This mix is versatile, though: swap in vodka, gin, or even amontillado sherry.

Lemon wedge
Lemon Pepper Salt (page 297)
1½ ounces Krogstad aquavit
5 ounces Normandie Club Bloody Mary Mix (page 296)
¼ ounce fresh lemon juice
¼ ounce fresh lime juice
Garnish: 1 cherry tomato and 1 lemon wedge on a skewer

Rub the lemon wedge along the upper ½ inch of a Collins glass, halfway around the circumference, then roll the wet portion in the Lemon Pepper Salt. Fill the glass with ice cubes. Add the remaining ingredients and stir a few times. Garnish with the cherry tomato and lemon wedge.

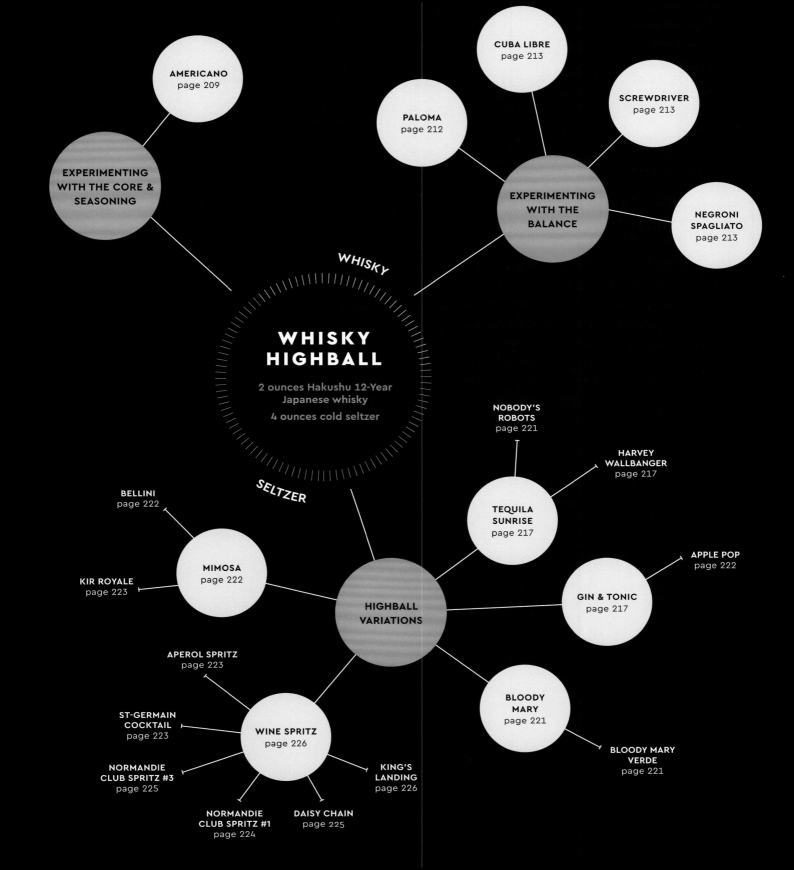

AMERICANO
page 209

EXPERIMENTING
WITH THE CORE &
SEASONING

CUBA LIBRE
page 213

SCREWDRIVER
page 213

PALOMA
page 212

EXPERIMENTING
WITH THE
BALANCE

NEGRONI
SPAGLIATO
page 213

WHISKY

WHISKY
HIGHBALL

2 ounces Hakushu 12-Year
Japanese whisky

4 ounces cold seltzer

SELTZER

NOBODY'S
ROBOTS
page 221

HARVEY
WALLBANGER
page 217

BELLINI
page 222

TEQUILA
SUNRISE
page 217

MIMOSA
page 222

APPLE POP
page 222

KIR ROYALE
page 223

GIN & TONIC
page 217

HIGHBALL
VARIATIONS

APEROL SPRITZ
page 223

BLOODY
MARY
page 221

ST-GERMAIN
COCKTAIL
page 223

WINE SPRITZ
page 226

BLOODY MARY
VERDE
page 221

NORMANDIE
CLUB SPRITZ #3
page 225

KING'S
LANDING
page 226

NORMANDIE
CLUB SPRITZ #1
page 224

DAISY CHAIN
page 225

TYSON BUHLER

Tyson Buhler is the bar director at Death & Co and a winner of the 2015 World Class bartending competition.

The Highball is probably the first drink every bartender learns. My introduction came from the old guys who drank whisky sodas at the golf course where I worked as a kid, always "easy on the soda."

Until recently, I still thought of whisky and soda as an old man's drink. But there's an entire culture of high-end Highballs coming our way from Japan. Highball bars are all the rage in Japan these days, and they get really specific about how to build the drink there. There's the *mizuwari* ("cut with water") ritual, in which you fill a glass with ice, stir it around to chill the vessel, then pour out the water that has melted, retaining the ice in the glass. Then you add whisky and stir exactly 13½ times, always clockwise. Finally, you add sparkling water and stir 3½ times. Some bartenders use one large piece of ice for the entire process; others add ice with every step. Don't even get me started on how fussy they are about the type of water they use. It's all very Zen.

If my grandpa saw this, he'd think it was hilarious. But these days American bartenders are drawn to this kind of exacting attention to detail, as well as the romanticism of the process. But

I have to admit, it's sometimes hard to convey our appreciation for these nuances to our guests. They see a two-ingredient drink that's mostly water, which can make it hard to understand the sophistication of the drink and the attention to detail in the glass. That's okay; they don't need to understand all of the minutiae if they enjoy the drink.

All of that said, the most beautiful thing about the Highball is its simplicity. You only need a spirit, a glass, some ice, and carbonated water. You don't need a shaker or mixing glass, fancy syrups, or bitters. Hell, you don't even need a proper barspoon. As a result, you can make a great Highball pretty much anywhere.

The simplicity of the template also leaves a lot of room to experiment, branching out into infinite other variations beyond the usual gin and tonics, rum and Cokes, and Palomas. So many branches, so little time . . . This recipe matches up soothing Calvados with the bright bitterness of tonic water, a combination that may sound surprising but is deeply refreshing and complex.

Calvados and Tonic

2 ounces Domaine de Montreuil Pays d'Auge Réserve Calvados

4 ounces cold Fever-Tree tonic water

Pour the Calvados into a Highball glass, then add 3 ice cubes. Stir for 3 seconds. Add the tonic and stir once. No garnish.

Bloody Mary

As mentioned earlier, a Highball can also be savory—and the Bloody Mary is the queen of all savory cocktails. Our baseline Bloody Mary is simple and requires minimal prep. Use this recipe as a template and adjust the drink to suit your preferences. It's also a great canvas for experimentation. You could add a splash of mezcal for smoke, or substitute manzanilla sherry for the vodka to up the savory ante and bring the ABV down (you don't *have* to get drunk at brunch). Or consider making it with our Roasted Garlic– and Pepper-Infused Vodka (page 292).

Kosher salt and pepper, for rimming

Lemon wedge

2 ounces Aylesbury Duck vodka

5 ounces Basic Bloody Mary Mix (page 295)

¼ ounce fresh lemon juice

Garnish: 1 lemon wedge and 1 celery stalk

On a small plate, mix equal parts of salt and pepper. Rub the lemon wedge along the upper ¼ inch of a pint glass, halfway around the circumference, then roll the wet portion in the salt and pepper. Fill the glass with ice cubes. Add the remaining ingredients and stir a few times. Garnish with the lemon wedge and celery stalk.

Bloody Mary Verde

DEVON TARBY, 2013

Call us classicists, but we don't often veer away from the tomato-based Bloody Mary mixes used in the previous cocktails. One exception is our tomatillo-based Verde Mix, which is the perfect match for a spicy infused tequila. This drink needs more sugar than you'd think, as cucumber and tomatillo are naturally less sweet than tomatoes, so we add honey to the mix, which also adds a slight earthiness that helps unify the rest of the ingredients.

Kosher salt and chile powder, for rimming

Lime wedge

5 ounces Verde Mix (page 296)

1½ ounces Jalapeño-Infused Vodka (page 291)

1 ounce fresh lime juice

Garnish: 1 cherry tomato and 1 lemon wedge on a skewer

On a small plate, mix equal parts of kosher salt and chile powder. Rub the lime wedge along the upper ¼ inch of a Collins glass, halfway around the circumference, then roll the wet portion in the salt mixture. Fill the glass with ice cubes. Add the remaining ingredients and stir a few times. Garnish with the cherry tomato and lemon wedge.

Nobody's Robots

ALEX DAY, 2013

Nobody's Robots is a nerdy evolution of the Screwdriver (page 213) made especially delicious by carbonating the entire cocktail. If you're equipped with a keg cocktail system (most people are, right?), this drink is a fantastic way to trick folks into drinking lots and lots of sherry. Overall, the flavors in this drink are more concentrated than those in a more typical Highball—a simple slug of booze topped with a mixer—which makes it feel more like a sophisticated cocktail.

1¼ ounces Absolut vodka

1 ounce Williams & Humbert Dry Sack sherry

1 ounce clarified orange juice (see page 146)

1 ounce Vanilla Lactic Syrup (page 286)

1 teaspoon Citric Acid Solution (page 298)

1 drop Terra Spice orange extract

2½ ounces cold seltzer

Garnish: 1 orange half wheel

Chill all the ingredients. Combine them in a carbonating bottle, charge with CO_2, and gently shake to help dissolve the CO_2 into the liquid (see page 228 for detailed carbonation instructions). Refrigerate the carbonating bottle for at least 20 minutes, and preferably for 12 hours, before opening. Pour into an ice-filled Highball glass and garnish with the orange half wheel.

Mimosa

In chapter 1, we delved (all too briefly) into the world of sparkling wines (see page 28). Because they can vary so widely in levels of acidity and sugar and display flavors that range from sharp to rich and yeasty notes, they often aren't interchangeable in cocktails. As with the Screwdriver (page 213), there's no comparing a Mimosa made with freshly pressed, in-season orange juice to one made with pasteurized juice. The former is bright and refreshing, while the latter often tastes flat. That said, oranges do vary in sweetness and acidity, so we include a bit of Citric Acid Solution to ensure that the drink has a bright, zippy flavor.

1 ounce fresh orange juice

3 drops Citric Acid Solution (page 298)

5 ounces cold dry sparkling wine

Combine the orange juice and Citric Acid Solution in a chilled flute. Pour in the sparkling wine, and quickly dip the barspoon into the glass to gently mix the wine with the cocktail. No garnish.

Apple Pop

DEVON TARBY, 2015

The Apple Pop is our take on creating a highbrow version of a straightforward Highball, inspired by the simplicity of a gin and tonic. We match an unaged French apple brandy with a touch of pear brandy and the herbal sweetness of blanc vermouth; a juicy homemade Apple Celery Soda stretches out these flavors for a refreshing Highball riff.

1 ounce Drouin Blanche de Normandie apple brandy

½ ounce Clear Creek pear brandy

1 ounce Dolin blanc vermouth

5 ounces Apple Celery Soda (page 295)

Garnish: 1 mint sprig and 1 celery leaf

Combine all the ingredients (except the soda) in a Highball glass, then add 3 ice cubes. Stir for 3 seconds. Add the soda and stir once. Garnish with the mint sprig and celery leaf.

Bellini

CLASSIC

Although Bellinis are served year-round in bars around the world, they're at their best when made with peaches at the peak of their ripeness—a privilege that few get to experience. Even the highest-quality commercial peach puree will taste dull in comparison to one made with peaches in their prime. Take note of when peaches are available at your local farmers' market, then seize the opportunity to make this classic cocktail. That said, the beauty of the Bellini is that it can be made with almost any fresh, ripe fruit, opening the door to numerous new creations.

1 ounce fresh peach puree (see sidebar)

5 ounces cold prosecco

Put the peach puree in a flute. Pour in the prosecco, and quickly dip the barspoon into the glass to gently mix the prosecco with the cocktail. No garnish.

MAKING FRUIT PUREES

To make fruit purees, you'll need a blender and a fine-mesh sieve. First, wash the fruit thoroughly. If the skins of the fruit have bitter or off-putting flavors, peel the fruit first. Also remove any pits or seeds. Fruits like peaches, pears, and apples tend to turn brown from contact with oxygen; for these, add ascorbic acid powder to the blender along with the fruit (½ teaspoon per 2 cups of fruit). Blend until smooth, then pass the puree through a fine-mesh sieve. Transfer to a storage container, cover, and store in the refrigerator, where it will keep for up to 1 week, or in the freezer, where it will keep for up to 1 month.

Kir Royale

CLASSIC

Another avenue for exploring Highball variations based on sparkling wines is to use fruit liqueur as a flavoring; just be careful not to add too much and oversweeten the drink. The classic Kir Royale strikes the right balance by using a restrained amount of crème de cassis, a black currant liqueur that retains the bright acidity of the fruit. That acidity makes it versatile for mixing, since it contributes both sweetness and sourness alongside its juicy fruit flavor. Although Champagne is traditional in this drink, Crémant de Bourgogne would also work well, and don't hesitate to venture farther afield, exploring the countless possibilities for pairing liqueurs with sparkling wines.

½ ounce Gabriel Boudier Crème de Cassis de Dijon

5½ ounces cold, dry Champagne

Pour the crème de cassis into a chilled flute, then pour in the Champagne and quickly dip the barspoon into the glass to gently mix the Champagne with the cocktail. No garnish.

St-Germain Cocktail

CLASSIC

The underlying principle in the St-Germain Cocktail is the same as that in the Aperol Spritz (see right). To ensure that the sparkling wine doesn't overpower the delicacy of the St-Germain, a fairly modest amount of sparkling wine is supplemented with seltzer, allowing for maximum effervescence and a balanced flavor profile that allows the St-Germain to shine through.

1½ ounces St-Germain

2 ounces cold dry sparkling wine

2 ounces cold seltzer

Garnish: 1 lemon twist

Pour the St-Germain into a Highball glass. Fill the glass with ice cubes, then pour in the sparkling wine and quickly dip the barspoon into the glass to gently mix the wine with the cocktail. Express the lemon twist over the drink, then place it into the drink.

Aperol Spritz

CLASSIC

The classic Aperol Spritz sits alongside the Americano as an indispensable aperitif cocktail—a drink consumed before a meal to stimulate the appetite. While we stand by our belief that sparkling wine makes everything better, too much can overpower delicate flavors. This drink, made with Aperol, the lightest of aperitifs, is a case in point. If it were to call for more sparkling wine, that would push it into boozy territory, so it also includes seltzer to ensure that it's refreshing and fizzy enough, without overly interfering with the flavor profile.

2 ounces Aperol

3 ounces cold prosecco or dry Champagne-style sparkling wine

2 ounces cold seltzer

Garnish: 1 grapefruit wedge

Pour the Aperol into a wineglass. Fill the glass with ice cubes, then pour in the sparkling wine and seltzer and quickly dip the barspoon into the glass to gently mix the wine with the cocktail. Garnish with the grapefruit wedge.

Normandie Club
Spritz #1

Daisy Chain

Normandie Club
Spritz #3

Normandie Club Spritz #1

DEVON TARBY & ALEX DAY,
THE NORMANDIE CLUB 2015

With fully clarified juices, it's easy to think this cocktail is just a simple spritz, but it's packed with bright, tart flavors and fantastically complex piney notes—thanks to the Clear Creek Douglas Fir eau de vie.

- **1½ ounces Dolin Blanc Vermouth**
- **½ ounce Clear Creek Douglas Fir Eau de Vie**
- **3 ounces clarified cucumber water (see page 146)**
- **½ ounce clarified lime juice (see page 146)**
- **½ ounce simple syrup (page 45)**
- **1 drop Salt Solution (page 298)**
- **½ ounce still water**
- **Garnish: 1 mint sprig**

Chill all the ingredients. Combine in a carbonating bottle, charge with CO_2, and gently shake to help dissolve the CO_2 into the liquid (see page 228 for detailed carbonation instructions). Pour over ice in a small white wine glass. Garnish with the mint sprig.

Daisy Chain

DEVON TARBY, 2015

The Daisy Chain takes an approach similar to the Normandie Club Spritz #3 (see right) to produce a cocktail that mimics the flavors of a glass of sparkling wine. The combination of bone-dry, salty manzanilla sherry, sweet and floral St-Germain, and juicy verjus could almost trick you into thinking you're drinking a dry Muscat. Bitter Suze is added to curb the candy notes of the St-Germain and add an aperitif quality, while the sparkling cider brings body and funk—qualities not found in seltzer or sparkling wine.

- **1½ ounces manzanilla sherry**
- **½ ounce St-Germain**
- **¼ ounce Suze**
- **½ ounce Fusion Napa Valley verjus blanc**
- **¼ ounce fresh lemon juice**
- **2 drops Salt Solution (page 298)**
- **3 ounces Normandy sparkling apple cider**
- **Garnish: 5 thin apple slices on a skewer**

Combine all the ingredients (except the cider) in a wineglass. Fill the glass with ice cubes and stir until chilled. Top with the cider and stir gently to combine. Garnish with the apple slices.

Normandie Club Spritz #3

DEVON TARBY, 2015

We took our Improved Wine Spritz (page 226) and expanded on the idea to come up with the Normandie Club Spritz #3, which has a split base of dry vermouth and St-Germain, accompanied by clarified juices to provide balance without altering the Champagne-like texture of the cocktail. We also chose to fully carbonate the cocktail, rather than simply pouring in seltzer. This infuses the drink with a uniform effervescence that makes it incredibly quaffable.

- **1 ounce Boissiere dry vermouth**
- **1 ounce St-Germain**
- **¼ ounce Pueblo Viejo blanco tequila**
- **¼ ounce Campo de Encanto Grand and Noble pisco**
- **¼ ounce Giffard Crème de Pamplemousse**
- **1 ounce clarified grapefruit juice (see page 146)**
- **½ ounce clarified lemon juice (see page 146)**
- **2½ ounces cold seltzer**
- **Garnish: 1 grapefruit half wheel**

Chill all the ingredients. Combine in a carbonating bottle, charge with CO_2, and gently shake to help dissolve the CO_2 into the liquid (see page 228 for detailed carbonation instructions). Refrigerate the carbonating bottle for at least 20 minutes, and preferably for 12 hours, before opening. Pour into an ice-filled Highball glass and garnish with the grapefruit half wheel.

Improved Wine Spritz

DEVON TARBY, 2016

Our Improved Wine Spritz demonstrates how we can integrate some of the principles from chapter 3, on Daiquiris and sours, to yield a superior Wine Spritz (see right) without veering too far from a Highball template. All we've done is add small amounts of lemon juice and simple syrup, but this brings an appealing sweet-sour balance to the drink, lifts the flavors of the wine, and gives the cocktail more body.

4 ounces cold, crisp white or rosé wine

¼ ounce fresh lemon juice

¼ ounce simple syrup (page 45)

2 ounces cold seltzer

Garnish: 1 lemon wheel

Combine the wine, lemon juice, and simple syrup in a wineglass. Fill the glass with ice cubes, pour in the seltzer, and stir gently to combine. Garnish with the lemon wheel.

Wine Spritz

CLASSIC

You can also use still wine as the core of a drink. Because its proof is so much lower and the flavor more mild than a spirit, the amount of wine should be increased, with the amount of seltzer being decreased accordingly. *Voilà!* The classic Wine Spritz, which is indeed a type of Highball. Though wines vary widely in their sweetness and acidity, sticking with a small measure of seltzer as the mixer generally works well, as it will stretch and carry the distinctive flavors of the wine. We love a Wine Spritz with no trace of shame. What's not to like about a glass of chilled wine topped with seltzer? It's a drink fit for moms and cocktail nerds alike.

4 ounces cold, crisp white or rosé wine

2 ounces cold seltzer

Garnish: 1 lemon wheel

Pour the wine into a wineglass. Fill the glass with ice cubes, then pour in the seltzer and stir once. Garnish with the lemon wheel.

King's Landing

ALEX DAY, 2013

In terms of its ingredients, the King's Landing may seem like a fairly typical sour-style cocktail, if a little lean in the sour department. But if you take a close look at the amounts called for, you'll see that cava and our birch-infused vermouth make up most of the volume of the cocktail, with relatively small amounts of lemon juice and pear liqueur being added for balance, keeping this cocktail firmly in Highball territory.

1½ ounces Birch-Infused Cocchi Vermouth di Torino (page 287)

½ ounce Clear Creek pear liqueur

¼ ounce fresh lemon juice

3½ ounces cold cava

Garnish: 1 lemon wheel

Combine the infused vermouth, pear liqueur, and lemon juice in a wineglass. Fill the glass with ice cubes, then pour in the cava and quickly dip the barspoon into the glass to gently mix the wine with the cocktail. Garnish with the lemon wheel.

King's Landing

NEXT-LEVEL TECHNIQUE: CARBONATING COCKTAILS

Our passion for all things bubbly has led us to explore a variety of techniques to help make drinks as effervescent as possible, making them even more delicious thanks to carbonation's impact on aroma and flavor. When you bring a bubbly drink to your nose, the bursting bubbles of carbon dioxide (CO_2) lift the drink's aromatic molecules, elevating your perception of flavor. As you take your first sip, the bubbles tickle your tongue. And as you consume the drink, the presence of CO_2 plays with your perception of acidity, making the drink seem more refreshing.

Carbonation can occur naturally or be introduced. While there are many excellent, high-quality carbonated mixers, sometimes we want to make our own—or carbonate an entire cocktail. Technology to the rescue! Using some inexpensive gear, we use a system that can make almost any drink effervescent. But before we tell you about that, let's look at how carbonation works and how best to accomplish it.

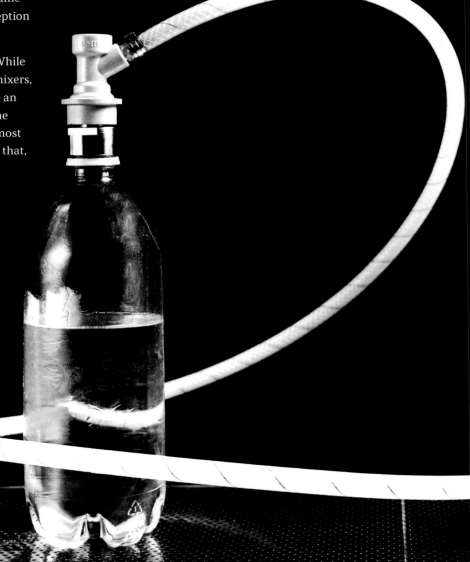

SOME BASIC PRINCIPLES OF CARBONATION

Carbonation is the presence of dissolved CO_2 in a liquid. When attempting to force CO_2 into solution in a liquid, it's important to keep three key variables in mind: clarity, temperature, and time.

Generally, transparent liquids are preferable for carbonation. Cloudiness yields less stable carbonation because any particles floating in a liquid, such as citrus pulp, create an escape route for bubbles, which attach to them and float to the surface of the liquid, where the CO_2 bubbles off. Therefore, we prefer to work with clear liquids, clarifying them before carbonating if need be. (See "Next-Level Technique: Clarifying," on page 144.)

The temperature of liquid also has a huge bearing on carbonation. Ever opened a warm bottle of soda? It probably fizzed everywhere because the higher the temperature of a liquid, the less CO_2 it can hold. A cold soda, on the other hand, will barely fizz when it's opened and will stay bubbly for longer. So before carbonating, we ensure that our ingredients are as cold as possible, and we keep them chilled after they've been carbonated.

Finally, there's no escaping time. Even when CO_2 is injected into very cold, clear liquid, the gas needs a bit of time to fully dissolve. We've noticed that our house carbonated cocktails have finer, tighter bubbles when they're allowed to rest for at least a day.

WHEN (AND WHEN NOT) TO CARBONATE

Just because a liquid is clear doesn't mean it's a good choice for carbonation. Not long ago, enthusiastic bartenders were carbonating everything in sight (guilty as charged!), including spirituous cocktails. And while there are few things in the world we love more than a Negroni and bubbles, separately, it really isn't appropriate to put them together. Here are some compelling reasons to steer clear of carbonating boozy cocktails.

Carbonated drinks are said to get drinkers tipsy more quickly. Although this hasn't been conclusively proven, we have found that people tend to drink effervescent cocktails far more quickly. Therefore, we gravitate toward carbonating cocktails that pack a lighter punch than other drinks.

Then, reflect back on how carbonation influences the drinker's experience of a liquid, altering its aroma, texture, and flavor. A cocktail such as a Negroni embodies a delicate balance of strong, sweet, and bitter, built from ingredients that have intense personalities. Carbonation would shift that balance, increasing the aromatic intensity of the Campari and vermouth, the perception of acidity, and the presence of alcohol on the palate. Ultimately, a carbonated Negroni isn't very tasty, and the drink certainly isn't improved by the process.

CARBONATION METHODS AND TOOLS

Shortly, we'll set forth three methods for home carbonation: using a soda siphon, building your own rig for carbonating bottled liquids (our favored method), or building a similar rig for carbonating entire kegs of cocktails. (Another option is the branded Perlini system, which utilizes a specialized shaker and either CO_2 cartridges or a CO_2 pressure tank.) You may wonder why you can't just use a SodaStream or other similar devices to carbonate cocktails. Perhaps you could, but we highly recommend against it. For one, using a SodaStream to carbonate cocktails will void the unit's warranty. Also, a SodaStream doesn't allow you to control the amount of pressure added to the liquid. We err on the side of control.

GENERAL NOTES ON PREPARING INGREDIENTS FOR CARBONATION

1 Prepare the ingredients: Filter and clarify (see page 144) any cloudy juices, infusions, or syrups.

2 Chill the ingredients: Place any spirits (40% ABV and above) in the freezer for at least 12 hours. Lower-proof ingredients (such as vermouth, still wine, and liqueurs) shouldn't be frozen; instead, refrigerate them or, for best results, chill in an ice bath for at least 1 hour. Syrups and juices should be refrigerated long enough that the liquid is thoroughly chilled but not so long that the juice oxidizes, ideally 1 to 4 hours.

3 Prepare your space and tools: Clean and assemble your carbonation rig (see below). If using an insulated soda siphon canister, place it in the freezer until it's cold. (Everything must be cold!) Set out a gram scale, bar towel, and measuring cup so you'll have them handy when it's time to start assembling the cocktail.

4 Prepare any auxiliary ingredients: In addition to the more voluminous ingredients that are chilled, your cocktail recipe may call for small amounts of other ingredients, such as bitters, flavor extracts, acid solutions, and so on. Make sure you have those handy.

5 Be smart with dilution: When carbonating a homemade cocktail, you're creating a finished drink, and you'll want it to be diluted similarly to the stirred or shaken version of that drink. We get our best results when we dilute the batch using very cold seltzer. Though the exact amount depends on the other ingredients in the cocktail, we tend to dilute carbonated cocktails so that 20 percent of the total volume of the batch is water.

6 Assemble the batch: One at a time, remove the ingredients from the freezer, refrigerator, or ice bath. Measure each and pour it into the vessel you're using for mixing, working quickly to keep everything cold. Now you're ready to carbonate using one of the methods described in detail below.

CARBONATED FRUIT

Carbon dioxide can also be used to introduce effervescence into solid ingredients to create unique garnishes. Using an iSi whipper (*not* the soda siphon), any fruit or vegetable that contains water (essentially, all of them) can be carbonated. The process is similar to what happens in a carbonated cocktail (or carbonated water, for that matter). When CO_2 and fruit are combined in a pressurized environment, the CO_2 will pass through the fruit's outer membrane and dissolve into the liquid within the fruit. What results is fruit with the unexpected sensation of a slight tingle on the tongue.

Because the opening of the whipper is small, one of the easiest fruits to use is grapes—a favorite of ours. Berries are too delicate and will break apart. Larger fruits will need to be cut into pieces; for citrus, we generally cut each segment into four pieces. Add the fruit to the whipper, filling it no higher than the "Max" line. Seal the top and charge with a CO_2 cartridge while holding the release valve open. This will purge the ambient gas from the canister. Then, with the valve closed, change the cartridge and charge with CO_2.

Place the whipper in an ice bath to chill the ingredients; the colder the liquid in the fruit, the more CO_2 it can hold. Let sit for at least an hour. The longer the fruit remains in the whipper, the more fizzy it will become—letting it sit overnight will result in *very* fizzy fruit.

If using whole fruits such as grapes, this process will probably burst the fruit, as the pressure of the gas exceeds the strength of the skin. One solution is to cut small fruits in half before carbonating them. Another is to add a complementary liquid to the whipper so the liquid will buffer the interaction and support the fruit's cell walls. With grapes, we use verjus; the result is carbonated grapes infused with the bright, acidic flavors of verjus.

One final note on fizzy fruit: It can be a mental trip. Our brains are hardwired at a very deep, animal level to interpret fizzy fruits as being fermented and therefore possibly decayed and dangerous. For some people, this reaction can be hard to overcome. For that reason, we often carbonate whole fruit using complementary liquids, as we do with grapes and verjus. This will reinforce the fresh qualities of the fruit, resulting in a pleasant and unique garnish.

SODA SIPHON

Soda siphons are thick-walled canisters made specifically for carbonating liquids. Our favorite is made by the iSi company (which also sells the N_2O cream whippers we use for rapid pressured infusions, discussed on page 97). To carbonate using a soda siphon, add liquid to the canister, being careful to fill it no higher than the "Max" line; this is important for both safety and optimum carbonation. Also, be sure to screw the lid on very tightly. Charge with one CO_2 cartridge, then shake vigorously. (Though the manufacturer doesn't recommend it, we always charge with a second charger and shake again for maximum effervescence.) Then refrigerate the canister or, for more rapid cooling, place it in an ice bath. Either way, let the siphon chill for at least 2 hours and preferably 6 hours, which will allow even more time for the CO_2 to go into solution.

The soda siphon is an inexpensive and versatile tool, but it has three major drawbacks. The first is that you can't remove the ambient air from the canister without wasting a full charger. The second is that you can't adjust the amount of pressure applied to the liquid, so you can't control the intensity of bubbles in the final drink. Third, there are the costs and environmental impacts of all those little canisters. That alone makes soda siphons a less that sustainable method, especially for a busy bar. That said, they can be a good off-the-shelf option for starting to explore home carbonation of cocktails.

DIY CARBONATION OF BOTTLED LIQUIDS

By far our favorite carbonation method, both at our bars and at home, is using a rig cobbled together from homebrew supplies, popularized by cocktail wizard Dave Arnold and Portland-based bartender Jeffrey Morganthaler. Luckily, this kind of rig is now popular enough that you probably won't need to search through a homebrew supply shop for the right parts while a confused shop clerk looks on. (Of course, these supplies are also available online should you not be fortunate enough to have a local homebrew shop.)

What we love most about this system is that, after a small upfront cost, making carbonated cocktails (or just having an endless supply of seltzer at home) becomes phenomenally cheap.

WHAT TO BUY FOR A
HOME CARBONATION RIG

- **CO₂ tank:** Purchase a 5-pound tank (about 14 inches tall by 5 inches wide) with a standard fitting or, if you're ambitious, a 20-pound tank, which will last for hundreds and hundreds of carbonations. Either way, once the tank is empty, you can swap it out for a full one for a small fee.

- **Primary CO₂ regulator:** This attaches to the coupler on the side of the CO_2 tank. Purchase a unit that has indicator dials for both the pressure (shown in PSI, or pounds per square inch) and the tank level, as well as a shutoff valve on the gas line. Ensure that the regulator can easily be adjusted either by a dial on the front or a screw, and that it will accommodate pressures up to 60 PSI. We prefer the regulators made by Micro Matic.

- **Hoses:** You'll need 5 feet of ⁵⁄₁₆-inch ID gas hosing (ID stands for "internal dimension"—in other words, the internal width of the hose). The commonly available red, flexible hoses will work, but we favor the thick-walled braided tubing available from Micro Matic because it's made to withstand the higher pressure we use when carbonating drinks. (Beer systems usually don't exceed 20 PSI.)

- **Gas ball lock connector:** This tiny plastic or stainless steel component connects the hose to the carbonation cap.

- **Worm clips:** You'll need at least two worm clips to secure the hose to the regulator and the gas ball lock connector. Buy extras!

- **Carbonation cap:** This is a one-way valve that connects the gas ball lock connector to a plastic bottle.

- **Plastic bottles:** This is the vessel in which you'll carbonate your cocktails. It's fine to use repurposed 1- to 3-liter PET seltzer or soda bottles, but if reusing a soda bottle, be sure to clean it thoroughly to remove any lingering flavors.

HOW TO CARBONATE BOTTLED LIQUIDS

1 Prepare your ingredients and ensure that they are all as cold as possible.

2 Funnel the ingredients into the plastic bottle, filling it no more than four-fifths full of liquid. Leaving some headspace provides space for the gas to interact with the liquid; if you fill it all the way to the top, you'll end up with a flat cocktail.

3 Squeeze the bottle in the middle to remove as much air as possible, then attach the carbonation cap and seal. Make sure the cap is tight—but not so tight that you won't be able to open it. (If carbonating multiple bottles, or if its ingredients aren't yet cold, refrigerate the bottle or put it in an ice bath.)

4 Turn on the gas and set the pressure on the primary regulator to 45 PSI.

5 Attach the gas ball lock connector to the carbonation cap, pressing until it locks into place. The bottle will expand within seconds as CO_2 rushes in.

6 Shake the bottle for 10 seconds while it's still attached to the tank, then disconnect the gas hose from the carbonation cap.

7 Place the bottle in the refrigerator or an ice bath for at least 2 hours before using.

8 For optimum results, consider carbonating the cocktail a second time. To do so, open the bottle after it has rested for 1 hour. Squeeze out the excess air and reseal, then repeat steps 4 through 7. Refrigerate or chill in an ice bath for another hour.

9 When you're ready to serve the cocktail, hold the bottle upright and carefully open the carbonation cap. It will make a loud hissing noise as the built-up CO_2 escapes. Serve quickly to preserve the bubbles.

DIY CARBONATION OF KEGGED LIQUIDS

A method similar to that for carbonating bottled cocktails can be used to carbonate an entire keg of cocktails. This just requires using a bigger setup, but because the volume is larger, a couple of additional steps are important for ensuring maximum carbonation.

Keg cocktails have become trendy in the cocktail world, and for good reason: by preparing a large batch of drinks in advance, a bartender can serve unique carbonated cocktails at incredible speed. The format can also open the door to manipulating cocktails in new ways; when they're batched in larger quantities, it's easier to make small adjustments that simply aren't possible in single cocktails. Just one word of caution: In a commercial establishment, serving liquor out of anything other than its original bottle may violate local laws, so be sure to check what's allowed in your region.

Through years of building these systems at our bars, we've made some key discoveries. Chief among them is that retrofitting a beer system for keg cocktails won't work in the long run. Traditional beer lines aren't designed to handle liquids like cocktails, which are more acidic and higher in proof. Plus, if you retrofit a beer system for cocktails, you'll quickly flavor the lines, which are a nightmare to clean or replace.

Keg cocktails are not just for bars; they can also be a great way to make a large volume of cocktails for a party, then let guests serve themselves. Are we lazy hosts? Yup! The same process we follow at our bars can be applied for home use, but instead of large 5-gallon kegs, we suggest purchasing a smaller 2½-gallon keg.

WHAT TO BUY FOR A KEG COCKTAIL RIG

- You'll need everything for the bottle rig (page 233) except the carbonation cap and plastic bottles.

- **Ball lock cornelius keg:** These kegs are available new or used from homebrew stores and various online sources, most commonly in the 5-gallon size, though smaller and larger ones are available. For professional bars, we recommend 5-gallon kegs; for home consumers, we recommend the more manageable 2½-gallon keg. Ensure that all the gaskets are clean and new and that the ball lock connectors are in good working order. It's very easy for the top opening to get bent during shipping, which will make it challenging to get a good seal and lead to poorly carbonated or uncarbonated cocktails. We prefer the stackable Torpedo kegs from Morebeer.com, which have sturdy handles that protect the connections from being jostled.

- **Carbonating lid:** This special top for cornelius kegs has a tube attached, with a carbonating stone at the end of the tube. When the top is secured onto the keg, the tube and carbonating stone are submerged in the liquid. The stone has tiny perforations that disperse CO_2 throughout the liquid in a more uniform way, speeding carbonation. (If you do a little research, you could modify a keg's gas-in connector to have an attached carbonating stone and save the expense of buying an additional lid.)

- **Tap for dispensing liquid:** A homebrew store can probably help you rig up a ball lock liquid connector to a hose and simple faucet, or there are many resources online: search for "beer faucet, cornelius ball lock disconnect."

HOW TO CARBONATE A KEG

1 Prepare your ingredients and ensure that they are all as cold as possible.

2 Prepare the keg by cleaning both the interior and the exterior well. Make sure all O-rings are in good condition and attached. (There's a large O-ring on the lid, and smaller O-rings on the ball lock connectors.)

3 Pour the cold ingredients into the keg, leaving enough room for dilution—it should be about half full.

4 Dilute your batch with very cold seltzer at the very last stage before the keg is sealed and carbonated—this gets us ahead of the game by having half of the batch already carbonated, while ensuring precision with measurement. Do not fill the keg more than four-fifths full. Leaving some headspace provides space for the gas to interact with the liquid; if you fill it all the way to the top, you'll end up with a flat cocktail.

5 Turn on the gas and set the regulator to 45 PSI.

6 Attach the gas-to-gas connector on the carbonating lid. This is the one in the middle of the lid, not the gas line to the side of the keg. Though you could carbonate using the connector on the side of the keg, in tandem with a standard lid (rather than a carbonating lid), it will take much longer to achieve full carbonation.

7 Allow the gas to disperse into the liquid for 1 minute.

8 Pull the release valve located on the lid for about 2 seconds to vent oxygen from the keg's headspace and replace it with CO_2. You'll hear the CO_2 injecting into the liquid.

9 If the line from your regulator to the keg allows, set the keg on its side and roll it back and forth for 5 minutes. Because the keg is taller than it is wide, laying it on its side increases the surface area of the gas-liquid interface, and keeping the liquid in motion speeds the rate at which the gas dissolves. If you want to carbonate very quickly, roll the keg back and forth for longer.

10 Let the keg rest. Ideally, it would remain attached to the carbonating line overnight to ensure maximum effervescence, but more importantly, it must be kept cold. If space allows, put the keg and carbonation rig into a refrigerator and let it rest under pressure. If space doesn't allow or you want to serve the cocktail sooner, put the keg in a bucket and completely surround it with ice, then add water to create an ice bath.

11 Just before dispensing, remove the gas line.

HOW TO DISPENSE A KEGGED COCKTAIL

1 Disconnect the gas line from the keg.

2 Pull the release valve on the lid. There will be a noticeably loud hissing sound. Don't worry! This only vents the gas built up in the keg's headspace, not what's dissolved into the cocktail—unless you hold it open for a long time. So, hold it open for about 10 seconds, until the hissing becomes minimal and steady, then close the release valve.

3 At this stage, you can replace the carbonating lid with the keg's standard lid, but there's no need to do so unless you want to use the carbonating lid for another keg.

4 Change the pressure on the primary regulator to 5 PSI. Attach the gas ball lock connector to the keg—*not* the carbonating lid ball lock connector that you used to carbonate the cocktail—and turn on the gas.

5 Vent the release valve one more time, again for about 10 seconds.

6 Attach a tap to the keg, making sure the liquid ball lock connector is in the *closed* position.

7 Carefully draw some liquid from the tap. If it's coming out slowly, increase the PSI in tiny increments until the liquid flows evenly without foaming. Conversely, if it's coming out too fast and foamy, decrease the PSI in tiny increments. The key is to take it slow, making only small adjustments to the pressure.

8 We advise keeping the keg on ice while serving—just like you did in college!

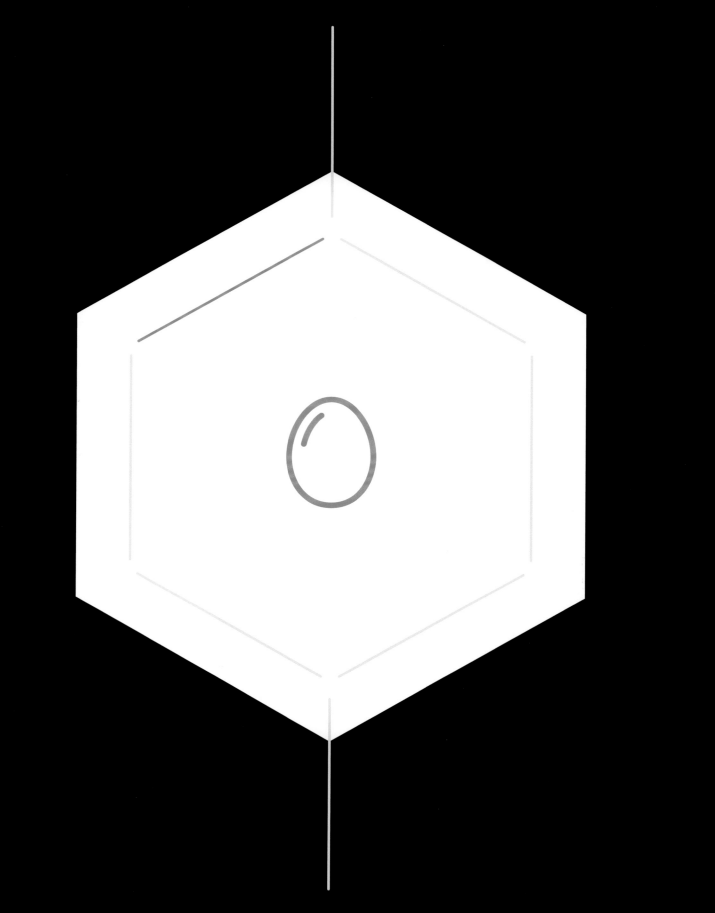

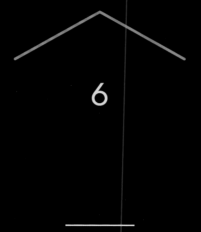

6

THE

FLIP

THE CLASSIC RECIPE

The origin of the Flip can be traced to seventeenth-century England, where beer, rum, and sugar were combined and heated to create a warming winter drink. That concoction, not yet called a Flip, became popular in colonial America, where after a couple of centuries of evolution, a method developed that involved plunging a red-hot iron poker into the liquid, causing it to violently froth, or "flip," thus christening the cocktail. Over time, the iron poker fell out of favor (thank goodness!), as did beer; the cocktail came to be served cold, not hot; and egg was introduced for reasons that remain historically murky. The end result is what today we refer to as a Flip—a drink comprised of booze, sugar, and whole egg, served cold.

Flip

2 ounces spirit or fortified wine
2 teaspoons demerara sugar
1 whole egg
Garnish: Nutmeg

Dry shake all the ingredients, then shake again with ice. Double strain into a chilled coupe. Garnish with a few grates of nutmeg.

spirit in our root Flip recipe because it was a prominent ingredient in the nineteenth-century heyday of cocktails, as well as a common component of the earliest Flips—and that would be true. However, we also admit that Flips made with a base of fortified wine are our favorites, especially those built upon oloroso sherry. So for our root recipe, we've chosen a deeply complex oloroso sherry and matched it with a rich demerara syrup. The result is a cocktail that, while decadent, is also surprisingly light and frothy.

Our Ideal Flip

2 ounces González Byass Matusalem oloroso sherry

½ ounce Demerara Gum Syrup (page 54)

1 whole egg

Garnish: Nutmeg

Dry shake all the ingredients, then shake again with ice. Double strain into a small white wine glass. Garnish with a few grates of nutmeg.

STRIKE IT RICH

Nowhere in the cocktail universe is unabashed decadence celebrated more than with the Flip and its extended family. There are many drinks that flirt with richness, but the Flip is singular in its total disregard for sound nutrition. It's dessert in a glass, often made with creamy ingredients and embracing flavors that have long been derided in fancy cocktail bars: sweet liqueurs with flavors such as chocolate, mint, and coffee. The Mudslide, the White Russian, the Grasshopper, and the Brandy Alexander—all are drinks that stem from the basic Flip. But in our opinion, those drinks aren't any less deserving of study than the finest craft cocktails. Indeed, these rich drinks have a heritage that stretches deep into cocktail history.

Though a Flip cocktail may look elaborate, there's nothing complicated about the recipe. It's just a slug of sherry (or another spirit), some sweetener, and an egg. Shake it up, and dust it with a bit of grated nutmeg, and that's it. The raisiny sherry offers dense fruit and woody flavors, demerara sugar creates a rich sweetness, and the egg, when shaken and emulsified, gives the drink its fatty, frothy texture. The way these three familiar ingredients commingle is like alchemy, creating something unique. This also makes it a launchpad for creativity. As just one example, add heavy cream to a Flip and it becomes a nog.

Flips have a reputation for being crude drinks in which richness and sugary sweetness overshadow the spirits. And while it's true that Flips are often both rich and sweet, a balanced Flip is a thing of beauty: the core flavor of the spirit takes center stage, with the egg, sugar, and sometimes cream playing supporting roles. Where the Old-Fashioned and Martini are contemplative drinks, and the Daiquiri, Sidecar, and Highball are invigorating, the Flip is all comfort—a featherbed for the senses.

When we play with riffs on the Flip, we begin with the flavor of the core, be it fortified wine or spirit, and keep its strength and sweetness in mind as we consider how to balance it with sugar, egg, cream, or other ingredients in harmonious proportions. In the 1862 first edition of *The Bar-Tender's Guide: How to Mix Drinks*, the godfather of modern mixology, Jerry Thomas, showcases myriad Flip recipes and variations. After setting the cold brandy Flip as the standard, he offers variations, both hot and cold, with substitutions of rum, gin, whiskey, port, sherry, and ale. In fact, those variations represent an early exploration along exactly the lines in this book: tweaking recipes to come up with balanced cocktails using different ingredients. Indeed, many Flip variations rely on the interplay between spirits or fortified wines and liqueurs and their affinity for rich ingredients.

UNDERSTANDING THE TEMPLATE

The classic recipe for a Flip reflects a careful balance between the personality of the core, the sweetness of the sugar, and the fat and frothiness of the egg. The egg provides a relatively static contribution, and whatever the source of the sweetness, the amount is usually a matter of personal preference. So the base ingredient, be it a spirit or fortified wine, becomes the main component to consider. If a light, unaged spirit, such as vodka, gin, or unaged rum, is used, a Flip will be overwhelmingly boozy and out of balance because the proof of the alcohol, rather than its lighter flavor, is front and center. Unaged spirits with a stronger personality, such as mezcal, tequila, or eau-de-vie, may have enough body and personality to commingle with the egg, but even they will probably need to be tempered with a rich fortified wine, such as a sweet sherry or port, for the drink to have the ideal full flavor. Typically, an aged spirit is a much better fit. The vanilla and spice notes in an aged brandy or whiskey are exactly the kind of flavors that make a Flip round and full.

As for the amount of liquor, we feel that 2 full ounces of a strong spirit (a typical portion for a cocktail), mixed with just a bit of sugar and an egg, still tends to produce a noticeably boozy Flip, even when an aged spirit is used. Therefore, we often decrease the alcohol content of Flip-style drinks a bit, either by lowering the amount of high-proof alcohol to just 1½ ounces or by using a low-ABV ingredient.

The beauty of fortified wines in cocktails is that they're highly flavorful and have enough proof to assert them-selves but aren't so boozy that they overwhelm. This is why they're so great in Flips. The choice of which fortified wine to use in a Flip follows the same line of thought as for spirits: those that have a rich body from either years in oak or from added sweetness are the best bet. A light fortified wine, such as fino sherry, wouldn't be robust enough to provide the dominant flavor. The perfect choice for a Flip is sherries such as amontillado, palo cortado, and oloroso, with their nutty and fruity flavors. Though these sherries are dry on their own, the fat from egg, along with an extra measure of sweetener, will allow their flavors to bloom in a satisfyingly decadent way. As a final touch, a grating of nutmeg on top of the cocktail will draw out the nut and spice flavors of the sherry.

THE CORE: FORTIFIED WINE

In chapter 2, we explored the wide world of vermouths: wines that have been both fortified and flavored with botanicals. In this chapter, we focus on unflavored fortified wines, a category that includes sherry, port, and madeira, among others. These wines are fundamental in our approach to making cocktails. They can act as the core spirit in a cocktail, creating the fundamental flavor profile, or they can be substituted for vermouth anytime it's used as a modifier. Even a tiny bit of unflavored fortified wine can add subtle complexity to just about any drink—be it the briny minerality of a fino sherry or the stewed fruit flavor of a ruby port.

SHERRY

Cocktails and sherry have a long shared history. Sherry was used extensively in mixed drinks starting in the late nineteenth century, when it was as common a base ingredient as other spirits. In addition to sherry-based Flips, drinks like the Sherry Cobbler (page 37) were stars of the era's cocktail boom. Sherry's popularity faded (along with that of other European wines) when vineyards were devastated by phylloxera (a rootstock-eating aphid) at the turn of the twentieth century. Add to that a lapse in production during World Wars I and II and American Prohibition, and sherry all but disappeared from the radar in the United States.

But now that high-quality sherry has made a triumphant comeback, it's become a valuable ingredient in cocktails. We've found that each style of sherry can bring a host of interesting contributions to a drink: fino offers dryness and salinity; amontillado lends aroma and a beguilingly dry finish; oloroso contributes density and a raisiny flavor; and Pedro Ximénez has a juicy sweetness. Sherry can range from bone-dry to supersweet, the result of two differing methods of aging: biological and oxidative.

All sherry is aged in oak barrels, but in contrast to other wines, where casks are filled to the top to limit the influence of oxygen, sherry casks are filled only four-fifths full. This allows a layer of yeast, called flor, to develop on the young wines inside the cask, creating a protective barrier on top of the wine that prevents oxidation. Meanwhile, the flor feeds off of the sherry as it ages, consuming some components and contributing others, giving sherry its distinctive flavor and texture. This is called biological aging, and it produces the driest forms of sherry: fino and manzanilla. It's also the first step in making amontillado and palo cortado sherries, which are subsequently aged in the presence of oxygen—in other words, they then undergo oxidative aging.

Other sherries never develop flor and are intentionally kept in casks with enough room for oxygen to interact with the sherry. Over time, the sherry oxidizes, developing nutty flavors, and as vapors evaporate out of the cask, the sherry becomes more concentrated. This is how richer sherries are made, such as oloroso and Pedro Ximénez.

Aside from biological and oxidative aging, sherries and a handful of other wines, such as port, are aged differently than most wines and spirits, using a process known as solera aging. While many wines, beers, and spirits are aged in barrels after distillation, then later bottled or blended (or even aged again in different casks), in solera systems, wines (and occasionally other spirits, such as rum or brandy) are aged by mixing multiple vintages in the same barrel, a process known as fractional aging. Solera systems were traditionally comprised of several stacked

HOW WE USE SHERRY IN COCKTAILS

We generally approach using sherry in cocktails in four ways:

As a simple substitution for a similar ingredient; for example, fino sherry in place of a dry vermouth, or oloroso sherry in place of a sweet vermouth.

As the drink's sole base, building a cocktail's flavor on the traits of a particular style or bottle of sherry.

As a split base, typically with slightly more sherry than spirit (1 or 1½ ounces sherry plus 1 ounce spirit)—a winning combination as a base for both citrusy and spirituous cocktails, as in the Fair Game (page 280), La Valencia (page 188), and Fuji Legend (page 280).

In tiny, nearly imperceptible amounts as a seasoning, an approach that works especially well with salty finos or amontillados.

layers of barrels, with new wine being introduced into the top layer of barrels, and each layer beneath holding progressively older blends. Today, the barrels often aren't stacked, but the process remains the same: Several times a year, some of the sherry from the oldest barrels (the solera for which the system is named) is bottled and replaced with the blend in the next-oldest barrels, which is in turn replenished by the blend in the next-oldest barrels, and so forth, with new wine, called *sobretabla*, being used to top off the uppermost barrels. None of the barrels is ever completely drained, and because of this, sherry from a solera can have trace amounts of extremely old wine, in some cases stretching back centuries. In addition to being very cool, this also produces wines that are amazingly consistent from year to year—a rarity in the wine industry.

FINO AND MANZANILLA

On the driest end of the sherry spectrum is fino sherry, made from the first pressing of Palomino grapes and fortified to about 15% ABV with the addition of a grape-based spirit. The place of origin of a sherry has a profound impact on its flavor—so much so that finos made in the seaside town of Sanlúcar de Barrameda are labeled as manzanilla, a subcategory that recognizes the noticeably briny aroma and flavor of wines from this region.

In cocktails, the delicacy of a fino or manzanilla can be lost among more powerful ingredients, such as spirits, so we tend to use them either as a base in low-ABV cocktails like spritzes or Highballs, or as a complement to less-assertive spirits, like vodka or blanco tequila. In fact, we often use these sherries in tiny amounts, adding between 1 teaspoon and ½ ounce to cocktails to add a subtle saltiness and creamy yeastiness that can be just the trick to bind flavors together and amplify aroma, as in the Celebrate (page 29).

Like vermouth, fino and manzanilla sherries are very fragile; once opened they will quickly oxidize, so they should be corked, stored in the refrigerator, and used within a week or so. They're also meant to be drunk soon after they're bottled, so look on the label for a bottling date and avoid any that are more than a couple years old. A fresh bottle will be vibrant and refreshing, whereas an older one will be dull and one-dimensional. If you ever see an open bottle of fino sherry on a back bar, run away.

RECOMMENDED BOTTLES

González Byass Tio Pepe Fino: An iconic brand with a long history, Tio Pepe is a benchmark fino sherry. Pop open a fresh, chilled bottle, and you'll notice its pale hay color, aroma of fresh bread, and extremely dry flavor with just a hint of nuttiness. The personality of Tio Pepe is straightforward, making it a good utility player in cocktails.

Hidalgo La Gitana Manzanilla: Produced a short stroll from the ocean, La Gitana is our go-to manzanilla sherry. Dry, salty, mildly yeasty, and bread-like in flavor, it's equally at home as the base of a cocktail or as a modifier.

Lustau Jarana Fino: The Lustau bodega produces large volumes of sherries in every style, and we're huge fans, thanks to the consistency and presence of all of their bottles. Their Jarana is a textbook fino—a dry, yeasty wine with a subtle almond flavor. Lustau also produces La Iña fino, which has slightly more body than the Jarana.

EN RAMA SHERRIES

More and more, sherry producers are exporting something that has traditionally been meant for the locals: *en rama* (raw) sherry. In order to keep exported sherry fresher, it has typically been filtered to remove any sediment, but *en rama* finos are bottled with very little filtration, giving them a yeastier flavor and silkier texture. Because they're less filtered, *en rama* sherries rapidly deteriorate even unopened, so getting the freshest bottle you can is key. We've tasted these straight from the cask in Jerez and in their bottled state here, and we can say that after only a couple of months, the flavor is significantly different. Unfortunately, quality *en rama* bottlings of finos and manzanillas are rarely available outside of Spain. We think it's worth a trip to Spain to try them at their source. We'll meet you there!

AMONTILLADO

Because amontillado sherries experience both biological and oxidative aging, they have all the benefits of the flor (dry and yeasty), as well as those of oxidation (concentrated aroma and flavor)—a confluence that gives them a noticeably nutty character. In addition to being some of the most pleasant wines to enjoy on their own (full disclosure: this book was largely written while consuming amontillado), they are also a valuable asset for cocktail making, being uniquely versatile thanks to their dry backbone and rich aroma. These sherries have a particularly strong affinity for aged spirits, especially bourbon and Cognac, with their nuttiness accentuating the characteristics of barrel aging (vanilla, baking spices).

RECOMMENDED BOTTLES

Barbadillo Príncipe Amontillado: While this bottle has the dried fruit aromas commonly associated with amontillados, its saltiness is always present, so it displays itself differently in cocktails than a Jerez amontillado, like Lustau's Los Arcos, providing an additional layer of seasoning that can draw out flavors in a fantastic way. Because saltiness can both brighten citrus and curb bitterness, this sherry is useful for adjusting those flavors in cocktails.

Lustau Los Arcos Amontillado: About a decade ago, only a few sherries were widely available in the United States, largely because Americans didn't know what to do with them. Then a handful of bar industry pros started putting quality sherries in front of bartenders—an act that profoundly changed the landscape of our cocktail making. This bottle was one of the first sherries to captivate our attention, and it continues to be a favorite. It has a rich nose but is surprisingly dry, with a distinct enough flavor to come through without tilting cocktails toward the sweet end of the spectrum.

PALO CORTADO

Palo cortado sherries are wrapped in mystical allure and prone to all sorts of marketing bluster. In the old days, every so often a cask meant to be a fino would suddenly lose its flor long before it was ready to evolve into an amontillado. If the sherry was of sufficient quality, it would be allowed to age in the presence of oxygen, eventually becoming a palo cortado. These days, many producers intentionally work to create palo cortados by steering finos in that direction.

While similar in many ways to amontillados, palo cortados have a richer aroma of coffee, along with slight molasses notes. And because they spend less time under flor, they have more of the raisiny aroma and flavor that you might expect from an oloroso (discussed on the next page), but with a dry finish. The easiest way to characterize palo cortados is that they smell like olorosos and taste like amontillados, which can be helpful in deciding how to use them. Importantly, because the key qualities of a palo cortado can be lost in a complicated cocktail, we often use it as the core to prevent it from being overpowered by ingredients with powerful flavors.

RECOMMENDED BOTTLE

Lustau Península Palo Cortado: Because they're rarer than amontillado sherries, palo cortados are often more expensive. While many of our favorite producers offer impeccable palo cortados, Lustau's is both reasonably priced and highly delicious. It gracefully teeters somewhere between the dryness of an amontillado and the richness of an oloroso, with a big dried fruit aroma and a deep, nutty flavor.

OLOROSO

Oloroso sherries lie on the richest end of the dry sherry spectrum. During production, wine—often from a second pressing of Palomino grapes (the first goes to fino production)—is added to a cask until it's nearly full, then fortified to a slightly higher alcohol strength (17% ABV) to stave off the development of flor. It's then aged in a solera system. Extensive contact with oxygen concentrates the liquid into a wine with a sweet nose, imbued with aromas of figs and raisins, but with a surprisingly dry backbone.

Because of their deeper personality, olorosos can be thought of much like sweet vermouth—minus the carefully layered spices, botanicals, bittering agents, and sweetener in the vermouth. So if you want to substitute an oloroso for sweet vermouth in a Manhattan variation, you'll need to find a way to add those qualities back into the mix. Olorosos also have enough body to be the focus of a cocktail, and because they tend to have a powerful aroma and flavor, they have the strength to stand up to the density of cream in decadent cocktails—like the cocktail at the heart of this chapter: the Flip.

RECOMMENDED BOTTLE

Lustau Almacenista Pata de Gallina Oloroso:
Lustau's entry-level oloroso (the Don Nuño bottling) is a fine sherry, but for a bit more money (around $25), you should be able to find their Almacenista Pata de Gallina. Regarding the term *almacenista*, it translates to "warehouse keeper" and is applied to sherries sourced from small, family-owned soleras and distributed by larger houses, such as Lustau. This bottling is phenomenal, miraculously balancing a bone-dry finish with a broad body that's chocolaty and spicy but not at all sweet.

SWEET SHERRIES

Sweet sherries are highly concentrated dessert wines made from Pedro Ximénez and Moscatel grapes. Pedro Ximénez is the sweetest style, made by first allowing the grapes to sun-dry until almost raisiny. As their moisture evaporates, sugars within the fruit become more concentrated, resulting in a highly viscous and naturally sweet wine. Fortified to halt further fermentation, the sherry is then aged in a solera system. This results in some of the sweetest wines in the world, defined by their ripe fig and date flavors. In cocktails, they should be used as you would a liqueur or sweetener. We often joke that Pedro Ximénez is nature's finest simple syrup, and it's true that an old bottle will be as dense and rich as any syrup we use in cocktails. Unlike syrups, however, it will add proof to the drink, so be mindful of the cocktail's balance when making that kind of substitution.

Moscatel sherries are also quite sweet, but due to the aromatic properties of the Muscat of Alexandria grape from which they're made, the resulting wine is not only dense but also has an intensely floral, perfume-like smell. Therefore, these sherries are best used in modest quantities to flavor a cocktail much like a floral liqueur.

RECOMMENDED BOTTLES

González Byass Noé Pedro Ximénez: With an average age of thirty years, this is an exceptionally intense bottle. The liquid is so reduced that it is noticeably viscous and has an unapologetically pungent flavor of raisins, figs, cinnamon, and anise. It's generally too expensive to mix into cocktails in any quantity, but because of its intense depth of flavor, just 1 teaspoon can go a long way. Try it in place of the sweetener in an Old-Fashioned made with rum, and you will not be disappointed.

Lustau San Emilio Pedro Ximénez: True to the style, Lustau's Pedro Ximénez is rich, sweet, and full-bodied. It smells and tastes of raisins, figs, nuts, molasses, and baking spices. The sweetness of the wine is balanced by a vibrant acidity, making it tasty and decadent on its own, as well as a good collaborator in cocktails, where it performs almost like a fruit liqueur, bringing a focused fruit personality, sweetness, and acidity. It balances beautifully with lemon juice, though we tend to use it in smaller doses (around ½ ounce), making up the difference with a syrup.

Lustau Emilín Moscatel: Lustau is one of the few bodegas that bottle a Moscatel, and this bottle is both affordable and widely available. Aged for eight years, it's sweet and rich, with the characteristic aroma of dried fruits, especially prunes, and an orangey flavor.

CREAM SHERRY

In addition to the many styles of sherry described above, there's also a long tradition of blending multiple styles. The term for these is *blends*—which can be dry, sweet, or somewhere in between—is *cream sherry*, and although this category is often associated with inferior commercial bottlings meant for cooking, some cream sherries are dynamic, excellent, and extremely useful in cocktails.

RECOMMENDED BOTTLES

González Byass Matusalem Oloroso: This is probably the priciest bottle of all the sherries we recommend for cocktails, but it's well worth the cost. Aged for an average of thirty years in a solera system (which means that it includes wines that are much older), the Matusalem is an odd mix of mostly Palomino grapes with some Pedro Ximénez grapes, making it technically a cream sherry, rather than a straight oloroso. It's quite sweet but intensely complex, with dried fruit, coffee, and cacao notes and a soft acidity.

Lustau East India Solera: A blend of mostly oloroso with a little Pedro Ximénez, this sherry is aged for three years in a slightly warmer part of the bodega in an effort to mimic the effects of longer shipping times in the past: after months of jostling at sea and exposure to higher temperatures, the sherry took on a different flavor. Lustau's modern-day warm aging enlivens the sherry with a woodsy bite, giving it added structure that works amazingly well in cocktails. It's a great stand-in for sweet vermouth, especially as a counterpoint to aperitif liqueurs like Aperol and Campari.

Williams & Humbert Dry Sack: The flagship bottle from one of the sherry industry's largest producers, Dry Sack can be found in almost every corner of the globe. A blend of amontillado, oloroso, and Pedro Ximénez sherries, it comes across much like an amontillado in aroma and flavor, with a slight rich undertone. When we can't get our hands on amontillado, Dry Sack is a solid stand-in.

PORT

Port is a fortified wine from Portugal's Douro Valley. One of the unique qualities of port is that it's made from a blend of different types of Portuguese grapes. It's typically a red wine, bottled and sold as either tawny, ruby, or vintage. (However, there are white and rosé ports out there, and they occasionally make their way into our cocktails.) The various grapes are usually harvested together and crushed in such a way that a great deal of color and flavor is extracted. When about half of the fermentable sugars have been consumed by yeast, the fortification process begins. A young grape brandy is added, raising the wine's strength to at least 17.5% ABV and preserving some of the sweetness of the grapes.

The wine is generally left to settle in neutral tanks, then evaluated for its quality. The character of the wine determines how long it will be aged and how it's categorized. Here's a quick breakdown of red port styles that show up on labels:

- **Ruby port:** A nonvintage port aged in wood for at least two years.

- **Vintage port:** Aged for at least two years in barrels, then aged for years in bottles. Bottle aging softens the aggressive tannins of a young port, allowing the fruitiness of the wine to develop and get progressively more complex.

- **Late-bottled vintage port:** Aged longer in barrels than vintage port (four to six years), then bottled, and generally intended to be drunk younger than vintage port. Some producers use this term for wines that are fruity and youthful, while others use it for those that are woody and clearly aged in barrel for years.

- **Tawny port:** A blend of multiple vintages, not intended to be aged in bottle.

- **Colheita port:** Wine from a single year aged extensively in barrels, also not intended to be aged in the bottle.

Ports are generally robust wines high in tannins and added alcohol, making them good substitutes for sweet vermouth in Manhattan-style cocktails. Port also has enough character to stand as the core in any style of cocktail; however, because it tends to be relatively sweet, the other ingredients will probably need to be adjusted accordingly.

A young tawny port can lend a remarkable depth of character to cocktails while still tasting fresh and juicy, thanks to the blending of multiple vintages. Older tawnies bring more structure to cocktails and can collaborate with the strong flavors of, say, a single-malt scotch, as in the classic Chancellor (page 279). We find that matching tawny ports with sweet vermouth accentuates the vermouth's hidden juiciness. Mixing with a ruby port depends on the style you choose. A young ruby port will be fresh and full of berry flavors that mix well with citrus, but it will probably lack the structure to shine through in spirituous cocktails. For those, you'll need to turn to a vintage or late-bottled vintage port.

RECOMMENDED BOTTLES

Graham's Six Grapes Ruby Port: The flavor of plums, raspberries, and blackberries is the first thing you'll taste, but underneath is a structured wine that has coconut notes. If you can only stock one bottle of ruby-style port, make it this one.

Sandeman Ruby Port: Sandeman produces phenomenally consistent and affordable ports, including this commonly available ruby port. It tends to be a bit sweeter than the Graham's, with a jammier flavor of bramble fruit (raspberry, blackberry).

Otima 10-Year Tawny Port: There's something very gentle about this port. It's aged just enough to develop a woodsy structure while still having fresh, vibrant berry flavors. Whereas older or denser ports can make a cocktail bland, the youthful Otima can be a complex contributor. We're particularly fond of mixing it with French brandies, such Cognac or Calvados, in Manhattan-style cocktails.

MADEIRA

Madeira is categorized by age, ranging from rainwater (a minimum of three years in oak) to older expressions. For use in cocktails, we steer toward lighter styles, particularly the rainwater madeiras. With a sweetness that falls between the driest and second-driest madeira styles, they have a whisper of residual sugar that boosts other ingredients while adding a slightly fruity flavor. Rainwater madeira has an impressive ability to lighten cocktails without making them seem diluted.

RECOMMENDED BOTTLES

Broadbent Rainwater Medium-Dry Madeira:
Broadbent's rainwater madeira is more complex than the Sandeman bottle described below. The aroma is more concentrated, with dried figs and a nutty note, but still characteristically light. The color is a dark copper tone, and it has a slight but noticeable sweetness combined with a bright, citrusy acidity. It reminds us of a tawny port in some ways—the influence of oak, its concentration, its relative dryness—but the unique flavor of the grapes used to make it shines through.

Sandeman Rainwater Madeira: Light-bodied, with a clean, nutty aroma and a crisp and complex taste, this bottle offers a great introduction to rainwater madeira. Because it has a light personality, it's great for stretching out dense flavors, as in the Golden Boy (page 11), where madeira is added to an Old-Fashioned made with Raisin-Infused Scotch (page 292) to make the cocktail slightly less rigid.

EXPERIMENTING WITH THE CORE

Of the Flip's three components—spirit, sugar, egg—its spirituous core offers the greatest opportunity to play with the flavor. Indeed, the recipes in classic cocktail books indicate that a Flip can be made with nearly any fortified wine or spirit. While that's certainly true in theory, in practice it brings some challenges.

Brandy Flip

CLASSIC

Our favorite version of the Flip is one made with sherry because of the wine's nutty aroma and raisiny finish. Another popular variation is the classic Brandy Flip. For our ideal version of this drink, we first fine-tune the core, choosing the woodsy juiciness of Cognac, which works well with the fattiness of the egg. Then, although some recipes for this drink do call for a full 2 ounces of brandy, we think the brandy's higher proof calls for dialing back on the spirits a bit: too much alcohol in a Flip and it just tastes like creamy hooch. Finally, we increase the amount of sweetener slightly to compensate for the oloroso sherry's missing sweetness.

1½ ounces Cognac
¾ ounce Demerara
Gum Syrup (page 54)
1 whole egg
Garnish: Nutmeg

Dry shake all the ingredients, then shake again with ice. Double strain into a chilled coupe. Garnish with a few grates of nutmeg.

Coffee Cocktail

CLASSIC

According to Jerry Thomas's 1887 *Bar-Tender's Guide*, this cocktail's name has nothing to do with its flavor (where's the coffee, after all?), but rather its appearance: it looks like a cup of coffee. Lucky for us, cocktail naming has come a long way in the past 150 years. Regardless, the drink is a great example of how the Flip's core can be split between a fortified wine and a spirit, marrying both the root, sherry-based Flip and the Brandy Flip above. Here, tawny port brings both a great deal of flavor and sweetness—requiring less syrup to balance—while the Cognac supports it with woodsy complexity.

1½ ounces tawny port
1 ounce Pierre Ferrand
Ambre Cognac
¼ ounce simple syrup (page 45)
1 whole egg
Garnish: Nutmeg

Dry shake all the ingredients, then shake again with ice. Double strain into a chilled coupe. Garnish with a few grates of nutmeg.

THE BALANCE: EGGS AND DAIRY

Eggs and dairy can bring unique flavors and textures to a cocktail, as well as impact the sweetness of a drink. Eggs bring both a fatty flavor (when using the whole egg or yolks), along with frothiness from the whites. Dairy has lots of flavor, and also brings sweetness and a frothy texture (when using high-fat cream). But these ingredients are also delicate and require careful attention to prepare well—and to avoid spoilage or curdling (see "Exploring Technique" on page 264).

EGG

Without eggs, a Flip would just be a glass of sweetened spirit shaken with ice. The egg adds body and texture, balancing the alcohol to create a smooth and pleasant cocktail. Beyond the Flip and its variations, eggs can be used in cocktails in a variety of ways to transform both flavor and texture, from adding a light foamy head to making a cocktail rich and decadent.

There's a lot of misinformation about egg safety. The largest risk of infection from raw eggs is a type of food poisoning caused by the bacteria *Salmonella enterica*, which can get into eggs in two ways: It can occur in undamaged eggs if the hen carries salmonella, as it can contaminate the interior of the egg before the shell is formed. But in this case, the amount of salmonella is likely to be very low, presenting little threat of illness. The second avenue for entry is via cracked or damaged shells.

Contrary to a somewhat common belief, the alcohol content in cocktails isn't high enough to kill bacteria, nor is there any evidence to suggest that the acidity in citrus kills bacteria. We recommend that you buy the freshest possible eggs, ensuring that they are clean and without cracks, and then refrigerate until you're ready to use them. Use them as soon as possible. The whites of fresh eggs will create stiff, strong foam that doesn't dissipate quickly, and the yolks will contribute deep flavor, as opposed to a lackluster richness. We opt for organic eggs and, when possible, purchase them from a local farm.

Certain cocktails include egg whites to impart a silky texture to the drink. The most famous are fizzes and sours such as the Ramos Gin Fizz (page 141) and the Pisco Sour (page 120). Foamy egg white will also increase the volume of the drink, stretching out its flavors. This is a great way to temper bitter flavors such as Campari, or to tone down the tannins in a spirit infused with tea. Unfortunately, egg white cocktails are sometimes plagued by an aroma reminiscent of a wet dog, due to how quickly egg whites oxidize when exposed to air. This is largely why bartenders decorate the top of an egg cocktail with a dash of bitters, as in the Pisco Sour, or a grating of nutmeg or cinnamon to add a pleasant aroma.

Far fewer cocktails call for egg yolk on its own. Egg yolks contain far less water than whites but much more protein, fat, and vitamins, bringing a rich eggy flavor to drinks. They also contain lecithin, an effective emulsifier that can bond disparate ingredients, such as spirits and cream, to create a smooth, thick, uniform texture, as in the New York Flip (page 257). Still, when the fattiness of the egg yolk is desired, recipes generally just call for the whole egg.

In fact, that's probably the most common approach—and the one associated with the classic Flip—using an entire egg to take advantage of the contributions of both the white and the yolk. This produces drinks that are both foamy and flavorful. A handful of classic sour-style drinks use a whole egg, such as the old-school Royal Fizz, Flips, nogs, and their variations.

An unconventional way to use whole eggs is to infuse them with flavor while they're still in their semipermeable shell. Place whole eggs in a sealed container with an aromatic ingredient, such as lavender, and the egg white will quickly absorb the aroma.

Our last tip when it comes to eggs: These cocktails generally need to be shaken longer than others, and they must be double strained.

DAIRY

Adding dairy to alcohol is an ancient way of making booze palatable, thanks to the richness of dairy and its lactic acid tang. When cream was first added to Flips, they became the creamy, rich cocktails now known as nogs.

While the term *dairy* can refer to the milk of any mammal, for cocktails we exclusively use cow's milk in various forms, particularly those with a high fat content, such as heavy cream. We also occasionally use butter. We prefer heavy cream over half-and-half or whole milk not just because it's rich (usually 35 to 40 percent fat) and perceived as sweet, but also because its higher fat content makes it less likely to curdle in the presence of acid. It's also more effective at carrying flavors over the tongue. True, heavy cream is more caloric, but that's precisely due to its higher fat content, which confers these desirable qualities.

Half-and-half, an equal mixture of cream and milk, usually has a fat content between 10 and 15 percent, whereas whole milk contains 3.5 percent fat. This makes half-and-half useful in certain cocktail applications, particularly in drinks that call for a significant amount of dairy, like the White Russian (page 267). In these drinks, using half-and-half rather than cream keeps the dairy from overshadowing the other flavors or making the drink too heavy.

One of the most critical considerations when using dairy in drinks is the temperature of the cocktail: whether hot or cold, the drink should be constructed in such a way that it's served at the ideal temperature, in a serving vessel that's been chilled or heated as appropriate. Furthermore, the volume should be small enough that the temperature won't change too much before the drink is finished. That means cold cocktails ought to be frosty and hot cocktails steaming—if dairy-based cocktails fall in the middle, they will be less than pleasant.

As with eggs, freshness and quality are key when using dairy products in cocktails. It makes sense that cows that are treated well and given a high-quality diet will produce milk that's more nutritious and delicious. Therefore, we recommend using organic dairy products and, if possible, seeking out local dairies that take pride in making the best possible product.

Then, as for technique, shaken cocktails that contain dairy are best when shaken slightly longer than usual; this will produce a frothy, smooth texture. We also recommend double straining these cocktails to ensure that they have a smooth, uniform texture, without any pesky ice chips.

DAIRY ALTERNATIVES

So many people can't or don't consume dairy, whether due to lactose intolerance or allergies, potential health impacts, or concerns about the treatment of animals or the environmental impacts of dairy. Thankfully, there are dairy alternatives that can offer a similar texture. We prefer nut milks because nuts contain more oils than many of the ingredients used to make nondairy milks. Therefore, nut milks most closely mimic the texture of heavy cream and carry flavor over the tongue.

Though nut milks can be used in place of dairy in certain cocktails, they are often thin and therefore must be used in a greater proportion than milk. We also add a bit more sweetener to drinks made with nut milks to make up for their lack of body. An important consideration with nut milks is that they reflect the flavor of their source ingredient, and because of that they produce wildly different results in drinks. We tend to use almond milk most often. Its flavor is mild and works well with a wide spectrum of spirits and liqueurs. While there are plenty of store-bought options available, it's easy to make nut milks at home. See our recipe for almond milk on the opposite page.

Almond Milk

600 grams sliced blanched almonds
7½ cups filtered water

In a blender, combine the almonds
and water. Blend until very smooth,
then strain through a fine-mesh sieve
with several layers of cheesecloth,
leaving the liquid to drain out for 1 to
2 hours. Don't press on the solids
until the end of the process, when the
pulp is mostly dry; this way, the pulp
that accumulates at the bottom of the
cheesecloth will further filter the milk.

EXPERIMENTING WITH THE BALANCE

There are two different branches of Flip variations that work with the balance to forge very different paths: those that don't contain dairy, and those that do. The second branch is further subdivided, containing some variations that include egg and some that don't.

Eggnog

CLASSIC

Dairy is a natural companion to the richness of an egg. Either can contribute to the texture of a cocktail in a dramatic way, and when they're combined the effect is amplified. Of course, Eggnog is the classic example. Though it's typically made in large batches that involve a lot of work—preparing a custard base and then spiking it (as in the Tom and Jerry, on page 268)—that isn't always convenient, so we've come up with this single-serving version of Eggnog that can be made quickly and without much prep.

¾ ounce Plantation Barbados 5-year rum

¾ ounce Pierre Ferrand Ambre Cognac

1 teaspoon Giffard Vanille de Madagascar

¾ ounce Cane Sugar Syrup (page 47)

1 ounce heavy cream

1 whole egg

Garnish: Cinnamon and nutmeg

Dry shake all the ingredients, then shake again with ice. Double strain into a chilled Old-Fashioned glass. Garnish with a few grates of cinnamon and nutmeg.

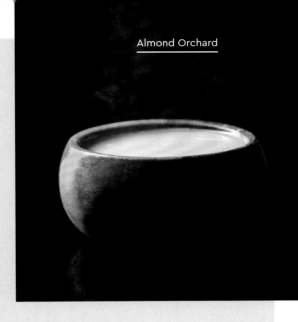

Brandy Alexander

CLASSIC

One way to experiment with the balance in Flip-style drinks is to omit the egg and rely solely on the richness of cream. In fact, this style of cocktail is even more common and varied than egg-based drinks. Perhaps the most famous of these is the Alexander, which itself has many variations based on different core spirits. Our favorite is the classic Brandy Alexander, a mixture of brandy, crème de cacao, and heavy cream, where a rich liqueur serves as the sweetener. As in our take on the Brandy Flip (page 252), we favor a rich Cognac in this drink. Note that because the cocktail has a slightly higher alcohol content, it must be shaken a bit longer so it will be diluted enough to fill a standard coupe.

1½ ounces Pierre Ferrand Ambre Cognac

1 ounce Giffard white crème de cacao

1 ounce heavy cream

Garnish: Nutmeg

Shake all the ingredients with ice. Double strain into a chilled coupe. Garnish with a few grates of nutmeg.

New York Flip

CLASSIC

Eggnog and other nogs have inspired a whole host of cocktails that incorporate both egg and cream. Some of these variations are called Flips, including the classic New York Flip, which takes inspiration from another classic: the New York Sour, a sour-style cocktail made with bourbon, lemon juice, and simple syrup, shaken and served in a coupe with a float of juicy red wine. The New York Flip is a more decadent articulation that replaces the lemon juice with heavy cream and an egg yolk: the same idea of a New York Sour expressed as a Flip with the bourbon and port as the connecting ingredients.

1 ounce Elijah Craig Small Batch bourbon

¾ ounce tawny port

¼ ounce simple syrup (page 45)

¾ ounce heavy cream

1 egg yolk

Garnish: Nutmeg

Dry shake all the ingredients, then shake again with ice. Double strain into a chilled coupe. Garnish with a few grates of nutmeg.

Almond Orchard

DEVON TARBY, 2015

For those who don't consume dairy or eggs, nut milks offer a similar creamy texture, along with unique flavor. The Almond Orchard is a soothing mix of a tea-infused young apple brandy and almond milk, spiked with a bit of lactic acid to ramp up the creaminess.

4¼ ounces Almond Milk (page 255)

1½ ounces A Field in Innsbruck Tea–Infused Apple Brandy (page 287)

¼ teaspoon Maraska maraschino liqueur

¾ ounce Demerara Gum Syrup (page 54)

2 drops Lactic Acid Solution (page 298)

1 drop Salt Solution (page 298)

Combine all the ingredients in a small saucepan over medium-low heat and cook, stirring frequently, until steaming but not simmering. Pour into a coffee mug, small wooden bowl, or large sake cup. No garnish.

THE SEASONING: AMARO

Though amaro doesn't show up in the classic Flip—or even some of its variations—it can be a wonderful ingredient to explore when creating Flip-style drinks. This is largely inspired by the spice garnish that adorns the top of a classic Flip: the aroma of freshly ground nutmeg perfumes the cocktail, but it also flavors the drink with each sip. Packed with spices and bitterness, amaro can serve the same purpose in a cocktail. So while amaro does not appear in the classic or root recipes at the beginning of this chapter, we hope the information here will help you take the Flip in new directions.

It's easy to categorize most types of alcohol, from spirits to liqueurs to wine. In any given category, similarities in ingredients, regional styles, and methods of production have a huge bearing on the booze's personality. But there is type of spirit that largely defies attempts at categorization: amaro.

Amaro (*amari* in the plural) takes its name from the Italian word for bitter. That hints at what to expect from them in flavor, but any similarities among amari generally stop there. Most are made by macerating herbs, barks, roots, flowers, citrus, and other botanicals in an alcoholic base (the strength and nature of which can vary, though usually neutral grain alcohol) to extract flavor. The spirit is then sweetened, and sometimes aged. The resulting spirits are as versatile as they are difficult to categorize. Are they all bitter? Mostly. Are they all sweet? Well, no, not really. Are they all unique? Without question. If we were pressed to define them, we'd have to simply say that an amaro is a bittersweet liqueur.

There are no universal regulations for the production or classification of amari, nor is there even much consensus (within Italy or beyond) on how they should be consumed. For our own purposes, we divide the ever-increasing options into groupings that reflect where they fall on the bitter and sweet spectrums and therefore indicate how particular bottles are likely to work in a cocktail: aperitivi, light amari, medium amari, and dense amari. Given how diverse they are, there are no hard-and-fast rules about how to use them in cocktails, but this is part of what makes them such a valuable addition to cocktails: they can play many roles, from seasoning and adding complexity to accenting a spirit or fortified wine to being at center stage as the core flavor.

APERITIVI

At the lightest end of the spectrum are aperitivo bitters, or aperitivi. In Italy, *aperitivo* is a term associated with leisurely before-meal drinking, when a low-alcohol beverage that's slightly bitter and relatively dry is served to stimulate the appetite. Aperitivi are the stars of many such cocktails, often in combination with seltzer or prosecco in a Highball or spritz.

RECOMMENDED BOTTLES

Aperol: At 11% ABV, Aperol is the lightest of all aperitivi bitters. It smells of fresh oranges and rhubarb and has a light flavor with a mild bitter undertone. We love Aperol for its versatility: it can be used in tiny amounts to boost the bitterness of grapefruit juice or grapefruit liqueur, as part of a split base, or even more refreshingly as the star of a drink. Though Aperol can work well in spirituous cocktails, especially Martini variations, we most often use it in citrusy cocktails like the classic Aperol Spritz (page 223) and other spritzes, and as a seasoning for sours, as in the High Five (page 133).

Campari: Oh, Campari, you are the wind beneath every bartender's wings. Without you, we wouldn't have the Negroni, and a world without Negronis wouldn't be a world worth living in. At 24% ABV, Campari sits smack in the middle of our recommended bottles for aperitivi, being fairly moderate in content, sweetness, and bitterness. This makes it well suited for many cocktail applications: light enough to use in larger quantities, yet strong enough to have a presence when used in small amounts. With a dark, ruby-red color and bright, floral orange flavor, Campari mixed with seltzer makes for a delicious and gorgeous Highball. It also works well in both citrusy drinks and spirituous cocktails.

Suze: The French also have a long tradition of making bitter liqueurs. We often think of Suze as French Campari, and while that comparison is simplistic, we tend to use it in similar ways. Suze is earthy, sweet, and citrusy, with a light body and bright yellow color. At 20% ABV, it's mild enough to mix into low-alcohol, citrusy cocktails, but it also has a strong personality that works well in spirituous cocktails—specifically Martini variations like the White Negroni (page 89)—thanks to gentian root, the ingredient that makes many amari bitter.

LIGHT AMARI

As mentioned, we categorize amari as light, medium, or dense depending on their alcohol content, intensity of flavor, and bitterness. The following recommended bottles of light amari balance a light sweetness with a pleasant bitterness, making them versatile cocktail ingredients—light enough to use as part of a split base in either citrusy or boozy cocktails, but with a presence that allows them to be used in smaller quantities to accent a core spirit much as a fruit or herbal liqueur might be used.

RECOMMENDED BOTTLES

Amaro Meletti: At 32% ABV, Meletti has a noticeably punchy aroma of cinnamon and orange and lemon peels, with a cool minty back note. This minty character carries through the flavor, along with burnt caramel notes and a long runway of citrusy tingle. Because of its light body, Amaro Meletti can accent the base spirit in both citrusy and boozy cocktails. It also can be used as part of a split base with vermouth in Martini- or Manhattan-style cocktails.

Amaro Montenegro: A perennial favorite in our cocktail making, Amaro Montenegro has a distinctive aroma of roses, cola, and burnt orange. When sipped, those rich flavors give way to a mild, lingering bitterness, almost like Coca-Cola with a lot less sugar. At 23% ABV, it has the lightness of body to mix beautifully with citrus, which we often do in drinks such as the Crop Top (page 179).

Amaro Nonino Quintessentia: We wax poetic about several specific bottles in this book, but Amaro Nonino ranks in the very top tier of all the spirits we use in cocktails. Though it's rather light in body, it's built upon grappa, a flavorful base that gives it a deeper backbone than other amari. On the nose it's a vibrant mix of fresh orange oil, herbs, and birch. The flavor is complex and slightly bitter, with the orange taking on more of an orange-candy quality. Nonino is delicious on its own, and phenomenal in cocktails. We're particularly fond of splitting the base of Manhattan-style cocktails with Nonino, as in La Viña (page 281). And because it's high in proof (35% ABV) but not too sweet, we also use it as the base in riffs on the Old-Fashioned, as in the Exit Strategy (page 11).

MEDIUM AMARI

In our categorization scheme, medium amari are those that have a bit more density than light amari, but not so much that they overpower other flavors. They're usually deep red or amber in color, with more sweetness and burnt caramel flavors and a more bitter finish. In cocktails, we generally use medium amari in smaller amounts as a seasoning. This can work quite well in riffs on Martinis or Manhattans, where amaro replaces some of the vermouth. In these cases, we skip the aromatic bitters.

RECOMMENDED BOTTLES

Amaro Averna: Not long ago, one of the few amari we could consistently get our hands on was Amaro Averna, which is extremely popular in Italy and widely distributed across the globe. It's quite a bit sweeter than most amari, but this helps balance its strong flavors of anise, lemon, juniper, and sage. For many people, Averna is a perfect introduction to amari, since its pronounced sweetness tempers its bitterness.

Amaro CioCiaro: With cola and orange aromas, a flavor that features burnt orange, and a moderate sweetness and ABV (30%), CioCiaro straddles a fine line: it isn't overly assertive, but it won't get lost in a complex cocktail. It's a versatile bottle for anyone's collection, and a favorite substitute for Amer Picon in classics like the Brooklyn (page 87) for those who cannot get Bigallet China-China Amer.

Bigallet China-China Amer: Falling somewhere between an amaro and a curaçao, this *amer* (French for "amaro") balances citrus, spice, and a pleasant lingering bitterness. A medium amount of sweetness boosts the mandarin orange character. We love to use it in small quantities, from 1 teaspoon to ¼ ounce, to add structure to drinks while also conferring a bright orange quality that lifts otherwise dense spirits, such as Cognac.

Cynar: Though it has a reputation as being extremely bitter, Cynar falls somewhere between the relative lightness of CioCiaro and the strength of the dense amari discussed next. The nose is distinctively vegetal and herbaceous. As its name implies, Cynar contains artichoke (in the genus *Cynara*), but that's a bit misleading; artichoke is just one of its many flavorings, but it does smell noticeably earthy. It has a eucalyptus flavor and a long-lasting bitter finish, which can help stretch the flavors of a cocktail.

Ramazzotti: With a noticeable aroma of woodsy birch, cooked citrus, and herbs, Ramazzotti is highly bitter. Sweet and earthy on the palate but surprisingly drying (thanks to the bittering agents), this amaro is bottled at 30% ABV. Ramazzotti's complex flavor and bitterness make it a great addition to Manhattan-style cocktails, such as Beth's Going to Town (page 87), where it replaces Angostura bitters and a portion of vermouth. Or in an Old-Fashioned, it can replace most of the sweetener while also supplementing the bitters, as in the Pop Quiz (page 17).

DENSE AMARI

Compared to all of the previous categories, dense amari can be sweeter, more bitter, or both. As such, all will be noticeably distinctive in a cocktail. We embrace this fact, often using them as a major component in drinks. Occasionally we use a tiny amount—just enough that their big personality is distinguishable beneath the surface of the core flavor, as in the Black Forest (page 278).

RECOMMENDED BOTTLES

Fernet-Branca: Fernet-Branca is an acquired taste. If you're new to Fernet-Branca, you may initially be overwhelmed by its bitter intensity, but with time it will reveal its nuances, the aroma transforming from terrifying to something hinting at caramel, coffee, and anise, and the intense flavor developing into a rich burnt orange elixir with a minty finish. Don't despair if it takes you a long time to appreciate Fernet. In fact, there are many in the spirits industry who, despite years of late-night shots of Fernet with cohorts, still view it as thinly veiled medicine. (At least we're taking our medicine, right?) Making cocktails with Fernet must be approached with the same caution as other dense amari; start with a small quantity as a seasoning, then add more, little by little, if you wish.

Luxardo Amaro Abano: Made with cardamom, cinnamon, bitter orange peel, cinchona, and other ingredients that remain a closely guarded secret, Amaro Abano has an extremely unique flavor profile. We sometimes think we can taste it from a mile away. Its aroma is citrusy and full of baking spices, while the palate leaves a tingling cinnamon flavor that lasts for minutes. Because this flavor will become a dominant component of any cocktail it's mixed into, we suggest using just a small amount; otherwise, it may take over the drink.

WAYS TO USE AMARI IN COCKTAILS

Seasoning: Highly bitter and flavorful amari can be used in tiny quantities, between a dash and a teaspoon, in much the same way as aromatic bitters. Their strength can bind ingredients that otherwise might not connect seamlessly, or add a unique seasoning that enhances the other ingredients.

Substitution for vermouth: This doesn't always work, but if an amaro is light enough, it can sometimes take the place of sweet vermouth in cocktails.

Substitution for a portion of vermouth and bitters: Instead of simply substituting vermouth for an amaro, we suggest removing the aromatic bitters and a bit of the vermouth from a Manhattan riff and replacing it with a small amount (between ¼ and ½ ounce) of amaro for an interesting variation.

In a split base: Depending on your tolerance for bitterness, any style of amaro can be used in a split base. That said, the bludgeoning power of a dense amaro like Fernet-Branca may make it too heavy-handed to collaborate well with another base spirit, though it could work with the right balance of ingredients.

As the base: Using an amaro as a base ingredient requires a higher-proof bottle (ideally 30% ABV or above) and enough inherent balance to accept the influence of other ingredients. We find that medium amari work best as the base in a cocktail.

EXPERIMENTING WITH THE SEASONING

In Flips and their variations, an amaro can serve as a powerful seasoning agent that can cut through the dense flavors of rich ingredients, like egg or dairy. On its own, an amaro is almost like a fully formed cocktail: it exhibits traits of strong, sweet, and sometimes sour, and always a layer of bitterness. You can use amari in cocktails in several ways, depending on the amaro's proof, sweetness, and bitterness. Because of these characteristics, amaro added to a Flip-style drink will interact with every ingredient and their proportions will need to be adjusted. In the Barnaby Jones (below), the addition of ½ ounce of Cynar necessitates lowering the Scotch to 1½ ounces, while the maple syrup amount finds balance at ½ ounce due to Cynar's sweetness.

Barnaby Jones

MAURA MCGUIGAN, 2013

The Barnaby Jones is a nog variation that introduces Cynar into the core for complexity. Shaking whole coffee beans with the cocktail adds a subtle coffee flavor while also helping to whip the cream, creating a smooth texture.

- **1½ ounces Famous Grouse scotch**
- **½ ounce Cynar**
- **½ ounce dark, robust maple syrup**
- **½ ounce heavy cream**
- **1 whole egg**
- **12 coffee beans**
- **Garnish: Cinnamon**

Dry shake all the ingredients, then shake again with ice. Double strain into a chilled coupe. Garnish with a few grates of cinnamon.

Jump in the Line

LAUREN CORRIVEAU, 2015

Here's a sophisticated nondairy riff on the tropical Piña Colada (page 269), with Amaro di Angostura being used to season a core of amontillado sherry. The result is a deeply complex poolside cocktail.

- **1 orange half wheel**
- **½ strawberry**
- **1½ ounces Lustau Los Arcos amontillado sherry**
- **½ ounce Amaro di Angostura**
- **¼ ounce La Favorite Ambre rhum agricole**
- **1 teaspoon Pierre Ferrand dry curaçao**
- **½ ounce House Coconut Cream (page 295)**
- **1 dash Angostura bitters**
- **Garnish: 1 pineapple leaf, 1 orange half wheel, and 1 mint sprig**

In a shaker, gently muddle the orange half wheel and strawberry. Add the remaining ingredients and short shake with ice, then double strain into a Collins glass. Fill the glass with crushed ice. Garnish with the pineapple leaf, orange half wheel, and mint sprig and serve with a straw.

TREVOR EASTER

Trevor Easter was general manager of the Walker Inn and the Normandie Club between 2016 and 2017, and previously worked at fine bars such as Bourbon & Branch and Rickhouse in San Francisco, and Noble Experiment in San Diego.

I actually remember the exact bar stool I sat on when I had my first Flip. I was in a bar called 15 Romolo in San Francisco. They had a drink that I ordered strictly because I thought the name was intriguing—the Sex Panther Flip. I can't recall what was in it, only that it was the first time I saw someone crack an egg at a bar and use the entire thing. When you throw a whole egg into a tin, people can't help but ask questions about it—*Are you training for a boxing match?*—questions that may just pique their interest, leading to the thought, *That looks interesting ... I think I'll have one.*

For bartenders, the Flip can be an annoying drink because making one is messy and slows down service. For this reason we don't typically put Flips on our menu, but I like using them as a bartender's choice whenever a customer asks for something decadent or dessert-y.

When I create Flip variations, I stick to that old-school Jerry Thomas mentality. I like to use an aged spirit as the base; I like what that woodiness does to the drink. I often add sherry or port, then play around with the sweetener— maybe maple syrup or honey instead of sugar to push it even further into the dessert category.

There's a certain stigma about the Flip and other drinks with a heavier texture. Many people associate richness with sweetness. But a balanced Flip isn't sweet, though it definitely is decadent. That's the cool thing about the Flip: it's somewhere between a cocktail and custard, making it the perfect drink if you want to imbibe after a meal instead of eating dessert.

One of the most important Flip-making techniques I've learned is to let the egg warm up just a bit before making the drink. I pull the egg out of the fridge right before I start to build the cocktail, and that minute or so of warm-up time helps ensure that the drink has that big, frothy head that everyone loves. Another thing I like to do is what I call the "David and Goliath shake." After dry shaking everything, I add a large block of ice to the tin, along with a Kold-Draft cube. Right out of the gate, that huge block obliterates the smaller cube. This brings the temperature down quickly, and then the large block can work like a piston to add air and texture.

Whenever I make a cocktail that calls for an egg white, I like to use the leftover yolk in a Flip-style drink that I give to a guest as an unexpected treat. Why throw out the yolk when you can use it to make someone's night?

I think the Flip is an untouched frontier for most bartenders. We spend a lot of time making Old-Fashioneds, Manhattans, and Daiquiris, and any decent bartender can easily rattle off riffs on those drinks, but ask them to make you a Flip-style drink, and you're likely to hit a dead end. To me, this indicates that there's tremendous potential in that category, with a lot of room for experimentation. Sometimes I dream of a world where I go to a cocktail bar and there's an entire section of Flips and other dessert drinks on the menu.

Bean Me Up Biscotti

- **1½ ounces aged rum**
- **½ ounce coffee liqueur**
- **¼ ounce Faretti Biscotti Famosi liqueur**
- **1 ounce heavy cream**
- **1 whole egg**
- **Garnish: Nutmeg**

Dry shake all the ingredients, then shake again with ice. Double strain into a small white wine glass. Garnish with a few grates of nutmeg.

EXPLORING TECHNIQUE: USING EGGS IN COCKTAILS

The proteins in eggs can make drinks frothy, but some special techniques are required to make the frothiest cocktails possible. When building cocktails that use raw eggs in any form, never add liquor or citrus on top of the egg. Acidity or alcohol will "cook" the egg if the ingredients are left standing too long, producing an off-putting texture and flavor. Therefore, we recommend that you first crack the egg into the larger shaker tin or separate the white into the larger tin. Then build the rest of the cocktail in the smaller shaker tin, keeping the ingredients separate from the egg. (Another advantage of keeping the egg separate in this way is that eggs can be tricky to work with: you'll probably mess up the cracking or separation at some point or need to fish out a small piece of shell.)

When you're ready to shake, bear in mind that ice inhibits foaming. So the first step is to shake the cocktail without ice—a technique known as dry shaking. So don't add any ice before you seal the tin. Then, be sure to seal it tightly. As the egg proteins expand to create all of that frothy goodness, the pressure inside the tin will increase and try to push it open. Once the shaker is tightly sealed, shake the drink vigorously for about five seconds.

Crack the tin open and peek inside. If you're using a whole egg or just the white, the mixture will be foamy. Transfer the foamy liquid to the small shaker tin, carefully add ice to the small tin to fill it to the top, then seal the shaker and shake vigorously once again. When you think you've shaken enough, shake for a few seconds longer. All of this agitation will both dilute and chill the drink, while also adding water and air that will be trapped by the egg's protein, creating stronger, more consistent foam.

Once shaken, open the tin and ensure that all the liquid is in the large shaker. We prefer to double strain all cocktails that contain egg. This will keep ice chips (as well as any errant bits of shell) out of a cocktail that's all about texture. In addition, the mesh of the sieve also helps aerate the drink even more, promoting further foaming.

A final and important step is to clean your tools properly. For working bartenders, simply dunking them in a sink filled with water is a big no-no. The egg clinging to the shaker and sieve will contaminate the water, so don't do it! Instead, rinse your shaker and tools independently and thoroughly, then smell them; if there's even a hint of egg aroma, wash them again.

We would be remiss not to mention that there's also a school of thought that it's preferable to invert the approach, first shaking the entire drink and egg with ice, then straining the drink and shaking it again without ice to froth it up just before pouring it into a glass. Called the reverse dry shake, this makes for beautifully frothy cocktails. Those who favor this technique claim the cocktail will have a more pronounced head and stay frothy longer, but we've found that the difference is marginal. Give each approach a try and decide which you like better. We prefer the regular dry shake because it involves fewer steps but yields similar results.

PRESSURIZED SHAKING AND

THE RAMOS GIN FIZZ REVISITED

Famous for its restorative properties, the Ramos Gin Fizz (page 141) is a creamy and floral drink that cures a hangover nearly as well as a Bloody Mary. Hailing from New Orleans and supposedly invented in 1888, its popularity has just as much to do with its nearly universally loved flavor as with the ritual of its preparation and the drama of its presentation. The nineteenth-century version was purported to be best when shaken for a full ten minutes—or longer! That extended shaking time beats the cream and egg into a fluffy froth, making for an ethereally light cocktail.

Taking ten minutes to shake a cocktail is both one hell of a workout and time that a bartender never has. Our trick in the past was to make a ritual of passing the shaker around the bar, having patrons join the fun and show off their shaking skills.

Then we stumbled onto the idea of using an iSi whipper (see page 97) to quickly infuse tiny bubbles of N_2O into the cocktail. The result is the fluffiest cocktail we've ever made. Because of its greater volume, a large glass (20 to 24 ounces) must be used.

It should be noted that this technique is in no way endorsed by iSi—and should only be undertaken with caution. We have made hundreds with no issue, but we have followed a strict safety protocol of always using large 1-liter canisters and never filling the canister more than half full (including ice).

N_2O Ramos Gin Fizz

2 ounces Plymouth gin
¼ ounce fresh lime juice
¼ ounce fresh lemon juice
1 ounce simple syrup (page 45)
1 ounce heavy cream
1 egg white
3 drops orange flower water
Cold seltzer

Combine all the ingredients (except the seltzer) in an iSi whipper; don't add any ice. Seal and shake for 20 seconds. Open, add five 1-inch ice cubes, then seal tightly once again. Charge with an N_2O cartridge, then shake for 10 seconds. Release the first burst of pressure into a cocktail shaker or other vessel, then turn the canister all the way upside down and dispense the cocktail into a large glass. Let settle for about 1 minute. Carefully add the cold seltzer, pouring it down a spoon to ensure that it goes directly to the bottom of the glass and lifts the foamy cocktail above the rim of the glass. No garnish.

This technique can be applied to any cocktail containing proteins that will bond around air when agitated (eggs and cream, for example) to make a frothy drink.

GLASSWARE: DEALER'S CHOICE

There's not a single glass that's best for the Flip and its extended family of cocktails, in part because these drinks take so many different forms: hot or cold, modest in volume or extravagantly frothy. This provides us with a good opportunity to talk about selecting the ideal serving vessel for different types of cocktails.

For the classic Flip and other cold cocktails made with eggs or dairy, we use a glass that's large enough to hold the extra froth, but not so large that there's a lot of extra headroom between the top of the drink and the rim of the glass. A glass that holds 7 to 8 ounces should do the trick. A glass with a stem is ideal, since it prevents the cocktail from being warmed by the drinker's hands. Lastly, the diameter of the rim should be fairly wide so there's enough surface area atop the drink for dusting it with spices or applying other garnishes, which are often an important component of this style of cocktail.

We often serve Flip-style drinks in a coupe or a small wineglass, such as those meant for white wine or rosé. A favorite of ours is the rosé glass made by Schott Zwiesel, which flares outward slightly at the top of the glass.

Just as cold cocktails need a stem, hot ones need a handle. For warm, creamy drinks like Irish Coffee (page 268) or a Tom and Jerry (page 268), we often reach for a clear toddy glass, which has the advantage of allowing the guest to see the gorgeous cocktail inside. But for others, such as the Almond Orchard (page 257), a decorative wooden bowl, coffee mug, or teacup can give the drink more character, just as tiki mugs do for tropical drinks.

FLIP VARIATIONS

Variations on the Flip have developed down a few different paths. As shown in the preceding sections, base spirits or fortified wines can be swapped in and out of the Flip template, eggs and dairy can be removed, or the sweetener can be manipulated. What's consistent in these variations on the root recipe is an overall richness and a creamy texture. Here we explore a handful of well-known variations that take the Flip orthodoxy and push it in different directions.

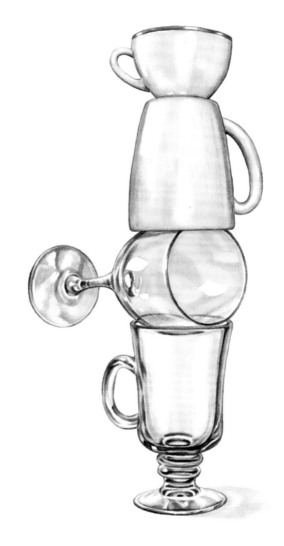

White Russian

CLASSIC

Some variations on the Flip template are simple concoctions that omit the egg, contain just a few ingredients, and are simply built in the serving glass. The classic White Russian is just such a drink. Because there's nothing complicated about these drinks, the quality of their ingredients is paramount. Like many other classic drinks in this chapter, the White Russian is often derided, but it's actually more carefully balanced than its reputation suggests. The fact that it calls for half-and-half, rather than cream, makes it light enough for everyday drinking; plus, if it called for heavy cream, the coffee flavor of the liqueur could be overwhelmed.

1½ ounces Absolut Elyx vodka
1 ounce Caffé Lolita coffee liqueur
1 ounce half-and-half
Garnish: 3 coffee beans

Combine the vodka and liqueur in a double Old-Fashioned glass. Fill the glass with ice cubes and stir briefly. Layer the half-and-half on top. Garnish with the coffee beans.

Irish Coffee

Irish Coffee

CLASSIC

In this Flip variation, the cream isn't mixed into the cocktail; instead, it's whipped and floated on top. Because the heat of the underlying ingredients unravels the structure of the whipped cream, causing it to seep into the liquid in a less-than-appealing way, we recommend whipping the cream until it develops soft peaks so it will hold up longer.

- **2 ounces heavy cream**
- **1½ ounces Jameson Irish whiskey**
- **¾ ounce Demerara Gum Syrup (page 54)**
- **3 ounces hot brewed coffee**

Using a bowl and whisk, whip the cream until soft peaks begin to form. Warm a coffee or toddy mug by filling it with boiling water, letting it sit a minute or two, then dumping out the water. Pour in the whiskey and syrup, then slowly add the coffee while stirring continuously. Carefully spoon all the whipped cream on top of the drink.

Grasshopper

CLASSIC

The Grasshopper is a rich but oddly refreshing liqueur-based cocktail. This cocktail and many others of its ilk have been relegated to dive bars for decades, but as high-quality liqueurs have come to the market—made with actual mint and cacao rather than artificial flavorings—we've revisited these classics and added some of them to our repertoire. In this cocktail, the fresh mint garnish provides both aromatic and visual reinforcement of the minty character of the cocktail.

- **1 ounce Tempus Fugit white crème de menthe**
- **1 ounce Giffard white crème de cacao**
- **1 ounce heavy cream**
- **8 mint leaves**
- **Garnish: 1 mint leaf**

Shake all the ingredients with ice. Double strain into a chilled coupe. Garnish with the mint leaf, placing it on top of the drink.

Tom and Jerry

CLASSIC

Long before central heat could protect us against the elements, humans had the bright idea to mix dairy with some booze to ward off the cold and rain. In fact, that may be how the Flip originated, as a heated mixture of egg, ale, and sugar. Although modern-day Flips are almost always served cold, the idea of a warm drink on a cold day remains appealing, and one of the most comforting warm drinks out there is the Tom and Jerry, a wintertime favorite packed with rum, Cognac, dairy, and eggs (which are a component of the Tom and Jerry Batter).

- **1 ounce El Dorado 12-year rum**
- **1 ounce Pierre Ferrand Ambre Cognac**
- **2 ounces Tom and Jerry Batter (page 296)**
- **2 ounces hot milk**
- **Garnish: Nutmeg**

Warm a coffee mug or teacup by filling it with boiling water, letting it sit a minute or two, then dumping out the water. Pour in the rum and Cognac, then add the batter. Stir until well combined, then slowly add the hot milk. Garnish with a few grates of nutmeg.

Golden Cadillac

CLASSIC

The classic Golden Cadillac is another chip off the Grasshopper block, with the vanilla and licorice flavors of the Galliano taking the cocktail in a different direction. A shaving of dark chocolate atop the drink accents the liqueur, drawing out some of its pleasantly bitter qualities.

1 ounce Galliano l'Autentico

1 ounce Giffard white crème de cacao

1 ounce heavy cream

Garnish: Dark chocolate

Shake all the ingredients with ice. Double strain into a chilled coupe. Garnish with a few grates of dark chocolate.

Piña Colada

CLASSIC

Though the Piña Colada is a famous cocktail associated with sandy beaches and thatched bars, analyzing the recipe reveals that it's basically another type of Flip. It was a shock to us to think of the Piña Colada as something other than a sour-style drink, but there you have it. The rum brings proof, coconut cream adds fat and sweetness, and the pineapple juice provides sweetness and acidity.

2 ounces Caña Brava white rum

½ ounce Cruzan Black Strap rum

1½ ounces fresh pineapple juice

1½ ounces House Coconut Cream (page 295)

Garnish: 1 pineapple wedge and 1 brandied cherry on an umbrella skewer

Combine all the ingredients in a shaker and whip, shaking with a few pieces of crushed ice, just until incorporated, then dump into a double Old-Fashioned glass and fill the glass with crushed ice. Garnish with the pineapple wedge and cherry and serve with a straw.

Piña Colada

EXTENDED FAMILY

The Flip's extended family pushes the template even
further. The template's reliance on richness is maintained,
but the form is played with in various ways. In the Indulge
(page 272), light almond milk replaces cream for a more
delicate riff on the Flip. The Hans Gruber (page 272) takes
inspiration from the classic White Russian (page 267) while
packing as much holiday flavors into a glass as possible.
Together, these drinks show just a few ways the Flip
format can be worked into your own cocktail creations.

Frozen Mudslide

DEVON TARBY, 2016

We know what you're thinking:
A Mudslide? What is this, 1985? Sure,
it's easy to make fun of this drink,
as it's essentially a boozy milkshake.
But then again, what's wrong with
that? The Mudslide probably got its
poor reputation because of how it's
usually made: a near-equal mix of
coffee liqueur, vodka, and Bailey's
Irish cream. While that's okay, we
prefer this version made with ice
cream, a rich and flavorful addition
that precludes the need to shake
with ice, which can quickly water
down the drink.

1 ounce Aylesbury Duck vodka

1½ ounces Bailey's Irish Cream

1 ounce Kahlúa coffee liqueur

3 scoops vanilla or coffee
ice cream

Garnish: finely grated dark
chocolate

Combine all the ingredients in a
blender and process until smooth.
Pour into a Collins glass and serve
with a straw and long spoon.
Garnish with grated dark
chocolate.

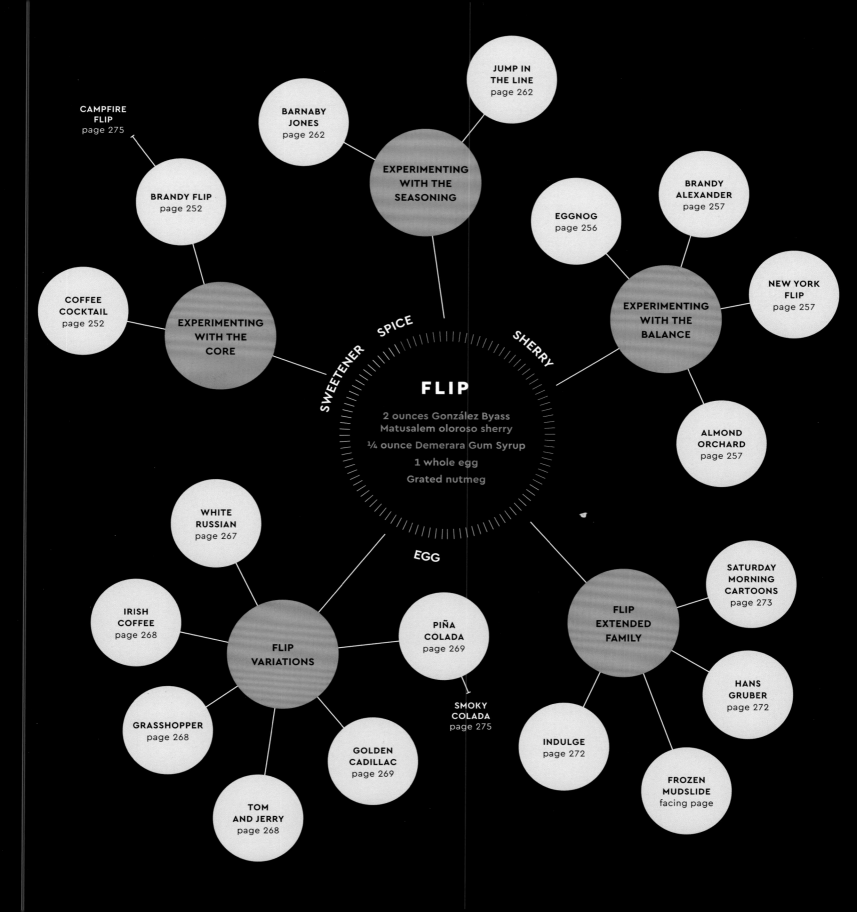

CAMPFIRE
FLIP
page 275

BARNABY
JONES
page 262

JUMP IN
THE LINE
page 262

BRANDY FLIP
page 252

EGGNOG
page 256

BRANDY
ALEXANDER
page 257

EXPERIMENTING
WITH THE
SEASONING

COFFEE
COCKTAIL
page 252

EXPERIMENTING
WITH THE
CORE

NEW YORK
FLIP
page 257

EXPERIMENTING
WITH THE
BALANCE

SPICE

SWEETENER

SHERRY

FLIP

2 ounces González Byass
Matusalem oloroso sherry
¼ ounce Demerara Gum Syrup
1 whole egg
Grated nutmeg

ALMOND
ORCHARD
page 257

WHITE
RUSSIAN
page 267

EGG

SATURDAY
MORNING
CARTOONS
page 273

IRISH
COFFEE
page 268

FLIP
VARIATIONS

PIÑA
COLADA
page 269

FLIP
EXTENDED
FAMILY

HANS
GRUBER
page 272

GRASSHOPPER
page 268

SMOKY
COLADA
page 275

INDULGE
page 272

GOLDEN
CADILLAC
page 269

FROZEN
MUDSLIDE
facing page

TOM
AND JERRY
page 268

Hans Gruber

DEVON TARBY, 2015

One of our favorite layered White Russian variations is the Hans Gruber, a cocktail that we created for a holiday-themed menu at the Walker Inn in 2015. In it, we've manipulated every component of the classic White Russian to create a sophisticated cocktail with the flavorful profile of pecan pie with ice cream. Though decadent, the toasted nuttiness of the pecan-infused rum and the implicit richness of the brown butter–infused brandy are balanced by the fig bomb of the Pedro Ximénez sherry. The maple-flavored whipped cream is one of our favorite revelations, with just a small amount of maple syrup flavoring the cream in a delicious way. We've also played with flavoring whipped cream with other ingredients, including orange curaçao and dry sherry. If you do the same, just be mindful of how much alcohol you add to the cream; anything more than around ½ ounce of alcohol per cup of cream will make the cream harder to whip.

2 ounces heavy cream

¼ ounce dark, robust maple syrup

1 ounce Toasted Pecan–Infused Plantation Rum (page 293)

¾ ounce Brown Butter–Infused Apple Brandy (page 287)

1 ounce Lustau San Emilio Pedro Ximénez sherry

1 teaspoon Giffard Vanille de Madagascar

¼ ounce Cane Sugar Syrup (page 47)

3 drops Salt Solution (page 298)

Garnish: 1 spritz of Cruzan Black Strap rum

Using a bowl and whisk, whip the cream and maple syrup together just until soft peaks start to form. In a mixing glass, stir the remaining ingredients with ice. Strain into a chilled coupe. Carefully spoon the whipped cream on top, then mist the blackstrap rum over the drink.

Indulge

DEVON TARBY, 2016

This Tom and Jerry–inspired cocktail demonstrates how the tang and creaminess of a few drops of Lactic Acid Solution can make a dramatic difference in a cocktail. The drink derives additional richness through two key ingredients—apple brandy infused with brown butter and creamy almond milk—with the amaretto providing some nuttiness. The result is an exceedingly smooth and rich drink.

4¼ ounces Almond Milk (page 255)

¾ ounce Brown Butter–Infused Apple Brandy (page 287)

¾ ounce Caña Brava 7-year rum

1 teaspoon Lazzaroni amaretto

½ ounce Spiced Almond Demerara Gum Syrup (page 56)

2 drops Lactic Acid Solution (page 298)

1 drop Salt Solution (page 298)

Combine all the ingredients in a small saucepan over medium-low heat and cook, stirring frequently, until steaming hot but not simmering. Pour into a coffee mug or small teacup. No garnish.

Saturday Morning Cartoons

DEVON TARBY, 2015

This cocktail, our tongue-in-cheek play on cereal milk, provides a great demonstration of how infusions and liqueurs can help bring the richness and sweetness of a classic Flip to a dairy-free concoction. Here, the cinnamon spice of Avuá Amburana cachaça is deepened by mixing it with a cacao nib tincture and a complex vanilla liqueur, all built on the backbone of homemade almond milk. In a twist, this cocktail isn't meant to be sipped (though you're more than welcome to): instead, pour it over cereal for a buzzy breakfast.

1 ounce Avuá Amburana cachaça

½ ounce Cacao Nib Tincture (page 297)

¼ ounce Giffard Vanille de Madagascar

¾ ounce Demerara Gum Syrup (page 54)

4 ounces Almond Milk (page 255)

Cereal

Combine all the ingredients (except the cereal) in a mixing glass and stir to mix well. Pour over cereal in a bowl and serve with a spoon. Be sure to lap up any remaining liquid!

NEXT-LEVEL TECHNIQUE: INTRODUCING SMOKY FLAVORS

What is it about smoke that's so comforting? Is there something deep in our animal brain that causes us to associate it with safety, warmth, and sustenance, perhaps activating our ancient hunter-gatherer heritage? Whatever it is, smoke is a powerful flavor and aroma in food, and it can be transformative in cocktails as well.

At the most basic level, smoke flavors can be introduced into cocktails via ingredients that have a smoky notes, particularly smoky spices, like paprika or cumin, and smoked ingredients, like chipotle chiles. These can be used as ingredients in syrups or infusions, or in powder form for rimming glasses. But that's hardly a next-level technique. So in this section, we'll discuss how the flavors of actual smoke can be infused into both cocktails and their ingredients.

You may wonder why we offer this technique in our chapter on Flips. Though smoking can add another layer of flavor to many styles of cocktails, Flips, thanks to their composition, can capture smoke in a way that no other cocktail can, since the fats in egg or dairy are ideal for trapping all sorts of flavors. The fat will absorb a wide range of the components that make up the personality of smoke, whereas introducing smoke into a lean drink, like an Old-Fashioned variation, may produce results that teeter on the edge of a liquid smoke flavor. In all cases, the key is to keep the particular cocktail

in mind and be very judicious: use too much and it will dominate a drink; use too little and it may have no impact. Also be aware that people have widely different tolerances for smokiness in a drink, so again, moderation is key.

Smoking a liquid ingredient or an entire cocktail may seem inconceivable, but in reality, it's quite easy. The basic method is to apply heat to wood until it's smoldering, then allow the smoke to interact with the surface area of the liquid. The smoke will infuse the liquid in a matter of minutes. Where the art comes in lies in specific choices, from choosing a cocktail that would benefit from the addition of smoke flavors, to selecting a type of wood or other smokable substance that has an affinity for the ingredients, to how you apply the smoke.

Hardwoods are the most common substance used for smoking food, as their smoke tends to be sweet and flavorful. But other dried ingredients can also be used, including teas and herbs.

As mentioned above, smoke has a powerful aroma and flavor that can easily overwhelm a cocktail, so we tend to infuse ingredients with only a modest amount of smoke, and then combine them with ingredients that have inherently complementary qualities, such as the vanilla richness of an oak-aged spirit, or that mimic flavors people are familiar with, such as the sweet smokiness of barbecue or the tobacco smoke of a cigar.

Campfire Flip

ALEX DAY, 2017

The Campfire Flip is a smoky riff on a classic Flip. We start with a smoked ingredient: Hickory-Smoked Cognac, which we pair with sherry and a bit of vanilla liqueur. The result is a rich drink with a smoked-woody complexity that plays off the barrel-aged flavors already present in both the Cognac and the sherry.

- **1 ounce Hickory Smoke–Infused Cognac (page 290)**
- **1 ounce Lustau Los Arcos amontillado sherry**
- **1 teaspoon Giffard Vanilla de Madagascar**
- **½ ounce Demerara Gum Syrup (page 54)**
- **1 whole egg**
- **Garnish: Cinnamon and nutmeg**

Dry shake all the ingredients, then shake again with ice. Double strain into a chilled coupe. Garnish with a few grates of cinnamon and nutmeg.

Smoky Colada

ALEX DAY, 2017

Smoky flavors need not be introduced via smoke itself; they can also be added by including ingredients that have smoky flavors conferred by cooking, such as grilling. One of our favorite ways of working with this in cocktails is to use a syrup made with grilled pineapple, as in this smoky variation on the Piña Colada (page 269). Substituting our Grilled Pineapple Syrup for some of the fresh pineapple juice takes this rich tropical drink in a slightly savory direction.

- **2 ounces Caña Brava white rum**
- **½ ounce Cruzan Black Strap rum**
- **¾ ounce fresh pineapple juice**
- **¾ ounce Grilled Pineapple Syrup (page 285)**
- **1 ounce House Coconut Cream (page 295)**
- **Garnish: 1 pineapple wedge and 1 brandied cherry on an umbrella skewer**

Combine all the ingredients in a shaker and whip, shaking with a few pieces of crushed ice, just until incorporated, then dump into a double Old-Fashioned glass and fill the glass with crushed ice. Garnish with the pineapple wedge and cherry and serve with a straw.

SMOKING TOOLS

Here are some of our favorite tools for adding smoke flavors to cocktails.

Smoking gun: There are several options on the market, but one of our favorites is PolyScience's Smoking Gun Pro. A small fan draws smoke from the burn chamber and directs it through a tube that can be submerged into a liquid or be used to smoke the space on top of or around a drink. The smoke is cold, so it won't heat drinks, and the smoke output can be adjusted to produce a lot of smoke or just a little. Because of its compact size, it's ideal for quickly adding smoke to an ingredient or an entire cocktail.

Wood stave or plank: In addition to seasoning ingredients with smoke, you can season glasses or other serving vessels. We love to do this using a wood stave from an old bourbon barrel to generate a rich smoldering smoke that evokes American whiskey. Place the stave on a heatproof surface, inner side up, and use a butane torch to light the surface on fire, toasting the stave until embers glow and smoke begins to waft. Then place a glass on top of the plank so the smoke's sweet vanilla and spice aromas will season it. It's a wonderful way to create a dramatic version of a Sazerac-style cocktail that has lingering aromas on the glass and a contrasting or complementary cocktail within.

Torch: A butane kitchen torch is a useful tool to have around. It's great for lighting wood chips in a Smoking Gun or other similar device, and it can also be used to ignite herbs for a smoky garnish, or to char a wood plank or stave (see above).

Grill: We sometimes cook fruits or vegetables on a wood-fired grill to impart a deeply smoky flavor, then use those ingredients as the base in a syrup or mix, as in our Grilled Pineapple Syrup (page 285). If you have a gas grill, don't fret: you can add smoke using wood chips in a foil pouch or metal box.

SMOKING WITH WOOD

By far the most common way to introduce smoke into cocktails is with wood smoke. We follow barbecue doctrine and use only hardwood chips, since soft woods like cedar, pine, fir, spruce, and hemlock produce a thick smoke that can be dangerous to inhale and creates an unpleasant flavor. Although different types of wood do produce different flavors, the amount of smoke they produce has a greater impact. Here are some of the most common woods used for smoking, arranged from least to most smoky:

Mild woods (cherry, apple, peach, pear, and birch): These woods produce sweet and fruity smoke and are best paired with lighter ingredients, such as fresh fruits to be used in syrups.

Medium woods (oak, hickory, maple, pecan, sarsaparilla): If you can choose only one wood for smoking, make it either oak or hickory. Both pair well with many ingredients and are noticeably smoky without being overwhelming. Oak is a natural accompaniment to any aged spirit, and hickory's sweet smoke will beautifully accent American whiskey or apple brandy.

Strong woods (mesquite, pimento, walnut): These woods, particularly mesquite, produce the strongest smoke, which can quickly overpower a cocktail. We recommend to either season a glass or the top of a cocktail, rather than to flavor an ingredient or the cocktail.

If using a Smoking Gun, you'll need small wood shavings. Pack them in an even layer in the gun's bowl, though not so tight that oxygen can't get through. Turn on the unit and light the chips using a torch. Let the first whiffs of smoke dissipate and wait for the visible flame to subside; though the wood is burning at this point, it isn't yet producing the smoke you're after. When the wood is smoldering and has red embers, it's producing flavorful smoke. At this point, insert the tube into the liquid, or above the liquid in a covered container, and smoke for ten seconds. Use a large enough container that will trap smoke when sealed. Allow the smoke to linger until it clears.

SMOKING WITH FLAMMABLE INGREDIENTS

Another way to introduce smoke flavors is to ignite certain ingredients that lend themselves to combustion. We primarily do this with tea leaves and herbs and spices.

Tea Leaves: Dried tea leaves are great for smoking using a Smoking Gun. Teas that already have a smoky flavor, such as Lapsang souchong, or tea blends with woodsy and fruity flavors, such as August Uncommon Tea's A Field in Innsbruck (see Resources, page 299), are particularly good choices. Experiment with different teas; some will act much like soft wood, producing a sweet smoke.

Herbs and Spices: Lighting herbs on fire and allowing them to perfume either the top of a cocktail or simply the air around the cocktail can be an incredibly powerful way to introduce a touch of smoke. Torched rosemary is one of our favorites. Take a long sprig of rosemary and, using a torch, light the leaves on fire. As they crackle, an intense woodsy aroma is released. This rosemary can be placed on the drink (be careful of burning embers!) or simply nearby; its aroma is powerful enough to perfume an entire room. You can use a similar approach with cinnamon.

Smoke-Infused Ice: Though a chunk of ice may seem impenetrable, it will absorb surrounding flavors and aromas. This is one reason why our bars have freezers dedicated solely to ice. (Yes, you should only use your home freezer for ice; please extend our apologies to your roommates or spouse.) To flavor ice with smoke, place the ice in a plastic container with a lid. Cover, leaving the top open just enough to slide in the tube from a Smoking Gun. Inject smoke inside so that it is dense enough not to see through, then seal the container and freeze for a few hours to allow the smoke to infuse the ice. It will have a subtle smoke flavor, making for a unique addition to an Old-Fashioned-style drink.

APPENDIX

COCKTAILS

Aces and Eights

JARRED WEIGAND, 2016

2 ounces El Tesoro
reposado tequila

½ ounce Amaro Meletti

1 teaspoon Galliano Ristretto

1 teaspoon Vanilla Lactic Syrup
(page 286)

1 dash Bittermens Xocolatl
mole bitters

Garnish: 1 orange twist

Stir all the ingredients over ice, then
strain into a double Old-Fashioned
glass over 1 large ice cube. Express
the orange twist over the drink, then
gently rub it around the rim of the
glass and place it into the drink.

Affinity

CLASSIC

2 ounces Compass Box Oak Cross
scotch

½ ounce Carpano Antica Formula
vermouth

½ ounce Dolin dry vermouth

2 dashes Angostura bitters

Garnish: 1 lemon twist

Stir all the ingredients over ice, then
strain into a Nick & Nora glass. Express
the lemon twist over the drink, then
set it on the edge of the glass.

Aviation

CLASSIC

2 ounces Plymouth gin

¼ ounce crème de violette

1 teaspoon maraschino liqueur

¾ ounce fresh lemon juice

½ ounce simple syrup (page 45)

Garnish: 1 brandied cherry

Shake all the ingredients with ice,
then strain into a chilled coupe.
Garnish with the cherry.

Berry Picking

DEVON TARBY, 2015

2 ounces Strawberry-Infused
Cognac and Mezcal (page 293)

1 ounce Lustau Los Arcos
Amontillado sherry

¾ ounce fresh lemon juice

¾ ounce Cinnamon Syrup
(page 52)

¼ teaspoon Campari

Garnish: 1 whole strawberry,
cut through the tip, leaving stem
end intact

Shake all the ingredients with ice,
then double strain into a chilled
double Old-Fashioned glass. Place the
strawberry on the edge of the glass.

Black Forest

BRYAN BRUCE AND
DEVON TARBY, 2016

¾ ounce Famous Grouse scotch

¾ ounce Brown Butter–Infused
Apple Brandy (page 287)

¼ ounce Clear Creek Douglas
fir brandy

¼ ounce Cacao Nib Tincture
(page 297)

1 teaspoon Luxardo Amaro Abano

1 teaspoon simple syrup (page 45)

1 drop Salt Solution (page 298)

Garnish: 1 spray of Cedar Tincture
(page 298)

Stir all the ingredients over ice, then
strain into a double Old-Fashioned
glass over 1 large ice cube. Mist the
top of the drink with the tincture.

Bobby Burns

CLASSIC

2 ounces Compass Box Asyla scotch

¾ ounce Carpano Antica Formula vermouth

¼ ounce Bénédictine

Garnish: 1 lemon twist

Stir all the ingredients over ice, then strain into a Nick & Nora glass. Express the lemon twist over the drink, then set it on the edge of the glass.

Campfire

DEVON TARBY, 2017

1¾ ounces Graham Cracker–Infused Elijah Craig Single-Barrel Bourbon (page 290)

½ ounce Cacao Nib Tincture (page 297)

1 teaspoon Giffard crème de cacao

1 pinch cherry wood chips (enough to fill smoker)

Stir all the ingredients over ice, then strain into a double Old-Fashioned glass over 1 large ice cube. Using a PolyScience Smoking Gun (see page 276), smoke the top of the drink with cherry wood smoke. No garnish.

Celery and Silk

ALEX DAY, 2014

1½ ounces Beefeater gin

½ ounce Linie aquavit

1 ounce Celery Root–Infused Dolin Blanc (page 288)

2 dashes Miracle Mile celery bitters

Stir all the ingredients over ice, then strain into a chilled Nick & Nora glass. No garnish.

Chancellor

CLASSIC

2 ounces Balvenie Doublewood 12-year scotch

1 ounce tawny port

½ ounce Carpano Antica Formula vermouth

1 dash Angostura bitters

Stir all the ingredients over ice, then strain into a chilled Nick & Nora glass. No garnish.

Class Act

NATASHA DAVID, 2015

1 ounce Pierre Ferrand Pineau des Charentes

½ ounce Singani 63

½ ounce St. George spiced pear liqueur

¾ ounce fresh pineapple juice

½ ounce fresh lemon juice

½ ounce simple syrup (page 45)

Garnish: 1 pineapple wedge

Shake all the ingredients with ice, then double strain into a chilled coupe. Garnish with the pineapple wedge.

Coco and Ice

MARY BARTLETT, 2014

1 ounce El Dorado 12-year rum

½ ounce Olmeca Altos reposado tequila

½ ounce Giffard Banane du Brésil

¼ ounce Caffé Lolita coffee liqueur

1½ ounces unsweetened coconut milk

Garnish: 1 banana chip

Shake all the ingredients with ice, then strain into a double Old-Fashioned glass over 1 large cube. Garnish with the banana chip.

Daisy Gun

ALEX DAY, 2013

2 ounces seltzer

1½ ounces Campo de Encanto Grand and Noble pisco

1 ounce Williams & Humbert Dry Sack sherry

¾ ounce fresh lemon juice

¾ ounce Clarified Strawberry Syrup (page 57)

¼ ounce Cinnamon Syrup (page 52)

Garnish: 1 lemon wedge and nutmeg

Pour the seltzer into a Collins glass. Short shake the remaining ingredients with ice for about 5 seconds, then strain into the glass. Fill the glass with ice cubes, then garnish with the lemon wedge and a few grates of nutmeg.

Dark Horse

JEREMY OERTEL, 2017

1½ ounces Appleton Estate 21-year rum

½ ounce Bordelet Calvados

½ ounce Amaro Nardini

½ ounce Grand Marnier

Garnish: 1 lemon twist

Stir all the ingredients over ice, then strain into a chilled Nick & Nora glass. Express the lemon twist over the drink, then set it onto the edge of the glass.

Endless Summer

DEVON TARBY, 2016

1 ounce Cimarrón blanco tequila

1 ounce Dolin blanc vermouth

¼ ounce Giffard Crème de Pamplemousse

¼ ounce Giffard blue curaçao

¾ ounce fresh pineapple juice

¾ ounce fresh lime juice

¼ ounce simple syrup (page 45)

Garnish: 1 grapefruit wedge

Shake all the ingredients with ice, then strain into a Collins glass filled with ice cubes. Garnish with the grapefruit wedge.

Fair Game

ALEX DAY, 2012

1½ ounces Williams & Humbert Dry Sack sherry

1 ounce Appleton Estate Reserve Blend rum

¾ ounce fresh lime juice

½ ounce simple syrup (page 45)

1 teaspoon orange marmalade

Garnish: 1 mint sprig

Combine all the ingredients in a shaker and whip, shaking with a few pieces of crushed ice, just until incorporated. Dump into a Collins glass and add crushed ice until the glass is about four-fifths full. Swizzle for a few seconds, then pack the glass with ice, mounding it above the rim. Garnish with the mint sprig and serve with a straw.

Fuji Legend

ALEX DAY AND DEVON TARBY, 2013

2 ounces seltzer

1 ounce Chamomile-Infused Blanco Tequila (page 288)

1 ounce manzanilla sherry

1 ounce fresh Fuji apple juice

½ ounce fresh lemon juice

½ ounce House Ginger Syrup (page 48)

1 teaspoon dark, robust maple syrup

Garnish: 3 thin apple slices on a skewer

Pour the seltzer into a Collins glass. Short shake the remaining ingredients with ice for about 5 seconds, then strain into the glass. Fill the glass with ice cubes, then garnish with the apple slices.

Ganymede

BLAKE WALKER, 2016

2 ounces Narutotai Ginjo Nama Genchu sake

¼ ounce Lustau Los Arcos amontillado sherry

1 teaspoon Cherry Heering

½ teaspoon Plymouth sloe gin

¼ ounce fresh lemon juice

¼ ounce Cane Sugar Syrup (page 47)

Garnish: 1 brandied cherry

Stir all the ingredients over ice, then strain into a chilled Nick & Nora glass. Garnish with the cherry.

Ginger Rogers

BRIAN MILLER, 2011

1 ounce Gosling's Black Seal rum

1 ounce Hine H Cognac

¾ ounce fresh lemon juice

¾ ounce House Ginger Syrup (page 48)

½ ounce simple syrup (page 45)

1 dash Peychaud's bitters

Shake all the ingredients with ice, then strain into a chilled coupe. No garnish.

The Greatest Dancer

NICK SETTLE, 2016

1½ ounces Honeydew-Infused Kappa Pisco (page 290)

½ ounce Plantation 3 Stars rum

½ teaspoon Chareau aloe liqueur

½ teaspoon Giffard Menthe-Pastille

¾ ounce fresh lime juice

½ ounce Cane Sugar Syrup (page 47)

6 drops Salt Solution (page 298)

Shake all the ingredients with ice, then strain into a chilled coupe. No garnish.

Jet Set

ALEX DAY, 2016

1 ounce Clear Creek pear brandy

½ ounce Clear Creek 2-year apple brandy

1 teaspoon Giffard Menthe-Pastille

1 dash absinthe

¾ ounce fresh lime juice

¾ ounce simple syrup (page 45)

Garnish: 1 mint sprig

Shake all the ingredients with ice, then strain into a double Old-Fashioned glass over 1 large ice cube. Garnish with the mint sprig.

La Viña

ALEX DAY, 2009

1 ounce Russell's Reserve rye

1 ounce Amaro Nonino

1 ounce Lustau East India Solera sherry

1 dash House Orange Bitters (page 295)

Stir all the ingredients over ice, then strain into a chilled Nick & Nora glass. No garnish.

Little Victory

ALEX DAY, 2013

1½ ounces Beefeater gin

½ ounce Absolut Elyx vodka

1 ounce Root Beer–Infused Cocchi Americano (page 292)

1 teaspoon orange marmalade

Garnish: 1 orange wedge

Stir all the ingredients over ice, then double strain into a double Old-Fashioned glass over 1 large ice cube. Garnish with the orange wedge.

Long-Distance Lover

LAUREN CORRIVEAU, 2016

1 orange half wheel

1 lemon wedge

1 pineapple wedge

¾ ounce House Orgeat (page 285)

1½ ounces Lustau Los Arcos amontillado sherry

¾ ounce St. George spiced pear liqueur

½ ounce Lustau Emilín Moscatel sherry

¼ ounce Copper & Kings unaged apple brandy

½ teaspoon kümmel liqueur

½ teaspoon Amaro di Angostura

Garnish: 2 pineapple leaves, 1 orange half wheel, 1 lemon wheel, and 1 cinnamon stick

In a shaker, gently muddle the orange, lemon, and pineapple with the orgeat. Add the remaining ingredients, shake with ice, then strain into a tall tiki mug filled with crushed ice. Garnish with the pineapple leaves, orange half wheel, lemon wheel, and cinnamon stick and insert a straw. Just before serving, torch the end of the cinnamon stick until it begins to smoke.

Malibu

DEVON TARBY, 2015

1 ounce Cabeza blanco tequila

½ ounce Campo de Encanto Grand and Noble pisco

½ ounce Lillet blanc

½ ounce Giffard Crème de Pamplemousse

1 teaspoon Campari

¾ ounce fresh lime juice

½ ounce fresh grapefruit juice

½ ounce Grapefruit Cordial (page 53)

3 drops Salt Solution (page 298)

Garnish: 10 toasted coconut chips

Shake all the ingredients with ice, then strain into a chilled coupe. Serve with the toasted coconut chips alongside.

Night Light

ALEX DAY, 2014

1½ ounces Campo de Encanto Grand and Noble pisco

½ ounce Dolin blanc vermouth

¼ ounce St-Germain

¾ ounce Fusion Napa Valley verjus blanc

Garnish: 1 grapefruit half wheel

Stir all the ingredients over ice, then strain into a double Old-Fashioned glass over 1 large ice cube. Garnish with the grapefruit half wheel.

Normandie Club Martini #2

DEVON TARBY AND TREVOR EASTER, 2016

1¾ ounces Absolut Elyx vodka

¼ ounce Linie aquavit

1 ounce Lustau Jarana fino sherry

1 teaspoon Giffard Abricot du Roussillon

1 teaspoon White Honey Syrup (page 286)

Garnish: 2 to 3 sprays of Rosemary Salt Solution (page 298)

Stir all the ingredients over ice, then strain into a chilled Nick & Nora glass. Mist the top of the drink with the salt solution.

Nurse Hazel

ALEX DAY, 2015

2 ounces Oolong-Infused Vodka (page 291)

¾ ounce Lustau Jarana fino sherry

½ ounce La Quintinye Vermouth Royal blanc

¼ ounce Cointreau

1 dash House Orange Bitters (page 295)

Stir all the ingredients over ice, then strain into a chilled Nick & Nora glass. No garnish.

Peach Boy

NATASHA DAVID, 2014

1½ ounces Krogstad aquavit

¾ ounce Mathilde peach liqueur

¾ ounce fresh lemon juice

½ ounce House Orgeat (page 285)

Garnish: 1 mint bouquet

Short shake all the ingredients with ice for about 5 seconds, then strain into a double Old-Fashioned glass. Top with crushed ice. Garnish with the mint bouquet and insert a straw.

Penicillin

SAM ROSS, 2005

2 ounces Famous Grouse scotch

¾ ounce fresh lemon juice

⅓ ounce Honey Syrup (page 45)

⅓ ounce House Ginger Syrup (page 48)

Garnish: 3 sprays of Islay scotch and 1 piece of candied ginger on a skewer

Shake all the ingredients with ice, then strain into a double Old-Fashioned glass over 1 large ice cube. Mist the top of the drink with the scotch, then garnish with the candied ginger.

Professor Hinkle

DEVON TARBY AND
ALEX DAY, 2015

1 ounce Neisson rhum
agricole blanc

½ ounce Clear Creek
raspberry brandy

½ ounce Dolin blanc vermouth

¼ ounce Aperol

¾ ounce fresh grapefruit juice

½ ounce fresh lemon juice

½ ounce House Orgeat (page 285)

Shake all the ingredients with ice, then
double strain into a teacup or chilled
coupe. No garnish.

Rendezvous in Chennai

ROBERT SACHSE AND
BLAKE WALKER, 2017

1½ ounces Madras Curry–Infused
Gin (page 291)

¾ ounce House Coconut Cream
(page 295)

¼ ounce Blume Marillen apricot
eau-de-vie

¼ ounce Rothman & Winter
apricot liqueur

1 teaspoon Giffard Crème
de Pêche

¾ ounce fresh lime juice

1 teaspoon House Ginger Syrup
(page 48)

Garnish: 1 orange twist

Stir all the ingredients over ice, then
strain into a double Old-Fashioned
glass over 1 large ice cube. Express
the orange twist over the drink, then
gently rub it around the rim of the
glass and place it into the drink.

Rob Roy

CLASSIC

2 ounces Balvenie Doublewood
12-year scotch

¾ ounce Carpano Antica Formula
vermouth

1 dash Angostura bitters

Garnish: 1 brandied cherry
on a skewer

Stir all the ingredients over ice, then
strain into a chilled Nick & Nora glass.
Garnish with the brandied cherry.

Root Beer Float

DEVON TARBY, 2015

2½ ounces water

1½ ounces Milk-Washed Rum
(page 291)

½ ounce Giffard Vanille
de Madagascar

½ ounce simple syrup (page 45)

⅛ teaspoon phosphoric acid
solution (see page 194)

2 drops Terra Spice root beer
extract

Chill all the ingredients. Combine
them in a carbonation bottle, charge
with CO_2, and gently shake to help
dissolve the CO_2 into the liquid (see
page 228 for setup and general
carbonation instructions). Place the
bottle in the refrigerator for at least
20 minutes before opening. To serve,
carefully pour into a Highball glass
with ice.

Rye Pie

DAVID FERNIE AND
MATTHEW BROWN, 2016

1½ ounces Rittenhouse rye

½ ounce St. George
raspberry brandy

¼ ounce Clear Creek
cherry brandy

1 ounce House Lemon Cordial
(page 285)

½ ounce simple syrup (page 45)

Garnish: 1 lemon wheel and
1 brandied cherry on a skewer

Shake all the ingredients with ice, then
strain into a double Old-Fashioned
glass filled with ice cubes. Garnish
with the lemon wheel and cherry.

Salvation Julep

JONATHAN ARMSTRONG, 2015

2 ounces Paul Beau VS Cognac

¾ ounce Sauternes wine

¼ ounce Grand Marnier

1 teaspoon Massenez Crème
de Pêche

½ teaspoon Giffard Menthe-
Pastille

Garnish: 1 mint sprig

Combine all the ingredients in a
Julep tin and fill the tin about halfway
with crushed ice. Holding the tin
by the rim, stir, churning the ice as
you go, for about 10 seconds. Add
more crushed ice to fill the tin about
two-thirds full and stir until the tin is
completely frosted. Add more ice
to form a cone above the rim. Garnish
with the mint sprig and serve with
a straw.

SS Cruiser

DEVON TARBY AND ALEX DAY, 2015

1 ounce Dolin blanc vermouth

¼ ounce St. George
raspberry brandy

¼ ounce Aperol

½ ounce fresh lemon juice

¼ ounce simple syrup (page 45)

1 teaspoon orange marmalade

3 ounces rosé crémant

Garnish: 1 mint sprig and
1 raspberry

Shake all the ingredients (except the crémant) with ice, then double strain into a wineglass filled with ice. Pour in the crémant, and quickly dip the barspoon into the glass to gently mix the wine with the cocktail. Garnish with the mint sprig and raspberry.

Thick as Thieves

JARRED WEIGAND, 2015

1 ounce Hine H Cognac

1 ounce Zacapa 23 rum

1 teaspoon Coffee-Infused Kalani
Coconut Liqueur (page 290)

1 teaspoon Marie Brizard white
crème de cacao

1 teaspoon Demerara Gum Syrup
(page 54)

Stir all the ingredients over ice, then strain into a chilled Nick & Nora glass. No garnish.

Troubled Leisure

ALEX DAY, 2016

2 ounces Oolong-Infused Vodka
(page 291)

¾ ounce Dolin blanc vermouth

¼ ounce Cointreau

1 dash House Orange Bitters
(page 295)

Garnish: 1 lemon twist

Stir all the ingredients over ice, then strain into a chilled Nick & Nora glass. Express the lemon twist over the drink, then set it onto the edge of the glass.

Unidentified Floral Objects

ALEX DAY, 2016

1 ounce Dupont Pays d'Auge
Original Calvados

½ ounce Wyoming whiskey

¼ ounce Laird's 100-proof straight
apple brandy

¼ ounce Blume Marillen apricot
eau-de-vie

1 teaspoon Demerara Gum Syrup
(page 54)

1 dash House Orange Bitters
(page 295)

Garnish: 1 orange twist

Stir all the ingredients over ice, then strain into a double Old-Fashioned glass over 1 large ice cube. Express the orange twist over the drink, then gently rub it around the rim of the glass and place it into the drink.

Warspite

MATT BELANGER, 2016

1¼ ounces Plymouth gin

½ ounce Plymouth sloe gin

¼ ounce Clear Creek
blue plum brandy

¾ ounce Aperol

1 teaspoon St. Elizabeth
allspice dram

Garnish: 1 orange twist

Stir all the ingredients over ice, then strain into a double Old-Fashioned glass over 1 large ice cube. Express the orange twist over the drink, then gently rub it around the rim of the glass and place it into the drink.

Wolf Tone

ALEX DAY, 2012

1 ounce Campo de Encanto Grand
and Noble pisco

¾ ounce Clear Creek Pinot Noir
grappa

¾ ounce St-Germain

1 dash House Orange Bitters
(page 295)

1 drop Terra Spice eucalyptus
extract

Garnish: 1 lemon twist

Stir all the ingredients with ice, then strain into a double Old-Fashioned glass over 1 large ice cube. Express the lemon twist over the drink, then place it into the drink.

SYRUPS AND CORDIALS

Basil Stem Syrup

500 grams water
50 grams basil stems
500 grams unbleached cane sugar

In a saucepan, bring the water to a boil. Remove from the heat, add the basil stems, and let steep for 30 minutes. Strain through a fine-mesh sieve lined with several layers of cheesecloth, then add the sugar and whisk until the sugar is dissolved. Transfer to a storage container and refrigerate until ready to use, up to 2 weeks.

Grilled Pineapple Syrup

1 pineapple
500 grams unbleached cane sugar
2.5 grams citric acid powder

Peel and cut the pineapple into ¾-inch-thick wheels, then grill over a wood fire until slightly smoky but not burned. Let cool, then run it through a juice extractor. Weigh out 500 grams of the juice, reserving the rest for another use. Combine the juice, sugar, and citric acid in a blender and process until smooth. Strain through a fine-mesh sieve lined with several layers of cheesecloth, then transfer to a storage container and refrigerate until ready to use, up to 4 weeks.

House Lemon Cordial

About 3 quarts lemon wheels or wedges, or the rinds of 10 lemons
600 grams white sugar
1,400 grams fresh lemon juice
Pectinex Ultra SP-L

Combine the lemon wheels or wedges and sugar in a large container. Cover and refrigerate for 2 days. Occasionally stir the mixture (the citrus oils will be extracted into the sugar and the mixture will liquefy).

Strain, then measure the weight of the liquid (discard the solids). Combine with the lemon juice, and stir until dissolved. Calculate 0.2% of the weight (multiply by 0.002) to get X grams. Stir in X grams of Pectinex, then cover and let sit for 15 minutes.

Divide the mixture evenly among your centrifuge containers. Weigh the filled containers and adjust the amount of liquid in each as needed to ensure their weights are exactly the same; this is important for keeping the machine in balance. Run the centrifuge at 4,500 rpm for 12 minutes.

Remove the containers and carefully strain the cordial through a paper coffee filter or Superbag, being careful not to disturb the solids that have collected on the bottom of the containers. If any particles remain in the cordial, strain it again. Transfer to a storage container and refrigerate until ready to use, up to 1 month.

House Orgeat

800 grams Almond Milk (page 255)
1.2 kilograms superfine sugar
14 grams Pierre Ferrand Ambre Cognac
18 grams Lazzaroni amaretto
3 grams rose water

Combine the almond milk and sugar in a saucepan over medium-low heat and cook, stirring occasionally, until the sugar has dissolved. Remove from the heat and stir in the Cognac, amaretto, and rose water. Let cool to room temperature, then transfer to a storage container and refrigerate until ready to use, up to 2 weeks.

Meyer Lemon Cordial

500 grams unbleached cane sugar
250 grams fresh Meyer lemon juice, strained
250 grams filtered water
100 grams Aylesbury Duck vodka
15 grams Meyer lemon zest
2 grams citric acid powder
0.5 gram kosher salt

Fill a large basin with water and place an immersion circulator inside. Set the circulator to 130°F.

Put all the ingredients in a bowl and stir until the sugar has dissolved. Transfer to a sealable, heatproof plastic bag. Seal the bag almost completely, then remove as much air as possible by dipping the bag (other than the unsealed portion) in the water. The counterpressure from the water will push the rest of the air out. Finish sealing the bag, then remove it from the water.

continued

continued

When the water has reached 130°F, place the bag in the basin and cook for 2 hours.

Transfer the bag to an ice bath and let cool to room temperature. Pass the cordial through a fine-mesh sieve. If any particles remain in the cordial, strain it again through a paper coffee filter or Superbag. Transfer to a storage container and refrigerate until ready to use, up to 2 weeks.

Raisin Honey Syrup

1 kilogram Honey Syrup (page 45)
200 grams golden raisins

Fill a large basin with water and place an immersion circulator inside. Set the circulator to 145°F.

Put the syrup and raisins in a bowl and stir to combine. Transfer to a sealable, heatproof plastic bag. Seal the bag almost completely, then remove as much air as possible by dipping the bag (other than the unsealed portion) in the water. The counterpressure from the water will push the rest of the air out. Finish sealing the bag, then remove it from the water.

When the water has reached 145°F, place the bag in the basin and cook for 2 hours.

Transfer the bag to an ice bath and let cool to room temperature. Pass the syrup through a fine-mesh sieve. If any particles remain in the syrup, strain it again through a paper coffee filter or Superbag. Transfer to a storage container and refrigerate until ready to use, up to 4 weeks.

Strawberry Cream Syrup

500 grams Clarified Strawberry Syrup (page 57)
500 grams Vanilla Lactic Syrup (see below)
130 grams Citric Acid Solution (page 298)

Put all the ingredients in a bowl and stir to combine. Transfer to a storage container and refrigerate until ready to use, up to 2 weeks.

Vanilla Lactic Syrup

500 grams simple syrup (page 45)
1 vanilla bean, split and scraped
0.5 gram salt
2.5 grams lactic acid powder

Fill a large basin with water and place an immersion circulator inside. Set the circulator to 135°F.

Put all the ingredients in a bowl and stir to combine. Transfer to a sealable, heatproof plastic bag. Seal the bag almost completely, then remove as much air as possible by dipping the bag (other than the unsealed portion) in the water. The counterpressure from the water will push the rest of the air out. Finish sealing the bag, then remove it from the water.

When the water has reached 135°F, place the bag in the basin and cook for 1 hour.

Transfer the bag to an ice bath and let cool to room temperature. Pass the syrup through a fine-mesh sieve. If any particles remain in the syrup, strain it again through a paper coffee filter or Superbag. Transfer to a storage container and refrigerate until ready to use, up to 4 weeks.

White Honey Syrup

500 grams raw white honey
500 grams hot water

Combine the honey and water in a heatproof bowl and stir until thoroughly blended. Transfer to a storage container and refrigerate until ready to use, up to 4 weeks.

INFUSIONS

A Field in Innsbruck Tea–Infused Apple Brandy

1 (750 ml) bottle Clear Creek 2-year apple brandy

20 grams August Uncommon Tea's A Field in Innsbruck Tea

Combine the brandy and tea in a bowl and stir to combine. Let stand at room temperature for 10 minutes, stirring occasionally. Strain through a fine-mesh sieve lined with several layers of cheesecloth, then funnel back into the brandy bottle and refrigerate until ready to use, up to 3 months.

Birch-Infused Cocchi Vermouth di Torino

4.75 grams Terra Spice birch extract

1 (750 ml) bottle Cocchi Vermouth di Torino

Add the birch extract directly to the bottle of vermouth. Seal, then gently tip the bottle upside down a few times to combine. Refrigerate until ready to use, up to 3 weeks.

Blood Orange–Infused Carpano Antica Formula

1 (750 ml) bottle Carpano Antica Formula vermouth

55 grams blood orange zest

Combine the vermouth and zest in an iSi whipper. Seal tightly. Charge with an N_2O cartridge, then shake the canister about five times. Change

the cartridge, then charge and shake again. Let stand for 15 minutes, shaking the canister every 30 seconds or so, then release the pressure. Point the canister's nozzle at a 45-degree angle into a container. Vent the gas as quickly as possible without spraying liquid everywhere; the quicker the venting, the better the infusion. When all of the gas is out, open the canister and take a listen. Once there is no longer audible bubbling, open the canister and strain the infusion through a paper coffee filter or Superbag. Funnel back into the vermouth bottle and refrigerate until ready to use, up to 4 weeks.

Brown Butter–Infused Apple Brandy

225 grams (2 sticks) unsalted butter, cut into cubes

1 (750 ml) bottle Clear Creek 2-year apple brandy

1 (750 ml) bottle Clear Creek 8-year apple brandy

Put the butter in a saucepan over medium heat and cook, stirring frequently, until it turns brown and smells nutty. Pour the butter into a heatproof container, add the brandy, and whisk until well blended. Cover the container and freeze for up to 12 hours, or overnight.

Remove the container from the freezer, poke a hole in the hardened butter, and drain the liquid out; reserve the butter for other uses (try it on popcorn!). Strain the infusion through a fine-mesh sieve lined with several layers of cheesecloth. Funnel back into the brandy bottles and refrigerate until ready to use, up to 3 months.

Cacao Nib–Infused El Tesoro Reposado Tequila

1 (750 ml) bottle El Tesoro Reposada Tequila

30 grams cacao nibs

Combine the tequila and cacao nibs in an iSi whipper. Seal tightly. Charge with an N_2O cartridge, then shake the canister about five times. Change the cartridge, then charge and shake again. Let stand for 15 minutes, shaking the canister every 30 seconds or so, then release the pressure. Point the canister's nozzle at a 45-degree angle into a container. Vent the gas as quickly as possible without spraying liquid everywhere; the quicker the venting, the better the infusion. When all of the gas is out, open the canister and take a listen. Once there is no longer audible bubbling, strain the infusion through a paper coffee filter or Superbag. Funnel back into the tequila bottle and refrigerate until ready to use, up to 4 weeks. (This infusion can also be prepared in a chamber vacuum machine following the instructions on page 97.)

Cacao Nib-infused Pear Brandy

1 (750 ml) Clear Creek Pear Brandy

30 grams Cacao Nibs

Combine the pear brandy and cacao nibs in an iSi whipper. Seal tightly. Charge with an N_2O cartridge, then shake the canister about five times. Change the cartridge, then charge and shake again. Let stand for 15 minutes, shaking the canister every 30 seconds or so, then release the pressure. Point the canister's nozzle

continued

continued

at a 45-degree angle into a container. Vent the gas as quickly as possible without spraying liquid everywhere; the quicker the venting, the better the infusion. When all of the gas is out, open the canister and take a listen. Once there is no longer audible bubbling, strain the infusion through a paper coffee filter or Superbag. Funnel back into the brandy bottle and refrigerate until ready to use, up to 4 weeks. (This infusion can also be prepared in a chamber vacuum machine following the instructions on page 97.)

Cacao Nib–Infused Ramazzotti

1 (750 ml) bottle Ramazzotti
30 grams cacao nibs

Combine the Ramazzotti and cacao nibs in an iSi whipper. Seal tightly. Charge with an N₂O cartridge, then shake the canister about five times. Change the cartridge, then charge and shake again. Let stand for 15 minutes, shaking the canister every 30 seconds or so, then release the pressure. Point the canister's nozzle at a 45-degree angle into a container. Vent the gas as quickly as possible without spraying liquid everywhere; the quicker the venting, the better the infusion. When all of the gas is out, open the canister and take a listen. Once there is no longer audible bubbling, strain the infusion through a paper coffee filter or Superbag. Funnel back into the Ramazzotti bottle and refrigerate until ready to use, up to 4 weeks. (This infusion can also be prepared in a chamber vacuum machine following the instructions on page 97.)

Cardamom-Infused St-Germain

1 (750 ml) bottle St-Germain
10 grams green cardamom pods

Place the St-Germain and cardamom in a bowl and stir to combine. Let stand at room temperature for about 12 hours. Strain through a fine-mesh sieve lined with several layers of cheesecloth, then funnel back into the St-Germain bottle and refrigerate until ready to use, up to 3 months.

Celery Root–Infused Dolin Blanc

1 (750 ml) bottle Dolin blanc vermouth
200 grams celery root, chopped

Combine the vermouth and celery root in an iSi whipper. Seal tightly. Charge with an N₂O cartridge, then shake the canister about five times. Change the cartridge, then charge and shake again. Let stand for 15 minutes, shaking the canister every 30 seconds or so, then release the pressure. Point the canister's nozzle at a 45-degree angle into a container. Vent the gas as quickly as possible without spraying liquid everywhere; the quicker the venting, the better the infusion. When all of the gas is out, open the canister and take a listen. Once there is no longer audible bubbling, strain the infusion through a paper coffee filter or Superbag. Funnel back into the vermouth bottle and refrigerate until ready to use, up to 4 weeks. (This infusion can also be prepared in a chamber vacuum machine following the instructions on page 97.)

Chamomile-Infused Blanco Tequila

1 (750 ml) bottle Pueblo Viejo blanco tequila
5 grams dried chamomile flowers

Place the tequila and chamomile in a bowl and stir to combine. Let stand at room temperature for 1 hour, stirring occasionally. Strain through a fine-mesh sieve lined with several layers of cheesecloth, then funnel back into the original bottle and refrigerate until ready to use, up to 3 months.

Chamomile-Infused Calvados

1 (750 ml) bottle Pierre Ferrand Ambre Calvados
5 grams dried chamomile flowers

Place the Calvados and chamomile in a bowl and stir to combine. Let stand at room temperature for 1 hour, stirring occasionally. Strain through a fine-mesh sieve lined with several layers of cheesecloth, then funnel back into the vermouth bottle and refrigerate until ready to use, up to 3 months.

Chamomile-Infused Cocchi Americano

1 (750 ml) bottle Cocchi Americano
5 grams dried Chamomile Flowers

Place the Cocchi Americano and the chamomile in a bowl and stir to combine. Let stand at room temperature for 1 hour, stirring occasionally. Strain through a fine-mesh sieve lined with several layers of cheesecloth, then funnel back into the original bottle and refrigerate until ready to use, up to 3 months.

Chamomile-Infused Dolin Blanc Vermouth

1 (750 ml) bottle Dolin Blanc Vermouth

5 grams dried chamomile flowers

Place the vermouth and chamomile in a bowl and stir to combine. Let stand at room temperature for 1 hour, stirring occasionally. Strain through a fine-mesh sieve lined with several layers of cheesecloth, then funnel back into the vermouth bottle and refrigerate until ready to use, up to 3 months.

Chamomile-Infused Rye Whiskey

1 (750 ml) bottle Rittenhouse rye

5 grams dried chamomile flowers

Place the Rittenhouse rye and chamomile in a bowl and stir to combine. Let stand at room temperature for 1 hour, stirring occasionally. Strain through a fine-mesh sieve lined with several layers of cheesecloth, then funnel back into the original bottle and refrigerate until ready to use, up to 3 months.

Cherry Wood–Smoked Almond Milk

1 liter Almond Milk (page 255)

1 pinch dried cherry wood chips (enough to fill smoker)

In a wide container with a lid, smoke the almond milk with cherry wood chips using a PolyScience Smoking Gun (see page 276). Cover immediately to capture as much smoke as possible. Let stand until the smoke has dissipated, about 10 minutes. Transfer to a container and refrigerate until ready to use, up to 3 hours.

Cocoa Butter–Infused Absolut Elyx Vodka

100 grams melted cocoa butter

1,000 grams Absolut Elyx vodka

Fill a large basin with water and place an immersion circulator inside. Set the circulator to 145°F.

Put the cocoa butter and vodka in a bowl and stir to combine. Transfer to a sealable, heatproof plastic bag. Seal the bag almost completely, then remove as much air as possible by dipping the bag (other than the unsealed portion) in the water. The counterpressure from the water will push the rest of the air out. Finish sealing the bag, then remove it from the water.

When the water has reached 145°F, place the bag in the basin and cook for 2 hours.

Transfer the bag to an ice bath and let cool to room temperature. Pass the infusion through a fine-mesh sieve lined with several layers of cheesecloth. If any particles remain in the infusion, strain it again through a paper coffee filter or Superbag. Transfer to a container, cover, and freeze for 24 hours. Strain again through a fine-mesh sieve lined with several layers of cheesecloth, then funnel back into the bourbon bottle and refrigerate until ready to use, up to 3 months.

Coconut-Infused Bourbon

50 grams unsweetened coconut flakes

1 (1-liter) bottle Old Forester 86 bourbon

Fill a large basin with water and place an immersion circulator inside. Set the circulator to 145°F. In a small skillet over medium heat, toast the coconut, stirring often, until slightly golden, about 4 minutes. Let cool slightly.

Put the coconut and bourbon in a bowl and stir to combine. Transfer to a sealable, heatproof plastic bag. Seal the bag almost completely, then remove as much air as possible by dipping the bag (other than the unsealed portion) in the water. The counterpressure from the water will push the rest of the air out. Finish sealing the bag, then remove it from the water.

When the water has reached 145°F, place the bag in the basin and cook for 2 hours.

Transfer the bag to an ice bath and let cool to room temperature. Pass the infusion through a fine-mesh sieve lined with several layers of cheesecloth. If any particles remain in the infusion, strain it again through a paper coffee filter or Superbag. Transfer to a container, cover, and freeze for 24 hours. (This will solidify the fatty coconut oils, allowing for a transparent coconut infusion.) Strain again through a fine-mesh sieve lined with several layers of cheesecloth, then funnel back into the bourbon bottle and refrigerate until ready to use, up to 3 months.

Coffee-Infused Carpano Antica Formula

1 (750 ml) bottle Carpano Antica Formula vermouth

15 grams whole coffee beans

Combine the vermouth and coffee beans in an iSi whipper. Seal tightly. Charge with an N₂O cartridge, then shake the canister about five times. Change the cartridge, then charge and shake again. Let stand for 15 minutes, shaking the canister every 30 seconds or so, then release the pressure. Point the canister's nozzle at a 45-degree angle into a container. Vent the gas as quickly as possible without spraying liquid everywhere; the quicker the venting, the better the infusion. When all of the gas is out, open the canister and take a listen. Once there is no longer audible bubbling, strain the infusion through a paper coffee filter or Superbag. Funnel back into the vermouth bottle and refrigerate until ready to use, up to 4 weeks. (This infusion can also be prepared in a chamber vacuum machine following the instructions on page 97.)

Coffee-Infused Kalani Coconut Liqueur

1 (750 ml) bottle Kalani coconut liqueur

15 grams whole coffee beans

Combine the liqueur and coffee beans in an iSi whipper. Seal tightly. Charge with an N₂O cartridge, then shake the canister about five times. Change the cartridge, then charge and shake again. Let stand for 15 minutes, shaking the canister every 30 seconds or so, then release the pressure. Point the canister's nozzle at a 45-degree angle into a container. Vent the gas as quickly as possible without spraying liquid everywhere; the quicker the venting, the better the infusion. When all of the gas is out, open the canister and take a listen. Once there is no longer audible bubbling, strain the infusion through a paper coffee filter or Superbag. Funnel back into the liqueur bottle and refrigerate until ready to use, up to 4 weeks. (This infusion can also be prepared in a chamber vacuum machine following the instructions on page 97.)

Graham Cracker–Infused Bourbon

2 (750 ml) bottles Elijah Craig Small Batch bourbon

408 grams graham crackers

Pectinex Ultra SP-L

Combine all the ingredients in a blender and process until smooth. Strain, then measure the weight of the liquid (discard the solids). Calculate 0.4% of the weight (multiply by 0.004) to get X grams. Stir in X grams of Pectinex, then cover and let sit for 15 minutes.

Divide the mixture among your centrifuge containers. Weigh the filled containers and adjust the amount of liquid in each to ensure the weights are exactly the same; this is important for keeping the machine in balance. Run the centrifuge at 4,500 rpm for 12 minutes.

Remove the containers and strain the infusion through a paper coffee filter or Superbag; be careful not to disturb the solids that have collected on the container bottoms. If any particles remain in the infusion, strain it again. Funnel back into the bourbon bottle and refrigerate until ready to use, up to 2 weeks.

Hickory Smoke–Infused Cognac

1 bottle Pierre Ferrand 1840 Cognac

1 pinch finely ground hickory chips (enough to fill smoker)

In a wide container with a lid, smoke the Cognac with hickory chips using a PolyScience Smoking Gun (see page 276). Cover immediately to capture as much smoke as possible. Let stand until the smoke has dissipated, about 10 minutes. Transfer to a container and refrigerate until ready to use, up to 3 hours.

Hickory Smoke–Infused Pierre Ferrand Ambre Cognac

1 (750 ml) bottle Pierre Ferrand Ambre Cognac

1 pinch finely ground hickory chips (enough to fill smoker)

In a wide container with a lid, smoke the Cognac with the hickory chips using a PolyScience Smoking Gun (see page 276). Cover immediately to capture as much smoke as possible. Let stand until the smoke has dissipated, about 10 minutes. Transfer to a container and refrigerate until ready to use, up to 3 hours.

Honeydew-Infused Kappa Pisco

1 (750 ml) bottle Kappa pisco

200 grams peeled ripe honeydew melon, cut into ¼-inch segments

Combine the pisco and honeydew in an iSi whipper. Seal tightly. Charge with an N₂O cartridge, then shake the canister about five times. Change the cartridge, then charge and shake again. Let stand for 15 minutes, shaking the canister every 30 seconds or so, then release the pressure. Point the canister's nozzle at a 45-degree angle into a container. Vent the gas as quickly as possible without spraying liquid everywhere; the quicker the venting, the better the infusion. When all of the gas is out, open the canister and listen. Once there is no longer audible bubbling, strain the infusion through a paper coffee filter or Superbag. Funnel back into the pisco bottle and refrigerate until ready to use, up to 4 weeks. (This infusion can also be prepared in a chamber vacuum machine, see page 97.)

Jalapeño-Infused Vodka

4 jalapeños

1 (1-liter) bottle Grey Goose vodka

Halve the jalapeños lengthwise, then scrape the seeds and membranes into a container. Add the flesh of 2 of the jalapeños (reserve the flesh of the other 2 for another use). Add the vodka and stir to combine. Let stand at room temperature for up to 20 minutes, tasting often to monitor the heat level. Strain through a fine-mesh sieve lined with several layers of cheesecloth, then funnel back into the vodka bottle and refrigerate until ready to use, up to 1 month.

Madras Curry–Infused Gin

1 (750 ml) bottle Dorothy Parker gin

5 grams Madras curry powder

Place the gin and curry powder in a bowl and stir to combine. Let stand at room temperature for 15 minutes, stirring occasionally. Strain through a fine-mesh sieve lined with several layers of cheesecloth, then funnel back into the gin bottle and refrigerate until ready to use, up to 3 months.

Milk-Washed Rum

1 (1-liter) bottle Flor de Caña 4-year white rum

250 ml whole milk

15 grams Citric Acid Solution (page 298)

Pectinex Ultra SP-L

Combine the rum and milk in a container and measure the weight of the liquid. Calculate 0.2% of the weight (multiply by 0.002) to get X grams. Let the mixture rest for 5 minutes, then stir in the Citric Acid Solution. Refrigerate for at least 12 hours.

Stir in X grams of Pectinex, then cover and let sit for 15 minutes.

Divide the liquid among your centrifuge containers. Weigh the filled containers and adjust the liquid in each to ensure their weights are exactly the same; this is important for keeping the machine in balance. Run the centrifuge at 4,500 rpm for 12 minutes.

Remove the containers and strain the infusion through a paper coffee filter or Superbag, being careful not to disturb the solids on the bottom of the containers. If any particles remain in the infusion, strain it again. Funnel back into the rum bottle and refrigerate until ready to use, up to 2 months.

Oolong-Infused Vodka

1 (1-liter) bottle Absolut Elyx vodka

20 grams oolong tea leaves

Place the vodka and tea leaves in a bowl and stir to combine. Let stand at room temperature for 20 minutes, stirring occasionally. Strain through a fine-mesh sieve lined with several layers of cheesecloth, then funnel back into the vodka bottle and refrigerate until ready to use, up to 3 months.

Raisin-Infused Rye

1 (750 ml) bottle Bulleit rye

150 grams golden raisins

Fill a large basin with water and place an immersion circulator inside. Set the circulator to 140°F.

Put the rye and raisins in a bowl and stir to combine. Transfer to a sealable, heatproof plastic bag. Seal the bag almost completely, then remove as much air as possible by dipping the bag (other than the unsealed portion) in the water. The counterpressure from the water will push the rest of the air out. Finish sealing the bag, then remove it from the water.

When the water has reached 140°F, place the bag in the basin and cook for 2 hours.

Transfer the bag to an ice bath and let cool to room temperature. Pass the infusion through a fine-mesh sieve lined with several layers of cheesecloth, then funnel back into the original bottle and refrigerate until ready to use, up to 3 months.

Raisin-Infused Scotch

1 (750 ml) bottle Famous Grouse scotch

150 grams golden raisins

Fill a large basin with water and place an immersion circulator inside. Set the circulator to 140°F.

Put the scotch and raisins in a bowl and stir to combine. Transfer to a sealable, heatproof plastic bag. Seal the bag almost completely, then remove as much air as possible by dipping the bag (other than the unsealed portion) in the water. The counterpressure from the water will push the rest of the air out. Finish sealing the bag, then remove it from the water.

When the water has reached 140°F, place the bag in the basin and cook for 2 hours.

Transfer the bag to an ice bath and let cool to room temperature. Pass the infusion through a fine-mesh sieve lined with several layers of cheesecloth, then funnel back into the scotch bottle and refrigerate until ready to use, up to 3 months.

Roasted Garlic– and Pepper-Infused Vodka

1 (750 ml) bottle Absolut vodka

12 grams roasted garlic, smashed into a paste

3 grams black peppercorns, crushed

Place all the ingredients in a bowl and stir to combine. Cover and refrigerate for at least 12 hours. Strain through a fine-mesh sieve lined with several layers of cheesecloth, then funnel back into the vodka bottle and refrigerate until ready to use, up to 3 months.

Root Beer–Infused Cocchi Americano

1 (750 ml) bottle Cocchi Americano Bianco

2.75 grams Terra Spice root beer extract

Add the root beer extract directly to the bottle of Cocchi Americano. Seal, then gently tip the bottle upside down a few times to combine. Refrigerate until ready to use, up to 2 weeks.

Sesame-Infused Rum

25 grams white sesame seeds

1 (750 ml) bottle El Dorado 12-year rum

In a small skillet over medium-low heat, toast the sesame seeds, stirring often, until fragrant and slightly golden, about 4 minutes. Let cool slightly. Place the sesame seeds and rum in a bowl and stir to combine. Let stand at room temperature for 5 minutes. Strain through a fine-mesh sieve lined with several layers of cheesecloth, then funnel back into the rum bottle and refrigerate until ready to use, up to 3 months.

Sour Cherry–Infused Rittenhouse Rye

1 (750 ml bottle) Rittenhouse rye

50 grams dried sour cherries

Pectinex Ultra SP-L

Combine the rye whiskey and cherries in a blender and process until smooth. Strain, then measure the weight of the liquid (discard the solids). Calculate 0.2% of the weight (multiply by 0.002) to get X grams. Stir in X grams of Pectinex, then cover and let sit for 15 minutes.

Divide the mixture evenly among your centrifuge containers. Weigh the filled containers and adjust the amount of liquid in each as needed to ensure their weights are exactly the same; this is important for keeping the machine in balance. Run the centrifuge at 4,500 rpm for 12 minutes.

Remove the containers and carefully strain the infusion through a paper coffee filter or Superbag, being careful not to disturb the solids that have collected on the bottom of the containers. If any particles remain in the infusion, strain it again. Funnel back into the original bottle and refrigerate until ready to use, up to 1 week.

Strawberry-Infused Cognac and Mezcal

625 grams Pierre Ferrand Ambre Cognac
375 grams Del Maguey Vida mezcal
700 grams hulled strawberries
Pectinex Ultra SP-L
10 grams ascorbic acid

Combine the Cognac, mezcal, and strawberries in a blender and process until smooth. Strain, then measure the weight of the liquid (discard the solids). Calculate 0.2% of the weight (multiply by 0.002) to get X grams. Stir in X grams of Pectinex and the ascorbic acid, then cover and let sit for 15 minutes.

Divide the mixture evenly among your centrifuge containers. Weigh the filled containers and adjust the amount of liquid in each as needed to ensure their weights are exactly the same; this is important for keeping the machine in balance. Run the centrifuge at 4,500 rpm for 12 minutes.

Remove the containers and carefully strain the infusion through a paper coffee filter or Superbag, being careful not to disturb the solids that have collected on the bottom of the containers. If any particles remain in the infusion, strain it again. Funnel back into the original bottle and refrigerate until ready to use, up to 2 weeks.

Thai Chile–Infused Bourbon

10 fresh Thai chiles
1 (750 ml) bottle Elijah Craig Small Batch bourbon

Halve the chiles lengthwise and scrape the seeds and membranes into a container. Add the flesh of 5 of the chiles (reserve the flesh of the other 5 for another use). Add the bourbon and stir to combine. Let stand at room temperature for up to 5 minutes, tasting often to monitor the heat level. Strain through a fine-mesh sieve lined with several layers of cheesecloth, then funnel back into the bourbon bottle and refrigerate until ready to use, up to 1 month.

Toasted Almond–Infused Apricot Liqueur

100 grams blanched slivered almonds
1 (750 ml) bottle Giffard Abricot du Roussillon

Fill a large basin with water and place an immersion circulator inside. Set the circulator to 145°F. In a small skillet over medium heat, toast the almonds until slightly golden, about 5 minutes. Let cool slightly.

Put the almonds and liqueur in a bowl and stir to combine. Transfer to a sealable, heatproof plastic bag. Seal the bag almost completely, then remove as much air as possible by dipping the bag (other than the unsealed portion) in the water. The counterpressure from the water will push the rest of the air out. Finish sealing the bag, then remove it from the water.

When the water has reached 145°F, place the bag in the basin and cook for 2 hours.

Transfer the bag to an ice bath and let cool to room temperature. Pass the infusion through a fine-mesh sieve. If any particles remain in the infusion, strain it again through a paper coffee filter or Superbag. Funnel back into the liqueur bottle and refrigerate until ready to use, up to 3 months.

Toasted Pecan–Infused Plantation Rum

150 grams pecans
1 (750 ml) bottle Plantation Barbados 5-year rum

Fill a large basin with water and place an immersion circulator inside. Set the circulator to 145°F. In a small skillet over medium heat, toast the pecans until slightly golden, about 5 minutes. Let cool slightly.

Put the pecans and rum in a bowl and stir to combine. Transfer to a sealable, heatproof plastic bag. Seal the bag almost completely, then remove as much air as possible by dipping the bag (other than the unsealed portion) in the water. The counterpressure from the water will push the rest of the air out. Finish sealing the bag, then remove it from the water.

When the water has reached 145°F, place the bag in the basin and cook for 2 hours.

Transfer the bag to an ice bath and let cool to room temperature. Pass the infusion through a fine-mesh sieve. If any particles remain in the infusion, strain it through a paper coffee filter or Superbag. Funnel back into the rum bottle and refrigerate until ready to use, up to 1 month.

Watercress-Infused Gin

1 (1-liter) bottle Fords gin
75 grams watercress leaves
Pectinex Ultra SP-L

Combine all the ingredients in a blender and process until smooth. Strain, then measure the weight of the liquid (discard the solids). Calculate 0.2% of the weight (multiply by 0.002) to get X grams. Stir in X grams of Pectinex, then cover and let sit for 15 minutes.

Divide the mixture evenly among your centrifuge containers. Weigh the filled containers and adjust the amount of liquid in each as needed to ensure their weights are exactly the same; this is important for keeping the machine in balance. Run the centrifuge at 4,500 rpm for 12 minutes.

Remove the containers and carefully strain the infusion through a paper coffee filter or Superbag, being careful not to disturb the solids that have collected on the bottom of the containers. If any particles remain in the liquid, strain it again. Funnel back into the gin bottle and refrigerate until ready to use, up to 1 week.

White Pepper–Infused Vodka

1 (750 ml) bottle Aylesbury Duck vodka
150 grams white peppercorns

Combine the vodka and peppercorns in an iSi whipper. Seal tightly. Charge with an N$_2$O cartridge, then shake the canister about five times. Change the cartridge, then charge and shake again. Let stand for 15 minutes, shaking the canister every 30 seconds or so, then release the pressure. Point the canister's nozzle at a 45-degree angle into a container. Vent the gas as quickly as possible without spraying liquid everywhere; the quicker the venting, the better the infusion. When all of the gas is out, open the canister and take a listen. Once there is no longer audible bubbling, strain the infusion through a paper coffee filter or Superbag. Funnel back into the vodka bottle and refrigerate until ready to use, up to 4 weeks. (This infusion can also be prepared in a chamber vacuum machine following the instructions on page 97.)

HOUSE MIXES AND SODAS

Apple Celery Soda

12 ounces water

9 ounces clarified Granny Smith apple juice (see page 146)

3 ounces clarified celery juice (see page 146)

7 ounces simple syrup (page 45)

1 ounce phosphoric acid solution (see page 194)

1½ ounces Malic Acid Solution (page 298)

Chill all the ingredients. Combine them in a carbonating bottle, charge with CO_2, and gently shake to help dissolve the CO_2 into the liquid (see page 228 for detailed carbonation instructions). Refrigerate the carbonating bottle for at least 20 minutes, and preferably for 12 hours, before opening.

Basic Bloody Mary Mix

1,100 grams organic tomato juice (bottled)

180 grams Worcestershire sauce

30 grams Magi seasoning

72 grams strained fresh lemon juice

72 grams strained fresh lime juice

30 grams Tapatío hot sauce

Place all the ingredients in a bowl and stir to combine. Transfer to a storage container and refrigerate until ready to use, up to 1 week.

Donn's Mix No. 1

400 grams strained fresh grapefruit juice

200 grams Cinnamon Syrup (page 52)

Combine the grapefruit juice and Cinnamon Syrup in a bowl and whisk until thoroughly blended. Transfer to a storage container and refrigerate until ready to use, up to 2 weeks.

Homemade Grapefruit Soda

5 ounces seltzer

1¾ ounces Grapefruit Cordial (page 53)

1 teaspoon Citric Acid Solution (page 298)

1 teaspoon phosphoric acid solution (see page 194)

1 drop Terra Spice grapefruit extract

Chill all the ingredients. Combine them in a carbonating bottle, charge with CO_2, and gently shake to help dissolve the CO_2 into the liquid (see page 228 for detailed carbonation instructions). Refrigerate the carbonating bottle for at least 20 minutes, and preferably for 12 hours, before opening.

House Coconut Cream

800 grams Coco Lopez coconut cream

200 grams unsweetened coconut milk

Combine the coconut cream and coconut milk in a bowl and stir to combine. Transfer to a storage container and refrigerate until ready to use, up to 3 months.

House Orange Bitters

100 grams Fee Brothers West Indian orange bitters

100 grams Angostura orange bitters

100 grams Regans' orange bitters

Place all the ingredients in a bowl and stir to combine. Transfer to a storage container and store at room temperature until ready to use, up to 1 year.

Milk & Honey House Curaçao

500 grams Grand Marnier

500 grams simple syrup (page 45)

Place the Grand Marnier and syrup in a bowl and stir to combine. Transfer to a storage container and refrigerate until ready to use, up to 6 months.

Normandie Club Bloody Mary Mix

6 ounces fresh tomato juice

2 ounces bottled tomato juice

2 ounces fresh celery juice

1½ ounces fresh red bell pepper juice

1 ounce Tomato Bouillon Concentrate (see below)

½ ounce fresh lemon juice

½ ounce fresh lime juice

½ ounce dill pickle juice (preferably from Bubbie's brand pickles)

4 teaspoons Worcestershire sauce

2 teaspoons Bragg Liquid Aminos

2 teaspoons Sriracha

2 teaspoons prepared horseradish (preferably Bubbie's brand)

Place all the ingredients in a bowl and stir to combine. Transfer to a storage container and refrigerate until ready to use, up to 1 week.

TOMATO BOUILLON CONCENTRATE

75 grams Knorr Tomato with Chicken Granulated Bouillon

25 grams boiling water

Combine the bouillon and water in a storage container and stir vigorously until the bouillon has dissolved. Refrigerate until ready to use, up to 6 months.

Normandie Club House Sweet Vermouth

25 ounces Carpano Antica Formula vermouth

7 grams Casa Mariol Vermut Negre

Place the vermouth and Vermut Negre in a bowl and stir to combine. Transfer to a storage container and refrigerate until ready to use, up to 3 months.

Tom and Jerry Batter

450 grams unbleached cane sugar

1 tablespoon ground cinnamon

1 tablespoon ground mace

1 tablespoon ground allspice

½ tablespoon ground cloves

12 eggs, separated

½ teaspoon cream of tartar

Put the sugar, cinnamon, mace, allspice, and cloves in a container and stir with a whisk to combine. Put the egg yolks in a large bowl and use an immersion blender to break them up. While still blending, slowly add the sugar mixture in a steady stream. When it's fully incorporated, cover and set aside in a cool place. In a separate clean, dry bowl, combine the egg whites and cream of tartar and beat or whisk vigorously until medium peaks form. Gently fold the egg whites into the egg yolk mixture. Transfer to a storage container and refrigerate until ready to use, up to 3 days.

Verde Mix

1,200 grams cucumber

1,000 grams tomatillo juice

650 grams green bell pepper juice

500 grams fresh pineapple juice

250 grams fresh lime juice

150 grams Salt Solution (page 298)

25 grams serrano chile, seeds removed

15 grams garlic

Peel, chop, and puree the cucumber. In a blender, combine the cucumber puree with the juices, salt solution, serrano chile, and garlic. Blend until smooth. Transfer to a storage container and refrigerate until ready to use, up to 1 week.

SALTS AND RIMS

Lemon Pepper Salt

20 grams dehydrated lemon slices

10 grams freshly ground
black pepper

50 grams kosher salt

Put the lemon slices in a spice grinder
or blender with the pepper and half
of the salt and process until powdery.
Transfer to a storage container, add
the remaining salt, seal, and shake to
combine. Store in a dry place until
ready to use. It will keep indefinitely.

Sugared Smoked Salt

25 grams Maldon smoked sea salt

25 grams unbleached cane sugar

Put the salt and sugar in a storage
container, seal, and shake to combine.
Store in a dry place until ready to use.
It will keep indefinitely.

SOLUTIONS, TINCTURES, AND CONCENTRATES

Après-Ski Tincture

250 grams vodka

20 grams 100 percent cedar
incense scrapings (see below)

10 grams crushed cinnamon sticks

Put all the ingredients in a jar, cover,
and shake to combine. Let sit in a
cool, dark place for 1 week. Strain
through a fine-mesh sieve lined with
several layers of cheesecloth, then
pour into a storage container and
refrigerate until ready to use, up to
3 months.

CEDAR INCENSE SCRAPINGS

It should be noted that this tincture
is all about a woodsy aroma on top of
the drink, and therefore is not to be
consumed in quantity on its own. We
recommend finding an incense that
lists cedar wood as its only ingredient
(with no other added chemicals!),
then scrape the cedar from the
incense stick for use in the tincture.

Cacao Nib Tincture

1 (750 ml) bottle Absolut vodka

75 grams cacao nibs

Combine the vodka and cacao nibs
in an iSi whipper. Seal tightly. Charge
with an N_2O cartridge, then shake
the canister about five times. Change
the cartridge, then charge and shake
again. Let stand for 15 minutes,
shaking the canister every 30 seconds
or so, then release the pressure. Point
the canister's nozzle at a 45-degree
angle into a container. Vent the gas as
quickly as possible without spraying
liquid everywhere; the quicker the
venting, the better the infusion.
When all of the gas is out, open the
canister and take a listen. Once there
is no longer audible bubbling, strain
the infusion through a paper coffee
filter or Superbag. Funnel back into
the vodka bottle and refrigerate until
ready to use, up to 4 weeks. (This
infusion can also be prepared in a
chamber vacuum machine following
the instructions on page 97.)

Cedar Tincture

1 (750 ml) bottle Absolut vodka

20 grams 100 percent cedar incense shavings (see Après-Ski Tincture, page 297)

Combine the vodka and cedar shavings in an iSi whipper. Seal tightly. Charge with an N_2O cartridge, then shake the canister about five times. Change the cartridge, then charge and shake again. Let stand for 15 minutes, shaking the canister every 30 seconds or so, then release the pressure. Point the canister's nozzle at a 45-degree angle into a container. Vent the gas as quickly as possible without spraying liquid everywhere; the quicker the venting, the better the infusion. When all of the gas is out, open the canister and take a listen. Once there is no longer audible bubbling, strain the infusion through a paper coffee filter or Superbag. Funnel back into the vodka bottle and refrigerate until ready to use, up to 4 weeks. (This infusion can also be prepared in a chamber vacuum machine following the instructions on page 97.)

Champagne Acid Solution

94 grams filtered water

3 grams tartaric acid powder

3 grams lactic acid powder

Combine all the ingredients in a glass bowl and stir until the powders have dissolved. Transfer to a glass dropper bottle or other glass container and refrigerate until ready to use, up to 6 months.

Citric Acid Solution

100 grams filtered water

25 grams citric acid powder

Combine the water and citric acid powder in glass bowl and stir until the powder has dissolved. Transfer to a glass dropper bottle or other glass container and refrigerate until ready to use, up to 6 months.

Lactic Acid Solution

90 grams filtered water

10 grams lactic acid powder

Combine the water and lactic acid powder in a glass bowl and stir until the powder has dissolved. Transfer to a glass dropper bottle or other glass container and refrigerate until ready to use, up to 6 months.

Malic Acid Solution

90 grams filtered water

10 grams lactic acid powder

Combine the water and malic acid powder in a glass bowl and stir until the powder has dissolved. Transfer to a glass dropper bottle or other glass container and refrigerate until ready to use, up to 6 months.

Rosemary Salt Solution

300 grams Absolut vodka

15 grams rosemary

100 grams Salt Solution (see below)

Combine the vodka and rosemary in a container with a lid and shake gently to combine. Let sit in a cool, dark place for 1 week. Strain through a fine-mesh sieve lined with several layers of cheesecloth. Transfer to a storage container, add the Salt Solution, and stir or shake to combine. Refrigerate until ready to use, up to 6 months.

Salt Solution

75 grams filtered water

25 grams kosher salt

Combine the water and salt in a storage container and stir or shake until the salt has dissolved. Refrigerate until ready to use, up to 6 months.

Sel Gris Solution

80 grams filtered water

20 grams sel gris

Combine the water and salt in a storage container and stir or shake until the salt has dissolved. Refrigerate until ready to use, up to 6 months.

RESOURCES

Art of Drink
(artofdrink.com)
For phosphoric acid solution, labeled "Extinct Acid Phosphate Solution."

Astor Wines & Spirits
(astorwines.com)
For a vast selection of spirits.

August Uncommon Tea
(august.la)
For loose-leaf teas, including A Field in Innsbruck.

Bar Products
(barproducts.com)
For all the bar equipment and tools under the sun.

Beverage Alcohol Resource
(beveragealcoholresource.com)
For aspiring bartenders and liquor professionals.

Chef Shop
(chefshop.com)
For honey, Fusion Napa Valley verjus, maraschino cherries, and other pantry staples.

Cocktail Kingdom
(cocktailkingdom.com)
For all matter of barware, as well as bitters, syrups, and cocktail books, including facsimiles of some vintage classics.

Crystal Classics
(crystalclassics.com)
For glassware from Schott Zwiesel and other brands.

Drink Up NY
(drinkupny.com)
For hard-to-find spirits and other boozy ingredients.

Dual Specialty Store
(dualspecialtystorenyc.com)
For spices, nuts, and bitters.

In Pursuit of Tea
(inpursuitoftea.com)
For rare and exotic teas.

Instawares
(instawares.com)
For an extensive assortment of bar tools, glassware, and kitchen supplies.

iSi
(isi.com)
For whippers, soda siphons, and chargers.

KegWorks
(kegworks.com)
For carbonation and draft cocktail tools, as well as acids, glassware, and bar essentials.

Libbey
(libbey.com)
For durable glassware.

MarketSpice
(marketspice.com)
For one-of-a-kind tea blends.

Micro Matic
(micromatic.com)
For keg cocktail equipment.

Modernist Pantry
(modernistpantry.com)
For Superbags, Dave Arnold's Spinzall centrifuge, carbonation tools, and powders used for infusions and clarifications.

Monterey Bay Spice Company
(herbco.com)
For bulk herbs, spices, and teas.

MoreBeer
(morebeer.com)
For keg cocktail equipment.

Ozark Biomedical
(ozarkbiomedical.com)
For refurbished medical centrifuges.

PolyScience
(polyscienceculinary.com)
For immersion circulators, the Smoking Gun, and other high-tech tools.

Steelite
(steelite.com)
For coupes and Nick & Nora glasses.

Terra Spice Company
(terraspice.com)
For an extensive selection of spices, sugars, dried fruits, and dried chiles.

T Salon
(tsalon.com)
For loose-leaf teas and tisanes.

Umami Mart
(umamimart.com)
For Japanese bar tools, glassware, and so much more.

COCKTAIL CODEX BOOKSHELF

Arnold, Dave. *Liquid Intelligence: The Art and Science of the Perfect Cocktail.* W. W. Norton, 2014.

Baiocchi, Talia. *Sherry: A Modern Guide to the Wine World's Best-Kept Secret, with Cocktails and Recipes.* Ten Speed Press, 2014.

Baiocchi, Talia, and Leslie Pariseau. *Spritz: Italy's Most Iconic Aperitivo Cocktail, with Recipes.* Ten Speed Press, 2016.

Bartels, Brian. *The Bloody Mary: The Lore and Legend of a Cocktail Classic, with Recipes for Brunch and Beyond.* Ten Speed Press, 2017.

Chartier, Francois. *Taste Buds and Molecules: The Art and Science of Food, Wine, and Flavor.* Houghton Mifflin Harcourt, 2012.

Craddock, Harry. *The Savoy Cocktail Book.* Pavilion, 2007.

Curtis, Wayne. *And a Bottle of Rum: A History of the New World in Ten Cocktails.* Crown, 2006.

DeGroff, Dale. *Craft of the Cocktail: Everything You Need to Know to Be a Master Bartender, with 500 Recipes.* Clarkson Potter, 2002.

DeGroff, Dale. *The Essential Cocktail: The Art of Mixing Perfect Drinks.* Clarkson Potter, 2008.

Dornenburg, Andrew, and Karen Page. *What to Drink with What You Eat: The Definitive Guide to Pairing Food with Wine, Beer, Spirits, Coffee, Tea—Even Water—Based on Expert Advice from America's Best Sommeliers.* Bulfinch, 2006.

Embury, David A. *The Fine Art of Mixing Drinks.* Mud Puddle Books, 2008.

Ensslin, Hugo. *Recipes for Mixed Drinks.* Mud Puddle Books, 2009.

Haigh, Ted. *Vintage Spirits and Forgotten Cocktails: From the Alamagoozlum to the Zombie—100 Rediscovered Recipes and the Stories Behind Them.* Quarry Books, 2009.

Jackson, Michael. *Whiskey: The Definitive World Guide.* Dorling Kindersley, 2005.

Lord, Tony. *The World Guide to Spirits, Aperitifs, and Cocktails.* Sovereign Books, 1979.

Madrusan, Michael, and Zara Young. *A Spot at the Bar: Welcome to the Everleigh: The Art of Good Drinking in Three Hundred Recipes.* Hardie Grant, 2017.

McGee, Harold. *On Food and Cooking: The Science and Lore of the Kitchen.* Scribner, 2004.

Meehan, Jim. *Meehan's Bartender Manual.* Ten Speed Press, 2017.

Myhrvold, Nathan, Chris Young, and Maxime Bilet. *Modernist Cuisine: The Art and Science of Cooking.* Cooking Lab, 2011.

Pacult, F. Paul. *Kindred Spirits 2.* Spirit Journal, 2008.

Page, Karen, and Andrew Dornenburg. *The Flavor Bible: The Essential Guide to Culinary Creativity, Based on the Wisdom of America's Most Imaginative Chefs.* Little, Brown, 2008.

Parsons, Brad Thomas. *Amaro: The Spirited World of Bittersweet, Herbal Liqueurs, with Cocktails, Recipes, and Formulas.* Ten Speed Press, 2016.

Parsons, Brad Thomas. *Bitters: A Spirited History of a Classic Cure-All, with Cocktails, Recipes, and Formulas.* Ten Speed Press, 2011.

Petraske, Sasha, with Georgette Moger-Petraske. *Regarding Cocktails.* Phaidon Press, 2016.

Regan, Gary. *The Bartender's Gin Compendium.* Xlibris, 2009.

Regan, Gary. *The Joy of Mixology: The Consummate Guide to the Bartender's Craft.* Clarkson Potter, 2003.

Stewart, Amy. *The Drunken Botanist: The Plants That Create the World's Great Drinks.* Algonquin Books, 2013.

Thomas, Jerry. *The Bar-Tender's Guide: How to Mix Drinks.* Dick and Fitzgerald, 1862.

Wondrich, David. *Imbibe!* Perigree, 2007.

Wondrich, David. *Punch: The Delights (and Dangers) of the Flowing Bowl.* Perigee, 2010.

ACKNOWLEDGMENTS

Long before we stepped behind the bar, a legion of bartenders, chefs, and culinary leaders were tinkering with the concepts that we've attempted to explore in these pages. This book represents the accumulated creative and professional work of so many people, and above all else, it must be acknowledged that it's just a modest step toward continuing a long tradition of asking "What's next?" in food, cocktails, and entertaining. Here's to many more steps forward from people like you.

This book would not have been possible without Devon Tarby. Even a cursory glance at the recipes within reveals that Devon is a prolific cocktail creator. Year after year, she has assembled dozens of innovative and delicious cocktails, but she has also been instrumental in shaping and cocreating our thoughts about flavor and the power of cocktails, and has done more than anyone to take the abstract and overwhelming topic of teaching these ideas to bartenders in a clear and impassioned way. Your mind and creativity are deeply entwined within this book, Devon—thank you for being our partner.

While they may have not mentored us directly, the work and friendship of industry legends have guided every aspect of this book. Dale DeGroff, Audrey Saunders, Gary Regan, Julie Reiner, Jim Meehan, and Eben Freeman, thank you for being friends, mentors (whether you know it or not), and supporters of our work from the beginning.

To our dearly departed Sasha Petraske, thank you for teaching us that simplicity is everything—and that the liquid in the glass is but one part of the equation. So much of how we view cocktails—as being both an integral part of our society and as works of art—was formed by listening to your words and heeding your endlessly helpful advice. You are missed.

Phil Ward, we can feel you squirming if ever you read these words, but the candor of your approach to cocktails—both as a drinks creator and as a mentor—is an integral part of everything we've built inside and outside of these pages. Brian Miller, Joaquin Simo, Jessica Gonzalez, and Thomas Waugh, thank you for tolerating Alex in those early Death & Co days and for continuing to be invaluable friends and colleagues as we all push the boundaries of what the hell it means to be a professional bartender.

There have been so many bartenders, chefs, operators, and guests who have been instrumental in forming our thoughts and opinions on what makes a great drink. By and large our biggest inspirations are the bar teams we've trained and managed over the years—thank you for allowing us to hone the perspective and method of this book through mad-dash openings (and a shot of sherry or two). The teams at Death & Co, Nitecap, the Normandie Club (special props for helping shoot the photos in this book!), Honeycut, and the Walker Inn are the best in the industry. Thank you for turning on the lights and filling the bins with ice every day. None of this means a thing without the craft of bartenders like you, who curate a room every night of the week. Likewise, thank you to our partners for your collaboration and endless patience: Ravi DeRossi, Craig Manzino, Natasha David, Cedd Moses, and Eric Needleman. To our managers currently and in the past, you're all angels for dealing with us—thank you for being the best in the business and for contributing your creativity to this book: Natasha David (again), Lauren Corriveau, Nick Settle, Tyson Buhler, Jillian Vose, Eryn Reece, Daniel Eun, Trevor Easter, Carrie Heller, David Fernie, Mary Barlett, Matt Brown, Matthew Belanger, Alex Jump, Nathan Turk, Willie Rosenthal, Wes Hamilton, and Kristine Danks.

The bar and restaurant industry is a close-knit group of misfits who care deeply about their craft and their community. The list of our friends and colleagues behind bars, in kitchens, and in the back offices of the world's best bars and restaurants is long—far too many to list here—but all of them have inspired us with their work and openness.

There's a strong connection between the people who serve booze and those who make and promote it. We've been privileged over the years to form close relationships with these folks, and in particular the teams at Pernod Ricard, Diageo, Clear Creek Distillery, Maison Ferrand, Singani 63, Del Maguey, Wyoming Whiskey, Back Bar Project, and Bacardi USA have been extremely generous in sharing their stories and supporting us as we learn more about spirits.

This book is more than just a collection of recipes and information about booze; it has taken a team of artists to direct and assemble it into something that can guide you with more than words. To our photographers, Dylan Ho and Jeni Afuso, thank you not only for your vision and creativity but also for being true collaborators (and so much fun to shoot with!). To our illustrator Tim Tomkinson, you never cease to amaze us with your brilliant eye and deft pen. Thank you to Kate Tomkinson for helping us create a beautiful cover.

A staggering amount of awe and gratitude goes to the team at Ten Speed Press. Thank you for allowing us a shot at a second book and for being patient as we shuffled our way through three years of writing. Emily Timberlake, while we mostly like talking about sci-fi books with you, your enthusiasm for this book and your guidance in pushing us to make it better with each revision has made this work what it is. Thank you, Betsy Stromberg and Emma Campion, for shaping our vision and corralling all of us into a cohesive design, and for Serena Sigona for seeing it through to production. Big ups to Ashley Pierce for jumping into editing late in the game—what, did we scare Emily off? Aaron Wehner, thanks for assembling this team of all-stars and for letting us work with them.

To our copyeditor, Jasmine Star, your contributions to and influence on this volume (and our last) deserves a more fitting title. Once again you went above to shape this mess into a real book. You'll never pay for a drink in any of our bars!

Thank you, Jonah Straus and David Black, our agents, for shepherding this project and for keeping us in check.

Finally, to our partners in life—thank you for your patience as we toiled away at this book for all these years. Andrew Ashey, you inspire Alex beyond words. Rotem Raffe, your patience during this process has been saintly. Jenna Kaplan, thank you for your support and consistent insights.

INDEX

Copyright © 2018 by David Kaplan, Alex Day,
and Nick Fauchald
Photographs copyright © 2018 by Dylan James Ho
and Jeni Afuso
Illustrations copyright © 2018 by Tim Tomkinson

Published in the United States by Ten Speed Press,
an imprint of the Crown Publishing Group, a division
of Penguin Random House LLC, New York.
www.crownpublishing.com
www.tenspeed.com

Ten Speed Press and the Ten Speed Press colophon are
registered trademarks of Penguin Random House LLC.

Library of Congress Cataloging-in-Publication Data
Names: Day, Alex, author. | Fauchald, Nick, author. |
  Kaplan, David (Bartender) author.
Title: Cocktail codex : fundamentals, formulas, and
  evolutions / Alex Day, Nick Fauchald, and David Kaplan.
Description: California : Ten Speed Press, [2018] | Includes
  bibliographical references and index.
Identifiers: LCCN 2018011137
Subjects: LCSH: Cocktails. | Flavor. | LCGFT: Cookbooks.
Classification: LCC TX951 .D3834 2018 |
  DDC 614.87/4—dc23
LC record available at https://lccn.loc.gov/2018011137

Hardcover ISBN: 978-1-60774-970-7
eBook ISBN: 978-1-60774-971-4

Printed in China

Design by Betsy Stromberg

12

First Edition